Policing Undocumented Migrants

Migration policing experiments such as boat turn-backs and offshore refugee processing have been criticised as unlawful and have been characterised as exceptional. *Policing Undocumented Migrants* explores the extraordinarily routine, powerful and above all lawful practices engaged in policing status within state territory. This book reveals how the everyday violence of migration law is activated by making people 'illegal'. It explains how undocumented migrants are marginalised through the broad discretion underpinning existing frameworks of legal responsibility for migration policing.

Drawing on interviews with people with lived experience of undocumented status within Australia, perspectives from advocates, detailed analysis of legislation, case law and policy, this book provides an in-depth account of the experiences and legal regulation of undocumented migrants within Australia. Case studies of street policing, immigration raids, transitions in legal status such as release from immigration detention, and character based visa determination challenge conventional binaries in migration analysis between the citizen and non-citizen and between lawful and unlawful status. By showing the organised and central role of discretionary legal authority in policing status, this book proposes a new perspective through which responsibility for migration legal practices can be better understood and evaluated.

Policing Undocumented Migrants will be of interest to scholars and practitioners working in the areas of criminology, criminal law, immigration law and border studies.

Louise Boon-Kuo is a Lecturer at the University of Sydney Law School. Louise researches in the areas of border policing, race and criminal justice.

International and Comparative Criminal Justice

Series Editors

Mark Findlay
Institute of Criminology, University of Sydney, Australia
Ralph Henham
Nottingham Law School, Nottingham Trent University, UK

This series explores the new and rapidly developing field of international and comparative criminal justice and engages with its most important emerging themes and debates. It focuses on three interrelated aspects of scholarship which go to the root of understanding the nature and significance of international criminal justice in the broader context of globalization and global governance. These include: the theoretical and methodological problems posed by the development of international and comparative criminal justice; comparative contextual analysis; the reciprocal relationship between comparative and international criminal justice and contributions which endeavor to build understandings of global justice on foundations of comparative contextual analysis.

Also in the series

The Dual State
Edited by Eric Wilson
978-1-4094-3107-7 (hbk)
978-1-1382-7384-9 (pbk)

Criminal Law Reform and Transitional Justice
Human Rights Perspectives for Sudan
Edited by Lutz Oette
978-1-4094-3100-8 (hbk)
978-1-1382-7223-1 (pbk)

Developing Restorative Justice Jurisprudence
Rethinking Responses to Criminal Wrongdoing
Tony Foley
978-1-4094-6533-1(hbk)
978-1-1382-5042-0 (pbk)

The Exclusionary Rule of Evidence
Comparative Analysis and Proposals for Reform
Kuo-hsing Hsieh
978-1-472-41067-2 (hbk)

Policing Undocumented Migrants

Law, Violence and Responsibility

Louise Boon-Kuo

Routledge
Taylor & Francis Group
LONDON AND NEW YORK

First published 2018
by Routledge

2 Park Square, Milton Park, Abingdon, Oxfordshire OX14 4RN

52 Vanderbilt Avenue, New York, NY 10017

Routledge is an imprint of the Taylor & Francis Group, an informa business

First issued in paperback 2019

British Library Cataloguing-in-Publication Data
A catalogue record for this book is available from the British Library

Library of Congress Cataloging-in-Publication Data
Names: Boon-Kuo, Louise, author.
Title: Policing undocumented migrants: law, violence and responsibility / Louise Boon-Kuo.
Description: Abingdon, Oxon; New York, NY: Routledge, 2017. | Series: International and comparative criminal justice | Includes bibliographical references and index.
Identifiers: LCCN 2017013934| ISBN 9781472435019 (hardback) | ISBN 9781315595337 (ebk)
Subjects: LCSH: Illegal aliens–Government policy–Australia. | Illegal aliens–Australia–Social conditions. | Detention of persons–Australia. | Emigration and immigration law–Australia. | Australia–Emigration and immigration–Government policy.
Classification: LCC JV9120.B66 2017 | DDC 364.1/370994–dc23
LC record available at https://lccn.loc.gov/2017013934

ISBN: 978-1-4724-3501-9 (hbk)
ISBN: 978-0-367-27936-3 (pbk)

Typeset in Galliard
by Wearset Ltd, Boldon, Tyne and Wear

Contents

Acknowledgements vi
List of abbreviations vii

Introduction: migrant illegality in legal records 1

1 Borders of responsibility 21

2 'You're just kidnapped': immigration 'arrests' and detention 47

3 Raids, searches and rapid removals 83

4 'Mums', 'mafia' and 'ransom money': release from immigration detention 113

5 Profiling bad character 142

Conclusion: 'the umbrella of legality' 181

Bibliography 191
Index 213

Acknowledgements

The research and writing of this book took place primarily on the land of the Gadigal people of the Eora nation in Sydney, and on Wurundjeri land in Melbourne. I offer my respect to the traditional owners and the knowledge embedded in Country.

I am indebted to all the interview participants who shared their expertise, time, trust and difficult experiences. The desire of interview participants with lived experience of illegality in Australia to have a wider audience for their experiences has driven the completion of this book. I want to extend respect to all those working in the field of border politics in Australia, from direct action, welfare and legal support, and campaigns against immigration detention, offshore refugee processing and border violence in all its formations.

The development of this research benefited greatly from the guidance, supervision and incisive reflections of Mark Findlay, Fleur Johns and Pat O'Malley, and from the critical engagement of Catherine Dauvergne, Phil Scraton and Eileen Baldry on an earlier version of the text. I am grateful to the many colleagues and friends who read drafts, posed astute questions and imparted encouragement. Particular thanks to Andrew Edgar, Arlie Loughman, Tanya Mitchell, Rayner Thwaites and Kimberlee Weatherall at Sydney Law School, and to research assistance at various times in the latter part of this project from Tom Kiat, Oscar Monaghan, Amanda Nguyen and Elle Triantafillou. The research and writing has benefited from lively discussions with Kata Japunčić, Dave Trudinger, Melissa McAdam, Gavin Sullivan, Sarah M. Harrison, Nassim Arrage, my former refugee law colleagues and everyone at Planet X. For the many stimulating conversations and challenging questions about the text from the beginning of this journey I am immensely thankful to Vicki Sentas and Meredith Williams.

The institutional support and collegiality of Sydney Law School, Sydney University has my appreciative acknowledgement. I would also like to thank Mel Eslick for her keen eye, and Routledge for their work in bringing this book to manifestation.

For their unflagging belief in me, I thank my parents Jacqualynne Boon and Graham Kuo, my siblings, and Cecily Briggs and Cheo Chai-Hiang.

Abbreviations

AAT	Administrative Appeals Tribunal
ABF	Australian Border Force
ACT	Australian Capital Territory
AFP	Australian Federal Police
AHRC	Australian Human Rights Commission
ALRC	Australian Law Reform Commission
ANAO	Australian National Audit Office
ASAS	Asylum Seekers Assistance Scheme
BRIS	Border Risk Identification System
BVE	Bridging E Visa
CDPP	Commonwealth Director of Public Prosecutions
Cth	Commonwealth of Australia
DIAC	Department of Immigration and Citizenship (2007–13)
DIBP	Department of Immigration and Border Protection (2013–Current)
DIEA	Department of Immigration and Ethnic Affairs (1976–87, 1993–96)
DILGEA	Department of Immigration, Local Government and Ethnic Affairs (1987–93)
DIMA	Department of Immigration and Multicultural Affairs (1996–2001, 2006–07)
DIMIA	Department of Immigration and Multicultural and Indigenous Affairs (2001–06)
Evidence Act	*Evidence Act 1995* (Cth)
IMA	illegal maritime arrival
IRT	Immigration Review Tribunal
ISS	Immigration Status Service
MIAC	Minister for Immigration and Citizenship
MIEA	Minister for Immigration and Ethnic Affairs
Migration Act	*Migration Act 1958* (Cth)
Migration Regulations	*Migration Regulations 1994* (Cth)
MILGEA	Minister for Immigration, Local Government and Ethnic Affairs

MIMA	Minister for Immigration and Multicultural Affairs
MIMIA	Minister for Immigration, Multicultural and Indigenous Affairs
MRT	Migration Review Tribunal
NSW	New South Wales
RFL	Risk Factor List
RPBV	Removal Pending Bridging Visa
RRT	Refugee Review Tribunal
Safeguards	Safeguards System
SHEV	Safe Haven Enterprise Visa
SRSS	Status Resolution Support Services
TPV	Temporary Protection Visa
UK	United Kingdom
UN	United Nations
UNHCR	United Nations High Commissioner for Refugees
US	United States
WA	Western Australia
Vic	Victoria

Introduction

Migrant illegality in legal records

> In August 2015, the Australian Border Force ('ABF') announced it would be joining Victoria Police, along with other agencies, to target 'everything from anti-social behaviour to outstanding warrants' as part of Operation Fortitude in Melbourne's city centre.[1] The ABF Regional Commander Victoria and Tasmania, Don Smith, announced it 'will be positioned at various locations around the CBD speaking with any individual we cross paths with.... You need to be aware of the conditions of your visa; if you commit visa fraud you should know it's only a matter of time before you're caught out'.[2] Within three hours the ABF released a further press release clarifying that the 'ABF does not and will not stop people at random in the streets and does not target on the basis of race, religion, or ethnicity'.[3] And within four hours of the initial announcement, protesters brought traffic to a standstill, chanting 'no to racism, no to hate this is not a police state'.[4] Half an hour later the operation was cancelled. It remained front-page news for a number of days, and memes circulated on social media. The public expressed a pronounced sense of shock about the planned action, and commentary associated the operation with the checkpoints of Nazi Germany, fascism and totalitarianism.[5]

The newly formed ABF, established within the Department of Immigration and Border Protection ('DIBP') as a frontline operational agency with responsibilities to enforce immigration and customs laws, presented Operation Fortitude as

1 Australian Border Force, 'ABF Joining Inter-Agency Outfit to Target Crime in Melbourne CBD', Media Release, August 28, 2015.

2 Ibid.

3 Australian Border Force, 'Clarifying Statement on Operation Fortitude', Media Release, August 28, 2015.

4 Alana Schetzer and Tammy Mills, 'Border Force: Operation Fortitude Cancelled as Protesters Take to Melbourne's CBD Streets', *The Age*. August 28, 2015, www.theage.com.au/victoria/border-force-operation-fortitude-cancelled-as-protesters-take-to-melbournes-cbd-streets-20150828-gja3mp.html#ixzz42qqBOuBw; ABC News, 'Timeline: How Operation Fortitude Unravelled', *ABC News Online*, August 28, 2015, www.abc.net.au/news/2015-08-28/timeline-of-how-operation-fortitude-unravelled/6733252.

5 David Holmes, 'What Does the "Border Farce" Tell Us about the Future of Crisis Politics in Australia?', *The Conversation*, August 31, 2015, https://theconversation.com/what-does-the-border-farce-tell-us-about-the-future-of-crisis-politics-in-australia-46865.

the 'first' involvement in a multi-agency operation of its kind. There were some differences between Operation Fortitude and earlier operations: the issue of a press release prior to the operation, and the impression the press release gave that ABF would be directly stopping people in the street for visa checks. But the truth is that immigration operations of this kind are far from unprecedented. Immigration, police and other authorities have conducted joint visits to homes and workplaces since at least 1997, when the Inter Agency Working Group on the Cash Economy was set up.[6] In the last 20 years, multi-agency approaches have developed further. A whole-of-government approach has been favoured to address unauthorised work,[7] and immigration has participated in large-scale multi-agency operations in a range of workplaces, as well as vehicle interceptions on the street.[8] Moreover, officers from a range of agencies, including state, territory and federal police, customs and immigration, hold the same powers as a function of their designation as 'officers' under the *Migration Act 1958* (Cth) ('*Migration Act*').[9] In various capacities ranging from information sharing, status checking and proactive operations, migration-related tasks have become part of the routine – though not uniformly operationalised work – of these agencies. The public surprise about the street-based strategy reflects the extent to which immigration compliance works under the radar within Australia. In contrast to maritime operations and immigration detention, it represents an immense area of policing that proceeds with very little public oversight.

The issues that arose in Operation Fortitude encapsulate the fundamental themes of this book. What does migration law say police and immigration officers can do? How are migration powers used in practice? How do migration legal practices become authoritative? In what ways does the law make and fail to make officers responsible for their exercise of power? And why do the violent experiences of particular parts of migration process leave only marginal notes in legal records? Important differences lie in the legal regulation of migration powers exercised by police, immigration officers and administrative tribunals arising from the broader regulatory context of their practice. What they have in common is that they involve

6 Department of Immigration and Multicultural Affairs ('DIMA'), 'Protecting the Border: Immigration Compliance' (Belconnen, 1999), chapter 8.

7 DIMA, 'Review of Illegal Workers in Australia: Improving Immigration Compliance in the Workplace' (Canberra, 1999), 47–8.

8 Department of Immigration and Multicultural and Indigenous Affairs ('DIMIA'), '175 Detained in Major Compliance Operations', Media Release, DPS 60/2001, December 20, 2001; Ursula Heger, 'Police, Immigration Officers Swoop on City Taxi Drivers', *The Courier-Mail.* June 10, 2010, www.couriermail.com.au/news/police-immigration-officers-swoop-on-city-taxi-drivers/story-e6freon6-1225878174694; Amanda Vanstone (Minister for Immigration and Multicultural and Indigenous Affairs), 'Taxi Rank Raid on Welfare Cheats', Media Release, September 16, 2002; Marissa Calligeros, 'Indian Taxi Drivers Investigated Following Sting', *Brisbane Times*, June 11, 2010, www.brisbanetimes.com.au/queensland/indian-taxi-drivers-investigated-following-sting-20100610-y14r.html; SBS, 'WA Police Raid Taxi-Drivers', *SBS News Online*, August 23, 2013, www.sbs.com.au/news/article/2003/10/04/wa-police-raid-taxi-drivers.

9 *Migration Act* s 5.

broad discretion, coercive power, often take place in low-visibility environments and involve status-based policing. Migration legal practices articulate an organised approach to state violence that differentiates and limits state responsibility promoted by legal rhetoric and available under other legal regimes. Migration legal practices also involve control of legal status for diverse reasons, making it a profound source of social, spatial and temporal regulation.

Police and immigration officers exercise powers that 'make people illegal'. This phrase, coined by Catherine Dauvergne,[10] as used in the book refers to making people illegal in the substantive legal sense by cancelling a visa after investigation finds a non-citizen in breach of visa conditions, or refusing a visa and thus making continued stay unlawful. It also refers to making people illegal in the social sense of taking action, which conditions the experience of those already formally 'illegal'. It is these two modes of legal regulation – substantive, and social – that I refer to as 'policing status'. Migrant illegality is not derived solely from illegal status, but arises from a 'palpable sense of deportability, which is to say, the *possibility* of deportation, the *possibility* of being removed from the space of the nation-state'.[11] In Australia, where the immigration detention of 'unlawful non-citizens' (the legislative term for those non-citizens present without a valid visa)[12] is mandatory, migrant illegality also arises from a sense of the possibility of detention. This possibility, and thus the social experience of migrant illegality, is shaped by policing practices that target non-citizens for apprehension, and which condone the presence and inclusion of illegal migrants in the community.[13] Non-citizens navigate the terrain of possible detention and deportation in diverse ways, some of which arose in my research in Australia and reflect findings elsewhere: social mimicry of regularity, strategies to avoid relevant authorities, careful adherence to rules, contravention of which risks exposure. This socio-legal study focuses on when those navigations fail and non-citizens come into contact with immigration authorities.

The discourse of 'illegal migrants' has been used by governments to dehumanise and undermine the political and social claims of non-citizens crossing borders without immigration authorisation and to legitimate harsh border-policing measures. Thus, many favour the term 'undocumented' as used in the title for this book. Yet the terms 'undocumented' or 'irregular' also position migration legal status as a problem of the lack of documentation or as 'deviant' migrant behaviour. Social movements across the globe have rightly stated that

10 Catherine Dauvergne, *Making People Illegal: What Globalization Means for Migration and Law*, Law in Context (New York: Cambridge University Press, 2008).

11 Nicholas P. De Genova, 'Migrant "Illegality" and Deportability in Everyday Life', *Annual Review of Anthropology* 31 (2002): 439 (emphasis added); Susan Bibler Coutin, *Legalizing Moves: Salvadoran Immigrants' Struggle for U.S. Residency* (Ann Arbor: University of Michigan Press, 2000), 27–47.

12 *Migration Act* ss 5, 189.

13 Coutin, *Legalizing Moves*; Kitty Calavita, 'A "Reserve Army of Delinquents": The Criminalization and Economic Punishment of Immigrants in Spain', *Punishment & Society* 5, no. 4 (2003); Monica W. Varsanyi, 'Documenting Undocumented Migrants: The Matrículas Consulares as Neoliberal Local Membership', *Geopolitics* 12, no. 2 (2007); Kate Hepworth, *At the Edges of Citizenship: Security and the Constitution of Non-Citizen Subjects* (Farnham: Ashgate, 2015).

'no one is illegal'. The use of the terms 'illegal' and 'unlawful non-citizen' throughout this book is consistent with the spirit if not the letter of this call – no one *is* illegal but the law *makes* some people illegal.[14] Using the term 'illegal' acknowledges: that it is law which constructs the problem of 'illegality'; that migration legal status is used instrumentally to organise how non-citizens should be treated; that it is illegal status itself that is responsible for much of the exploitation of non-citizens; and that illegal status grants officers expansive powers. In other words, the term provides a constant reminder that migration legal status is the product of a process of illegalisation, and thus foregrounds migrant illegality as a social relation, not as a static or inherent identity.

Policing Undocumented Migrants argues that migration law and policing is organised in ways that effectively marginalises responsibility for its violence. It identifies how this marginalisation is the outcome of various structures that are integral parts of administrative and immigration law and legal practices. To investigate this thesis, it examines the very practices that represent the 'hard end' of immigration ('arrest', detention, raids, visa refusal or cancellation), or are proximate to it (such as release from immigration detention). These practices regulate migration legal status via two modes: the use of 'police-like' powers to identify and apprehend suspected unlawful non-citizens and those in breach of visa conditions; and the use of legal status and visa conditions as a means of control.

Guided by original empirical research, *Policing Undocumented Migrants* provides an in-depth account of the experiences and legal regulation of migrant illegality within Australia. It draws on 27 interviews with people with lived experience of illegality and advocates, as well as documentary, policy and case law analysis in order to identify significant features of migration legal practice in Australia in the period spanning 1996–2016. This research is not intended to document how migration law and policing is routinely practiced by immigration, police and other immigration decision-makers, such as the Immigration Minister. That is an empirical question requiring broader study. It takes particular overlooked experiences of policing status as a starting point to comprehend how legal conventions, doctrines, procedures and institutions make it difficult for the voices of those with lived experience of illegality to leave a mark in legal records, and to cast light on the migration law's violence and responsibility for that violence.

By situating diverse experiences of the production of illegal (or marginally legal) status in their broader legal contexts, this book charts the saturation, constitution and affirmation of discretionary authority in four sites of migration control: immigration detention as 'arrest'; immigration searches and raids; release from immigration detention; and character determination. It contends that, across these sites, legal strategies for the disavowal of responsibility for the law's violent effects are part of the ordinary organisation of migration law. It is organised through a

14 See Dauvergne, *Making People Illegal*, 4, see also 9–10; Peter Nyers, 'No One Is Illegal between City and Nation', *Studies in Social Justice* 4, no. 2 (2010); Harald Bauder, 'Why We Should Use the Term "Illegalized" Refugee or Immigrant: A Commentary', *International Journal of Refugee Law* 26, no. 3 (2014). Note that throughout the book the quotes around 'illegal' are implied.

concentration of discretion at the front end of migration processes and the diverse enactment of temporal borders, through the migration policing network of both state and civil actors that institutionalise and normalise the policing of status, and is masked by formal legal rhetoric that (at least on some issues of liberty) enunciates the same protections for citizens and aliens. These are long-standing features of migration law and policing's production of migrant illegality. The manifestations examined are necessarily historically, politically and site specific, but the book offers a methodology useful beyond the Australian context. By centring discretionary legal authority, it proposes a new perspective through which responsibility for migration legal practices can be better understood and evaluated.

This research is driven by three main impetuses. First, border policing is a legally, institutionally and technologically dynamic arena of migration policy. The negotiations between migration and state practices are creating new legal questions about state power and the adequacy of existing forums of responsibility, and broader questions about the role of migration policies in perpetuating or ameliorating global inequalities. The general growth in migration from the Global South to the North since 1990, and the trend towards long-term *temporary* migration in Australia as well as other Global North states,[15] makes focus on practices within the state a productive one to explore these questions.

Second, although there is a substantial literature on immigration detention in Australia and on its exterior border policing, both sites in which the designation of illegality has already effectively been accomplished, little is known about the practices of interior migration policing.[16] Legal scholarship has not examined the effects on the subjects of Australian migration policing and, by foregrounding the experiences of police-like powers and transitions in legal status, the book endeavours to redress that absence.

Third, the book seeks to understand how the law marginalises the violent effects of migration law and policing from legal records and naturalises the limited accountability and responsibility for these practices. It draws on critical legal resources to understand how the scale and jurisdiction of migration law make limited responsibility appear natural. In the analysis developed, it raises questions about the implications of migration authority developed at the interrelation of laws, powers and procedures. What significance does migration law, as a specific legal discipline, hold in making people invisible and in regulating the lives of unlawful non-citizens and non-citizens in breach of visa conditions?

Invisible people

The population of non-citizens living without a visa in Australia is largely invisible, atomised and socially isolated. One interviewee, Stephen, explains his isolation was partly self-imposed. 'I just stayed away from everyone', but also because

15 Stephen Castles, 'International Migration at a Crossroads', *Citizenship Studies* 18, no. 2 (2014): 193.
16 A notable exception is Leanne Weber, *Policing Non-Citizens* (Oxford: Routledge, 2013).

'nobody wants to really give you help because they're scared'.[17] This was a common story among those I interviewed. Many also explained that they kept away from communities with whom they shared ethnic or spiritual bonds because of their deep fear that social intimacy would result in them being reported to immigration. Interviewee Rachel describes how the fear of the 'dob-in' breaks relationships of trust in workplaces and ethnic communities.[18] Having been accused of reporting another to immigration, Rachel quickly fled Sydney in tears to escape threats to her life and of being reported herself. One of the hardest things about living without a visa was the constant pressure to, in Rachel's words 'hide', but also

> if you have enemies and know what your situation that's the worst thing – they can dob you in … that's why you have to be friendly with them, even if you really hate them, you have to be [here Rachel gestured towards her simulation of a 'happy face'].

The invisibility and isolation of non-citizens living without a visa or in breach is not unique to Australia. A vocabulary of stigmatising terms – such as 'clandestine' 'illegal', 'unauthorised', 'irregular' – has become commonplace, devaluing the political claims of these groups. But the demographics of the population in Australia may have some part to play in the marginalisation of 'illegal' migrants in political and legal discourse. The number of individuals living without a visa in Australia is small compared with other countries,[19] which has been attributed to strict controls supported by the absence of national land borders in the island continent of Australia. From 1980 to 2011, the figure was roughly around 50 000, bar a few spikes in the late 1980s and early 1990s, which recorded numbers of up to 90 000 persons.[20] Since 2011, the estimate has remained about 60 000 persons, a

17 Interview with M10.

18 Interview with M11.

19 For comparative data on the undocumented population in various nations, see Platform for International Cooperation on Undocumented Migrants, 'PICUM Submission to the UN Committee on the Protection of the Rights of All Migrant Workers and Members of Their Families: Day of General Discussion on the Role of Migration Statistics for Treaty Reporting and Migration Policies' (Geneva, April 22, 2013).

20 The assessment of trends in this paragraph is derived from Joint Standing Committee on Migration Regulations, 'First Report: Illegal Entrants in Australia – Balancing Control and Compassion' (Canberra: Commonwealth of Australia, September 1990); DIMA, 'Annual Report 1996–97' (Canberra, 1997); 'Annual Report 1997–98' (Canberra, 1998); 'Annual Report 2000–01' (Canberra, 2001); DIMIA, 'Annual Report 2001–02' (Canberra, 2002); 'Annual Report 2002–03' (Canberra, 2003); immigration annual reports covering the period 2003–16 at DIBP, *Annual Reports*, www.border.gov.au/about/reports-publications/reports/annual; DIMA, 'Review of Illegal Workers 1999'; DIMIA, 'Managing the Border: Immigration Compliance 2003–04 Edition' (Belconnen, 2005); 'Managing the Border: Immigration Compliance 2004–05 Edition' (Belconnen, 2005); Stephen Howells, 'Report of the 2010 Review of the *Migration Amendment (Employer Sanctions) Act* 2007' (Belconnen: Commonwealth of Australia, 2011), 26; Department of Immigration and Citizenship ('DIAC'), 'Australia's Migration Trends 2011–12' (Belconnen, 2013); DIBP, 'Australia's Migration Trends 2012–13' (Belconnen, 2014); DIBP, 'Australia's Migration Trends 2013–14' (Belconnen, 2014).

miniscule 0.003 per cent of the Australian population. More than 99 per cent of non-citizens depart Australia before their visa expires.[21] In recent years, for the period 2010–15, the vast majority of those who did remain after visa expiry stayed for over a year, and about half have remained without a visa for five or more years.[22] Because of the period of overstay immigration assumes that most non-citizens without a visa will be working without permission,[23] and overall a larger number of between 50 000 and over 100 000 non-citizens are estimated to be working without permission at any one time.[24]

Contrary to popular perception, most people living without a visa *arrived* in Australia holding a visa. Since at least 1990, the overwhelming majority formerly held a visitor visa. Former visitor visa holders accounted for about three-quarters of the unlawful non-citizen population in 2010–14, and the next largest demographic in this period was former student visa holders, who accounted for about 16 per cent.[25] Reflecting the multiplicity of nationalities who arrive as visitors or students, the population living without a visa is culturally and linguistically diverse. Together these factors provide some explanation for why the experiences and claims of undocumented migrants receive little political attention in Australia.

Much of the exploitative conditions and difficulties of the lives of illegalised migrants have been attributed to living 'off the books'. Driving and defining the lives of 'illegal' migrants is the potential for deportation, which conditions the social relations of those with illegal status.[26] Illegal status contributes to precarious and exploitative employment conditions and, in Australia, contradictory legal approaches to labour rights and protection.[27] It is associated with the lack of documentation of residence – non-citizens living without a visa may choose not to be the named lease holder if renting a home, may not have a driver's licence, may undertake employment without a written contract or under an alias, may employ similar precautions in school enrolment, and so on.

In some places, such as the United States ('US'), where long-term residence is a factor in legalisation processes, the inability to document long-term

21 See, for example, DIBP, 'Annual Report 2014–15', 2.

22 Howells, 'Report of the 2010 Review of the *Migration Amendment (Employer Sanctions) Act 2007*', 99; Australian National Audit Office ('ANAO'), 'Managing Compliance with Visa Conditions: Department of Immigration and Border Protection, ANAO Report No. 13 2015–16, Performance Audit', (Barton, 2015), 22.

23 Howells, 'Report of the 2010 Review of the *Migration Amendment (Employer Sanctions) Act 2007*', 23.

24 Ibid., 12. Note, however, this is a very small proportion of the non-citizen population and a minute proportion of the Australian workforce: ibid., 24.

25 Joint Standing Committee on Migration Regulations, 'First Report: Illegal Entrants in Australia'; DIAC, 'Australia's Migration Trends 2011–12', 86; DIBP, 'Australia's Migration Trends 2012–13', 77; DIBP, 'Australia's Migration Trends 2013–14', 69.

26 De Genova, 'Migrant "Illegality" and Deportability in Everyday Life', 439.

27 Kitty Calavita, 'Immigration, Law, and Marginalization in a Global Economy: Notes from Spain', *Law & Society Review* 32, no. 3 (1998); Laurie Berg, *Migrant Rights at Work: Law's Precariousness at the Intersection of Immigration and Labour* (Abingdon: Routledge, 2016).

residence while living without a visa undermines the potential for non-citizens to legalise their status.[28] In Australia, long-term residence is not an explicit criterion for legalising status. If a person has spent time without a visa, eligibility for a substantive visa depends a range of factors, notably whether the person has applied for a visa within varied specified time periods of becoming unlawful.[29] Lack of social documentation may pose a drawback for unlawful visa applicants who have missed the time limit for lodging an application for some visas, and also affects a limited range of decisions in which the Immigration Minister has discretion to take credible social ties into account.[30] The more important effect in Australia is the way in the apparent 'legal nonexistence'[31] of illegal migrants introduces uncertainty about which legal discipline has precedence and the circumstances in which non-migration laws are relevant. The low visibility of migration policing practices compounds the problem of ascertaining how the interrelation between legal disciplines works in practice.

Invisible policing

It has often been remarked that political and media attention focuses on people seeking safety arriving without visas by boats as the source of 'illegal' migration, rather than those who remain after their visa has expired or cancelled. Australian maritime border policing policies and practices have involved novel and often spectacular legal forms to prevent the 'influx' of people seeking safety in Australia, notably the Pacific Solution operational from 2001 to 2008, and 2012 to now. The Pacific Solution includes physical measures of interception at sea followed by turnaround or removal to offshore detention in Nauru and Papua New Guinea's Manus Island, legal measures that prevent those arriving by boat from lodging a valid refugee protection application,[32] and relatedly the excision of 5000 islands and eventually the mainland itself from the Australia migration zone.[33] Both major Australian political parties have presented these policies as necessary to address the

28 Coutin, *Legalizing Moves*, 27–47; Saskia Sassen, 'The Repositioning of Citizenship: Emergent Subjects and Spaces for Politics', in *Empire's New Clothes: Reading Hardt and Negri*, ed. Paul A. Passavant and Jodi Dean (New York: Routledge, 2004).

29 For an overview on the regularisation of unlawful status, see Mary Crock and Laurie Berg, *Immigration, Refugees and Forced Migration: Law, Policy and Practice in Australia* (Annandale: The Federation Press, 2011), 453–66.

30 *Migration Act* ss 417, 351, 501.

31 Coutin, *Legalizing Moves*, 27–47.

32 *Migration Act* s 46A. This was considered by the High Court in *Plaintiff M61/2010E* v. *Commonwealth of Australia; Plaintiff M69 of 2010* v. *Commonwealth of Australia* [2010] HCA 41; (2010) 243 CLR 319.

33 Moira Coombs, 'Excising Australia: Are We Really Shrinking?' *Research Note*, no. 5, Information and Research Service (Canberra: Parliamentary Library, 2005); Moira Coombs, 'Excisions from the Migration Zone-Policy and Practice' *Research Note*, no. 42, Information and Research Service (Canberra: Parliamentary Library, 2004).

security threat of large numbers of persons arriving by boat, and to act as a deterrent to those seeking safety, positioning these practices as exceptional measures to deal with an exceptional problem.

In contrast, practices of identification and apprehension of 'illegal' migrants within Australia have received comparatively little political attention. Political discourse has not stigmatised 'illegal' migrants within Australia to the same degree as those seeking safety by boat. Coercive police-like powers are exercised in low-visibility contexts and are subject to only limited ad hoc judicial oversight. The broad discretion to make people illegal through visa cancellation and refusal (and otherwise shape the conditions associated with lawful status) supports the arbitrary exercise of powers. Overall, the harmful effects of policing, such as the direct violence involved in arrest, investigation and even release practices, the subjugation, as well as protections that are differentiated on the basis of the legal regime they effect, are elided because they are made, through a series of legal sleights of hand discussed in Chapter 1, to appear natural.

Making visible: ways of seeing, hearing and reading law

When I started this research I was working as a refugee lawyer at a community legal centre in Sydney, NSW, that provided free legal assistance to people seeking safety. I was frustrated because the legal centre had limited resources to assist clients with many of the issues that arose while they were unlawful, in their apprehension and during later detention. I was also involved in refugee and border campaigns and projects and was similarly struck by the way in which campaigns were organised around state-defined visa categories: refugee, worker, student. Identity-based orientation can be of great value in better understanding the unique dilemmas faced by migrants.[34] But experiences of migration control potentially affect any non-citizen regardless of what visa they hold, and disciplinary segregation makes it more difficult to identify and explain the nature of the problems that arise.

I adopted the lens of policing status to analyse the experiences of migrants within Australia. It allows for study of a broader scope of practices and experiences than that established through refugee law perspectives and enables connections to be drawn between the experiences of refugees, permanent migrants, temporary migrants, undocumented migrants and even citizens. The multifaceted impetuses and contexts in which officials suspect individuals to be non-citizens living unlawfully (and act on that suspicion) emphasise that migration law and policing view migrant illegality as more than the absence of lawful non-citizen status. Concern that migration policing casts a broad net has been borne

34 See, for example, Berg, *Migrant Rights at Work*; Fethi Mansouri and Melek Bagdas, *Politics of Social Exclusion: Refugees on Temporary Protection Visa in Victoria* (Geelong: Deakin University Centre for Citizenship & Human Rights, and Victorian Arabic Social Services, 2002); Simon Marginson *et al.*, *International Student Security* (Melbourne: Cambridge University Press, 2010).

out in the past. The Ombudsman recorded 15 Australian citizens and 13 permanent residents among 70 persons unlawfully detained in 2000–06; only two of the 70 detained were in fact unlawful non-citizens.[35] The value of policing status as an analytic is that it does not engage any preconceived ideas about the subject population of migration processes, nor does it separate 'procedural' matters of enforcement from 'substantive' matters of visa determination.

Turning attention to the laws and policing practices that 'make people illegal' might be seen simply as a shift in the subject of study – from refugee rights or migrant workers' rights to migration control. Nevertheless, it is a productive shift because it allows the clash between experiences of legal practices and policing and legal frameworks for accountability to really come to the fore. It is this clash that I contend is critical to understand why immigration compliance work takes place largely outside of independent scrutiny within Australia. It is a shift that sidesteps some of the tricky normative issues that have sustained much thinking around the legitimacy of differentiation between the rights of citizens and non-citizens: whether all those present on a particular territory should have access to the same rights, whether rights accrue with longevity of residence or through labour force participation, and so on. Instead, it focuses attention to the question of state responsibility for the exercise of power.

This qualitative study is not an ethnography of illegal migrants, but might be considered 'an ethnography of a legal process'.[36] It approaches migration law as a set of practices formed via interaction between law (legislation and case law) and social processes that condition how 'law is imagined, produced, formalized, enforced, reformed, or made meaningful for different political constituencies and individuals in any given community'.[37] As should be clear, much of what my research covers are processes not fully disclosed by law in the books. I learned about how these processes are made meaningful by talking to those involved (detailed below), reading about how they view their roles and responsibilities,[38] and the expectations of those making immigration decisions detailed in volumes of non-binding procedure manuals for immigration officers, along with binding ministerial directions, which generally provide guidance through listing requisite considerations for decision-makers.[39]

35 Commonwealth and Immigration Ombudsman, 'Department of Immigration and Citizenship Report into Referred Immigration Cases: Detention Process Issues' (Canberra, 2007), 2.

36 Coutin, *Legalizing Moves*, 23.

37 Eve Darian-Smith, *Laws and Societies in Global Contexts: Contemporary Approaches* (New York: Cambridge University Press, 2013), 2. See also Alan Hunt, *Governance of the Consuming Passions: A History of Sumptuary Law* (New York: St. Martin's Press, 1996), 3, 319.

38 For example, evidence given by immigration portfolio staff in Parliamentary settings, as well as Ministerial policy statements in a range of forums. Secondary sources utilised include ad hoc governmental inquiries, such as those of the Ombudsman, the Australian Human Rights Commission (formerly the Human Rights and Equal Opportunity Commission) and annual reports (of the Immigration Department, Commonwealth Department of Public Prosecutions, the Australian Federal Police and the Commonwealth and Immigration Ombudsman).

39 DIAC, *Procedures Advice Manual 3*, and Ministerial Directions made under *Migration Act* s 499.

From discussions with non-citizens living without a visa I decided on four sites of analysis that involve transitions in legal status or the legal enforcement of status (in other words, different aspects of the production of migrant illegality): apprehension in the street; apprehension in organised migration raids; release from immigration detention; and character determination in migration decision-making. My intent was to study how people are made or found to be illegal in different contexts in order to identify commonality between the contingent conditions and practices that produce migrant illegality.[40] My findings reveal that discretionary authority over migrant illegality is organised in particular ways that concentrate power in the hands of administrators and diminish responsibility for those practices.

In any legal practice relationship there are two main actors: those exercising particular powers, which for convenience are referred to as 'policing agents' but include police and immigration officers, as well as civil actors and tribunal members; and the policed subjects. Except for some 'responsibilised' civil actors in Chapter 5, I have not interviewed policing agents. In adopting the view 'from above' of the policing agent I rely on public and parliamentary statements, uncontested evidence in court cases, other official sources and, where relevant, an exploratory empirical study into policing and immigration migration law work that was undertaken at the same time as my research.[41] Because I am interested in showing the *possibilities* allowed by the legal framework (not developing the argument that particular practices predominate), omitting interview of policing agents does not undermine the salience of my findings. Note that during the period of my research and writing the name of the immigration portfolio changed several times as it merged with portfolios including Labour, Local Government, Ethnic, Multicultural and Indigenous Affairs, Citizenship and finally, from 2013, Border Protection,[42] developments which themselves provide insight into the political positioning of the merged portfolios.[43] Because of the frequent name changes, I have used the abbreviation of 'Immigration

40 For discussion of comparative contextual analysis, see Mark Findlay, *The Globalisation of Crime: Understanding Transitional Relationships in Context* (Cambridge: Cambridge University Press, 1999), 1–19; Mark Findlay and Ralph Henham, 'Integrating Theory and Method in the Comparative Contextual Analsis of Trial Process', in *Research Methods for Law*, ed. Mike McConville and Wing Hong Chui, *Research Methods for the Arts and Humanities* (Edinburgh: Edinburgh University Press, 2007).

41 Leanne Weber interviewed 13 Department of Immigration and Citizenship staff, 40 law enforcement staff (mostly NSW Police) and a few individuals from other federal, state and local government agencies, as well as members of the tertiary education sector, with most interviews undertaken in 2008 and 2009. Weber also undertook a survey of 371 operational police in NSW: see Weber, *Policing Non-Citizens*, 17–21.

42 See the abbreviations list at the front of the book for the full titles at different periods.

43 See, for example, Jeremy Bruer and John Power, 'The Changing Role of the Department of Immigration', in *The Politics of Australian Immigration*, ed. James Jupp and Marie Kabala (Canberra: AGPS, 1993); Jeremy Moon and Anthony Sayers, 'The Dynamics of Governmental Activity: A Long-Run Analysis of the Changing Scope and Profile of Australian Ministerial Portfolios', *Australian Journal of Political Science* 34, no. 2 (1999).

Minister' and 'immigration' (to reference the department) for brevity and because the policies described cover the periods of multiple departmental name changes.

Resisting silence, listening and tracing hidden processes

The starting point of my research was to learn about how migration law and policing is made meaningful for those living without a visa. I drew on interviews with such individuals as insider experts to develop my research direction,[44] as well as to chart instances of how migration law has been articulated. From 2008 to 2010 I undertook semi-structured interviews with 12 individuals who were living without a visa at the time, or who had lived in Australia without a visa in the past. I interviewed eight men and four women, from nine countries of origin, representing nine from Asia (including the sub-regions of Southern Asia, Western Asia and South-Eastern Asia), one from Europe, one from Africa, and one person who was stateless.[45] Some had spent just a short time living without a visa, others had remained unlawful for up to ten years, and individuals came to official notice in diverse ways. Participants describe experiences spanning a time period between 1996 and 2010.

Discussion focused on how persons were detected or otherwise became unlawful and, where relevant, how persons became lawful, and participants' identification of justice problems and solutions. It also covered whether and how living without a visa had shaped individuals' relationships with family, friends and communities, work, accommodation, health, and other aspects of life. Some interviews were supplemented with personal immigration files (obtained by Freedom of Information requests and provided by participants). Participants selected pseudonyms or asked me to do so to protect their identity, I have not specified the country of origin of participants, and where necessary other measures have been taken to ensure participants cannot be identified. The experiences explored are a small proportion of the estimated 60 000 undocumented migrants in Australia at any one time. While not statistically representative, the experiences reported are consistent with community and legal insider experts' knowledge of migration control within Australia. Documentation of migration policing in case law, reports and inquiries supplement the individual narratives relayed to me in interview. Assembling the disparate glimpses into the

44 See, for example, discussion in Giorgia Doná, 'The Microphysics of Participation in Refugee Research', *Journal of Refugee Studies* 20, no. 2 (2007): 212.

45 The geographical region and sub-region classifications used are set out in the United Nations publication, *Standard Country or Area Codes for Statistical Use, Revision 4* (United Nations publication, Sales No. 98.XVII.9). Excerpts may be accessed at United Nations Statistics Division, 'Composition of Macro Geographical (Continental) Regions, Geographical Sub-Regions, and Selected Economic and Other Groupings'. Last modified September 26, 2016, http://unstats.un.org/unsd/methods/m49/m49regin.htm. Note that the Southern and Western Asia categories include countries colloquially referred to as the 'Middle East'.

policing of migrant illegality in this book attempts to redress the absence of 'illegal' voices, and to contribute to the work of peer organisations such as Refugees, Survivors and Ex-Detainees ('RISE') which formed after this research was undertaken.

Most of the interviews were conducted with the assistance of interpreters, which poses particular challenges. Interpretation of meaning may be particularly fraught within an environment of contested definitions such as 'illegal' migration. I had become aware of this prior to undertaking this research through involvement in a plain-language community legal publication as 'living without a visa' was initially translated as 'illegal', a translation which, in an interview context, would have implied a wrongdoing that I did not mean to convey and undermined the trust needed for candid discussion. Far from being merely technical, the act of translation involves a third person in the interview process.[46] I invited interpreters after discussion with interview participants because participants needed to be confident of the interpreter's commitment to confidentiality (especially acute due to the matters being discussed, and for those with refugee claims), and because of potential shared cultural and linguistic communities between the interpreter and participant. Professional accredited interpreters were utilised as well as non-accredited interpreters nominated by the interview participant.

I interviewed 15 advocates in the period 2007–10. This included seven immigration lawyers and migration agents, based in Sydney and Melbourne, who represented non-citizens across Australia. The immigration law experience of practitioners ranged between three to over 30 years, and participants were selected because their daily work entailed contact with non-citizens living unlawfully. I also interviewed eight non-legal advocates based in Sydney and Melbourne who were involved in supporting non-citizens living unlawfully, including sponsorship of detainees' release from detention and in community volunteer-run support schemes. The majority of these advocates were involved in organisations that were informal in character. They provided support on an unpaid basis, and most were engaged in such activity as their main activity. Some non-legal advocates were community organisation workers who had contact with a specific population that included non-citizens living unlawfully. While most legal advocates participated as named interviewees, almost all non-legal advocates sought anonymity as a condition of their participation, as many felt their future advocacy work in the migration field might otherwise be adversely affected.

Lastly, I drew on my own involvements in the refugee and migrant sector. While undertaking this study, at various times I was a full-time refugee lawyer, occasional remote detention centre lawyer and a volunteer at the centre's

46 Bogusia Temple and Rosalind Edwards, 'Limited Exchanges: Approaches to Involving People Who Do Not Speak English in Research and Service Development', in *Doing Research with Refugees: Issues and Guidelines*, ed. Bogusia Temple and Rhetta Moran (Bristol: The Policy Press, 2006).

evening advice service. I spoke at various conferences, not solely about my academic work, but also to deliver peer-based migration legal education. I was also involved in supporting migrant and refugee action through facilitating contact between various persons and bodies, and campaigns. In these capacities, I undertook legal research and writing, and was exposed to dilemmas facing non-citizens living without visas, which later informed this investigation.

Challenges in researching 'illegality'

The ethical issues that arose in the research process revealed and reflected the contemporary Australian politics of migrant illegality, and underscore the oft-cited impossibility of research objectivity.[47] For instance, at the commencement of the study, my advertisements about the research, participant information statements, consent forms and other public documents all introduced the research focus as with 'migrants living without visas in Australia'. The research ethics committee expressed concern about my safety given the subject of my research, and suggested that my email address be removed from all public documents as a protection measure. This was the diametric opposite to the ethical concerns I held in relation to the research.

The most pressing concern for me was that the Immigration Minister could require me to breach confidentiality and disclose the identity and location of those believed to be non-citizens living unlawfully, refusal being a criminal offence punishable by a maximum of six months' imprisonment.[48] I addressed this through strict anonymity measures for the participation of non-citizens and did not collect residential contact details. Apart from this concern, informed by studies into the ethics of research with refugees, 'illegal' migrants and other vulnerable groups, I was acutely aware of the unequal political, systemic and individual power dynamic involved in the participation of non-citizens living without a visa. To address this issue, I avoided imposing pressure to participate by not directly recruiting participants. The conversations we shared in this research, however, were not easy and at times covered traumatic experiences from the past and the present. Yet participants did not solely express anger, frustration and despair; they also expressed pride in sharing their political strategies and involvements, and confidence in their assessment of the political and moral culpability of immigration and government for personal wrongs done to them, as well as the government's broader cynical manipulation of border security for electoral gain:

> Border security is throwing harpoons to the fisher boats during the election bringing up a fishing boat with ... some sort of lure and then sending the Federal Police to throw harpoon to sink their boat ... then using it in

47 Andrea Fontana and James H. Frey, 'The Interview: From Neutral Stance to Political Involvement', in *The Sage Handbook of Qualitative Research*, ed. Norman K. Denzin and Yvonna S. Lincoln (Thousand Oaks: Sage Publications, 2005).

48 *Migration Act* ss 18, 21.

> the television as if giving a flavour that we stopped an invasion: 'So we are the heroes, give us votes'.[49]

This emphasised to me the veracity of psychological research on the impact of trauma research participation upon survivors of physical violence or disaster that indicates that the majority do not regret their participation or experience negative impact from their participation.[50]

A broader ethical dilemma that underlies research with vulnerable groups is whether research can be ethical if it is of no direct benefit to participants. Good arguments have been put forward that academic research involving refugees and other vulnerable groups must go further than 'do no harm' to be ethically justifiable, and must explicitly aim to alleviate that suffering.[51] Certainly, upon starting my research, I grappled with this question given that I did not have confidence that my research would directly lead to political reform. But I was also cognisant of the need to respect the political agency and multifaceted identity of non-citizen participants to determine what 'benefit' from research might look like. Indeed, this was emphasised to me by those participants who saw their participation as political, as an opportunity to correct mistaken beliefs, or as a learning opportunity helpful in their own legal journey:

> Well I'm against capital punishment but still I think they [specific immigration officers] should be in prison at least for a few years, and if we are strong enough and we're focused then it is possible, it is not impossible. Presidents even go to jail, prime ministers go to jail. So the time has come actually to try them, to try real criminals.[52]

> I'm happy to be on the TV … put in a camera and I will speak. I swear, I'm happy with that.[53]

49 Interview with M1.

50 Elana Newman and Danny G. Kaloupek, 'The Risks and Benefits of Participating in Trauma-Focused Research Studies', *Journal of Traumatic Stress* 17 (2004); Michael G. Griffin *et al.*, 'Participation in Trauma Research: Is There Evidence of Harm?', *Journal of Traumatic Stress* 16, no. 3 (2003); Elana Newman and Elizabeth Risch, 'Ethical Issues in Trauma-Related Research: A Review', *Journal of Empirical Research on Human Research Ethics* 1, no. 3 (2006).

51 Richard Hugman, Eileen Pittaway and Linda Bartolomei, 'When "Do No Harm" Is Not Enough: The Ethics of Research with Refugees and Other Vulnerable Groups', *British Journal of Social Work* 41 (2011); David Turton, 'Migrants and Refugees', in *In Search of Cool Ground: War, Flight, and Homecoming in Northeast Africa*, ed. Tim Allen (Trenton: Africa World Press, 1996); Newman and Kaloupek, 'The Risks and Benefits of Participating in Trauma-Focused Research Studies'; Michael G. Griffin *et al.*, 'Participation in Trauma Research'; Newman and Risch, 'Ethical Issues in Trauma-Related Research'; Franck Duvell, Anna Triandafyllidou and Bastian Vollmer, 'Ethical Issues in Irregular Migration Research, Clandestino, European Union Citizens and Governance in a Knowledge-Based Society', in *CLANDESTINO Undocumented Migration: Counting the Uncountable, Data and Trends Across Europe* (Research DG, 2008); Valerie J. Smith, 'Ethical and Effective Ethnographic Research Methods: A Case Study with Afghan Refugees in California', *Journal of Empirical Research on Human Research Ethics* 4 (2009).

52 Interview with M1.

53 Interview with M12.

> I want to help for other people … Yeah, I don't want to like me, the same like me. Everybody want a work permit. Yeah, everybody need the work permit.[54]

It is important not to restrict an understanding of benefit to vulnerable populations within a limited framework of policy recommendations or reform. Susan Bibler Coutin reflected that fieldwork is never merely, nor even primarily, research.[55] The issue of 'benefit' must be understood within the broader context of research that can be just as much a legal, political and social practice. Here the process of the research itself made some steps towards realising one of my underlying motivations for this research – to make space for the voice of illegalised migrants to be heard.[56] At the time the interviews were undertaken and at the time of writing for publication, no peer organisation or community organisation or campaign exclusively focused on this group, although some community groups did engage with issues facing illegal migrants. Introducing this research to community legal centres, lawyers and migration agents, refugee advocates, union staff and broader community organisations implicitly challenged common delineations of those worthy of support. Simply framing this research on experiences of 'illegality', rather than identity-based legitimacy such as refugee status, has contributed to debate within different community sectors as to whether and how their activities should incorporate the unlawful non-citizen population. The research itself thus became part of political discussions and involved, in effect, an incidental advocacy.

Involvement in the research process also had political and legal consequences for those non-citizen participants living without a visa. A number later sought my assistance in linking them with legal assistance for matters that arose in our discussions. In one instance, this led to an interview participant pursuing compensation for his unlawful detention. Another participant supplemented his request to the Immigration Minister for intervention with information that I had shown interest in during our discussions. Although I was careful not to provide migration advice, it was clear that some interview participants found participation in the interview helped orient their understanding of their own immigration status and Australian migration law, and I did provide referrals. One interview participant, who had spent ten years living without a visa, now has a permanent visa and is sponsoring the migration of his elderly parents. Others I understand have since left Australia. As is evident, the ethics approach I adopted meant I had ongoing contact with those who sought a continued

54 Interview with M5.

55 Susan Bibler Coutin, 'Reconceptualising Research: Ethnographic Fieldwork and Immigration Politics in Southern California', in *Practicing Ethnography in Law: New Dialogues, Enduring Methods*, ed. June Starr and Mark Goodale (New York: Palgrave Macmillan, 2002).

56 David Brown, 'Giving Voice: The Prisoner and Discursive Citizenship', in *The Critical Criminology Companion*, ed. Thalia Anthony and Chris Cunneen (Sydney: Hawkins Press, 2008).

connection.[57] Contact over a longer timeframe confirms the absolute imbrication of research processes in the social processes they study. Participation in the research did play a role, for some, in the process of legalisation of status, and for others it played a small role in extending their social participation.

As an Australian citizen, a lawyer, an academic, it is important to situate myself in the research. I am an outsider to the experiences and struggles that I study.[58] Advocate and non-citizen participants treated me in a range of different ways – as 'Australian', as a lawyer, as a political ally, and as someone with potentially common experiences because of my non-Anglo background (I am of Chinese-Australian ethnicity). I was asked by most of the non-citizen participants about my own ethnic background and sometimes about my immigration history. I shared with a couple of the interview participants my own experience of being questioned on the street by police as a suspected illegal migrant, and all these factors formed part of the dialogue in which these stories emerged.

Important political questions arise for researchers who are outsiders to the communities affected by their research, and on this it is worth noting that the limited political debate on unlawful non-citizens within Australia is very different from the US, Canada and Europe. One reason for this is that the population of non-citizens living without visas in Australia is relatively small, and not vital to the national economy. In the US, 'illegal' migrants make up 3.6 per cent (or about 11.4 million) of the total US resident population, and the vast majority are Spanish speaking.[59] Demonstrations in 2006 by immigrants, both 'legal' and 'illegal', have been heralded as the largest social protests in the US.[60] The situation in Australia could not be more different and thus research on the regulation of migrant illegality poses more challenges than the acknowledged and pragmatic difficulty of access.[61] The lack of an organised political community of 'illegal' migrants at the time of my research provoked questions for this research such as: How should I understand the political claims of unlawful non-citizens from the stories I am hearing? How can I centre these voices as authors of knowledge? What aspects of policing are most pressing? And how do I act in solidarity with these struggles? I hope that spotlighting the extraordinary

57 An ethical approach to research with vulnerable people means being aware that the cessation or maintenance of contact with participants at the conclusion of fieldwork influences whether participants feel they are treated merely as sources of data: Hugman, Pittaway and Bartolomei, 'When "Do No Harm" Is Not Enough', 1278.

58 Bruce A. Collet, 'Confronting the Insider-Outsider Polemic in Conducting Research with Diasporic Communities: Towards a Community-Based Approach', *Refuge* 25, no. 1 (2008).

59 This is a 2012 estimate by the US Department of Homeland Security: see Jie Zong and Jeanne Batalova, 'Frequently Requested Statistics on Immigrants and Immigration in the United States', *Migration Information Source*. Last modified April 14, 2016, www.migrationpolicy.org/article/frequently-requested-statistics-immigrants-and-immigration-united-states#Unauthorized Immigration.

60 Juan Gonzalez, *Harvest of Empire: A History of Latinos in America* (New York: Penguin Books, 2011); Nicholas De Genova, 'The Queer Politics of Migration: Reflections on "Illegality" and Incorrigibility', *Studies in Social Justice* 4, no. 2 (2010): 102, 21.

61 Duvell, Triandafyllidou and Vollmer, 'Ethical Issues in Irregular Migration Research', 10.

power to make people illegal and tracing migration's law development of arenas of non-responsibility for coercive practices enables a better understanding of both the experience of migration policing and the law's role in disavowing responsibility for its effects.

Outline of the book

Policing Undocumented Migrants argues that migration law and policing practices marginalise and disavow the violent effects of their operation. Because virtually nothing is known about people's experience of illegal status outside the institution of immigration detention centres, the book develops accounts of how unlawful non-citizens are 'arrested', searched, detained and removed, as well as how people are made illegal or made marginally legal. The case study chapters follow a trajectory conventionally understood as moving from procedural police-like powers (Chapters 2 and 3) towards substantive visa determination (Chapter 5), with a study of a marginal form of legality (Chapter 4) acting as a transition between these two apparent divisions, and in doing so, the studies undermine the salience of this division.

Chapter 1 sets out the central conceptual concern of this book: How and why do migration legal practices disavow responsibility for the violent effects of their power? It begins with a case of immigration's breach of privacy in order to situate the gulf between non-citizens' experience of discretionary power and what the law claims is a just approach to responsibility. Drawing on policing and administrative law scholarship, the chapter proposes three lens though which the organisation of discretionary authority in migration control registers with greater clarity: the concentration of power at the front end of the migration process, the targeting of status, and the masking of differentiation through legal rhetoric of equality. Turning to issues of responsibility for power, the chapter contends that conceptualising the plural legalities of migration law using the tools of legal scale and jurisdiction is productive for identification of the disjuncture between frameworks of responsibility and migration laws effects. The conceptual approach in this chapter founds the inquiry and analysis in the chapters that follow, each of which develop the themes discussed to explain how the significance of discretionary authority is diminished, official legal wrongdoing is sanctioned and notions of wrongdoing are limited.

Chapter 2 is the first of two chapters discussing coercive migration policing powers and the regulation of these powers. Australia is somewhat unusual in that police have been involved in immigration enforcement since the nation federated in 1901. Today police hold many of the same powers as immigration officers. But police and immigration officers exercise the same powers in very different social scenarios and in the context of very different arrays of investigation and enforcement powers, and these chapters focus on the implications of these differences. In Chapter 2, the focus is on police and immigration officers' practices in taking people into immigration detention, that is in effecting immigration 'arrest' of people known or reasonably suspected to be unlawful non-citizens. It argues that migration law marginalises recognition of the violence engaged in these encounters through three perspectives. By foregrounding accounts of apprehension by police or immigration officers, it shows how detention proceeds as an experience of violence which lacks the conventional safeguards associated with arrest. Through examination of common ways that detention proceeds it illuminates how interplay between varied immigration powers and between criminal and migration powers, renders the requirement of reasonable suspicion of unlawful status meaningless in fundamental respects. Lastly, based on doctrinal analysis, it contends that the model of policing responsibility invoked by migration powers limits police and immigration officers' powers in particular ways. Evidence of the concentration of discretionary authority in the hands of police and immigration officers, and temporality as an organising principle for responsibility, are elaborated as connecting themes that emerge further in the following chapters.

Chapter 3 furthers the book's argument that migration law marginalises recognition of the violence it effects. This chapter examines scenarios of raids, searches and rapid removals, where the violent effects of policing are acknowledged, but legal responsibility is disavowed. It takes legal decisions and conventions as the primary source for analysis, and identifies the institutional and procedural conventions of administrative law which hinder accounts of migration law's violence from being documented in tribunal and judicial records. The first scenario examines how the law responds to a rare glimpse offered by two reported cases of immigration's breach of search warrant powers in raids of homes, and traces features that structure disregard for officers' contravention. The second case study focuses on rapid removal practices empowered through the interrelation of various migration procedures. It traces the constitution of legal authority for temporal control in the absence – or even contradiction – of policies with an explicit time dimension.

Chapter 4 analyses release from immigration detention or, in other words, the conditions that make a person marginally lawful. It involves the policing of status through examining the conditionality of the legal status of those released from detention. It is concerned with practices connected to detention but nevertheless peripheral, which have not received the extent of concerted advocacy as immigration detention. It is clear from listening to former detainees' experiences of and after release, as well as accounts of community advocates involved in sponsoring detainees' release, that release is not equivalent to liberty. Nor does it mean the end of conditions of the kind that defined incarceration. This chapter examines three features that have dominated the conditions of release on a bridging visa at various times: the constraints imposed by sponsorship requirements, the denial of work rights, and the requirement for unauthorised maritime arrivals to abide by a code of behaviour since 2013. These features produce a restricted form of liberty, subject to arbitrary controls, which make legal status precarious.

The precarious legal status that bridging visas afford reveals that, in the context of release from detention, legal status itself does not hold the central place afforded to it by the policy of mandatory detention of all unlawful non-citizens and the requirement that all non-citizens in Australia hold a visa. The relative insignificance of legal status in the context of release from detention was even more directly illustrated by instances when the state enforced illegality. Taking these constraints imposed on release seriously suggests that legal status may be utilised as a means of control, one that gains its violent effect through diverse means including by making compliance with rules materially impossible or creating uncertainty about what rules require for compliance.

The final case study, in Chapter 5, shifts the vantage point from the 'procedures' that produce migrant illegality to the substantive visa requirement that all non-citizens satisfy the character test. The character test sets out criteria that, if not satisfied, means a visa may be refused or cancelled. This chapter argues that stereotypes associated with 'nationality' have been utilised as a way to particularise and stabilise the broad subjective discretion empowered by the general conduct provision in the character test. In tribunal decisions from 1997 to 2006 'nationality' is deployed to interpret and organise disparate factors, to make sense of a person's honesty, and to evaluate the potential deterrent effect of visa refusal on others. These decisions show how 'common sense' implications derived from a person's nationality are made authoritative. The law of character also demonstrates that profiling, regarded as a procedural mechanism, animates discretion in court rooms over substantive visa determination just as much in the streets and in raids.

Migration law and legal practices involve extraordinary powers to make people illegal which are often overlooked as a consequence of their discretionary nature and of legal conventions of its administrative jurisdiction. Far from discretionary authority operating with residual flexibility to deal with exceptional matters, it is organised in particular ways that enhance its power and obscure responsibility for its effects. The conclusion to this book draws together how discretionary authority and non-responsibility have been organised through the policing of status. It argues that if, as a number of scholars have argued, the differential regimes of entitlements produced by migration laws bolster a system of 'global apartheid', then it is even more important that the law's work in marginalising the voices of those it makes illegal be resisted.

1 Borders of responsibility

It was 7pm one night in 2004 when a team of immigration officers raided a Sydney massage parlour, accompanied by media including a journalist and a photographer.[1] Vivienne was working that night. She had been in Australia for five years and her visa had been valid until a month before the raid.[2] A photographer kept shooting during the raid, transport and interviews at the immigration offices, disregarding the objections Vivienne expressed to both the photographer (who at the time she believed was an immigration officer) and to immigration officers. Immigration raided two sex industry workplaces accompanied by media that night. Ten days later, a sensational tabloid news article was published with an attention-grabbing headline referencing 'sex slaves'. It featured an image taken the night of the raid of the back of one of the women interviewed in a distinctive jacket, referenced the nationality of the women detained, where they were taken, and reported details of immigration's interviews with the women.[3] As soon as it was published, it was handed around those in detention and the women were harassed and abused. In 2006, immigration acknowledged it failed to protect Vivienne's privacy and issued a letter of apology. But the harm could not be undone.

Being identified as a sex worker changed Vivienne's life. The local diasporic community and her family in her country of origin 'all turned their backs' on Vivienne.[4] Because of her profile in her country of origin, she believed her capacity to find employment on return was ruined. After lodging a visa application, Vivienne spent more than two years in detention while it was being processed, reviewed and appealed. During that time, her mental health deteriorated, she started taking medication for anxiety and depression, and she was seriously assaulted by another individual in detention.

1 The details in this account are derived from Interviews with M4, perusal of documents from the interview participant's immigration file, obtained by her by freedom of information request, news sources (details not provided here to protect anonymity) and Commonwealth and Immigration Ombudsman, 'Report for Tabling in Parliament by the Commonwealth and Immigration Ombudsman: Under S4860 of the *Migration Act 1958*, Personal Identifier 226/07, Tabled in Parliament 13 February 2008' (Canberra: Commonwealth and Immigration Ombudsman, 2007).

2 Vivienne had not realised the visa had expired because she had understood from the tribunal reviewing her case that immigration would be in contact with her prior to its expiry.

3 To protect Vivienne's anonymity reference to this article is not included.

4 Commonwealth and Immigration Ombudsman, 'Report for Tabling in Parliament by the Commonwealth and Immigration Ombudsman'.

I met with Vivienne on a number of occasions in 2008, two years after immigration's apology. At that time, Vivienne held a bridging visa, which had enabled her release from detention. She had asked the Immigration Minister Chris Evans to use his personal discretion to grant her a permanent visa on the basis of exceptional and compelling humanitarian grounds because of immigration's actions. The bridging visa gave Vivienne permission to stay temporarily in the Australian community while awaiting the Immigration Minister's response to her request, but provided no guarantee that she would not be taken back into detention when she attended immigration for visa renewal. In this extended period of negotiating the complexities of migration law and complaints systems, Vivienne learned what many non-citizens do: that there is a fundamental incompatibility between the expectations of justice for the harms experienced by non-citizens and the legal framework of responsibility.

The disconnect between expectations of justice and responsibility for the impact of the exercise of power is encapsulated in the view Vivienne's psychiatrist in Villawood Immigration Detention Centre expressed to her when he said, 'Well you know, you can't get compensated for your time in detention … because you put yourself voluntarily in this position'. Vivienne explained:

> Till the very day today the Department is denying that it's [my situation] a consequence of what they've done. They're telling me it's wrong, 'you end up in detention because you overstayed'. Okay, so they refuse to make connection between what they done and my prolonged detention and it's very hurtful. You think you've wasted – you've lost two years in this bloody hole and they said 'Well that was your choice' basically. What was my other choice? To go home? What home? I don't have a home after what you've done. What am I going to do? 'Well we can give you a visa to come on the court'. I said if you can give me visa from [my country of origin], do you think I'm going to have every couple of months $2000 or $3000 to attend the court? … You know that it's not realistic.… They isolate you and they don't give you the right information; they don't give information at all. Basically all they're telling you constantly that you don't have rights and your only way is home and that's their answer for everything. When this thing [the privacy breach] happened, they presented [me] with a ticket to leave.[5]

From Vivienne's perspective, the damage was done. Justice required that immigration accept responsibility and make amends by granting her a permanent visa to stay in Australia. From the perspective of immigration, remedy for the breach of privacy was a matter separate to that of visa decision-making. Vivienne was ineligible for the only permanent visas open to her and, as mentioned, her only prospect to stay relied on the Immigration Minister's personal discretion. Law

5 Interview with M4.

and outsider narratives of justice can appear, as illustrated in the contrasting perspectives expressed above, to be 'incommensurable languages'.[6]

Law is important to study because it occupies a prominent place in normative hierarchies. Legal rules and procedures describe what the law *expects* of officials and what the law *allows* officials to do.[7] It claims to exclusively delineate what constitutes justice. It is inherently coercive, which bolsters its socially normative force.[8] At stake in the policing and legal regulation of migrant illegality is the justice system not being able to *recognise* the harm that non-citizens suffer. This issue is not unique to migration control.[9] Scott Veitch, for example, argues that the law itself is complicit in the production of large-scale human suffering such as widespread human rights violations, environmental and nuclear devastation and forms of colonialism.[10] Veitch offers an analysis that reverses the conventional focus on law as a source of obligation and responsibility and instead traces the way in which legal institutions and practices organise irresponsibility, or create a 'zone of non-responsibility'.[11] The administrative forum of migration law has its own conventions, doctrines and institutional organisation that make such an analysis necessary in order to understand how non-citizens' experiences of migration control are marginalised in law and legal records.

This chapter proposes that two main conceptual sites in the migration legal order are key to understanding how migration law's *violence*, also defined, is authorised. Analysis of these two sites exposes *how* the government perspective and government practices come to exclusively define the narrative of justice. The first site is that of discretionary authority. Discretionary authority by definition can never be fully articulated by legal text. Analysis of discretionary *practice* is required for its contours to be rendered clear. The argument in this part of the chapter unfolds through examining three central modes of organisation of discretion that render its practice legally authoritative: (i) the concentration of discretion at the front end of a socio-temporal process that marginalises recognition of its violence; (ii) targeting practices that normalise differential treatment

6 George A. Martinez, 'Philosophical Considerations and the Use of Narrative in Law', *Rutgers Law Journal* 30 (1999): 688.

7 Doreen J. McBarnet, *Conviction: Law, the State and the Construction of Justice* (London: Macmillan, 1981), 6–7.

8 Robert Alexy, 'A Defence of Radbruch's Formula', in *Recrafting the Rule of Law: The Limits of Legal Order*, ed. David Dyzenhaus (Oxford: Hart, 1999), 27; also discussed in Scott Veitch, *Law and Irresponsibility: On the Legitimation of Human Suffering* (New York: Routledge-Cavendish, 2007), 24–7; Martinez, 'Philosophical Considerations and the Use of Narrative in Law'.

9 This has also been particularly vivid in feminist analyses of how the criminal trial mobilises social myths of sexual abuse and assault through seemingly neutral evidentiary rules on sexual history and corroboration: see, for example, S. Caroline Taylor, *Court Licensed Abuse: Patriarchal Lore and the Legal Response to Intrafamilial Sexual Abuse of Children* (New York: Peter Lang, 2004); Janet Galbraith, 'Processes of Whiteness and Stories of Rape', *Australian Feminist Law Journal* 14, no. 1 (2000): 71–89.

10 Veitch, *Law and Irresponsibility: On the Legitimation of Human Suffering*.

11 Ibid., 21.

on the basis of migration legal status; and (iii) the masking of differential treatment in practice by legal rhetoric of equality.

The second site for analysis is that of the plural legalities involved in immigration practices. A key problem in responsibility for migration law's violence is that its logic and practice does not match with the framework of oversight it has established. This part of the chapter argues that the tools of legal scale and jurisdiction help disentangle the plural or 'interlegalities' involved in immigration practices. The analytical tools introduced in this chapter are developed further in the case study chapters in order to raise questions about the usefulness of the administrative legal framework for addressing the violence experienced by those made illegal by migration law and policing. Before turning to these perspectives, let us investigate the meaning of 'violence'.

The violence of migration law and policing

Migration law and policing no doubt involve violence. The violence of law should be understood 'first and foremost in its embodiment and effects on embodied subjects'.[12] It is 'utterly real'.[13] It includes, as Robert Cover rightly elaborates, pain such as the loss of freedom through incarceration, physical pain, psychological pain, the separation of a parent from their child, and the deprivation of property, which itself has some role in the conditions of life and survival. Migration law and policing encompasses the gamut of these forms of violence. Every non-citizen interview participant relayed an experience of migration law's violence, and in many the psychological and somatic effects were inseparable, as in the accounts below of terror, stress and sweat:

> It was such a terrible experience [having officers come to my house and detain me in the police station because my visa had expired]. I mean if I'm in front of a lion I will not be that much terrified. I mean the way they terrified me, the whole thing was organised to terrify. It's just terrifying people. They're playing on the psychology so that they give up.[14]

> All the guys they coming, all Aussie and a couple of Asian, they come in the kitchen and two of my friend was illegal, me and the other guys.... And I'm like whoa, I can't do anything; all my body sweats. This is – we're getting busted, getting busted, getting busted, and it was lucky the guys is not immigration, the guys is like – because the boss wanted to sell the business.[15]

12 Austin Sarat, 'Situating Law between the Realities of Violence and the Claims of Justice: An Introduction', in *Law, Violence, and the Possibility of Justice*, ed. Austin Sarat (Princeton: Princeton University Press, 2001), 8.

13 Robert Cover, 'Violence and the Word', *Yale Law Journal* 95(1986): 1609.

14 Interview with M1.

15 Interview with M8.

The law enacts violence every day – either as part of the explicit means through which it expresses its authority (such as indefinite immigration detention) or by providing implicit acquiescence or justification (such as the absence of criminal culpability for acts done in self-defence).[16] The instrumental use of violence has been understood as 'law-preserving' violence – violence that guarantees the law's enforcement, promotes the law's monopoly over violence and thus makes the law's continued existence possible.[17] While not every legal relation involves the instrumental use of violence (notably fines), 'the normal abnormality of bureaucratic abstraction'[18] may mask the violence engaged by legal interpretation. Violence is implicated in immigration processes and decisions that make people illegal, the subject of this book, because unlawful status is a trigger for mandatory immigration detention and removal. Even in instances where force is not explicitly used, it remains residually present to endorse the authority of law.[19] Thus, although visa cancellation is not an act of violence itself, because it results in unlawful migration status and thus occasions detention and authorises subsequent removal from Australia, it, as Cover states of legal interpretation more generally, 'takes place in a field of pain and death'.[20] In practice, the official mandatory nature of detention is ameliorated by discretion. But the legislative mandate that requires detention of all non-citizens without a visa keeps detention proximate and the restricted temporary legal status afforded as an alternative to detention institutes conditions of violence. This book seeks to develop a broader understanding of the law's organisation of responsibility for the violence of migration law and policing outside immigration detention centres.

Organised authority: discretion in migration control

In its simplest sense, discretion is the permission to make a decision, the 'room for decisional manoeuvre';[21] 'a sphere of autonomy within which one's decisions are in some degree a matter of personal judgment and assessment'.[22] Discretion permeates immigration processes. The Immigration Minister has delegated discretion to immigration officers to grant and cancel visas, and statute provides officers with detention and other powers to conduct what is referred to as 'compliance' activities. In so doing, immigration reflects the modern state,

16 Sarat, 'Situating Law', 3.

17 Walter Benjamin, 'Critique of Violence (1920–1)', in *One Way Street and Other Writings* (London: New Left Books, 1979).

18 Sarat, 'Situating Law', 3.

19 Ibid.; Stephen Skinner, 'Stories of Pain and the Pursuit of Justice: Law, Violence, Experience and Jurisprudence', *Law, Culture and the Humanities* 5, no. 1 (2009): 139.

20 Cover, 'Violence and the Word', 1601.

21 Jeffrey Jowell, 'The Legal Control of Administrative Discretion', *Public Law* (1973): 179.

22 Denis J. Galligan, *Discretionary Powers – A Legal Study of Official Discretion* (Oxford: Clarendon Press, 1986), 8.

characterised by the conferral and reliance on officials' delegated discretion to make decisions and thus maintain the wide variety of regulatory activities of the state.[23] Despite the acknowledgement of the existence of discretion, its profound significance as a source of violence and organised legal authority is not sufficiently appreciated. The orthodox narrative of the development of immigration law provides some explanation for this neglect, as does the influence of legalistic conceptual frames that treat discretion as separate to law or in isolation from the social and legal dimensions that organise discretion as legally authoritative. Each of these issues will be addressed in turn.

The historical trajectory of immigration law in Australia has been portrayed as progressively, to borrow the terminology of Kenneth Culp Davis, confined (by restricting its scope), structured (through setting out a procedure and standards for the exercise of discretion) and checked (by scrutiny and review options).[24] It is true that the law has moved on from the early days of immigration control in Australia. The 1901, the *Immigration Restriction Act 1901* (Cth) embedded extraordinary discretion over the entry and prohibition of immigrants, most infamously through the dictation test used to exclude non-white immigration, and which was abolished in 1958.[25] Even in the 1970s, decision-making was idiosyncratic, guided by the *Migration Act 1958* (Cth) ('*Migration Act*') which simply empowered officers to 'grant to the immigrant an entry permit'. Although policy manuals guided decision-making, they were not published, which undermined the predictability of decision-making.[26] Prior to 1989, the Immigration Minister's power to grant an entry permit was simply that, a power, and the law was, as Kathryn Cronin stated, mere 'machinery' to authorise that power.[27]

Reforms in the 1970s and 1980s informed the sense that immigration law was appropriately fettered. In the 1970s, a series of Commonwealth committees reviewed Australia's administrative law system[28] and the resulting administrative reform introduced a merits review tribunal of general jurisdiction, the

23 Ibid., 72–84.

24 Kenneth Culp Davis, *Discretionary Justice: A Preliminary Inquiry* (Baton Rouge: Louisiana State University Press, 1969).

25 Kathryn Cronin, 'A Culture of Control: An Overview of Immigration Policy-Making', in *The Politics of Australian Immigration*, ed. James Jupp and Marie Kabala (Canberra: AGPS, 1993), 91.

26 Ian Freckelton, *Administrative Decision-Making in Australian Migration Law* (ANU eText, 2015), 29; Mary Crock and Laurie Berg, *Immigration, Refugees and Forced Migration: Law, Policy and Practice in Australia* (Annandale: The Federation Press, 2011), 113; Andrew Metcalfe, 'Administrative Law Evolution: An Administrator's Point of View', *Admin Review* 59 (2010): 43.

27 Cronin, 'A Culture of Control'.

28 See Commonwealth Administrative Review Committee, 'Commonwealth Administrative Review Committee Report', Parliamentary Paper No. 144 (Canberra: Commonwealth of Australia, 1971) ('Kerr Committee Report'); Committee on Administrative Discretions, 'Final Report of the Committee on Administrative Discretions', Parliamentary Paper No. 316 (Canberra: Commonwealth of Australia, 1973) ('Bland Committee Report'); Committee of Review of Prerogative Writ Procedure, 'Report of the Committee of Review of Prerogative Writ Procedure', Parliamentary Paper No. 56 (Canberra: Commonwealth of Australia, 1973) ('Ellicott Committee Report').

Commonwealth Ombudsman[29] and a statute governing judicial review,[30] often referred to as the 'new administrative law'. An immigration-specific committee review followed[31] and ushered in reforms in 1989 that codified existing policy into legally binding Regulations, set out clear visa classes and objective criteria for application which sought to remove discretion for officers, and almost entirely removed Ministerial discretion. Codification of visa criteria was designed to respond to earlier governmental review that found 'excessive discretionary features'[32] were creating uncertainty in visa decision-making. The 1989 reforms also introduced access to immigration-specific merits review beyond that which had been available. In this new immigration law system, the Immigration Minister retained certain powers to grant visas not otherwise permitted under legislation, but the limitation of these powers to the Minister's personal discretion indicated they were powers of an 'exceptional, last resort, or residual kind'.[33]

There is truth to the argument that current discretion in migration has been confined, structured and checked much more than in former times. But despite detailed legal criteria, guidance and merits review, an extraordinary discretion remains over the production of illegal mobile subjects – in other words, migrant illegality. The challenge in enabling this discretion to come into view is captured by Denis Galligan's comment that, despite the widespread permeation of discretion, 'an analysis of discretionary power has not been a major concern of legal theory. Discretionary authority is generally thought of as peripheral to the core of settled rules in terms of which legal order is characterized'.[34] Centring discretionary authority as productive of illegal migrants means dismantling one key legalistic epistemology: that some clear distinction can be made between 'discretion' and 'law'.

The argument that there is a bright line between types of discretion and law was most strongly put by Ronald Dworkin. Dworkin argued that judges do not truly exercise discretion, and thus judges do not make law, but discover the pre-existing rights of the parties.[35] While judges ordinarily exercised what Dworkin referred to as weak discretion – meaning discretion that involved *judgment* to interpret or apply a standard or *finality* in that it could not be reviewed nor reversed – when faced with the absence of a standard for application judges did

29 Administrative Appeals Tribunal (established July 1, 1976); Administrative Review Council (established in 1975).

30 *Administrative Decisions (Judicial Review) Act 1977* (Cth).

31 Committee to Advise on Australia's Immigration Policies, 'Immigration: A Commitment to Australia', Parliamentary Paper No. 335 (Canberra, 1988) ('FitzGerald Report').

32 Joint Management Review, 'Immigration Functions Related to Control and Entry' (Canberra: Commonwealth of Australia, July 1978), 115; Committee to Advise on Australia's Immigration Policies, 'Immigration: A Commitment to Australia', 112–13.

33 *Plaintiff S10/2011* v. *Minister for Immigration and Citizenship* [2012] HCA 31; (2012) 246 CLR 636 [111] (Heydon J), [30] (French CJ, Kiefel J), [55] (Gummow J).

34 Galligan, *Discretionary Powers*, 1.

35 Ronald Dworkin, *Taking Rights Seriously* (London: Duckworth, 1978), 31–9, 68–71.

not utilise a strong sense of discretion to create such standards but were instead guided by legal principles. But as Galligan rightly stated, there is little to distinguish weak from strong discretion – even ostensibly 'weak' discretion involved in the interpretation of standards may involve 'strong' policy-style choices between competing standards.[36] This observation is particularly germane in the administrative field, where administrators are often required to achieve 'broadly defined policy goals in individual cases'.[37]

Approaches that view discretion as categorically distinct from 'law', or even orient discretion by reference to law, promote the flawed policy notion that legislative or policy-based reform fundamentally changes administrative activities. In practice, more finely tuned rules do not necessarily equate to greater predictability and may compel legalistic adherence in favour of reasoned decisions directed towards organisational ends.[38] Moreover, the presence of discretion throughout all processes of a legal bureaucracy like immigration means that controls themselves may not necessarily manage discretion, but rather lead to 'the phenomenon of displacement. Squeeze in one place and, like tooth-paste, discretion will emerge at another'.[39]

Discretion is present in all aspects of the decision-making of legal and bureaucratic institutions; it is 'woven into a broader process'.[40] Because it involves the freedom to 'make a choice among possible courses of action or inaction'[41] it cannot be completely articulated by legal text. This is why, as a form of authority, discretion has been characterised by its 'amorphousness' and its 'undefineability'.[42] It must be understood as a social phenomenon that is constituted by its social and legal relations, whereby practices that assert the power of law are backed by the potential of coercion and are treated as law by those subjected to it. The notions of 'finality' and 'judgment' are not important for distinguishing types of non-law like discretion but are important in understanding the sociological effects of discretion as legal authority.

How discretion is exercised is socially and historically specific, but insights from policing scholarship open up questions relevant to the immigration setting. In the 1960s, Anglo-American scholars found that police utilised discretion through careful observational studies of police-work,[43] and the understanding that discretion

36 Galligan, *Discretionary Powers*, 14–20.

37 Ibid., 63.

38 Jowell, 'The Legal Control of Administrative Discretion', 192–4.

39 Robert Baldwin and Keith Hawkins, 'Discretionary Justice: Davis Reconsidered', *Public Law* (1984): 582.

40 Ibid., 580; Jowell, 'The Legal Control of Administrative Discretion'.

41 Davis, *Discretionary Justice*, 4.

42 Markus D. Dubber, *The Police Power: Patriarchy and the Foundations of American Government* (New York: Columbia University Press, 2005), xi, xv.

43 See, for example, J. H. Skolnick, *Justice without Trial* (New York: John Wiley & Sons, 1966); Egon Bittner, *The Functions of Police in Modern Society* (Chevy Chase, MD: National Institute of Mental Health, 1970); James Q. Wilson, *Varieties of Police Behavior: The Management of Law and Order in Eight Communities* (Cambridge: Harvard University Press, 1968).

is 'a policeman's daily task' soon became the grounding assumption of police scholarship.[44] Policing and criminal justice literature, which has engaged with the social, spatial, temporal and legal contexts of discretion, thus provides insights useful when considering how discretionary practices become legally authoritative.

By 'authoritative', I mean that practices act and are treated as legally authorised, that is as law, not that these practices are legitimate. Discretionary practices may become legally authorised, for example, by their explicit or implicit endorsement in a court or where their practice is never reviewed and thus represents finality for a matter. In the migration law and policing of illegal non-citizens, three analytical lenses reveal crucial ways in which the organisation of discretion produces such practices as legally authoritative. By becoming legally authoritative government practice comes to exclusively define justice and marginalises the violent effects of migration law and policing.

Concentrating power: front-end discretion

The concept of 'front-end' discretion provides a helpful interpretive frame to understand the concentration of discretion as a process unfolding through time, which, in the immigration environment, is mobilised in specific sites as part of a layered and constantly shifting border. The term 'front end' was used by Markus Dubber in order to locate where the bulk of power is exercised in procedural criminal law.[45] In criminal law and trial process in the US, Dubber contended, the 'center of gravity lies at the front-end of the process'.[46] The term captures an important argument in criminal law scholarship which challenges the traditional view that positions the trial as the dominant forum in criminal process. This body of literature draws attention to the concentration of discretion in pre-trial actors, such as police and prosecutors, and processes such as arrest, bail and charge negotiation.[47] Front-end discretion has two distinguishing features:

44 Leslie George Scarman, *The Scarman Report: The Brixton Disorders 10–12 April 1981 Report of an Inquiry* (Harmondsworth: Penguin, 1982), [4.58].

45 Markus D. Dubber, 'The Possession Paradigm: The Special Part and the Police Power Model of the Criminal Process', in *Defining Crimes: Essays on the Special Part of the Criminal Law*, ed. R. A. Duff and Stuart Green (Oxford: Oxford University Press, 2005), 93; see also Markus D. Dubber, 'The New Police Science and the Police Power Model of the Criminal Process', in *The New Police Science: The Police Power in Domestic and International Governance*, ed. Markus D. Dubber and Mariana Valverde (Stanford: Stanford University Press, 2006); Markus D. Dubber, *The Police Power*.

46 Dubber, 'The Possession Paradigm', 93.

47 See, for example, Richard Ericson, *Reproducing Order: A Study of Police Patrolwork* (Toronto: University of Toronto Press, 1982), 3–11, 206; Robert Reiner, *The Politics of the Police*, 2nd edn (Hertfordsire: Harvester Wheatsheaf, 1992), 139–46; Gail Travis, 'Police Discretion in Law Enforcement: A Study of Section 5 of the NSW *Offences in Public Places Act 1979*', in *Issues in Criminal Justice Administration*, ed. Mark Findlay, Sandra J. Egger and Jeff Sutton (Sydney: George Allen and Unwin, 1983); Malcolm M. Feeley, *The Process Is the Punishment: Handling Cases in a Lower Criminal Court* (New York: Russell Sage Foundation, 1992), 34; Dubber, 'The New Police Science', 136; Dubber, 'The Possession Paradigm', 94; Mark Neocleous, *The Fabrication of Social Order: A Critical Theory of Police Power* (London: Pluto Press, 2000), 105.

it is a site where discretionary decisions invoke the 'finality' Dworkin associated with weak discretion by the judiciary; and, because of the finality involved, it is of low visibility.

In immigration, 'front-end' discretion is the product of both its temporal and socio-spatial location in immigration processes. This is apparent from the discourse of the immigration portfolio, which at least since the early 2000s, has envisioned its work as adopting a 'layered' approach to the border. The Australian Border Force recently stated: 'We consider the border not to be a purely physical barrier separating nation states, but a complex continuum stretching offshore and onshore, including the overseas, maritime, physical border and domestic dimensions of the border'.[48] It envisages a series of administrative processes and multiple actors involved in filtering visa applicants and exercising discretion to effect exclusion in decisions that range from visa refusal, refusing to board a passenger overseas with suspect documents, and turning back a person after cancelling their visa on arrival. The transnational nature and disaggregated spatiality of the border is well recognised, as is its production by many acts of bureaucratic and legal performance.[49] But a more comprehensive understanding of front-end discretion requires integration of these spatial insights with the temporal locus of discretion in immigration processes.

Thinking through the analytic of 'front-end' discretion allows the concentration of administrative power to surface more fully. It moves the site for analysis backwards from the review tribunal and the court and also situates the actions of officers of first contact within immigration-related legal processes. The front-end analytic thus invests the actions of officers empowered under the *Migration Act*, including immigration, police and customs officials, with significance as part of the legal process. Actions that begin and end with the officer of first contact are of 'low visibility'.[50] This is acute in circumstances where police decide not to invoke the criminal process. Police decisions not to investigate nor report an apparent criminal offence are overwhelmingly not subject to review or public oversight. Officers' decisions and conduct in such scenarios evidently involve aspects of finality. In criminal justice, early actions in the process, such as settling a charge, have more weight over the outcome of a trial than the trial itself.[51] In immigration, this

48 Australian Border Force, 'About the Australian Border Force', accessed December 1, 2016, www.border.gov.au/australian-border-force-abf/who-we-are.

49 Leanne Weber and Benjamin Bowling, 'Policing Migration: A Framework for Investigating the Regulation of Global Mobility', *Policing and Society* 14, no. 3 (2004); Sandro Mezzadra and Brett Neilson, *Border as Method, or, the Multiplication of Labor* (Durham: Duke University Press, 2013); Connal Parsley, 'Performing the Border: Australia's Judgment of "Unauthorised Arrivals" at the Airport', *The Australian Feminist Law Journal* 18 (2003); Alison Kesby, 'The Shifting and Multiple Border and International Law', *Oxford Journal of Legal Studies* 27, no. 1 (2007).

50 Joseph Goldstein, 'Police Discretion Not to Invoke the Criminal Process: Low-Visibility Decisions in the Administration of Justice', *Yale Law Journal* 69, no. 4 (1960): 12; Ericson, *Reproducing Order*.

51 See, for example, Mike McConville, Andrew Sanders and Roger Leng, *The Case for the Prosecution: Police Suspects and the Construction of Criminality* (London: Routledge, 1993).

holds true. For example, in street policing, once identification of an unlawful non-citizen has been made, the law *requires* immigration detention.[52] The front-end analytic brings the concentration of discretion in the identification stage to the fore, and thus opens up questions about the adequacy of the immigration law framework in guiding and providing oversight over officers' actions. Officers under the *Migration Act* utilise the same immigration powers, but they operate in different spaces, with different objectives, institutional routines and cultures, with different impetus for initial intervention and in the context of different, broader powers at their disposal. Chapter 2 illustrates how the interaction between multiple sources of authority for policing practices concentrates discretion at the front end of the process.

The front-end analytic is relevant not only to policing encounters. The finality involved in finding and characterising facts in visa determinations by immigration officers and tribunals also involves powerful discretion. Some do not view the finding of facts as part of discretionary legal authority. But it should be seen this way because the tasks of finding facts and applying legal standards cannot be separated. The application of a legal standard to facts first requires the finding of the facts (which involves 'judgment')[53] and in so doing constructs a version of reality produced for adjudication or other decision.[54] This is particularly apparent in immigration decision-making, where the credibility of a visa applicant's narrative is an important part of visa assessment at all level of administrative decision-making and necessarily involves a high degree of subjective judgment, as is explored in Chapter 5.[55] The legislative restriction of judicial review over immigration matters to matters involving jurisdictional error, such as errors of law, further concentrates the factual determination in the front end of the process.[56]

52 *Migration Act* s 189. Note there is more subtlety to the mandatory detention policy in practice: see Chapter 4.

53 Galligan, *Discretionary Powers*, 34–5.

54 Baldwin and Hawkins, 'Discretionary Justice', 34–5; Galligan, *Discretionary Powers*, 33–7; McConville, Sanders and Leng, *The Case for the Prosecution*.

55 See also Catherine Dauvergne and Jenni Millbank, 'Burdened by Proof: How the Australian Refugee Review Tribunal Has Failed Lesbian and Gay Asylum Seekers', *Federal Law Review* 31 (2003); Jenni Millbank, 'From Discretion to Disbelief: Recent Trends in Refugee Determinations on the Basis of Sexual Orientation in Australia and the United Kingdom', *The International Journal of Human Rights* 13, no. 2 (2009); '"The Ring of Truth": A Case Study of Credibility Assessment in Particular Social Group Refugee Determinations', *International Journal of Refugee Law* 21, no. 1 (2009); Laurie Berg and Jenni Millbank, 'Constructing the Personal Narratives of Lesbian, Gay and Bisexual Asylum Claimants', *Journal of Refugee Studies* 22, no. 2 (2009).

56 See the privative clause in *Migration Act* s 474, and the High Court's interpretation in *Plaintiff S157/2002* v. *Commonwealth of Australia* [2003] HCA 2; (2003) 211 CLR 476; 195 ALR 24; and discussion in Caron Beaton-Wells, 'Judicial Review of Migration Decisions: Life after S157', *Federal Law Review* 33, no. 1 (2005); Duncan Kerr, 'Privative Clauses and the Courts: Why and How Australian Courts Have Resisted Attempts to Remove the Citizen's Right to Judicial Review of Unlawful Executive Action', *Queensland University of Technology Law and Justice Journal* 5, no. 2 (2005); Mary Crock, 'Judging Refugees: The Clash of Power and Institutions in the Development of Australian Refugee Law', *Sydney Law Review* 26, no. 1 (2004).

An important implication of the concentration of front-end discretion is that the traditional distinction between procedural and substantive law is less stable and less relevant. An orthodox view regards migration provisions such as search and detention as procedural powers that assist the administration of the visa regime, not as part of the substantive law of visa criteria which dictates who will hold a visa. In criminal justice, the blurred distinction between procedural and substantive law is vividly illustrated by the role police play in defining conduct that amounts to broadly worded offences such as 'offensive behaviour'.[57] In migration, the conventional distinction between procedural and substantive law becomes unstable in various ways. Chapter 2 discusses a case in which legal practices that are ostensibly procedural (the form of notification of visa cancellation) materially affected access to substantive lawful status. Substantive visa decision-making can also take on procedural features, as is explored in Chapter 5.

The significance of discretion in immigration is overlooked partly because, unlike the separation between judicial and executive power threatened by the front-end concentration of power in the criminal justice process, administrative processes are *intended* to hold broad discretion over the regulation of non-citizens and it is part of the lawful remit of administration. The normality itself prevents discretion from being taken seriously. The analytic of front-end discretion illuminates how discretion concentrates, and through finalising aspects of decision-making, becomes legally authoritative. Drawing on this analytic the chapters that follow examine points in the legal process – such as the practice of taking a person into custody, the final merits review determining visa eligibility or cancellation – to explore the extent to which the violent effects of these practices register in law.

Normalising differentiation: policing status

> It's not legal. It's policy. So all I discovered, like they target a group of people. Like now the students will be arrested. That's policy, that's not legal. There has to be a rule of law, a consistent rule of law everywhere. Now that's not happening in the *Migration Act*.[58]

The analytic of profiling or targeting is crucial to understand the significance of discretionary power in policing status. Targeting involves discrimination as part of its practice. Government has framed targeting practices as those oriented towards unlawful non-citizens, non-citizens in breach, and management of non-citizens' adherence to visa conditions more generally. These practices are important, but must be understood as always contingent upon a more general targeting of migration legal status, which is an essential part of how differentiated treatment on the basis of status becomes normalised. This section starts by explaining how

57 Travis, 'Police Discretion in Law Enforcement'.
58 Interview with M1.

immigration plans and understands its own targeting practice, and then proposes key methods, both legal and social, which are essential components to understand how migration legal practices target and normalise the policing of status.

Immigration's approach

Immigration frames its targeting practice as including visa administration, such as visa grant and cancellation (often referred to as *visa integrity programmes*); the promotion and support of voluntary compliance (often referred to as *visa status resolution services* or *compliance*); and field activities in order to locate those living without a visa or in breach of visa conditions (often referred to as *compliance operations*). On this view, the effectiveness of profiling is assessed in terms of the apparently rational or statistical basis for its focus[59] and, on this measure, it fails. In Australia, immigration does not plan its operations to locate 'illegal' non-citizens and those in breach of visa conditions on the basis of predictive risk analysis identification of which segments of the population are likely to be non-compliant. This was evident from audits in 2004 and 2015, despite the formal adoption in 2011 of a compliance strategy that modelled integrated engagement in a 'feedback loop' between the prevent/deter/detect/respond stages of compliance.[60]

Various government reports over the years have documented instead that immigration utilises intelligence from other government institutions, civil actors and community sources to identify individuals for compliance action.[61] It also focuses its fieldwork attention on industry as a site of illegal work in general as well as on specific industries. This relationship- and industry-based strategy emphasises the role of front-end discretion and targeting structured on broader institutionalised suspicion. Particular industries have been consistently targeted for various compliance operations because they are viewed as industries considered to 'traditionally' employ illegal workers based on casual or seasonable demand, low-skill requirements and high worker turnover.[62] The most consistent and top-ranking targets have been hospitality (including accommodation, restaurants, clubs and cafes), the sex industry, factories and rural industries.[63]

59 Karen S. Glover, *Racial Profiling: Research, Racism and Resistance*, Issues in Crime & Justice (Lanham: Rowman and Littlefield, 2009), 43.

60 Australian National Audit Office ('ANAO'), 'Managing Compliance with Visa Conditions: Department of Immigration and Border Protection, Performance Audit' (Barton, 2015), 25, also citing the DIBP Compliance Strategy 2012–15.

61 See, for example ANAO, 'Onshore Compliance: Visa Overstayers and Non-Citizens Working Illegally Department of Immigration and Multicultural and Indigenous Affairs' (Canberra, 2004), 47.

62 ANAO, 'Managing Compliance with Visa Conditions', 70.

63 See, for example, the top workplaces in which people were found to be working without immigration authorisation in 1998–99: DIMA, 'Review of Illegal Workers in Australia: Improving Immigration Compliance in the Workplace' (Canberra, 1999), 21; the industries most subject to employer awareness sessions and most issued warning notices following immigration having found illegal workers in their employ in 2002–03: ANAO, 'Onshore Compliance', 70–2.

Within this bureaucratic frame, institutions and actors other than immigration are positioned in a subsidiary role feeding information to immigration in an 'intelligence led, risk-based' visa compliance strategy set out in the Department of Immigration and Border Protection's (DIBP) 2015–19 Corporate Plan.[64]

Policing status through visa conditions

Targeting is evident in migration law and policing in a number of dynamics missed in a narrow focus on fieldwork. Attaching conditions to visas is a method to police status. Visa conditions target 'risk' through imposing individualised conditions upon grant or variation of a non-citizen's visa. Visa conditions police status, as explored in Chapter 4, by making release from detention into the community conditional. In some instances, conditions such as the prohibition on work pose impossible conditions for compliance, and produce a constant state of incipient illegality. In others, visa conditions produce a metaphysical prison for non-citizens despite their release from immigration detention. Other conditions, such as prohibition on further stay at the conclusion of a visa period, are imposed on whole classes of visa holders or on those who fit particular risk profiles. The imposition of conditions provides a flexible way through which individuals may be grouped as targets and are subject to limitations on entitlements (such as period of stay, social entitlements and freedom of movement to return after departure from Australia). The targeting engaged via visa conditions suggests that a continuum-based risk approach exists to mediate the presence of non-citizens in Australia, although risk prediction had not achieved prominence in informing fieldwork deployments by 2015.

Status-based discretion in law

Migration law primarily targets migration legal status, not conduct. This is crucial to understand the significance of discretionary power in migration. A status-based focus activates a broad and flexible discretionary authority in selecting the proper subject of migration policing practice. A status-based focus has long been a feature of Australian migration law, despite the shift from illegal status as a criminal offence to illegal status as an administrative classification.

From 1901 to 1994, it was a criminal offence to enter or be found in Australia as a prohibited immigrant.[65] In 1953, the High Court expressed some ambivalence as to whether the offence involved wrongful conduct, traditionally required for criminalisation alongside mental fault. Chu Shao Hung, a Chinese national, had been deemed a prohibited immigrant on the basis of immigration legislation that stipulated that a person could become a 'prohibited immigrant'

64 ANAO, 'Managing Compliance with Visa Conditions', 24–6, 74; DIBP, 'Corporate Plan 2015–19' (Belconnen, 2015).

65 *Immigration Restriction Act 1901* (Cth) ss 5 (if also fails the dictation test), 7 (1901–33).

if they failed to accurately transcribe 50 words of a language selected by a migration officer (known as the 'dictation test').[66] Williams ACJ explained that, despite the offence being made out by failure of the dictation test, this did not appear to amount to a conduct element of the offence:

> The giving of a dictation test to an immigrant is not for the purpose of testing his education. It is given so that his failure to pass the test (and it can be assumed that he will fail), will convert into an immigrant deemed to be a prohibited immigrant offending against the Act.[67]

Williams ACJ's statement reflects the understanding of the role of the dictation test at the time. It enabled designated officers to distinguish between those morally respectable white immigrants who were not its intended targets, and the undesirable non-white others perceived to pose a threat to white Australia. As Kitto J comments, the culpability of Chu Shao Hung did 'not necessarily involve any element of wrongdoing.... His offence under s.5 (6) is complete, even though ... his conduct has been exemplary'.[68] It was his status, not his conduct, that was at issue.

As a status-based criminal offence, the historical offence of being found to be a 'prohibited immigrant' empowered flexible intervention analogous to that of vagrancy laws. Vagrancy is regarded as an exemplar of status offences. Status offences characteristically depart from criminal law principles that make a person liable on the basis of their conduct and subjective mental fault. By making a person's status, not specified conduct, central to the offence, vagrancy laws enabled police to distinguish between the morally respectable working poor, who were not its intended targets, and the idle and socially undesirable poor perceived to be a threat to urban order.[69] Status offences thus have been regarded as broad discretionary powers to 'identify and eliminate threats',[70] and as better typified as police powers not as a substantive criminal law offence.[71]

The decriminalisation of unlawful status has not changed the law's focus on status not conduct. From 1994, the criminal offence of being an 'illegal entrant' (a designation that superseded the 'prohibited immigrant') was abolished and replaced with a 'binary structure', a classification structure for status within Australia.[72] Non-citizens are either 'lawful non-citizens' or 'unlawful non-citizens'.[73] Hayne J states that the *Migration Act* 'provides no middle ground'.[74] Despite

66 Ibid., s 3.
67 *Chu Shao Hung* v. *R* [1953] HCA 33; (1953) 87 CLR 575, 583 (Williams ACJ).
68 Ibid., 589 (Kitto J).
69 Kimber, 'Poor Laws', 538.
70 Dubber, *The Police Power*, 136.
71 Alex Steel, 'Consorting in New South Wales: Substantive Offence or Police Power?', *University of New South Wales Law Journal* 26, no. 3 (2003).
72 *Plaintiff M47/2012* v. *Director-General of Security* [2012] HCA 46; (2012) 251 CLR 1; 292 ALR 243, 291 [176]–[178] (Hayne J).
73 Ibid.
74 Ibid., 291 [178] (Hayne J).

political rhetoric of the putative illegality implicated in unlawful non-citizen status, the courts have been clear that the terms 'lawful' and 'unlawful' do not 'refer to any breach of a law which expressly prohibited the conduct of entering or remaining in Australia without permission'.[75] 'Unlawful non-citizenship' embeds broad discretion in policing by requiring a focus only on status not conduct.

Institutionalising status-based classification

Today, the targeting of status is aided and enabled by legal and bureaucratic measures that institutionalise classification of persons by migration legal status in many social arenas. Strategies that recruit government and civil actors in immigration practices of visa verification, monitoring or reporting represent the enactment of the border in the nation's interior by more finely regulating a non-citizen's access or exclusion to entitlements. In bureaucratic language, it is what is referred to as a whole-of-government and community policing approach to the 'problem' of illegal migration. It brings citizenship and migration status into being as a normalised target of surveillance in general community and civil life.

In practical terms, for some government actors, this is achieved by the delegation of powers (such as the power to detain) or by memoranda of understanding and institutional routes to share information (such as prisons advising of the date and details of a non-citizen's release). Even where these formal measures have been instituted, a smooth governmental system that classifies persons in terms of their migration legal status upon contact has by no means been achieved. Coordination between government departments remains patchy and in many areas is characterised by informal agreements and inconsistency nationally.[76] As Leanne Weber comments: 'Rather than acting from a shared commitment to border control, the government and non-government actors who participate in migration policing networks maintain distinct organisational objectives that sometimes converge in the identification of unlawful non-citizens'.[77]

Bringing migration legal status into civil life has been addressed with legal and bureaucratic vigour through strategies of 'responsibilisation'. Policing through neoliberal techniques of 'responsibilisation' or 'governing at a distance'

75 *Al-Kateb* v. *Godwin* [2004] HCA 37; (2004) 219 CLR 56, 73 (Hayne J).

76 See, for example, ANAO, 'Managing Compliance with Visa Conditions'; ANAO, 'Administering the Character Requirements of the Migration Act 1958: Department of Immigration and Citizenship' (Barton, 2011), 60–1; ANAO, 'Onshore Compliance' (2004); Commonwealth and Immigration Ombudsman, 'Department of Immigration and Multicultural Affairs Administration of S501 of the *Migration Act 1958* as it Applies to Long-Term Residents' (Canberra: Commonwealth Ombudsman, Commonwealth of Australia, 2006), 40, 60; DIBP, 'Annual Report 2013–14' (Belconnen, 2014), 248.

77 Leanne Weber, *Policing Non-Citizens* (Oxford: Routledge, 2013), 161.

is intended to enhance the authority and extend the reach of policing.[78] Private and civil involvement in policing is generally understood to have become more widespread and important as governments in the Anglo-American world have come to lose confidence in their capacity to control crime and, as David Garland argues, respond to this predicament by outsourcing these functions.[79] Migration control reflects this trend.

The establishment of structures to streamline civil actors checking individuals' migration legal status and community reporting of those believed to be unlawful has been an important mechanism to institutionalise status-consciousness. In the early 2000s, communication between immigration and community and industry bodies ranged in formality and depended on the development of personal relationships. For example, by June 2001, immigration's relationship with the construction industry had progressed to the point that immigration provided the NSW Secretary of the Construction Forestry Mining and Energy Union with a regular contact in the Employer Awareness Unit for information on illegal workers.[80] It was not until 2004 that immigration embarked on a more deliberate institutional strategy for receiving community information on the identity and whereabouts of 'illegal' migrants with the introduction of the 'Immigration dob-in line' which remains in operation today.[81] Although reporting is voluntary, the Immigration Minister at the time emphasised the 'wealth of knowledge in public hands that is vital to the operation of our compliance activities',[82] and the media appealed to the public's sense of competition and self-interest when it presented it as a launch of an 'immigration cheat' and 'illegal immigrant' hotline'.[83] An analogous initiative was introduced in 2006 but to facilitate a whole-of-government consciousness of migration legal status, and continues to operate today. The 24-hour Immigration Status

78 Pat O'Malley, 'Risk, Power and Crime Prevention', *Economy and Society* 21, no. 3 (1992); Pat O'Malley, 'Risk and Responsibility', in *Foucault and Political Reason: Liberalism, Neo-Liberalism, and Rationalities of Government*, ed. Andrew Barry, Thomas Osborne and Nikolas Rose (London: UCL Press, 1996); Pat O'Malley and Darren Palmer, 'Post-Keynesian Policing', *Economy and Society* 25, no. 2 (1996); David Garland, *The Culture of Control: Crime and Social Order in Contemporary Society* (Oxford: Oxford University Press, 2001), 124–7; Mariana Valverde, *Law's Dream of a Common Knowledge* (Princeton: Princeton University Press, 2003), 141–66.

79 Garland, *The Culture of Control*, 110; Tim Newburn, 'The Commodification of Policing: Security Networks in the Late Modern City', *Urban Studies* 38, no. 5–6 (2001).

80 Richard Steven Konarski (DIMIA), 'Statutory Declaration' (Melbourne: Royal Commission into the Building and Construction Industry, 2002); see also DIMIA, 'Royal Commission into the Building and Construction Industry Discussion Paper Eleven – Working Arrangements – Their Effects on Workers' Entitlements and Public Revenue' (Melbourne: Royal Commission into the Building and Construction Industry, 2002).

81 Amanda Vanstone (Minister for Immigration and Multicultural and Indigenous Affairs), 'Immigration Dob-in Line Launched', Media Release, February 19, 2004. Note that the 'dob-in' is Australian vernacular for turning a person in to the authorities.

82 Ibid.

83 McConville, Sanders and Leng, *The Case for the Prosecution*; Kerr, 'Privative Clauses and the Courts'.

Service ('ISS') provides a dedicated hotline for police and other government agencies to seek information about non-citizens' visa status.[84]

Legal measures to compel or encourage civil actors to check migration legal status are also a vital part of the mechanism for embedding status-consciousness in key arenas of civil life. Institutions providing education services to overseas students are required by law to monitor student compliance with visa conditions, which require students to maintain satisfactory attendance and course progress.[85] Should a student visa holder breach these conditions, the education provider is charged with issuing a notification to the student to report to immigration within a set timeframe, failure of which leads to automatic student visa cancellation.[86] The legal requirements on employers do not obligate direct monitoring, but from 2006, it has been an offence for an employer to hire a non-citizen in breach of their work restrictions.[87] Although the sanctions do not specifically require employers to request evidence of immigration status and work permission, sanctions operate as a 'legal lever'[88] to encourage alignment with immigration goals to prevent illegal work. Immigration encourages *universal* work entitlement checks as the 'easiest way to avoid [racial] discrimination' and avoid committing the reckless form of the offence.[89]

The involvement of non-immigration government agencies develops a 'whole of government' consciousness of migration legal status. For education institutions and employers, obtaining citizenship and visa details reflects civil actors' material investments to avoid sanctions. For Australian citizen community members, status consciousness encourages identification with 'Australian citizenship' and protection of the privileges that entails by ensuring those benefits are not accessed by others.[90] The distribution and coordination of migration controls outside the immigration department normalises status-based classification and differentiation on the basis of migration legal status.

Masking differential practices: legal rhetoric of equality

A third lens which helps spotlight the significance of discretionary power in migration control is the contrast between legal rhetoric or ideology and legal

84 Ibid., 39–40.

85 See the National Code of Practice for Providers of Education and Training to Overseas Students 2007, established under the *Education Services for Overseas Students Act 2000* (Cth).

86 *Migration Act* s 137J.

87 *Migration Act* ss 245AB, 245AC, introduced by *Migration Amendment (Employer Sanctions) Act 2007* (Cth).

88 Ibid.

89 DIMA, 'Review of Illegal Workers 1999', 43; DIAC, 'Do Your Employees Have a Valid Visa to Work in Australia?' (Canberra, 2007), 5, 9; Senate Legal and Constitutional Legislation Committee, 'Migration Amendment (Employer Sanctions) Bill 2006' (Canberra: Commonwealth of Australia, 2006), 15.

90 Aileen Moreton-Robinson, *The White Possessive: Property, Power, and Indigenous Sovereignty* (Minnesota: University of Minnesota Press, 2015).

practices.[91] This is not the same as a distinction between 'law in the books' and 'law in action' as legislation, case law and policing practices are all, sociologically, legal practices. Rhetoric here refers to high and general principles that are assumed to guide legal practice, whereas legal practices are all those procedures and rules that compose the mechanics through which law is practised.[92] Doreen McBarnet highlights the value of exploring the contrast between legal rhetoric and legal practices as one which reveals the politics of law:

> To question whether the law incorporates its own rhetoric is to ask whether deviation from standards of justice and legality are not merely the product of informalities and unintended consequences at the level of petty officials, but institutionalised in the formal law of the state.[93]

It is a lens that is helpful because, at first glance, the ideological mandate of migration law reads as unrelentingly flexible; its legislative object is to: 'regulate, in the national interest, the coming into, and presence in, Australia of non-citizens'.[94] In other words, its premise is to manage differential access to social, territorial and, through migration provisions, legal entitlements, in order to articulate distinctions between citizens and non-citizens, and between classes of non-citizens. It does this through the minutiae of visa criteria and visa restrictions, notably prohibitions on work and state subsidised medical care, the power to refuse or cancel a visa on broad grounds, and from 1994 the statutory power to indefinitely detain a non-citizen present in Australia without a visa.

On closer examination, there are limits to the extent of differentiation authorised. Prior to 1985, the unconditional power to deport prohibited immigrants signified that the principles of natural justice were not intended to apply to the deportation of prohibited immigrants.[95] This position changed after one of the most important judicial decisions for unlawful non-citizens, the High Court decision of *Kioa* v. *West*,[96] which was made when it was a criminal offence to be found a 'prohibited immigrant', and the principal finding of which continues to apply to unlawful non-citizens today. In this case Deane J infamously stated, 'An alien who is unlawfully within this country is not an outlaw',[97] and is not bereft of the law's protection. Deane J went on to outline the law's constraint of administrative action regarding aliens:

91 McBarnet, *Conviction: Law, the State and the Construction of Justice*, 8, 154–68; Doreen McBarnet, 'Legal Form and Legal Mystification: An Analytical Postscript on the Scottish Criminal Justice Act, the Royal Commission on Criminal Procedure, and the Politics of Law and Order', *International Journal of the Sociology of Law* 10 (1982).

92 McBarnet, *Conviction: Law, the State and the Construction of Justice*, 6.

93 Ibid., 8.

94 *Migration Act* s 4.

95 *Salemi* v. *Mackellar (No 2)* [1977] HCA 26; (1977) 137 CLR 396 [27]–[28] (Gibbs J).

96 *Kioa* v. *West* [1985] HCA 81; 159 CLR 550; 62 ALR 321.

97 Ibid., 631 (Deane J).

> Nor is such an alien without status or standing in the land. He can invoke the protection of the law, including the protection of the writ of habeas corpus, against any government official or private citizen who acts unlawfully against him or his property. *He can look to, and demand the observance of, the ordinary restraints which control the exercise of administrative power* including, unless they be excluded by reason of statutory provision or the special nature of the case, the standards of procedural fairness which are recognised as fundamental by the common law.[98]

In a case two years later, Deane J further emphasised this issue:

> The common law of Australia knows no lettre de cachet or executive warrant pursuant to which either citizen or alien can be deprived of his freedom by mere administrative decision or action. Any officer of the Commonwealth Executive who, without judicial warrant, purports to authorise or enforce the detention in custody of another person is acting lawfully only to the extent that his conduct is justified by clear statutory mandate.... It cannot be too strongly stressed that these basic matters are not the stuff of empty rhetoric. They are the very fabric of the freedom under the law which is the prima facie right of every citizen and alien in this land. They represent a bulwark against tyranny.[99]

Such entitlements are due even to those in immigration detention.[100]

These big-picture principles do not map easily onto migration policing practice. It is not always clear what legislative authority officials are reliant upon in, for example, depriving a non-citizen of their liberty. It is extremely rare, however, for migration policing practices to face legal challenge. In reality, what is permitted, encouraged and required by the routines, conventions and practice of migration law and policing differentiates treatment of the subjects of migration policing from that held out by general principles. The legal rhetoric of equal treatment functions to mask the reality of such differential treatment and differential access to protection.

These three analytical lenses – front-end discretion, policing status and legal rhetoric – provide insight into how discretionary authority is constituted and maintained. These lenses show how the organisation of discretion concentrates and normalises its operation and, for some practices, proceeds under the masking rhetoric of equality. The next part of the chapter turns to the site of the plural legalities of migration practice and its relationship with legal frameworks of accountability. This furthers understanding of migration's discretionary authority

98 Ibid., 631 (Deane J), 564 (Gibbs CJ) (emphasis added).

99 *Re Bolton; Ex parte Beane* [1987] HCA 12; (1987) 162 CLR 514, 528–529; see also *Ruddock* v. *Taylor* [2005] HCA 48; (2005) 222 CLR 612 [138] (Kirby J).

100 *Soh* v. *Commonwealth* [2008] FCA 520; (2008) 101 ALD 310 [82].

because authority is always produced through the socio-legal negotiations between the empowerment of discretion and its constraint. The constitutive relation between these dynamics is captured in Mark Findlay's concept of 'boundaries of permission', which positions discretionary police dominion as the outcome of the interrelation between the opportunity for that policing activity (shaped by its aspirations and processes) and control mechanisms of accountability as a brake on police authority.[101] The control mechanisms of interest here are those frameworks of responsibility for administrative practice.

Ordering frameworks of responsibility

Legal conventions organise and order systems that make the imposition of responsibility appear natural, and consequently create 'zones of non-responsibility'.[102] Two main theoretical tools help clarify how the plural legalities regulating migrant illegality produce non-responsibility for the violent effects of migration law and policing. The notion of legal scale provides resources to disentangle the logics and accountability frames respectively at work in citizenship law and policing legal practice. The problem for illegal migrants is that the logic of migration law and policing escapes the national scale of citizenship, and, theorising jurisdiction as the 'governance of legal governance',[103] further elaborates the problem by showing how the separation between legalities is made to appear natural, thus obscuring the gaps in responsibility practices.

Boaventura de Sousa Santos introduced the cartographic tool of scale for study of how laws are organised and ordered so that their regulation of objects appears natural.[104] As a tool that translates geographic three-dimensional realities into the two dimensions of paper, Santos argues scale performs a similar task by distinguishing between scales of laws and, in doing so, creates an organised and orderly misreading of reality.[105] In this view, local laws like council ordinances are large scale. In local laws, social reality is captured in minute detail. Local laws regulate by closely representing objects and activities and where they should be and what they should do.[106] In contrast, international law involves small-scale legality. It is low on detail, operates through generalisations, and regulates by orienting, for example, by providing universal standards by which to judge position, and direct aspirations.

101 Mark Findlay, 'The Ambiguity of Accountability: Deaths in Custody, and the Regulation of Police Power', *Current Issues in Criminal Justice* 6, no. 2 (1994).

102 Veitch, *Law and Irresponsibility*, 21.

103 Mariana Valverde, 'Jurisdiction and Scale: Legal "Technicalities" as Resources for Theory', *Social and Legal Studies* 18, no. 2 (2009): 141.

104 Boaventura de Sousa Santos, 'Law: A Map of Misreading. Toward a Postmodern Conception of Law', *Journal of Law and Society* 14, no. 3 (1987): 281.

105 Ibid., 282.

106 Ibid., 287–91.

Critical for identification of how responsibility for migration law's violence is marginalised is that, although these different forms of law create different legal objects of regulation, it is ordinary for multiple orders to act upon the same social object. For Santos, this requires attention to the interaction and intersection between legal orders. Because of the multiplicity at work, 'one cannot properly speak of law and legality but rather of interlaw and interlegality'.[107] In the legal regulation of migrant illegality, it is the intersection between the legal orders of citizenship and policing, each of which operate as 'interlaw', that is at issue. Scale provides a resource to unpack the multiple legal scales simultaneously at work and thus better identify how the violent effects of migration law fail to register as unlawful.

Legal geography approaches have been taken up by scholars focusing on citizenship practices in order to unpack changes in citizenship practices. Traditionally, citizenship represents a classically national scale law. Citizenship frames the legal status of individuals in terms of state membership within the nation. 'Citizenship' here is meant broadly to include citizenship and migration laws. Both laws regulate the terms and social entitlements of state membership within the nation. Both are instrumental in producing normative political closure at the national level (note that the *Migration Act* is the only source of right for non-citizens to enter or remain in Australia).[108] Yet citizenship is not produced solely at the national scale. The plural legality of citizenship law is evident through critiques that the formal legal entitlements of citizenship have in practice differentiated benefits on racialised and gendered terms. The plural legality of citizenship law is more dramatically illustrated through recognition of the membership claims of 'illegal' non-citizens, being those with ostensibly no legal claim on the state.

A legal geography analysis of citizenship has been taken up prominently by scholars in the US, perhaps because of the political and legal context in which more than 11 million residents are illegal migrants.[109] The phenomenon of 'sanctuary cities' in the US, which offer refuge and protection for undocumented migrants, has prompted much debate on this issue. In these cities, some police departments have decided not to enforce immigration law on the basis that enforcing immigration laws frustrates their competing objective to encourage victims of crime to report to police regardless of their immigration status.[110] Further, growing number of US city police agencies accept 'matrículas consulares', identity cards issued by the Mexican government to its citizens living in

107 Ibid., 288.

108 *Migration Act* s 4.

109 Jie Zong and Jeanne Batalova, 'Frequently Requested Statistics on Immigrants and Immigration in the United States', *Migration Information Source*. Last modified April 14, 2016. www.migrationpolicy.org/article/frequently-requested-statistics-immigrants-and-immigration-united-states# Unauthorized Immigration.

110 Jennifer Ridgely, 'Cities of Refuge: Immigration Enforcement, Police, and the Insurgent Genealogies of Citizenship in U.S. Sanctuary Cities', *Urban Geography* 29, no. 1 (2008).

the US, as identification.[111] In other words, these practices by government officials have extended social and political inclusion beyond that to which illegal migrants are legally entitled. In a series of papers, Monica Varsanyi reflects on city-based practices that effect a partial inclusion of illegal migrants in the US. Varsanyi argues such measures gesture towards development of 'citizenship-as-inhabitance' or 'urban citizenship':[112]

> In effect, local communities are collapsing the processes of immigration and naturalization into 'local neoliberal membership moments', which enable the presence and residence of undocumented migrants within their communities without giving them firm and permanent purchase in the United States.[113]

Although Varsanyi doesn't go so far as to say that local laws are producing national citizenship laws, she posits that it illustrates the multi-scalar nature of citizenship.[114] Equally these practices illustrate the multi-scalar nature of policing.

The migration law and policing practices analysed in this book present an especial challenge for classification of legal scale. On the one hand, these practices are concerned with the entitlements dictated at the national scale. Migration law and policing seeks to ensure that individuals access only eligible entitlements: no study or work unless permitted, visa cancellation upon breach of visa conditions, detention of those without a visa, release of those upon visa grant, and so on. In other words, migration policing involves the enforcement of nuanced differential legal regimes of entitlements determined by status, and reflects the national scale of citizenship.

On the other hand, practices of 'enforcement' can never be simply described as the application of law; these practices always involve discretion that does not easily map onto the national scale of citizenship. As will be discussed and explored in Chapter 2, the range of actors involved in identifying, locating and apprehending unlawful non-citizens in Australia might be motivated by suspicion of drug possession, public order concerns and other factors distant from concerns about status and membership. But nor can these concerns be reduced to the minor concerns of local law. A strong argument running through Mariana Valverde's work is that the urban and local should not be collapsed into a single concept, and that urban regulation involves a qualitatively different type of governance than that at the state

111 See Monica W. Varsanyi, 'Interrogating "Urban Citizenship" vis-à-vis Undocumented Migration', *Citizenship Studies* 10, no. 2 (2006): 242.

112 Ibid., 239–40.

113 Monica W. Varsanyi, 'Rising Tensions Between National and Local Immigration and Citizenship Policy: Matrículas Consulares, Local Membership and Documenting the Undocumented', in *Working Paper 140* (San Diego: The Center for Comparative Immigration Studies (University of California), 2006), 21.

114 Monica W. Varsanyi, 'Rescaling the "Alien", Rescaling Personhood: Neoliberalism, Immigration, and the State', *Annals of the Association of American Geographers* 98, no. 4 (2008); Varsanyi, 'Interrogating "Urban Citizenship"'.

level.[115] For Valverde, the kind of regulatory and preventative logic exhibited by the continental police science of the seventeenth century epitomised urban regulation. This earlier form of police held a remit that partly overlaps with contemporary local government tasks (including garbage collection, hygiene, good order and crime prevention), which Michel Foucault, reflecting on the domain of the French police, explained were 'urban' because they addressed issues that existed only in towns, arose because of a town, or were prominent in towns.[116] The urban regulation of police logic was characterised by flexibility over its temporal orientation, directed towards the future through education, prevention and risk management as well as towards the past through enabling punishment for past wrongs.[117] Migration law and policing, like other forms of policing, cannot be constrained to a single legal scale.

Migration law and policing within Australia also function as part of the broader management of the circulation of people across the globe. Foucault talks about circulation as a technology of power utilised by biopolitical practices of security.[118] Biopolitical power is a mode of population level governance which distributes life's chances through producing the conditions where some are made to live and others 'let die'. On this understanding, the problem for characterising migration law and policing as a particular legal scale is that the object being secured through the management of circulation is not the juridical-political citizen.[119] The referent object of biopolitical security is the biological mass of the population, that is, the human species.[120] Contemporary analysis of Australian immigration suggests a varied manifestation of this – that managed migration is integral to strengthening the Australian population conceived as an economic not a genetic entity.[121] In either perspective, the logic of migration law and policing escapes the national scale of citizenship.

115 Valverde, 'Jurisdiction and Scale'; Valverde, 'Seeing Like a City: The Dialectic of Modern and Premodern Ways of Seeing in Urban Governance', *Law & Society Review* 45, no. 2 (2011); Markus D. Dubber and Mariana Valverde, 'Perspectives on the Power and Science of Police', in *The New Police Science: The Police Power in Domestic and International Governance*, ed. Markus D. Dubber and Mariana Valverde (Stanford: Stanford University Press, 2006); Mariana Valverde, 'Police, Sovereignty, and Law: Foucaultian Reflections', in *Police and the Liberal State*, ed. Markus D. Dubber and Mariana Valverde (Stanford: Stanford University Press, 2008).

116 Michel Foucault, *Security, Territory, Population: Lectures at the Collège De France, 1977–78*, ed. Michel Senellart, gen ed. François Ewald and Alessandro Fontana, English series ed Arnold I. Davidson, trans. Graham Burchell (Houndmills: Palgrave Macmillan, 2007), 335.

117 Dubber and Valverde, 'Perspectives on the Power and Science of Police'.

118 Michel Foucault, *Society Must Be Defended: Lectures at the Collège De France 1975–1976*, ed. Mauro Bertani *et al.*, trans. David Macey (London: Penguin Books, 2004); Michel Foucault, *Security, Territory, Population: Lectures at the Collège De France, 1977–78*, 15, 45; Mark B. Salter, 'To Make Move and Let Stop: Mobility and the Assemblage of Circulation', *Mobilities* 8, no. 1 (2013): 9.

119 Michael Dillon and Luis Lobo-Guerrero, 'Biopolitics of Security in the 21st Century: An Introduction', *Review of International Studies* 34 (2008): 273–4.

120 Ibid.

121 Mark Kelly, 'Racism, Nationalism and Biopolitics: Foucault's Society Must Be Defended, 2003', *Contretemps* 4 (2004).

The notion of scale is useful for analysis of the mismatch between a particular exercise of power and the legal scale of its accountability framework, but it does not completely explain how responsibility for the violence of migration law is marginalised. Many of the violences in migration law potentially give rise to grounds for civil litigation. Why then do the voices of illegal migrants and their experiences remain largely outside the legal record? It is not solely because illegal non-citizens and non-citizens more generally face significant barriers to initiating litigation. The answer can also be found in the organisation of legal frameworks of responsibility and by appreciating that 'the governance of legal governance is the work of jurisdiction'.[122]

Analysis of the *organisation* of legal responsibility is supported by Valverde's contention that the technical notion of jurisdiction offers resources for theorising legal governance that she argues adds to that of Santos's approach to scale.[123] Jurisdiction draws in the relevance of who is empowered, where power may be exercised, what is empowered to be done, and how power should be exercised.[124] Valverde explains that the relationship between these moves – the unfolding 'chain reaction' of jurisdiction – makes the simultaneous operation of very different rationalities of legal governance appear natural, provided these powers are exercised by a particular authority and in a particular place.[125] In practical terms this means that

> [t]he conflicts between the constitutional rights that operate at the level of the nation-state and the legal governance processes that operate at the local/urban scale very seldom erupt into view. Why? Because of the blackboxing of both scales and jurisdictions that is an integral, constitutive part of 'interlegality'.[126]

The temporalities, referent objects, knowledges, logics of migration law and policing constitute an 'interlegality' subject to limited accountability because it does not match the legal logics of local, national or international law. This is explored further in Chapter 3, but informs the enquiry throughout all the case studies into the legal conventions, meanings, institutions and structures that obscure migration law's violence from legal records and thus from responsibility. It is this 'blackboxing' that represents an organised, structured marginalisation and non-responsibility for migration law's violence.

Conclusion

> At that time [when immigration issued an apology] they did not admit, they were just using terms like 'alleged breach of privacy', in a sense like

122 Valverde, 'Jurisdiction and Scale', 141.
123 Ibid.
124 Ibid., 144, 41.
125 Ibid., 142–4.
126 Ibid., 150.

> 'sorry for everything that you went through' and 'allegedly disturbed you' and it was everything in terms like 'alleged, alleged, alleged, alleged, alleged', but at the time already the Ombudsman made the report on my case, a recommendation of compensation and apology. So I got apology but I didn't get released; another four months I was still sitting in detention and in these four months I think I broke.[127]

For Vivienne, the clash between the justice that was delivered and her belief in the justice that was owed is captured in the drawn-out four months she spent after immigration apologised for breaching her privacy. From her experience, it is easy to see the 'blackboxing' between the respective interlegalities of citizenship and policing, and the harm that separation sustains. As such, Vivienne's experience reveals many of the features that organise discretionary power and the plural legalities at work in migration law and policing. The concentration of discretion at the front end of the process was evident from immigration's invitation to media to attend. More importantly, Vivienne's experience reveals how formal 'visibility' on many occasions, such as through media coverage, does not ensure accountability, and shows the impact of normalising migration legal status as a policing target. Immigration's conduct of her interview in the presence of media and the relay of details demonstrates how many of the protections afforded to suspects in criminal justice are not extended to those subject to migration policing, despite legal rhetoric of equal protection from state intrusion. The two years Vivienne spent in detention, only to be released on a bridging visa which provided only short periods of lawful status before requiring application for renewal, reflects the slippery purchase of migration law and policing on the scale of citizenship.

The law plays a vital role in ordering how justice is practised, and how violence is part of that practice, coupled with disavowal of responsibility for that violence. Taking discretion seriously means turning to practices that are not completely captured in legal text and that take shape through their social relation and their relation to frameworks of oversight and accountability. It means examining how discretion is organised, enlivened and extended. And it means analysing the work of scale and jurisdiction in ordering legal frameworks of responsibility to consider how migration law's violence comes in and out of law's view, structuring the purchase of legal accountability. In the case study chapters that follow, the organisation of responsibility and non-responsibility through the features of temporality and spatiality is developed in both the conceptual sites of discretion and plural legalities discussed in this chapter. The analytical tools introduced in this chapter are developed further in the case study chapters in order to raise questions about the usefulness and limitations of the administrative legal framework for addressing the violence experienced by those 'made illegal' by migration law and policing.

127 Interview with M4.

2 'You're just kidnapped'

Immigration 'arrests' and detention

Mohammad was working as a security guard at a bus depot when New South Wales (NSW) Police handcuffed and removed him in front of his colleagues on the basis that he did not hold a valid visa. Many aspects of Mohammad's apprehension by police are typical of those in a public place, particularly his concern regarding what it communicated to his colleagues with whom he had friendly relationships of mutual respect:

> They handcuff me, the police, in the bus depot and I'm a security officer. All the bus depot people, they're looking at me ... [They were thinking] Oh I'm a drug dealer? ... They're thinking this guy committed some crime, because it's the police, it's not the immigration. When the police come, they think it's something else, because when they see the uniform they think something else.[1]

Stephen, who was stopped by NSW Police while he was driving and was also found not to hold a visa, reported a similar experience. He was initially pulled over by one police wagon, but, soon after, six wagons and two or three sedans came when police called for back-up, a number Stephen felt was excessive given his compliance with police directions. Police drove his girlfriend (who had been in the car with him) to her parents' house and, while talking with her parents, described Stephen as 'a criminal' despite his lack of criminal history. Stephen explained: 'Makes me feel like an idiot too, the way they go through everything. How will I show my face to the family?'[2]

There is little public awareness in Australia that police as well as immigration officers have the power to detain people under migration laws. In fact, NSW Police and immigration officers, as designated 'officers' under the *Migration Act 1958* (Cth) ('*Migration Act*'), both hold various immigration powers analogous to the powers police hold in exercising their criminal jurisdiction.[3] The most impactful is the power to detain. Immigration detention is a key and controversial site of border violence, but its practice outside its institutional confines – that

1 Interview with M2.

2 Interview with M10.

3 *Migration Act* s 5.

is, its use as a power that authorises taking individuals into custody – is remarkably neglected by scholars and activists. The same provision and the same words that authorise the entire regime of mandatory immigration detention also gave police authority to take Mohammad and Stephen into custody, as the *Migration Act* provides that '[i]f an officer knows or reasonably suspects that a person ... is an unlawful non-citizen, the officer *must* detain the person'.[4]

For those detained, although the experience of detention by immigration or police mimics that of arrest for a criminal offence, the law does not treat detention for unlawful migration status as arrest. Police do not rely on the power to arrest without a warrant for a criminal offence because living without a visa is not a criminal offence in Australia. However, this was not always the case. Historically, particular definitions of illegal status amounted to a criminal offence (for example, 'prohibited immigrant' and later 'illegal entrant') and, for these matters, police, immigration and customs officers were empowered to arrest and detain individuals.[5] In doing so, officers were statutorily required to abide by conventional safeguards on arrest, including informing the person of the reason for their arrest and taking the person before a magistrate (or other prescribed authority) within 48 hours, which thus inserted the court's supervision of the arrest. In practice, at least in 1994 when the Department of Immigration and Ethnic Affairs (DIEA) explained its practice to a parliamentary committee, about one-third of the 'illegal entrants' (those who had generally entered Australia lawfully but subsequently lost their lawful status) arrested and detained were never brought before a magistrate because they either departed or were released within 48 hours.[6] If the person was brought before a magistrate, the magistrate was authorised to continue detention for a maximum of seven days (which could be extended) if satisfied that reasonable grounds existed to suppose the individual was an illegal entrant, or to otherwise release the individual.[7] However, anecdotal evidence from the early 1990s suggests it was extremely rare for magistrates to release detainees and when they did so it was because they were satisfied that detainees held a valid entry permit or they saw continued detention as 'inappropriate',[8] not, it would seem, because of improper arrest practices.

The contemporary legal framework regulating detention commenced in 1994 with migration law reforms that decriminalised the presence of non-citizens unlawfully in Australia by doing away with a complex system of 'illegal'

4 Ibid., s 189 (emphasis added); see also discussion in Chapter 4.
5 See, for example, *Migration Act* s 38 (1958–89), s 92 (1989–94).
6 Joint Standing Committee on Migration, 'Asylum, Border Control and Detention' (Canberra, February 1994), 77–9.
7 *Migration Act* s 92. Although disputed by the Department of Immigration, Local Government and Ethnic Affairs at the time, some courts interpreted the statute as permitting courts to release 'presumptive illegal entrants' upon the imposition of an undertaking on future conduct: see, for example, *Grech* v. *Heffey* [1991] FCA 50; (1991) 34 FCR 93 [13]; see also Michael Clothier, 'Changing Custody Regimes for Illegal Entrants', in *The Criminal Justice System in a Multicultural Society* (Melbourne: Australian Institute of Criminology, 1993).
8 Joint Standing Committee on Migration, 'Asylum, Border Control and Detention', 79.

status based on whether individuals were regarded in law as having 'entered' Australia, and replacing it with two statuses for non-citizens: 'lawful non-citizens' (who held a valid visa) and 'unlawful non-citizens' (who did not hold a valid visa).[9] Rather than being a criminal offence, unlawful non-citizenship is merely an administrative classification of migration legal status.[10] The radical aspect of these wide-ranging reforms is well known: it marked the start of mandatory immigration detention in Australia in the form that we now know it. The decriminalisation of migrant illegality also marked a change in the type of supervision structured into the legal regulation of detention. Regardless of the practical limitations of the pre-1994 system, making detention for unlawful status a purely administrative matter has instituted an opaque regime for taking people into immigration custody.

Police and immigration officers detain people in diverse social settings, using various processes and under disparate legal powers. Nevertheless, these practices are authorised and regulated by the same framework of migration law, which raises important questions about how the detention power sits with these varied practices. In practice, police undertake much of the migration policing (and immigration detention) in the street. Leanne Weber's exploratory qualitative study of policing non-citizens found that the Department of Immigration and Citizenship (DIAC) viewed police as their 'eyes and ears on the ground', and that state police involvement in locating those holding unlawful status primarily takes place in an 'opportunistic' manner as part of everyday police duties.[11] Targeted operations are typically conducted by immigration officers, and may involve detention as part of search warrant visits to homes and workplaces, or multi-agency operations. Officers may use direct physical force to effect detention and, since the 2015 establishment of the Australian Border Force within the Department of Immigration and Border Protection (DIBP), in some circumstances officers may carry firearms.[12] Officers may hold persons in immigration detention in a police station, watch house, prison or immigration detention centre.[13] In all these settings, detention remains an exercise of migration power and is thus not subject to the legal safeguards imposed on arrest in the criminal jurisdiction. The discrepancy between the frameworks governing arrest and detention highlights the central quandary of this chapter: how does migration law impose constraints on and responsibility for the exercise of the immigration detention power in the streets and in immigration fieldwork colloquially referred to as 'raids'?

Surprisingly little case law guidance exists for immigration detention as a practice of taking an individual into custody (that is, as a policing power). The

9 *Migration Act* ss 13, 14.

10 See Chapter 1.

11 Leanne Weber, *Policing Non-Citizens* (Oxford: Routledge, 2013), 62.

12 *Migration Act* s 5; *Customs Act* 1901 (Cth) ss 4, 189A; *Australian Border Force Act* 2015 (Cth) ss 3, 4.

13 *Migration Act* s 5.

overwhelming focus of judicial, scholarly and policy attention has been on the legality of indefinite detention and the conditions within immigration detention centres.[14] In contrast, much of the routine work of locating and detaining those known or suspected to be unlawful non-citizens or in breach of visa conditions has occurred under the radar of public and judicial scrutiny. Migration policing detention practices attract little visibility because, like other policing practices that do not involve criminal charge (such as move-on directions or questioning), their purpose is not to pursue a criminal offence. Instead, the object of migration policing is the identification, apprehension and detention of individuals under administrative imprimatur. These migration policing practices involve the actions of officers of first contact with non-citizens and are positioned at the 'front end' of immigration process. The discretionary decisions officers make to stop, question and search individuals on the street and in raids determine, with a sense of finality, whether a person will be detained. Analysis of migration policing practice within its statutory framework and the available case law reveals the specific ways that detention practices are made invisible and thus elude responsibility. By focusing on immigration detention as a power and as a practice, this chapter turns attention to the everyday violence of migration powers outside immigration detention centres.

Study of the legal framework for authority and responsibility for practices of detention power by police and immigration is long overdue. Police use of migration detention powers is especially important because it occurs in an already low visibility context. Police have been empowered to detain unlawful non-citizens alongside criminal investigation powers since the commencement of the contemporary mandatory detention provision in 1994. Although some Local Area Commanders in NSW Police presented immigration status checking as part of standard procedure in information-gathering, whether with a suspect, victim or witness, the extent and uniformity of integration of migration powers into general police work remains unclear, as does the issue of whether police have become more involved in immigration enforcement.[15] It is clear that police perform two main immigration-related tasks as part of their ordinary work: calling immigration's status check hotline to check an individual's visa status; and identifying and detaining unlawful non-citizens and then referring them to immigration. The need to reflect on the authority of immigration practices is made more urgent by the recent increase in proactive immigration operations.

14 For an analysis of the legality of indefinite detention in Australia, see Rayner Thwaites, *The Liberty of Non-Citizens: Indefinite Detention in Commonwealth Countries* (Oregon: Hart Publishing, 2014), 37–119. For analysis of the experiences and conditions of immigration detention centres in Australia, see, for example: Human Rights and Equal Opportunity Commission, 'Those Who've Come Across the Seas: Detention of Unauthorised Arrivals' (Sydney, 1998); 'A Last Resort? The National Inquiry into Children in Immigration Detention' (Sydney, 2004); Australian Human Rights Commission, 'The Forgotten Children: National Inquiry into Children in Immigration Detention (2014)' (Sydney, 2014).

15 Weber, *Policing Non-Citizens*, 71, 89.

In 2009–10, immigration conducted 2708 field actions to locate unlawful non-citizens or non-citizens in breach of visa conditions, in 2014–15 the number of operations had reached 4437.[16] Involving powers predicated on suspicion of status, migration policing marks a dangerous arena of discretionary power.

This chapter argues that the regulation of the immigration detention power in the street and in raids marginalises its violent effects. Rendering what is effectively 'arrest' as detention in law reveals how the law marks its violence as insignificant, as well as the law's authorisation of differential protection of individuals based on the legal power exercised. Drawing on the interpretive frame of front-end discretion as a means to analyse practices of taking a person into immigration detention, it traces policing practices in the street and in raids that involve finality because they are never reviewed. The concern is with what and how discretion becomes legally authorised. It finds that detention commonly proceeds in contexts of interaction between multiple sources of authority which concentrate discretion at the front end of the process into the hands of police and immigration officers. The chapter articulates the legal formation of 'zones of non-responsibility' for policing practice.[17] It analyses the forms of responsibility over officers' actions in taking people into immigration custody that the doctrinal approach forecloses. Tracing the legal work that goes into defining violence and delimiting responsibility for harm that arises from detention as arrest shows the material and ideological labour of the law in making status-based differentiation invisible.

The questions explored in this chapter have been driven by interviews with seven migrants with personal experience of being apprehended by police or immigration without a visa. Most arrived in Australia holding a visa; some initially held a visitor visa, others student or work visas, and one arrived on a false passport. Some of these experiences are referenced in this chapter and are supplemented by publicly reported accounts. The chapter also draws on interviews with seven advocates who have worked with people who have been apprehended by either immigration or state police. Interviews with non-legal advocates were richer in this regard, which makes sense because of the few legal opportunities to challenge apprehension practices, as discussed in Chapter 3. Although the small sample size makes these accounts anecdotal rather than representative, they capture the dilemmas raised by the law's institutionalisation of broad discretionary migration powers.

The argument that migration law marginalises recognition for the violence of immigration 'arrest' advances through three perspectives. The first part of this chapter details the ways in which detention proceeds, to foreground it as an experience of violence outside the formal detention setting, which lacks the conventional constraints associated with arrest. It collates accounts of interview

16 Ibid., 173. Note these figures do not include fieldwork undertaken by immigration compliance officers to educate employers regarding their obligations to avoid breach of immigration law.

17 See Chapter 1 and Scott Veitch, *Law and Irresponsibility: On the Legitimation of Human Suffering* (New York: Routledge-Cavendish, 2007).

participants and those emerging from sporadic public reports to develop an overall picture of the experience of detention not otherwise available. The second part demonstrates how the practice of detention in street policing within the broader legal framework of police powers risks trivialising the significance of specific legal authority to detain and thus the liberty of those detained. The third part closely examines the limited retrospective models of policing responsibility invoked by migration powers when wielded by police in the context of criminal investigation and more generally by officers with migration powers.

The moment of detention and the violence of arrest

The *Migration Act* does not use the language of 'arrest'; nor is the term used in the policies and procedures that guide *Migration Act* officers. The *Migration Act* equivalent is the power to detain. The meaning of 'detain' includes acts that 'take into immigration detention', and 'immigration detention' not only means being held within a detention centre, it also means 'being in the company of, and restrained by' an officer.[18] In the common law, an arrest for a criminal offence takes place when an officer makes it clear through words and conduct that the person is no longer at liberty, and has been taken into custody by police.[19] It is hard to refute that arrest is what is involved in the process of taking a person into detention and the courts, in the context of interpreting the executive and statutory power to detain non-citizens, have at times used the terms 'arrest' and 'detention' as holding the same meaning.[20] This part of the chapter seeks to sensitise the reader to the experience of the moment of being taken into immigration detention, and highlight qualities that mirror those in arrest absent procedural safeguards.

Although the function of arrest for a criminal offence is different from that of immigration detention, at least in terms of how they are legally conceived neither practice is intended to be punitive. In criminal justice, punishment is the province of the court via sentencing, and the rationale for the deprivation of liberty as part of arrest is solely to achieve efficient criminal justice administration. In migration, mandatory detention is constitutionally justified on the basis that it is reasonably capable of being necessary for immigration visa processing and removal, that is, for the effective administration of migration process.[21] The

18 *Migration Act* s 5. See also *Minister for Immigration and Multicultural and Indigenous Affairs* v. *VFAD* [2002] FCAFC 390; (2002) 125 FCR 249 [150] in which Black CJ, Sundberg and Weinberg JJ explain that s 189 of the *Migration Act* provides the power to take a person into detention, and s 196 provides for the keeping of a person in detention until a particular event such as visa grant or removal from Australia.

19 *R* v. *Inwood* [1973] 2 ALL ER 645; (1973) 57 Cr App R 529; *Alderson* v. *Booth* [1969] 2 QB 216; (1969) 53 Cr App R 301.

20 See, for example, *Chu Kheng Lim* v. *Minister for Immigration* [1992] HCA 64; (1992) 176 CLR 1, 19 (Brennan, Deane and Dawson JJ); *CPCF* v. *Minister for Immigration and Border Protection* [2015] HCA 1; (2015) 316 ALR 1, 39 [148], [149] (French CJ).

21 *Chu Kheng Lim* v. *Minister for Immigration* [1992] HCA 64; (1992) 176 CLR 1.

characterisation of both arrest and detention as ostensibly non-punitive administrative practices provides a strong basis for expectation that the deprivation of liberty should be subject to the same legal safeguards. But this is not the case.

Arrest powers across Australia are significantly more regulated than detention powers. Statutes provide for how arrests must take place, restrict the permitted purposes for arrest, stipulate requirements for the issue of cautions and limit the period of detention after arrest for investigatory purposes. The common law principle – that arrest is to be treated as a last resort and used only if a summons would not be effective – recognises the violence involved in the sudden deprivation of liberty itself:

> Arrest is an additional punishment involving deprivation of freedom and frequently ignominy and fear. The consequences of the employment of the power of arrest unnecessarily and inappropriately and instead of issuing a summons are often anger on the part of the person arrested and an escalation of the situation leading to the person resisting arrest and assaulting the police.[22]

If police make an arrest when a summons was appropriate (such as if police knew the suspect's details and the alleged criminal offence was minor), the arrest itself may be found unlawful because it was not used as a last resort.[23] The principle allows the quality of violence involved in arrest to register as distinct from ongoing institutional incarceration more generally.

In contrast, although the legal framework of detention acknowledges the seriousness of detention in particular ways, it is not restrictive because ultimately the decision not to detain remains the discretion of immigration. For instance, immigration officers may grant a bridging visa to enable temporary lawful status rather than detain, but this power is discretionary.[24] Various principles, designed to guide when unlawful non-citizens should be detained, have also been gradually introduced, but remain statements of aspiration rather than mechanisms that impose consequences for an officer's detention decision. In 2005, the *Migration Act* adopted the commitment that 'Parliament affirms as *a principle* that a minor shall only be detained as a measure of last resort',[25] but as a principle only it does not provide a foundation for the detention of children to be unlawful. In mid-2008, immigration detention values were established as a matter of policy, stating (among other values) that only those unlawful non-citizens who present unacceptable risks to the

22 *Director of Public Prosecutions* v. *Carr* [2002] NSWSC 194; (2002) 127 A Crim R 151 [35] (Smart AJ).

23 See, for example, *Director of Public Prosecutions* v. *Carr* [2002] NSWSC 194; (2002) 127 A Crim R 151.

24 See Chapter 4 for discussion of bridging visas granted for release from immigration detention.

25 *Migration Act* s 4AA (commenced June 29, 2005) inserted by *Migration Amendment (Detention Arrangements) Act 2005* (Cth) s 3 and Sch 1 item 1, with effect from June 29, 2005 (emphasis added).

community or who have repeatedly refused to comply with their visa conditions ought to be detained. However, again, these values have been enunciated as policy, not binding law.[26] Lastly, some recognition for the violence of 'arrest' in immigration detention is achieved through litigation for damages in tort law, which may award damages for the 'initial shock of being arrested' but only if the courts find a non-citizen to have been falsely imprisoned under migration powers.[27] If detention itself is lawful, the violence engaged in first taking a person into custody does not make it unlawful. These initiatives and laws are important as statements of value in immigration detention. However, they are limited, and do not institute the legal force of statutory procedural requirements or allow courts to call for account as in arrest for a criminal offence. These principles fail to constrain the legality of the detention power and consequently do not take the initial sudden violence involved in apprehension seriously. Yet interviewees' accounts illustrate that being taken into custody has a character distinct from ongoing detention.

The most prominent quality that emerges from accounts of detention by police or by immigration is the sense of shock, disruption and dislocation connected with the event. Apprehension involves an immediate physical and social removal from one's existing life; in the words of one interview participant located by immigration, 'you're just kidnapped ... you're evicted from your house and then you disappear'.[28] The interview participants apprehended outside the home were not allowed to return home before they were taken to the immigration detention centre,[29] though a return home en route is not unheard of.[30] Removal from the community involves all the violences of any sudden incarceration. For one interview participant who had lived alone and was located by immigration at her workplace, her two cats and fish were left locked inside the house, and she was unable to arrange for their food, water or care.[31] Almost all interview participants lost all their possessions when they were apprehended, such as clothes, computer, furniture, cars and other possessions, as well as legal and educational documents.[32]

26 See Chapter 4 for further discussion of the key detention values; see also DIAC, 'Annual Report 2008–09' (Belconnen, ACT, 2009), 7, 17, 118.

27 *Ruddock* v. *Taylor* [2003] NSWCA 262; (2003) 58 NSWLR 269, 279 [49] (Spigelman CJ) citing *Thompson; Hsu* v. *Commissioner of Police of the Metropolis* [1997] EWCA Civ 3083; [1998] QB 498, 515. Note, however, that an approach that sees the effect of imprisonment as progressively diminishing should not be treated too rigidly: see *Fernando* v. *Commonwealth* [2014] FCAFC 181, 29 [110]; (2014) 231 FCR 251.

28 Interview with M1.

29 Interviews with M2, M4, M12, M3, M9 and A8.

30 Amanda Woodard and Anne Davis, 'School Friends' Removal Hurting Pupils', *The Sydney Morning Herald*, March 17, 2005, www.smh.com.au/news/National/School-friends-removal-hurting-pupils/2005/03/16/1110913672248.html.

31 Interview with M4.

32 Interviews with M1, M2, M4, M12, M3, M9 and A8.

Non-citizens may be detained even though their identity and whereabouts are known and their words and actions indicate they intend to report to immigration as soon as possible. For example, Ahmed's visa was automatically cancelled because, due to the post office mistakenly cancelling his post box, he had not received notification that his student visa was to be cancelled and missed the period for response to that notification.[33] Ahmed contacted the Department of Immigration and Multicultural and Indigenous Affairs (DIMIA) as soon as he was aware of this, advised immigration of his address, and that he would attend the closest immigration office which, because he resided in country NSW, was a few hours drive away. Despite this indication of compliance, three immigration officials came to his home and detained him. Ahmed was held overnight in a police station (defined as a place of immigration detention), and he was transferred to an immigration detention centre about six hours distance by road the following day.[34] Although Ahmed was taken into custody prior to the introduction of the key detention values into policy, the law of detention prior and after such policy change remains the same.

Reports show that the violence involved in non-citizens being taken into immigration custody mirrors issues addressed by legislative safeguards for criminal investigations. Unlike arrest for a criminal offence, migration law does not require officers to inform the person of the right to contact a lawyer or friend upon immigration detention. Authorities are required to provide reasonable facilities for individuals detained to obtain legal advice in relation to their detention but only if the person makes this request.[35] In some instances immigration officers have denied permission for those detained to contact partners or carers. For example, in 2005, police stopped Maria while she was driving on her way to pick fruit with her parents, and when immigration arrived, Maria explained:

> They locked us in a car and we were there for three hours. My mother felt very sick because she has high blood pressure. I asked them if I could contact my husband and children and asked for medication for my mother, but they refused.[36]

Also in 2005, a school principal was not permitted to contact the children's carer when immigration removed two girls aged six and 11 from a school in Sydney's inner west.[37] It was around 2005 that the removal of children from

33 Interview with M1.

34 *Migration Act* s 5.

35 Ibid., s 256; *Wu Yu Fang* v. *Minister for Immigration and Ethnic Affairs* [1996] FCA 106; (1996) 64 FCR 245.

36 Amanda Woodard, 'Labouring in the Shadows: Illegal Immigrants Form the Backbone of a Much-Needed Workforce for Many Industries', *The Sydney Morning Herald*, April 28, 2005, www.smh.com.au/news/National/Labouring-in-the-shadows/2005/04/27/1114462103530.html.

37 AAP, 'Outcry over School "Raids" to Detain Children', *The Sydney Morning Herald*, March 16, 2005, www.smh.com.au/news/National/Outcry-over-school-raids-to-detain-children/2005/03/16/1110913654553.html.

schools first commenced. Although on another occasion the principal of Stanmore Public School was permitted to explain to the children removed from school that they were to go with the officer to detention, immigration officers refused to allow an 11-year-old boy to say goodbye to his friends at the school he had attended for seven years.[38] The statutory principle that children should be detained as a last resort was later introduced in 2005, as mentioned above, but even after enactment immigration has detained children from school on some occasions. For instance, in 2014, immigration took two children from an Adelaide school into mainstream detention after they had resided in community detention for over a year.[39] In 2015, armed immigration officials took 21-year-old Mojgan Shamsalipoor from her Brisbane high school without notice. She had been attending high school on day release while held in immigration detention in Brisbane, and had been brought to school by a guard each day. Immigration had refused her application for refugee protection and, at the time immigration officials came to her school, the federal government had decided to re-detain those Iranian nationals whose refugee claims had been refused and who did not voluntarily return to Iran.[40] Her husband, Milad Jafari, an Australian resident, said Mojgan was 'dragged on the ground' when she asked officers to call her husband, and was transferred to detention in Darwin, Northern Territory, and he was not permitted to say goodbye to his wife.[41] The refusal to permit communication exacerbates the violent effect of removing children from the school environment. Removal from school itself undermines notions of safety and care associated with school and in some situations has created such fear that non-citizen students have gone missing following the removal of fellow students from the school.[42]

The frightening character of raids is evident even from those not directly subject to detention, and is made more dramatic by reports that immigration officers do not always identify themselves to all those affected by their operations. Grape grower and farm owner Tony Natale explained that in a 2005

38 Woodard and Davis, 'School Friends' Removal Hurting Pupils'; Jo McKenna, 'Immigration Raid Angers Community', *The 7.30 Report* (transcript, March 23, 2005), www.abc.net.au/7.30/content/2005/s1330414.htm.

39 Tory Shepherd, 'Adelaide Schoolchildren Reported Missing from Northern Suburb School after Their Friends Were Taken into Immigration Detention', *The Advertiser*, June 27, 2014, www.adelaidenow.com.au/news/south-australia/adelaide-schoolchildren-reported-missing-from-northern-suburb-school-after-their-friends-were-taken-into-immigration-detention/news-story/30acbf5ebedb4174f49a299531b504f2.

40 Kent Gordon, 'Mojgan Shamsalipoor: Peter Dutton Won't Intervene in Case of Iranian Asylum Seeker Student', *ABC News Online*, July 25, 2016, www.abc.net.au/news/2016-07-25/peter-dutton-refuses-to-help-iranian-asylum-seeker/7655866.

41 Tony Moore, 'Brisbane Asylum Seeker Accepts Year 12 Certificate Behind Detention Bars', *Brisbane Times*, November 18, 2015, www.brisbanetimes.com.au/queensland/brisbane-asylum-seeker-accepts-year-12-certificate-behind-detention-bars-20151117-gl1cb9.html; Eric Tlozek, 'Asylum Seeker School Student "Dragged on Ground", Put in Detention in Lieu of Deal to Return Iranian Citizens, Husband Says', *ABC News Online*, August 8, 2015, www.abc.net.au/news/2015-08-08/iranian-asylum-seekers-devastated-by-return-to-detention/6682210.

42 Shepherd, 'Adelaide Schoolchildren Reported Missing'.

evening raid on his premises in Robinvale in a horticultural region in north-western Victoria, the nine plain-clothes immigration officers involved did not notify him, identify themselves or show a warrant, but simply proceeded to the sleeping quarters of the fruit pickers.[43] Natale said, 'They might have the legal right [to raid the property] but ... it can be a scary situation.... They walk on to anyone's property, they're not recognisable, not in uniform. They make no effort to contact the owner of the property'.[44] In criminal investigation, statute obliges police to identify themselves, but no such safeguard exists in immigration law, merely in immigration policy and procedures.

The other most common feature of detention operations is the direct use of force. Unlike the matters discussed thus far, the power to use force in immigration detention faces the same legislative constraint as the police use of force in arrest. Officers are permitted to use such force as is 'reasonably necessary' to detain or keep a person in immigration detention and it is not unusual for immigration officials or state police to use force in raids and other operations.[45] Officers may also use 'reasonable force' or 'such force as reasonably necessary' to enable an identification test, search a detained person, and utilise authorised entry, search and seizure powers with and without a warrant.[46] Of the seven interview participants in the study who had been apprehended by police or by immigration (or both), five experienced some use of force, from mild restraint to rough handling and the use of handcuffs (by immigration and police), which are also used in transporting detainees and persons being deported.

Over the years, there has been criticism of the extent of force used. In 2003, the construction union was critical of an early-morning armed immigration raid by police on a building site, stating it was too violent and the context made it 'very dangerous'.[47] In 2005, a 4 am farm raid in rural northern Victoria involved forced entry, the breaking of windows and doors.[48] In extreme circumstances immigration raids might result in death, such as occurred in 2004, when six immigration officers attended a Sydney house and Seong Ho Kang, 37, whose visa had expired, ran and was hit by a car.[49] Similarly, in 2006, South Australian police had undertaken a random alcohol breath test of Wah Aun Chan,

43 ABC News Online, 'Immigration Raids Spark Farmer Anger', *ABC News Online,* February 10, 2005, http://mobile.abc.net.au/news/2005-02-10/immigration-raids-spark-farmer-anger/1516732.

44 Elizabeth Colman, 'Anger over Immigration Raids', *The Australian*, February 17, 2005, 2.

45 *Migration Act* ss 5, 189, 192, 253.

46 Ibid., ss 261AE, 252, 223, 251.

47 ABC News Online, 'Protocols Were Followed in Immigration Raids: Ruddock', *ABC News Online*, February 20, 2003, www.abc.net.au/news/2003-02-20/protocols-were-followed-in-immigration-raids/2689002.

48 Michelle Grattan, '"Picking on" Fruit Pickers', *The Age*, February 14, 2005, http://fddp.theage.com.au/news/Immigration/Picking-on-fruit-pickers/2005/02/13/1108229854898.html.

49 See Geesche Jacobsen, 'Immigration Death Sparks Training Queries', *The Sydney Morning Herald*, August 29, 2005, www.smh.com.au/news/national/immigration-death-sparks-training-queries/2005/08/28/1125167552329.html. Note that the Coroner's Inquest into Kang's death was not released: Rebecca Powell, Leanne Weber and Sharon Pickering, 'Counting and Accounting for Deaths in Australian Immigration Custody', *Homicide Studies* 17, no. 4 (2013): 403.

aged 27.[50] Upon Chan's presentation of his passport, police checked his immigration status, found his visa had expired, and attempted to detain him. A struggle ensued in which police used capsicum spray on him, Chan fled and was found dead nine days later. The Coroner found that Chan was evading apprehension at the time of his death, which appeared to be the result of falling off a nearby cliff top and drowning in the Murray River. In Kang's case, the Coroner expressed surprise at immigration officers' lack of training, and in Chan's case the Coroner found that the police's use of force was reasonable.

Even if the extent of force used is found by the authorities to be reasonable and thus lawful, it may be experienced as humiliating. One interview participant explained of the cuffs used on him in transporting him by plane to another detention centre:

> [The handcuffs were] very tight, the plastic ones. When you go to the toilet you have to tell the officer and you can't do anything, so you just put your hand like this [gesturing].... The officer has to, you know, zip it for you.[51]

A sense of humiliation pervades the experience of detention reported by interview participants. In one instance discussed in Chapter 1, this was made particularly acute by media accompanying immigration officers in a raid of a massage parlour.[52] Media published photographs of the raid as well as personal details of those detained that were sufficient to identify the interview participant, and resulted in a complaint to the Ombudsman that immigration had not protected her privacy. Humiliation by the act of detention, like the use of force, is characteristic of arrest for a criminal offence, and a large part of why the common law views it should be a measure of last resort.

The utter disruption to all facets of life caused by apprehension, use of force and humiliation is testament to the significance of the moment of detention. Detention is an important state practice where the unlawful non-citizen is produced as 'illegal'. Until that time, unlawful non-citizens achieve a modicum of social inclusion through work, presence in the community and so on. Detention is the moment of 'illegalisation', which achieves a literal, physical and social erasure. The legal framework governing detention achieves specific forms of erasure. A single power authorises both the moment of taking a person into immigration custody and ongoing immigration detention arrangements, obscuring the different character of the violences implicated in a sudden deprivation of liberty.

50 South Australia State Coroner, 'Finding of Inquest: An Inquest Taken on Behalf of Our Sovereign Lady the Queen at Adelaide in the State of South Australia, on the 3rd Day of July 2008 and the 16th Day of October 2008, by the Coroner's Court of the Said State, Constituted of Mark Frederick Johns, State Coroner, into the Death of Wah Aun Chan' (2008); Jamie Walker, 'Police Cleared over Malaysian Migrant's Death', *The Australian*, October 16, 2008, www.theaustralian.com.au/news/sa-police-cleared-over-migrants-death/story-e6frg6p6-1111117769281.

51 Interview with M12.

52 Interview with M4.

Further, immigration favours policy and procedural guidelines, rather than the statutory safeguards associated with arrest for a criminal offence, which communicates that although detention and arrest produce the same violent effects on those taken into custody, immigration detention is viewed less seriously.

For police, who hold both migration and criminal justice powers, the discrepancy in power afforded officers in these two fields is stark. In the criminal arena, police have a series of options to address a suspected criminal offence: not to charge at all, to issue an on-the-spot fine if available, and proceeding by summons or arrest for a criminal offence in which case the process is governed by legal safeguards. By contrast, in immigration, police are *required* to detain those they know or reasonably suspect to be unlawful non-citizens if they form reasonable suspicion of unlawful status (police do not share immigration officers' power to grant bridging visas to unlawful non-citizens). In other words, unlike addressing a suspected criminal offence, police dealings with suspected unlawful non-citizens are institutionalised as consistently involving the deprivation of liberty, but in the absence of statutory safeguards. Moreover, particular features of the legal context of street policing where police locate and detain unlawful non-citizens run the risk of minimising the importance of needing a legal basis for detention.

Migration policing practices – trivialising detention?

The power to detain, like other policing powers under the *Migration Act*, has been drafted devoid of the context of its use. It provides legal authority for quite divergent practices of detention – in the street, in immigration raids and operations targeting a specified individual. Migration policing powers are thus used in radically different contexts, and must be analysed in those contexts. Developing its focus on street policing and immigration raids, this part of the chapter examines common ways that detention proceeds in order to explore the interplay first between the immigration identification and detention powers, and second between criminal and migration powers. Detention practices by both immigration and police rely on the individual's 'consent' to bolster the legal authority to detain in circumstances where detention may not otherwise be lawful, emptying out the need to justify the legal basis for detention, and trivialising the deprivation of liberty at stake.

The *Migration Act* immigration detention power allows police or other officers under the Act to initiate contact if they know or reasonably suspect a person is an unlawful non-citizen. The concept in law is that the immigration detention power may be expected to be used in planned operations that target a specific individual. In scenarios such as street policing or workplace raids, the law envisages that officers use the immigration identification power before the detention power.[53] The former provides a less coercive investigatory power that allows

53 *Ruddock* v. *Taylor* [2005] HCA 48; (2005) 221 ALR 32 [46] (Gleeson CJ, Gummow, Hayne and Heydon JJ).

officers to gather information that might lead to the requisite suspicion to detain, but is not restricted to those suspected to be unlawful. Officers may require a 'person whom the officer knows or reasonably suspects is a non-citizen' to show evidence of being a lawful non-citizen.[54] In practice, however, the immigration identification power does not play much of a role in preceding immigration detention in the street or in raids.

It seems impossible for police to lawfully rely on the immigration identification requirement to initiate an encounter on the street. Citizenship is simply a conferred form of legal status. Perceptions that a person is a non-citizen cannot legitimately be based on a person's appearance of ethnicity, language or accent. The identification power must also be understood in the context of countless statutes that empower police (or other officers) to require identification, oftentimes making refusal an offence. Police may require identification of individuals driving a car (or motorbike, bicycle), on public transport without a ticket, at a hotel or somewhere else alcohol is being sold, if police believe a person has information that could assist in the investigation of a serious crime or reasonably suspect a person has committed an offence or is carrying prohibited items such as drugs or weapons and more. Pragmatically, the sheer volume of identification powers available makes it difficult for an individual, and even police, to know if a legal *requirement* to provide identification exists in a given circumstance, and thus might partly explain why it is also a power that often proceeds with the apparent consent of the individual. In Australia, no requirement to carry national identification exists and it has been subject to sustained political resistance. The Hawke Labor government proposals for an 'Australia Card' failed in the 1980s and became a trigger for a double dissolution election in 1987. Twenty years later, the Howard Coalition government decided against pursuing an identity card as well as a smart access card for access to government health and social services due to public concerns about privacy and security safeguards.[55] Yet the status-based trigger for the migration identification power appears to institute a de facto Australia card.

Accounts of immigration compliance visits to workplaces describe a practice that appears to effect detention of all present in the premises being searched, *before* checking identification, and with little regard to ensuring that the requisite suspicion has been reached for each person. Immigration raids are generally authorised by search warrant, which does not provide the power to detain anyone.[56] Yet interview participants reported instances of raids conducted by closing the doors at the entry and exit of premises, and then categorically checking the identity of all occupants irrespective of their presence as customers,

54 *Migration Act* s 188.

55 Roy Jordan, 'Identity Cards and the Access Card', *E-brief* (Canberra: Parliamentary Library, 2006).

56 DIAC, 'Procedures Advice Manual 3' (Canberra: Commonwealth of Australia, 2010) National Compliance Operational Instructions [P A135.16], 16.1.

clients or visitors, or staff in restaurants, brothels or factories.[57] The commonality of a categorical approach to identification checking in raids is evident from action taken by a brothel owner who placed a laminated sign in his waiting area stating:

> Attention visitors the Department of Immigration may visit this brothel at any time. The Department will ask everyone to provide ID and some kind of evidence that they are lawfully in Australia. This applies to the customers, the receptionist and the workers in this premise.[58]

Note that in the context of a brothel workplace, often neither workers nor clients take their identification because of privacy and confidentiality issues, so identification checks can take some time. Questioning as to identity frequently takes places in front of workers' colleagues, which is problematic because often workers adopt a work alias, and have not shared their personal information with colleagues, regardless of their lawful immigration status.[59]

On other occasions, it appears that immigration officers were more selective in requiring identification, having sought identification solely from non-Caucasian staff.[60] In all these circumstances it is difficult to see how officers could reasonably develop a suspicion immediately upon entering that all those in the premises were non-citizens unlawfully in Australia subject to detention, or even non-citizens subject to identification checks. In practice, the whole concept of an immigration raid where immigration officers anticipate finding at least some unspecified non-citizens living unlawfully or in breach of visa conditions appears predicated on a non-existent categorical authority to detain for the duration of the operation.

In street policing, police requests for identification often occur in a context where individuals acquiesce without requiring police to articulate their authority, and where the legal prerequisites for the immigration identification power cease to be practically relevant. Effectively, police officers rely on a generalised power to require identification, rather than specific powers. In immigration raids, far from the identification power being used to gather information to inform an officer's view of a person's migration legal status, identification checks

57 Interviews with M4, M7, M12, A8 and A6; Elena Jeffreys (President, Scarlet Alliance) in discussion with the author, August 5, 2008; Maria McMahon (Sex Work Policy Advisor, ACON) in discussion with the author, August 5, 2008; Peter Bollard (Bollard and Associates) in discussion with the author, March 19, 2008. See also Freya Peterson, 'Immigration Casts its Net at Doyles', *The Sydney Morning Herald*, May 14, 2004, www.smh.com.au/articles/2004/05/13/1084289821930.html.

58 Maria McMahon (Sex Work Policy Advisor, ACON) in discussion with the author, August 5, 2008.

59 The importance of privacy in sex work contexts was also highlighted in Fiona David, 'Trafficking of Women for Sexual Purposes', in *Research and Public Policy Series* (Canberra: Australian Institute of Criminology, 2008).

60 Peter Bollard (Bollard and Associates) in discussion with the author, March 19, 2008; Peterson, 'Immigration Casts its Net at Doyles'.

are used improperly to justify what appears to be the detention of all those present at a premise during the raid. In both scenarios, officers seem to rely on the apparent consent of individuals to check identification in circumstances where they are not at liberty to leave, which raises alarm bells as to the quality of consent in these circumstances. The effect of force cannot be denied and it is the police capacity to use force that has been said to give police the unique flexibility to intervene in situations that may not be illegal, and bolsters police authority in circumstances where it might not be apparent.[61]

More often, police detain persons after having initiated contact for non-migration-related reasons. It is the latter, more 'opportunistic' uses of migration powers that appear to characterise at least NSW state police involvement in migration policing.[62] A number of interviewed non-citizens relayed being stopped by state police on the street and while driving, following ticket validation checks aboard public transport, apprehended thus by state police as a consequence of non-migration-related policing priorities. These experiences accord with NSW Police reports that they routinely check immigration status checks in patrolling stops, in the course of criminal investigations, following reports of crime by victims and in response to reports from the public.[63] In other words, state police used migration powers alongside other police powers as part of a dynamic investigative process.

In the context of multi-institutional migration policing, the danger is that the potential justification of detention on multiple grounds may facilitate a disregard for the legal basis for detention by police. This argument is most compelling if a person has been detained in circumstances where it is unclear whether a criminal arrest has been made or whether they are being detained under immigration powers.

Immigration detention as a 'placeholder'

The complex relationship between authority, coercion and consent is highlighted in the experience of one of the interview participants. NSW Police stopped Stephen while he was driving in Sydney's western suburbs.[64] Initially police advised him the stop was to conduct a random breath test to assess his blood alcohol level. Stephen did not believe the stop was random, rather that it was influenced by his Asian ethnicity and because he was driving a sports car at 4.30am on a weekday. The police questioning of Stephen after he was stopped suggested police suspected he possessed drugs or illegal items, such as weapons. After undertaking a body and bag

61 Egon Bittner, 'The Capacity to Use Force as the Core of the Police Function', in *The Police and Society: Touchstone Readings*, ed. V. E. Kappeler (Illinois: Waveland Press Inc., 1995), 129; Carl B. Klockars, *The Idea of the Police* (California: Sage Publications, 1985); P. A. J. Waddington, *Policing Citizens* (London: UCL Press, 1999), 20.

62 Weber, *Policing Non-Citizens*, 62.

63 Ibid., 69–71.

64 Interview with M10.

search, police determined that Stephen was driving without a licence and seized a Medicare card in Stephen's possession (which provides access to state-subsidised healthcare). At some point during this encounter police formed the suspicion that Stephen was an unlawful non-citizen. From what police told Stephen, it was clear they preferred him to be dealt with by immigration not criminal law and process.[65] Police told Stephen that if immigration advised he held lawful status, they would charge him with defrauding the Australian public health system on the basis of his possession of his brother's Medicare card.

From the time police determined that Stephen was driving without a licence Stephen was under the impression that he was not at liberty to leave. Yet, at this time and for the duration of his transport to the police station, Stephen was not formally arrested or charged with a criminal offence, nor did police tell Stephen that he was legally obliged to attend the station. Stephen's experience highlights issues that have long been present in criminal justice: whether a person is under arrest or has volunteered to assist police with their investigations.[66] If a person gives consent, then police are not required to rely on a legal basis for their exercise of power. Whether consent is in fact informed and genuine will depend on the circumstances, and in practice encounters with police often engage elements of both coercion and consent that make consent a contested notion.[67] The asymmetry in power between non-citizens and police is arguably heightened as police phrasing may impress that cooperation is legally required and perceptions that a person has consented may be compromised by cultural and linguistic factors.[68] The factors at play in Stephen's experience were less nuanced. Soon after

65 For discussion of NSW Police perceptions that administrative removal is preferable to criminal prosecution for minor criminal matters, see Weber, *Policing Non-Citizens*, 95–6. In relation to the criminal offence of working without permission, see Louise Boon-Kuo, 'The Policing of Immigration: Raids, Citizenship and the Criminal Law', in *Criminalisation and Criminal Responsibility in Australia*, ed. Thomas Crofts and Arlie Loughnan (Melbourne: Oxford University Press, 2015). For the UK, see Ana Aliverti, 'Making People Criminal: The Role of the Criminal Law in Immigration Enforcement', *Theoretical Criminology* 16, no. 4 (2012): 424. For the US, see Juliet P. Stumpf, 'The Process Is the Punishment in Crimmigration Law', in *The Borders of Punishment: Migration, Citizenship and Social Exclusion*, ed. Katja Franko Aas and Mary Bosworth (Oxford: Oxford University Press, 2013), 58, 62.

66 David Dixon, *Law in Policing: Legal Regulation and Police Practices* (New York: Clarendon Press, 1997); David Dixon, Clive Coleman and Keith Bottomley, 'Consent and the Legal Regulation of Policing', *Journal of Law and Society* 17, no. 3 (1990).

67 Victoria Sentas, *Traces of Terror: Counter-Terrorism Law, Policing, and Race* (Oxford: Oxford University Press, 2014), 194–237.

68 Dorothy K. Kagehiro, 'Perceived Voluntariness of Consent to Warrantless Police Searches', *Journal of Applied Social Psychology* 18, no. 1 (2006). This has been particularly documented in relation to Indigenous Australians and migrants in immigration settings: see Heather Douglas, 'The Cultural Specificity of Evidence: The Current Scope and Relevance of the Anunga Guidelines', *University of New South Wales Law Journal* 21 (1998). Studies of refugee application interviews, although in the context of bureaucratic interviews rather than police street stops, provide a wider sense of the inequality of communication that informs these processes: see, for example, Jan Blommaert, 'Investigating Narrative Inequality: African Asylum Seekers' Stories in Belgium', *Discourse Society* 12, no. 4 (2001): 413.

Stephen was stopped, six police wagons and two or three police cars attended the encounter, strongly giving him the impression he had no choice but to remain in police custody.

At the time Stephen was located by police he had been living in Australia for ten years, most of that time without a visa. However, police did not inform Stephen that he was under immigration detention, and it remained unclear whether their suspicion reached the standard of reasonableness that would authorise his immigration detention until sometime after they arrived at the police station. If, as it appears, Stephen had not consented to being detained, serious questions remain as to the legal authority of his detention in the period until police gained sufficient information to detain him under the immigration detention power.

The potential for police to conduct arrest for a criminal offence or immigration detention amplifies the problems of legal authority presented by the tension between coercion and consent in policing encounters. Because the deprivation of liberty may be lawful if certain formal steps take place, the availability of multiple custodial powers facilitates these powers being used as later justification for custody (as 'presentational rules'),[69] rather than as powers with legal prerequisites for lawful custody. This potential generates a kind of 'placeholder' practice of detention that masks the reality that a person is detained, and diminishes the significance of the deprivation of liberty it entails. It is also likely that the mandatory nature of immigration detention itself plays a role in how police address the custody of suspected unlawful non-citizens, and delay making the reason for custody explicit. The potential for arrest on criminal grounds might be referenced, as in Stephen's case, in such a way that it lends forceful authority to custodial periods that otherwise do not have an explicit legal basis, even though if Stephen was a citizen and criminal charges were pursued, it is less likely he would have been taken to the station for suspected fraud.

The mandatory nature of detention

In considering the mandatory nature of the detention power in facilitating a disregard for the deprivation of liberty in these circumstances, it is helpful to reflect upon insights from studies into immigration officers' exercise of detention powers. In 2005, former Police Commissioners Mick Palmer and Neil Comrie reported on their inquiries into the ten-month wrongful detention of Australian permanent resident Cornelia Rau ('Rau report'),[70] and the wrongful detention and removal of Australian citizen Vivian Alvarez Solon as well as DIMIA's failure to rectify that

69 See, for example, the discussion of law that acts as 'presentational rules' in David John Smith, Jeremy Gray and Policy Studies Institute, *Police and People in London: The PSI Report* (Aldershot: Gower, 1985), 440–2.

70 Mick Palmer, 'Inquiry into the Circumstances of the Immigration Detention of Cornelia Rau' (Canberra: Commonwealth of Australia, 2005).

mistake for two years ('Alvarez/Solon report').[71] The reports drew on interviews with immigration staff at all levels of the institution, state and federal police, as well as policy, procedures and law, to develop their findings.

Rau was initially detained by police, but at the direction of DIMIA, whereas Alvarez Solon was detained by DIMIA. In both cases the reports focused on the deficiencies in immigration's steps to identify the person detained. The fundamental problem, the Rau and Alvarez/Solon reports argued, did not arise from an absence of policy or procedure, but from the fact that immigration officers did not correctly interpret the legal and procedural requirements:

> DIMIA officers, from field level to senior executive, seemed to have had little understanding of their responsibilities under the Act – other than a mistaken belief that they must detain a person and that when the person is detained the detention is absolute.[72]

Officers directly involved in detaining people were found to have little understanding of how to apply 'reasonable suspicion' in factual scenarios.[73] At least some officers viewed the correct process as to first detain and then obtain evidence to support that detention, rather than to first obtain evidence to support a reasonable suspicion of unlawful status.[74] Investigation into the basis for detention was treated as 'a matter of process' without urgency.[75] The Ombudsman's subsequent review of 247 cases of wrongful detention confirmed a mistaken understanding of legal responsibilities to be widespread, finding the basis for suspicion of unlawful status was not adequate in many of these cases.[76]

The Rau report's most scathing comments were directed at the 'overly self-protective and defensive' culture of DIMIA.[77] It noted that Australia's immigration policy requires the detention of all people known or reasonably suspected of being non-citizens and unlawfully in Australia, but also proceeded on the assumption that the government intends that policy be achieved fairly and justly.[78] Both reports viewed institutional culture as the ultimate culprit in the failure to effectively exercise detention powers with integrity:

71 Commonwealth and Immigration Ombudsman, 'Inquiry into the Circumstances of the Vivian Alvarez Matter: Report under the *Ombudsman Act 1976* by the Commonwealth Ombudsman, Prof. John McMillan, of an Inquiry Undertaken by Mr Neil Comrie AO APM' (Canberra, 2005). Note that 'Vivian Alvarez' is the name under which Vivian first came to the Immigration attention that led to her removal, but after her earlier marriage she used the name 'Vivian Solon Young'. As commentary variously refers to her as 'Alvarez' and 'Solon', both names are used throughout this book.

72 Ibid., 69.

73 Palmer, 'Inquiry into Cornelia Rau', 24.

74 McMillan, 'Inquiry into Vivian Alvarez', 69.

75 Palmer, 'Inquiry into Cornelia Rau', 25, 171.

76 Commonwealth and Immigration Ombudsman, 'Department of Immigration and Citizenship Report into Referred Immigration Cases: Detention Process Issues' (Canberra, 2007), 3.

77 Palmer, 'Inquiry into Cornelia Rau', ix.

78 Ibid., 171, 60–82. Note that the Inquiry into the Circumstances of the Vivian Alvarez Matter agreed with the assessment of DIMIA culture by Palmer.

> [T]he DIMIA management approach to the complexities of implementing immigration detention policy is 'process rich' and 'outcomes poor'.... Many of these practices have been in operation for a long time and seem to have given rise to an immigration detention culture that, in the opinion of the Inquiry, constrains thinking, flexibility and initiative and concentrates on functions, process and quantitative measurement to the detriment of the achievement of policy outcomes.[79]

The weakness of this approach is that it positions law itself as unproblematic, as though fairness and efficiency would result if police practice only reflected the law.[80] Yet the Rau and Alvarez/Solon report findings that DIMIA misunderstood the law cannot and should not be quarantined from the legal provisions themselves. It was the mandatory nature of detention that overshadowed officers' appreciation that the detention power 'operates in a mandatory way only *after* an officer has formed the requisite "reasonable suspicion" that a person "is" an unlawful non-citizen'.[81] Senior DIMIA staff had explained that

> detention powers were administrative, not criminal, and not subject to review; that the section was mandatory in its effect; and that the only way a person detained under its provisions could be released from detention was if an event [such as a visa grant] occurred.[82]

These insights suggest that the overall legal framework itself shaped officers' perceptions of the loss of liberty as 'a consequence of both the operation of the Act and the detainee's own doing and circumstances brought about by the detainee's own actions', minimising the impact of officers' decisions.[83] These observations flag the role of law in diminishing the significance of the loss of liberty, signalling the need to be vigilant of how other agencies use the very same powers.

The immigration detention power is used in contexts that amplify the problem of consent and coercion in the development of legal authority. When detention is undertaken by police as part of ordinary police work, the multiple bases for potential lawful custody run the risk of supporting a more generalised sense of legitimacy for detention that devalues the liberty of those policed. The practice of workplace immigration raids also minimises the deprivation of liberty involved in the very

79 Palmer, 'Inquiry into Cornelia Rau'.

80 Doreen J. McBarnet, 'The Police and the State: Arrest, Legality and the Law', in *Power and the State*, ed. Gary Littlejohn *et al.* (London: Croom Helm, 1978); Doreen J. McBarnet, *Conviction: Law, the State and the Construction of Justice* (London: Macmillan, 1981). For an overview of the long-running debate in policing scholarship as to whether it is law or institutional culture that explains what police do, see Dixon, *Law in Policing*, 1–48.

81 Palmer, 'Inquiry into Cornelia Rau', 21.

82 Ibid.

83 McMillan, 'Inquiry into Vivian Alvarez', 69.

process. In these contexts, the content of the main constraint in the detention power – reasonable suspicion of unlawful status – is rendered meaningless in fundamental respects. It fails to constrain initial contact with individuals in the street and fails to shape the practice of raids. The low visibility of such policing practices makes it profoundly important to consider how the law makes officers responsible for their powers and the harm to those detained.

Migration law's 'snapshot' model for officers' retrospective responsibility

In practice, the use of migration powers by non-immigration officers, and in specific ways also by immigration officers, is judged on the use of those powers in the moment, rather than taking a longer view of the event and its implications. This is evident from the legal structures of review and doctrinal approach as to what may ground an officer's 'reasonable suspicion' of unlawful status. The legal framework determines responsibility for the use of powers and recognises harm to those detained based on a 'snapshot' of the moment of detention itself. But does examining the use of the detention power only in that moment provide sufficient account of the powers being utilised in policing practices? Permitting only a narrow scope of examination does not engage with the reality that migration powers are often used as part of a sequence of police powers. Nor does it allow for legal recognition of the harm done to those apprehended and subsequently detained.

The term 'snapshot' was coined by criminal law scholar Peter Alldridge to reference the doctrine of contemporaneity or temporal coincidence in criminal law, which holds a person criminally liable only if at the instant he or she performs the criminal conduct, the person also holds the relevant mental state to be culpable. Alldridge argued that 'the criminal law takes snapshots and does not make videos'.[84] This chapter borrows the terms 'snapshot' and 'video' to visualise the time period migration law implicitly deems relevant in assessing whether an officer's action of taking an individual into immigration detention is lawful. A 'snapshot' approach to policing responsibility is evident in a couple of scenarios where detention powers are used, where: (i) police initially intervene on non-migration-related grounds and subsequently detain a person under the *Migration Act*; (ii) police or immigration officers detain a person based on a legal view of a person's migration legal status that was correct at the time, but is later found by the court to be mistaken. This part of the chapter turns to how the legal regulation of each of these scenarios embeds a 'snapshot' approach and the forms of responsibility it hinders. But it is first necessary to elaborate on the key constraint embedded in the detention power itself.

An officer is required to detain if the officer 'knows or reasonably suspects' that a person is an unlawful non-citizen. This constraint or standard is

84 See Peter Alldridge, *Relocating Criminal Law* (Aldershot: Ashgate, 2000), 87–90.

familiar as the principal trigger for police powers more generally. The majority joint judgment in the 2005 High Court decision in *Ruddock* v. *Taylor*,[85] which considered the immigration detention provision, did not explicitly reference the criminal law jurisprudence on the meaning of 'reasonable suspicion'. But the majority finding that 'what constitutes reasonable grounds for suspecting a person to be an unlawful non-citizen must be judged against what was known or reasonably capable of being known at the relevant time'[86] reflects the existing authority guiding requisite suspicion for criminal investigations. Further, McHugh J's dissenting judgment referenced approaches in Australian and United Kingdom ('UK') criminal cases on the interpretation of suspicion itself.[87] A suspicion itself is 'more than a mere idle wondering ... it is a positive feeling of actual apprehension or mistrust'.[88] Police must form their reasonable suspicion based on fact,[89] and its reasonableness is determined by objective criteria.[90] A reasonable suspicion must amount to more than a possibility,[91] but less than a reasonable belief.[92] Police may rely on material that is inadmissible in evidence, including hearsay, provided that evidence is probative (that is, it affects the probability of the existence of a fact in issue).[93]

More may be required of immigration officers than police in the formation of reasonable suspicion. The higher standard required reflects assessment of immigration officers' roles and experience and the planned nature of immigration operations, both of which affect how courts interpret what amounts to a 'reasonable' basis for suspicion. An immigration officer 'in forming a reasonable suspicion is obliged to make due inquiry to obtain material likely to be relevant to the formation of that suspicion'.[94] This is appropriate, the Court reasoned, because the scheme rests the decision for indefinite detention pending removal with administrators.[95] Thus, in *Goldie* v. *Commonwealth* an experienced immigration officer detained Goldie after examining a computer record that indicated he did not currently hold a visa, but in 2002 the Full Federal Court held this detention was not

85 *Ruddock* v. *Taylor* [2005] HCA 48; (2005) 221 ALR 32.

86 Ibid., 32 [40] (Gleeson CJ, Gummow, Hayne and Heydon JJ); applied in *Akpata* v. *Minister for Immigration and Citizenship* [2012] FCA 806; (2012) 206 FCR 120, 127.

87 *Ruddock* v. *Taylor* [2005] HCA 48; (2005) 221 ALR 32 [70]–[100] (McHugh J).

88 *Queensland Bacon Pty Ltd* v. *Rees* [1966] HCA 21; (1966) 115 CLR 266, 303 (Kitto J) cited by *George* v. *Rockett* (1990) HCA 26; (1990) 93 ALR 483, 490.

89 *George* v. *Rockett* [1990] HCA 26; (1990) 93 ALR 483, 490 (unanimous joint judgment).

90 *Anderson* v. *Judges of the District Court of New South Wales* (1992) 27 NSWLR 701, 714 (Kirby P., Meagher and Sheller J. J. A agreeing); *Hyder* v. *Commonwealth of Australia* [2012] NSWCA 336; (2012) 217 A Crim R 517 [15] (McColl JA) ('*Hyder*').

91 *R* v. *Rondo* [2001] NSWCCA 540; (2001) 126 A Crim R 562 [53] (Smart AJ) (Spigelman CJ and Simpson J in agreement in separate judgments) ('*Rondo*').

92 *George* v. *Rockett* [1990] HCA 26; (1990) 93 ALR 483, 490; *Rondo* [2001] NSWCCA 540; (2001) 126 A Crim R 562 [53].

93 *Rondo* [2001] NSWCCA 540; (2001) 126 A Crim R 562 [53] (Smart AJ).

94 *Goldie* v. *Commonwealth* [2002] FCA 433; (2002) 117 FCR 566 [6].

95 Ibid.

objectively justified.[96] The officer had disregarded other facts in forming his suspicion including official information that treated Goldie as if he held a current visa. The officer also did not make sufficient inquiries; he based his suspicion on a computer record that was incomplete and out of date, in a context which would have alerted the officer to the need undertake further inquiry.[97]

The reasonableness of suspicion is a matter of factual evaluation and it will depend on each case as to whether the circumstances were enough to prompt other inquiries before the requisite suspicion could be formed.[98] Because police and others who are not immigration officers have different levels of access to information, less may be required for their suspicion to be reasonably grounded than is required of immigration. If police or, for example, detention staff can show evidence they knew a person held unlawful status (for instance, the person had knowledge of a visa cancellation)[99] or relied on information from a credible source such as immigration, this would likely be enough to lawfully ground suspicion.[100]

The legal standard allows for a broad range of information to ground the formation of reasonable suspicion, but whether evidence meets the standard will depend on the circumstances. The decision in *Goldie* suggests that the Court would have found detention on the basis of suspicion of status unjustified in some scenarios investigated by the Ombudsman. In one such instance, Australian citizen Mr E was detained for four days, despite providing evidence of citizenship (Australian passport, Australian citizenship certificate and the passport from his birth country), because immigration found that evidence was outweighed by information provided to them that the person claiming to be Mr E was in fact an unlawful non-citizen.[101]

In contrast to targeted detention operations, far less information is available to officers encountering a suspected unlawful non-citizen in the street without prior knowledge. This appears to be what McHugh J, one of the minority in *Ruddock* v. *Taylor*, had in mind when he suggested what appears to be a low bar in the culturally and linguistically diverse Australian community:

> If, for example, an officer finds an adult person in the migration zone who cannot speak English, who appears to have no residential address or employment with Australia and who fails, when asked, to produce a visa, the officer may 'reasonably suspect' that the person is an 'unlawful non-citizen'. If no more appears, that is a clear case of reasonable suspicion. Many less compelling facts may establish reasonable suspicion.[102]

96 Ibid., 566 [6]–[20] (Gray and Lee JJ).
97 Ibid., 566 [9], [17], [19].
98 *Hyder* [2012] NSWCA 336; (2012) 217 A Crim R 517 [15], [17] (McColl JA).
99 See the discussion in *Fernando* v. *Commonwealth of Australia* [2010] FCA 753; (2010) 271 ALR 521 [88]–[110].
100 *Hyder* [2012] NSWCA 336; (2012) 217 A Crim R 517.
101 McMillan, 'Detention Process Issues', 10–11.
102 *Ruddock* v. *Taylor* [2005] HCA 48; (2005) 221 ALR 32, 53–4 [108].

But McHugh J's comments must be read in light of his overall dissenting judgment that an officer's suspicion could not be reasonably founded if the facts upon which the officer relies to form suspicion are incapable in law of making the person an 'unlawful non-citizen', and a mistaken understanding of law (which will be discussed below) could not provide reasonable grounds for suspicion.

Immigration training to external agencies (such as state police) in the proper exercise of *Migration Act* powers advises the bar is somewhat higher than that offered by McHugh J:

> Training modules that are provided for the police by DIAC inform officers that their suspicions about unlawful status must be 'based on objective evidence and not on assumption', and … instructors' notes … explain that factors such as language proficiency or ethnicity fall under the category of 'assumptions'.[103]

In practice, in street contexts, police suspicion of a person's migration legal status is not formed in isolation, but as part of an unfolding series of suspicions.

Police responsibility for initial intervention on the street

Initial encounters between police and unlawful non-citizens often start on a basis other than an officer's suspicion that a person is unlawful. This is implied by the calls police make to the Immigration Status Service, an immigration telephone hotline established in 2006 which provides information on the status of named individuals to external agencies. Most queries were instigated by police doubt over a person's identity, because they held foreign documents, or were unable to speak English,[104] facts that would be apparent only after some interaction between police and the individual. The invisibility and concomitant undermining of responsibility for that initial contact is evident from John's account of his apprehension.

John was apprehended as an illegal migrant in early 2006 shortly after the Cronulla 'riots' of December 11, 2005.[105] A decade has since passed, but the Cronulla riots, a racist attack on people viewed as 'Middle Eastern' followed by clashes between Caucasian and 'Middle Eastern' Australians, remain an important landmark event in Australian race politics and a distinct policing event.[106] The

103 Weber, *Policing Non-Citizens*, 75. Weber cites the training materials 'Immigration Compliance: DIAC and Police Working Together' provided to the researchers by the Department of Immigration and Citizenship.

104 Weber, *Policing Non-Citizens*, 68–73.

105 This account is developed from the author's interview with M9, as well as documents from M9's immigration file, which he had obtained via a freedom of information request.

106 See, for example, Gregory Noble, ed. *Lines in the Sand: The Cronulla Riots, Multiculturalism and National Belonging* (Sydney: Sydney Institute of Criminology, 2009), 1; Scott Poynting, 'What Caused the Cronulla Riot?', *Race & Class* 48, no. 1 (2006); Chris Cunneen, 'Law, Policing and Public Order: The Aftermath of Cronulla', in *Lines in the Sand: The Cronulla Riots, Multiculturalism and National Belonging*, ed. Greg Noble (Sydney: Sydney Institute of Criminology, 2009).

circumstances in which John was stopped made it clear it was part of the post-Cronulla riot policing, as will become apparent.

By way of background, the immediate precursor to the riot is generally attributed to a conflict at Cronulla beach between a number of off-duty lifesavers and a group of 'Middle Eastern' men, which resulted in injury of the lifesavers and controversial media coverage.[107] Various commentators have remarked that the emblematic Australian icons of the beach and lifesavers were recruited to energise anti-Arab sentiment as a form of nationalism. On December 11, 2005, about 5000 people attended Cronulla Beach ostensibly to protest against reports of assaults and perceived intimidating behaviour by persons described by the crowd as 'Middle Eastern' people from the western suburbs of Sydney. The gathering became violent as the crowd chased and assaulted a number of persons perceived to be 'Middle Eastern'.[108] That night, the 'reprisal attacks' (the terminology used by police and media) commenced, and clashes between 'Middle Eastern' and Caucasian Australians continued the next day and to a lesser extent in the days that followed.[109] The events attracted national and even international attention. A few days later, Parliament passed new laws to grant police emergency powers to address large-scale public disorder in authorised 'target' areas,[110] and supplemented existing police powers. There were 104 people charged, 51 in relation to the attacks of December 11, 2005, and 53 in relation to the events that followed.[111] The police investigations included stops and searches of people of 'Middle Eastern' appearance, particularly in the south-west Sydney suburbs of Bankstown, Punchbowl, Campsie and Chester Hill.

John believed he was stopped and searched because of his ethnicity as police had been checking many people of 'Middle Eastern appearance' in the area following the Cronulla events. The police officer locating John advised immigration that the impetus for the stop was that John was 'looking lost'.[112] But John explains that police in a patrol car singled him out while he was walking down a quiet residential street to buy cigarettes. The police stopped him and no others who were in the street at the time, and asked him for his identification and mobile phone. Nothing in the police records retained in John's immigration file indicate that John was stopped due to suspicion about his immigration status, but at some point in seeking identification police requested John's passport.

107 Norm Hazzard, 'Strikeforce Neil Cronulla Riots: Review of the Police Response, Vol 1', (Sydney: NSW Police, 2006); Gregory Noble, 'Where the Bloody Hell Are We? Multicultural Manners in a World of Hyperdiversity', in *Lines in the Sand: The Cronulla Riots, Multiculturalism and National Belonging*, ed. Greg Noble (Sydney: Sydney Institute of Criminology, 2009).

108 Hazzard, 'Strikeforce Neil Cronulla Riots', 39–45.

109 Ibid., 54.

110 The emergency powers (inserted into the *Law Enforcement (Powers and Responsibilities) Act 2002* (NSW) ss 87A–87P) were adopted in a special sitting of Parliament on December 15, 2005 and commenced the same day.

111 Hazzard, 'Strikeforce Neil Cronulla Riots', 54.

112 Documents from the immigration file of M9, Immigration file note, 2006 (exact date anonymised).

Moreover, police also checked John's mobile phone for text messages, which formed a strong theme in the post-Cronulla riot-related policing.

The priority police placed on checking mobile phones post-Cronulla was novel, and reflected the new profile attained by mobile phones as key to 'rioting for a tech-savvy generation'.[113] Over 270 000 SMS messages had been transmitted inciting the events of December 11.[114] SMS messages called for 'every Aussie in the Shire get down to North Cronulla to help support Leb and wog bashing day'[115] and relayed, 'These skippy aussies want war. Bring ur guns and knives and lets show them how we do it'.[116] Police identified mobile phones not only as central to the planning and coordination of attacks, but also to the evasion of police.[117] Introducing new police powers to confiscate mobile phones, the NSW Police Minister Carl Scully explained these powers would 'take away any tools that people may use to feed this unrest'.[118] During the authorisation of emergency powers on December 15 and 17–19, 2005, 113 mobile phones were checked,[119] and in the latter period police records show seizures of 56 mobile phones.[120]

In terms of criminal justice, John's experience reflects that of many reported by Arabic-speaking communities in the Canterbury-Bankstown area, where John was stopped, that they had been 'unfairly targeted by police following the Cronulla incidents'.[121] In the absence of a full account by police, it is impossible to be certain, but from the information available from John's account and details recorded in his immigration file, it did not appear that police held the requisite objectively based suspicion at the time they stopped John. After he was held at the police station for about three hours, the police told John they had no criminal interest in him, then police informed John that his visa had expired, unbeknownst to him, as he had believed his temporary bridging visa was continuing while he was awaiting the Minister of Immigration and Multicultural and Indigenous Affairs (MIMIA) decision on an intervention request he had submitted. He was then taken into immigration detention.

This kind of intervention by police, which does not result in charge, is typical of what is referred to as 'low visibility' police decisions, because such decisions do not result in criminal prosecution and the judicial scrutiny afforded in the

113 Gerard Goggin, 'SMS Riot: Transmitting Race on a Sydney Beach, December 2005', *M/C Journal* 9, no. 1 (2006): para 8.
114 Hazzard, 'Strikeforce Neil Cronulla Riots', 35.
115 Cited by Poynting, 'What Caused the Cronulla Riot?', 86–7.
116 Hazzard, 'Strikeforce Neil Cronulla Riots', 35.
117 NSW Ombudsman, 'Review of Emergency Powers to Prevent or Control Disorder' (Sydney, September 2007), 45.
118 Cited in NSW Ombudsman, 'Review of Emergency Powers to Prevent or Control Disorder', 45.
119 Ibid., 39–40.
120 These figures do not provide the complete picture. As noted by the Ombudsman, record-keeping requirements for police exercises of power were unclear: ibid., 6, 59–60.
121 Community Relations Commission, 'Submission to the NSW Ombudsman Law Enforcement Legislation Amendment (Public Safety) Act 2005 Review', February 21, 2007.

subsequent trial.[122] The immigration decision to detain is in many ways paradigmatic of low visibility policing. Unlike a criminal arrest, persons are not detained for the purpose of commencing proceedings, nor are they detained for judicial determination of status.[123] Persons are simply detained under 'administrative fiat'.[124] If no charge is laid or if a person is dealt with under migration law not by way of criminal charge, a 'video' model of responsibility embedded in a criminal trial is not engaged. In a criminal trial, the court has discretion to exclude evidence that has been obtained improperly or as a consequence of an improper act.[125] The potential to exclude improperly obtained evidence engages a 'video' model of responsibility for the police exercise of power because the court is able to call police to account for their use of power in a *sequence* of events. Thus, if police stop a vehicle without authority and then conduct a lawful search that locates drugs, and they proceed to charge, the court may nevertheless exclude evidence of the drugs in the trial against the accused because they were found only as a consequence of an unlawful stop.[126] In other words, the legality of a single exercise of power may rely on prior exercises of power.

This model of retrospective responsibility for police intervention is lost when it results in immigration detention, rather than criminal charge. If initial intervention by police on criminal justice grounds is improper, and police then utilise *Migration Act* policing powers, legal responsibility shifts to a 'snapshot', rather than a 'video', model. In migration law, police exercise of the immigration detention power will be judged solely on the use of the detention power in that moment. If its justification is contested, the legality of police action will be confined to the question: did the officer know or reasonably suspect the unlawful non-citizen status of the individual? It will not encompass the question of the legality of initial police powers to intervene (such as stop and search), and in this way migration law lacks capacity to deter illegal police action and encourage lawful investigatory methods. Certainly, the policed may initiate civil litigation for trespass or false imprisonment for the initial police intervention, although extensive practical barriers exist.

In practice, the problems of accountability for use of the immigration detention power reflect those underlying police practice in the criminal jurisdiction generally. At a systemic level, much police work occurs through informal means, does not proceed to charge and thus lies outside the 'video' model for retrospective responsibility offered by the criminal trial. Powers that do not result in charge are part of the broader activities of police in 'handling the situation',[127]

122 Joseph Goldstein, 'Police Discretion Not to Invoke the Criminal Process: Low-Visibility Decisions in the Administration of Justice', *Yale Law Journal* 69, no. 4 (1960): 12; Richard Ericson, *Reproducing Order: A Study of Police Patrolwork* (Toronto: University of Toronto Press, 1982).

123 *Goldie* v. *Commonwealth* [2002] FCA 433; (2002) 117 FCR 566 [6].

124 Ibid.

125 See, for example, *Evidence Act 1995* (Cth) s 138; see also the discussion in Chapter 3.

126 See, for example, *Rondo* [2001] NSWCCA 540; (2001) 126 A Crim R 562. Other dimensions of the use of evidence law as a mechanism of police responsibility are discussed in Chapter 3.

127 James Q. Wilson, *Varieties of Police Behavior: The Management of Law and Order in Eight Communities* (Cambridge: Harvard University Press, 1968), 31.

addressing a 'problem' defined by police. An extensive and well-established literature on the role of police in producing and maintaining order illustrates the great diversity of informal tactics police use to produce order – moving people along in the street, mediating disputes, using threats, intimidation or reassurance, and disrupting social and religious affiliations.[128] In street policing particularly, police patrol has been found to be primarily about order maintenance achieved other than by law enforcement.[129] The immigration detention power adds another tool for police to achieve a particular kind of order or objective.

Accountability for the detention power also encapsulates pervasive tensions between the police practice of suspicion and the law's requirement that suspicion be reasonable. Policing scholarship has highlighted that police form suspicion not only in relation to gathering evidence for a specific crime, but as part of broader policing surveillance of people whose activities and behaviours are out of step with what is considered to be normal in the particular context of the place, time and activity.[130] 'Suspicion is built up and dispersed', developed cumulatively, and thus does not fit neatly with legal requirements that reasonable grounds for suspicion be established before detention.[131]

It is important not to overstate the contrast between responsibility for police powers in the criminal jurisdiction and for the immigration detention power. Indeed, the strong resonances between the extensive discretion afforded officers in each realm evidence an arena of power that remains largely invisible and unregulated. However, with respect to matters that proceed to criminal trial, the contrast is dramatic. Retrospective inspection of police practice in criminal trials does instil some responsibility for what is required for lawful intervention, but even this level of police responsibility is lost when police wield migration powers. The 'snapshot' approach to the officer's responsibility in migration reduces the visibility of the initial reason for intervention, and quite artificially isolates the reasons for intervention from review.

Responsibility for detention based on a misunderstanding of legal status

Importantly, the law provides that the reasonableness of an officer's suspicion must be assessed against what was known or reasonably capable of being known at time the officer formed their suspicion.[132] In criminal justice, the

128 See, for example, Michael Banton, *Policeman in the Community* (New York: Tavistock, 1964); William Ker Muir, *Police: Streetcorner Politicians* (Chicago: University of Chicago Press, 1977); Ericson, *Reproducing Order*; Sentas, *Traces of Terror*.

129 Ericson, *Reproducing Order*, 3–11, 206; Robert Reiner, *The Politics of the Police*, 2nd edn (Hertfordshire: Harvester Wheatsheaf, 1992), 139–46.

130 David Dixon *et al.*, 'Reality and Rules in the Construction and Regulation of Police Suspicion', *International Journal of the Sociology of Law* 17, no. 2 (1989).

131 Ibid., 189.

132 *Ruddock* v. *Taylor* [2005] HCA 48; (2005) 221 ALR 32 [40]; see also *Rondo* [2001] NSWCCA 540; (2001) 126 A Crim R 562 [53]; *Hyder* [2012] NSWCA 336; (2012) 217 A Crim R 517 [15], [17].

common law principle that the legality of the officer's action only be judged on what they knew at the time reflects a balance between protection of individual liberties and the need for efficiency in criminal justice at a preliminary stage of investigations. In migration, the very issue officers are required to determine is one that may be subject to change in legal interpretation – immigration status. The question thus becomes what, if any, responsibility should be imposed if it is later found that the person did hold lawful status in these circumstances? In 2005 the majority of the highest appellate court in Australia, the High Court, found in *Ruddock* v. *Taylor* that the legality of formation of a reasonable suspicion could not be retrospectively affected by a later judicial finding that a person in fact holds lawful status.[133] This decision means that people in these circumstances do not have access to the tort of false imprisonment even if the courts find they held lawful status at the time they were apprehended.

Graham Ernest Taylor was born in the UK and had arrived in Australia as a child but never obtained Australian citizenship. As an adult, he pleaded guilty to serious criminal offences and served a sentence of imprisonment. On two occasions after his release on parole, the Minister for Immigration and Multicultural Affairs (MIMA) purported to cancel Taylor's visa on grounds that he did not meet the character test (in November 1999 and June 2000) and detained him for the purpose of deportation.[134] On both occasions the Court later quashed the visa cancellation decision.[135]

Taylor then brought an action for the two periods he was detained, which amounted to 316 days, arguing that his detention was unlawful because it was the consequence of invalid decisions to cancel his visa. He argued that suspicion that a person is an unlawful non-citizen could not be reasonable if based on a mistake of law (even if the mistake was only found after detention had commenced). However, the majority of the High Court found the invalid visa cancellation did not make his detention unlawful. In construing the meaning of the statute, it held that suspicion might be based on a mistake of law or fact and still remain reasonable because the detention provision does not provide any basis for distinguishing between these types of mistakes.[136] The detention provision simply allows for detention on the basis of reasonable suspicion of unlawful status. The majority noted that often no distinction could be drawn and the error will be both one of fact and law, '[e]specially is that task difficult where, as here, the subject-matter of the relevant suspicion is a statutory status – being an unlawful non-citizen'.[137] By confining the

133 *Ruddock* v. *Taylor* [2005] HCA 48; (2005) 221 ALR 32.

134 For discussion of the character test, see Chapter 5.

135 *Re Patterson; Ex parte Taylor* [2001] HCA 51; (2001) 207 CLR 391 [1], [52], [136], [223], [318], [377].

136 *Ruddock* v. *Taylor* [2005] HCA 48; (2005) 221 ALR 32, 41 (Gleeson CJ, Gummow, Hayne and Heydon JJ).

137 Ibid.

reasonableness of suspicion to that known at the time, the *Ruddock* v. *Taylor*[138] approach frames officers' responsibility for taking a person into immigration custody in a 'snapshot' model.

Despite the *Ruddock* v. *Taylor* majority, even at the time of the decision there was robust authority for the proposition that detention effected pursuant to an administrative decision later found by courts to have misapplied the law would make that detention unlawful.[139] The reasoning rests on the principle that when a court quashes an administrative decision, it makes the decision void from the date of the decision itself so that the decision has no legal effect (*void ab initio*).[140] In the view of the dissenting judgment of Kirby J in *Ruddock* v. *Taylor*, it is not reasonable for a suspicion to be founded on a misunderstanding of law, because, as noted in the UK House of Lords decision of *Brockhill*,[141] a judicial decision about what the law is in effect declares what the law has always been. The UK authority explains that there is a difference between situations where administrators have wrongly interpreted a valid law (though it was in accordance with the law as it was understood at the time such as the situation in *Ruddock* v. *Taylor*),[142] and those where a decision has been made in accordance with law that is later held to be invalid.[143] A decision in the former situation is void because it is a decision of an administrator (such as the Minister or delegate) that has been found to be mistaken in law, whereas if, for example, detention was the result of High Court orders, these remain binding until they are set aside or stayed because of the constitutional role of the High Court as final arbiter.[144] In contrast to this approach, the trend in the Australian High Court has been to 'avoid the labels of "voidness" and "nullity" ',[145] and simply reference the consequence of the remedy of *certiorari* (which quashes a decision), which allows for redecision.

What is at stake in a snapshot approach to officers' responsibility in these circumstances? Immigration has detained and even removed numerous people from Australia following a visa cancellation, which the court has later found to

138 Ibid.

139 See, for example, *Park Oh Ho* v. *Minister for Immigration and Ethnic Affairs* [1989] HCA 54; (1989) 167 CLR 637; *R* v. *Governor of Brockhill Prison; Ex parte Evans (No 2)* [2000] UKHL 480; [2000] 4 All ER 15 ('Brockhill') cited in *Ruddock* v. *Taylor* [2005] HCA 48; (2005) 221 ALR 32 [162]–[166] (Kirby J). See also Steven Churches, 'Civil and Political Rights: Flow-on from Findings of Lack of Legislative Reach or Invalidity: False Imprisonment and Compulsory Examinations Founded in Invalid Summonses', *Australian Journal of Administrative Law* 16 (2008): 13.

140 See *Ruddock* v. *Taylor* [2005] HCA 48; (2005) 221 ALR 32, [160] (Kirby J).

141 *Brockhill* [2000] UKHL 48; [2000] 4 All ER 15, 18–20, 20–2, 24–5; *Ruddock* v. *Taylor* [2005] HCA 48; (2005) 221 ALR 32 [165]–[166].

142 For example, as in *Brockhill* [2000] UKHL 48; [2000] 4 All ER 15 [27D]–[27F] (Lord Browne-Wilkinson), [45H]–[46C], [46G]–[46H], [47E]–[47F] (Lord Hobhouse).

143 For example, as in *Percy* v. *Hall* [1997] QB 924.

144 *Ruddock* v. *Taylor* [2005] HCA 48; (2005) 221 ALR 32, [170]–[172] (Kirby J).

145 Susan Kneebone, 'Before the High Court: Ruddock and Others v. Taylor', *Sydney Law Review* 27, no. 1 (2005): 155.

be an invalid cancellation. For example, the Federal Magistrates Court held in *Uddin* v. *Minister for Immigration and Multicultural and Indigenous Affairs*[146] that an educational institution had issued notice of automatic student visa cancellation in a form that did not meet the mandatory legal requirements and so did not effect visa cancellation. Following this decision, it became apparent that educational institutions had provided incorrect notifications to 8450 student visa holders in the period May 2001 to August 2005.[147] In August 2005, DIMIA reversed all the automated cancellations in this period, which effectively reinstated the lawful status of those students (unless their student visas had expired).[148] Yet by the time this correction was made, over 5200 of those affected were outside Australia and no longer held a valid student visa because the reinstated visa had already expired, and thus they could not automatically travel to Australia and resume study.[149] By October 2005 only 625 people held a student visa resurrected under this process.[150] This mistake was extremely disruptive for students' life aspirations as they were forced to abandon study and leave Australia at great personal and financial cost, and it would be expected that many would have been detained as a consequence of visa cancellation.[151]

A number of other court decisions similarly found the interpretation of legal status that authorised an individual's detention was mistaken. In one such case, the non-citizen Ahmed El Masri was detained for an extensive period, almost three years in the period November 2002 to October 2005. El Masri was released in October 2005 after being identified as one of 13 affected by the decision in *Nystrom* v. *Minister for Immigration and Multicultural and Indigenous Affairs*,[152] where the court had found immigration had erred and not validly cancelled Nystrom's visa. Similar to *Nystrom*, immigration found that El Masri held a valid absorbed person visa for the entire period of his detention, and released him 104 days after that decision.[153] A year later the High Court

146 *Uddin* v. *Minister for Immigration and Multicultural and Indigenous Affairs* [2005] FMCA 841.

147 Senate Legal and Constitutional References Committee, 'Inquiry into the Administration and Operation of the Migration Act 1958' (Canberra: Commonwealth of Australia, 2006), 315.

148 *Uddin* v. *Minister for Immigration and Multicultural and Indigenous Affairs* [2005] FMCA 841.

149 DIAC, 'Advice to Education Providers Regarding Federal Court Decision', Commonwealth of Australia, https://web.archive.org/web/20110602000930/www.immi.gov.au/business-services/education-providers/advice_providers.htm.

150 Senate Legal and Constitutional References Committee, 'Inquiry into the Administration and Operation of the Migration Act 1958', 315.

151 Note that arrangements were made for affected students located by immigration whose visas had expired to be offered bridging visas while they applied for a substantive visa: ibid., 316.

152 *Nystrom* v. *Minister for Immigration and Multicultural and Indigenous Affairs* [2005] FCAFC 121; (2005) 143 FCR 420; Question Taken on Notice, Immigration and Multicultural and Indigenous Affairs Portfolio, Senate Legal and Constitutional References Committee Inquiry into the Administration of the Migration Act 1958, October 11, 2005.

153 Australian Human Rights Commission, '2009 El Masri v. Commonwealth (Department of Immigration and Citizenship): Report into Unlawful and Arbitrary Detention and the Right of People in Detention to Humane Treatment (2009) AUSHRC 41' (Sydney, 2009).

overturned the *Nystrom* decision,[154] and immigration took El Masri into detention again although he was not affected by the High Court's decision.

In yet another instance, the Minister for Immigration and Citizenship purported to cancel the Transitional (Permanent) visa held by Charles Sales, but the Federal Court (in a decision three years after *Ruddock* v. *Taylor*[155]), found that regardless of whether Sales 'held' that visa, the cancellation was invalid.[156] The cancellation was invalid because the character power does not authorise cancellation of a visa 'held' by a person, it authorises cancellation only where a visa has been 'granted' or deemed to have been granted which wasn't the case in this instance.[157] As a result of the *Sales* decision, 23 people were released from detention because, like Sales, they held a visa.[158] Two months after the *Sales* decision, legislative amendments commenced that overruled that decision, which not only provided that the type of visa held by Sales be deemed to be granted (and thus able to be cancelled), but also retrospectively validated any purported cancellations of such visas.[159] By amending the *Migration Act* post-*Sales*, the legislature sent a clear message against the retrospective operation of judicial law-making on the legality of detention, and thus restricted state accountability.

What is important to note about these cases is that those affected by the ilk of the *Sales* and *Nystrom* decisions do not necessarily have access to damages for their periods of imprisonment. This is because an invalid visa cancellation that precipitated detention does not make the detention unlawful per se. Provided detention was based on reasonable suspicion of unlawful status, it may be lawful. And so, despite his long and tumultuous history of immigration detention, El Masri received compensation for only 90 days of his detention, commencing 14 days after the *Nystrom* decision, which is the date at which the Australian Human Rights Commission determined that immigration's suspicion that El Masri was an unlawful non-citizen became unreasonable.[160]

A recent UK High Court decision, *Mohammed*,[161] flags potential for change to the Australian approach in *Ruddock* v. *Taylor*.[162] In an analogous case, *Mohammed* found that an erroneous view of the law could not amount to

154 *Minister for Immigration and Multicultural and Indigenous Affairs* v. *Nystrom* [2006] HCA 50; (2006) 228 CLR 566.

155 *Ruddock* v. *Taylor* [2005] HCA 48; (2005) 221 ALR 32.

156 *Sales* v. *Minister for Immigration & Citizenship* [2008] FCAFC 132; (2008) 171 FCR 56 ('*Sales*').

157 Ibid.

158 Sarah Smiles, 'Ban on Deportations Reversed', *The Age*, October 10, 2008, 3 cited by Michelle Foster, '"An 'Alien' by the Barest of Threads" – the Legality of the Deportation of Long-Term Residents from Australia', *Melbourne University Law Review* 33, no. 2 (2009): 487.

159 *Migration Legislation Amendment Act (No 1) 2008* (Cth).

160 Australian Human Rights Commission, '2009 El Masri v. Commonwealth', 37.

161 *Mohammed* v. *The Secretary of State for the Home Department* [2014] EWHC 4317 (Admin); [2015] WLR 3349 ('*Mohammed*').

162 [2005] HCA 48; (2005) 221 ALR 32.

'reasonable grounds for suspecting' that an unaccompanied minor was liable to removal. It followed the streams of authority favoured by the dissenting judgments in *Ruddock* v. *Taylor*, judgments that the UK Court found more persuasive than the majority. Because it found an official's decision based on a misunderstanding of law does not provide a defence to false imprisonment,[163] the *Mohammed* approach means officials are made responsible for decisions based on a misapprehension of law. This alternative approach expresses a 'video' approach to officers' responsibility, but has not yet been considered by Australian courts.

The form of responsibility enabled by the tort of false imprisonment in these circumstances would not have much impact on how officers exercise their powers in either responsive street policing or targeted operations. After all, at the time officers take a person into detention, they can only do so based on how they understand the law at the time; they cannot know whether and how the courts will interpret an individual's migration legal status. Rather, the tort of false imprisonment makes authorities responsible for compensating the harm experienced by the individual detained: '[T]he focus of this civil wrong is on the vindication of liberty and reparation to the victim, rather than upon the presence or absence of moral wrongdoing on the part of the defendant'.[164] To emphasise, the tort requires only that the act is intended and caused by the respondent, not that detention was effected in bad faith.[165] Excluding the availability of this tort is significant both for legal doctrine and practical redress as shown by the cases just discussed. The tort of false imprisonment has been regarded as one of the 'important constitutional safeguards of the liberty of the subject against the executive'.[166] The denial of this form of legal redress prevents recognition of the harm that was done by often lengthy deprivation of liberty itself. In so doing, it also denies the person detained access to damages for false imprisonment.

Legal theorists today point to a broader role for tort law beyond financial redress. Tort law can be instrumental in setting standards and changing the conduct of individuals and organisations.[167] Optimistically, if Australia adopted the *Mohammed* approach to decisions based on a misapprehension of law, the risk of adverse financial consequences might act as a serious disincentive to government commitment to immigration detention itself. At the least it would provide legal recognition that the state caused the harm experienced by the individual.

163 *Mohammed* [2014] EWHC 4317 (Admin); [2015] WLR 3349, 3349 [93].

164 *Ruddock* v. *Taylor* [2005] HCA 48; (2005) 221 ALR 32 [140]; see also *Marshall* v. *Watson* [1972] HCA 27; (1972) 124 CLR 640.

165 *Macpherson* v. *Brown* (1975) 12 SASR 184, 190–1; *Brockhill* [2001] 2 AC 19; [2000] 4 All ER 15 [33F]–[35F], [37B].

166 Ibid., 43.

167 Janet Ransley, Jessica Anderson and Tim Prenzler, 'Civil Litigation against Police in Australia: Exploring its Extent, Nature and Implications for Accountability', *The Australian and New Zealand Journal of Criminology* 40, no. 2 (2007): 147.

In sum, two main implications arise from the limited temporality (the 'snapshot' model) migration law deems relevant for determining state responsibility for the violence of detention. First, it intensifies the invisibility or low visibility of street policing encounters. Making the legality of detention dependent only on whether an officer holds reasonable grounds for detention means that even if police improperly stop a person in the street, this will not be relevant for the legality of detention. The lawfulness of initial stops is an ongoing issue in street-based policing more generally and migration law is certainly counter to addressing this problem. Second, the snapshot model of responsibility means that even if a court later finds that a non-citizen was detained based on a misapprehension of the individual's legal status, this does not make detention unlawful. The former dynamic enhances discretionary power in migration policing and the latter disregards the impacts of discretionary power on those detained. As practices at the front end of migration process, both amplify the problems of responsibility associated with initial 'low visibility' policing encounters. Both prompt important questions as to whether a snapshot mode of responsibility encourages officers to dismiss the significance of articulating the authority for detention at any one time. It is apparent overall that the law imposes dramatically less responsibility for coercive powers utilised in the immigration context than it does for criminal law arrest.

Conclusion

This chapter focused on a key and controversial site of border violence – immigration detention – and examined the legal regulation of its practice outside institutional confines to better understand its character as a power to apprehend those known or suspected to be unlawful non-citizens. As the empirical starting point for this book, the work of the detention power illustrates the book's argument that migration law marginalises recognition of its violence. This marginalisation is achieved through legal practices which concentrate discretion at the front end of migration process, equipping officers with broad powers to decide who should be detained and how detention ought to proceed. The concentration of discretion in the front end is facilitated by the *Migration Act* which mandates immigration detention once an unlawful non-citizen has been identified. It is strengthened by rendering what in practice operates as arrest simply as detention, as such not warranting any of the procedural safeguards afforded arrest for a criminal offence.

The far-reaching implications of discretion held by officers in their first contact with individuals has been well recognised in the criminal justice literature, and many of the same issues arise in the police use of immigration powers in street settings. Police apprehension of individuals as suspected unlawful non-citizens in the street is imbricated with other policing projects and routines. As an additional custodial tool for police, the immigration detention power runs the risk of amplifying problems reported in street policing more generally. It extends the potential consequences for those deemed suspect by police, and raises serious questions about the impact of status-based suspicion on police practices. It is hard to escape the implication that race and ethnicity become cemented as part of the constellation of factors that police use to identify a person being 'out of place'.

Because police rarely use immigration powers to *initiate* a street stop, the requirement that officers form reasonable suspicion before immigration detention has no impact in constraining the initial street stop. The observation that legal requirements of 'reasonable suspicion' do little to regulate police stop and search practices on the street is not new. When the immigration detention power is added in the police powers mix it further decreases the visibility of street policing practice generally (as it provides an additional justification for intervention that does not result in charge for a criminal offence) and it intensifies the lack of visibility of street policing on a particular population – those suspected to be non-citizens and unlawful non-citizens.

For immigration officers, the 'detention first, identification second' approach that seems to occur in some raids illustrates the disjuncture between the *Migration Act*'s legalistic approach requiring individualised suspicion and the messy social reality of a raid. No court has considered this practice, so it is uncertain whether it would be regarded as unlawful detention, but those caught up in these processes certainly felt they were not at liberty to depart the premises during the compliance operation. In targeted operations, the courts have demanded more of immigration officers to demonstrate an objective basis for suspicion of status, which, though it makes sense as immigration officers have more information and experience, nevertheless emphasises the alarmingly expansive discretion held by police given the broad context of routine police practice.

For both police and immigration, the concentration of discretionary authority over detention practices is constituted through the interrelation between legal powers. This emphasises the need to understand migration policing practices as generated through interlegalities, overlaps and the spaces between legal powers, not solely from explicit designation of powers. These interrelations are productive of diverse practices including the capacity for police to trivialise immigration detention by using it as a 'placeholder' or back-up justification during broader investigations, the institution of a de facto Australian identity card, and the sidelining of the immigration detention power as a mechanism to target individuals in an immigration raid.

Migration law further marginalises recognition of its violence through the legal structures of review and doctrinal approach to responsibility for taking people into detention. The 'snapshot' model of responsibility embedded in migration legal practice for officers' use of detention powers reveals the significance of temporality as a feature that organises policing responsibility, or rather zones of non-responsibility. Temporality as an organising feature of policing responsibility is a connecting theme throughout the book. In this chapter it emerges in two senses. First, the limited timeframe of police practices subject to judicial review in immigration matters artificially isolate officers' responsibility to the immediate circumstances of its use. The analysis of officers' retrospective responsibility starkly illustrates that different standards of responsibility for coercive powers are required of police, which means police have more discretion and less responsibility in how they conduct immigration detention than when using arrest powers. Second, the legality of detention does not rely on officers' conduct preceding detention, nor is compensation available for detention effected on what later becomes known as a misunderstanding of an individual's legal status which limits recognition and vindication of the harm suffered by detention.

The next chapter explores another manifestation of the relationship between temporality and officers' responsibility: how speeding up migration processes changes the character of migration practice, but without the imposition of responsibility. It also develops the book's focus on front-end policing practices turning to search warrant visits ('raids') of homes.

3 Raids, searches and rapid removals

It's night-time on December 18, 2002. Mahabub Alam, an information technology student at Central Queensland University and a national of Bangladesh, is at home, relaxing. There is a knock on the door and immigration officers ask for his name, which he provides along with his passport. Without Alam's permission and without a warrant, the officers enter his house and search it, and they do not let him leave. The officers find pay slips from his work and decide he has worked more than the hours he is permitted. They refuse to allow Alam to put on a shirt over his singlet before they take him to the immigration office in the city of Sydney. It's now close to 11 pm and Alam ends up detained in Villawood Immigration Detention Centre for almost three weeks. Despite judicial acknowledgement that the officers undertook an illegal search, committed trespass and falsely imprisoned Alam during the search, the officers' wrongdoing has no impact on whether Alam's visa is cancelled.[1]

In this case, *Alam* v. *Minister for Immigration and Multicultural and Indigenous Affairs*, the Court was highly critical of the officer's actions in the raid, but as one of the few accounts of an officer's improper use of power recorded in a judicial decision, it raises serious questions as to why so few similar stories surface. In comparison to complaints about and challenges to immigration detention, there are relatively few complaints about officers undertaking operations outside detention.[2] Operations undertaken by the officially named 'compliance' section of immigration include planned search warrant operations in homes, workplaces and schools, with other agencies, as well as bridging visa grants, which permit temporary stay in Australia while awaiting a substantive visa decision or to make arrangements to depart. These practices are the mainstay of the interior border work of immigration. It is hard to know the extent of wrongdoing or violence by officers in migration policing because it leaves so

1 *Alam* v. *Minister for Immigration and Multicultural and Indigenous Affairs* [2004] FMCA 583; (2004) 187 FLR 120 ('*Alam (2004)*') (and the associated case of the *Minister for Immigration and Multicultural and Indigenous Affairs* v. *Alam* [2005] FCAFC 132; (2005) 219 ALR 629 ('*Alam (2005)*').

2 Leanne Weber, *Policing Non-Citizens* (Oxford: Routledge, 2013), 45.

little trace on the official record. The potential harm resulting from officers' actions is serious. Aside from the indignities and violation of search and apprehension, officers' actions frequently result in a non-citizen being detained and removed from Australia. Moreover, law and legal bodies fail to adequately impose responsibility for the violent effects of officers' actions, and are implicated in the routine production of border violence.

This chapter explores two forms of disavowal of law's responsibility for the violent experiences of non-citizens present in migration law and policing. The first mobilises sanctioned disregard for violations of the law. It involves the formal promotion of protection of liberty, but a structured marginalisation of recognition of law's violation. By examining the regulation of immigration raids, the chapter develops the argument that structural disregard for the non-citizen's experiences of violence in these contexts amounts to authorisation of officers' wrongdoing. The second form normalises the authority of discretionary power generated by the interrelation between delegated powers, processes and legal conventions. Understanding what power is authorised here requires analysis of policing practice because explicit delegation of power is only one part of its constitution. Officers' engagement with the gaps between express delegations of powers under the *Migration Act 1958* (Cth) ('*Migration Act*') constitutes a particular practice of immigration 'arrest' and rapid removal that is not explicitly envisioned by migration law, but is nevertheless supported. Imposing weak constraints on policing power supports the power of institutions and officers to decide the boundaries of their own authority, and the chapter thus jurisprudentially charts selected arenas of relatively uncontrolled power. Conceptually, this chapter continues the book's investigation of whether and how migration law 'organises irresponsibility' and creates 'zones of non-responsibility' for officers' use of migration powers.[3]

In order to evaluate the imposition of legal responsibility for migration policing, this chapter adopts the standpoint of the affected non-citizen whose focus is on visa-related litigation. Thus it aims to explore the relationship between police power and the retrospective address of that power within the legal framework of visa-related litigation, but not to evaluate all the varied options for bringing policing practices to account. It focuses on visa-related tribunal and judicial litigation because migrants are already engaged in these forums in challenging decisions to cancel or refuse visas. These forums represent an opportunity for oversight that is integrated into routine legal processes and are often the only accessible option for non-citizens. But the remit of visa-related tribunal and court matters does not encompass many of the exercises of migration police-like powers in practice, some of which fail to register as distinct acts of power.

Key features of the administrative regime of migration law constrain accountability for migration policing practices. To articulate the structural limitations of

3 Scott Veitch, *Law and Irresponsibility: On the Legitimation of Human Suffering* (New York: Routledge-Cavendish, 2007).

the administrative regime, the first part of this chapter explores the jurisdiction and procedural rules of administrative institutions via a rare insight offered by two cases where there has been a clear breach of search powers. The applicability of evidence law to arenas of legal discipline must be understood here as not only producing more informal forums for legal resolution, but also differentiating arenas of varied official responsibility. The second part considers the policing control over the timing of series of actions as an embedded form of power that articulates a structured disavowal of responsibility for the speed of policing actions. It examines a case of sudden immigration 'arrest' and removal, which of itself is not unusual, but which surfaced in legal records because the non-citizen, unusually, pursued legal remedy. This chapter draws on reported cases not linked to the research interviews outlined in this book. The view is primarily from 'above', and thus adopts a different perspective though the concerns being traced mirror those identified by interview participants in the last chapter.

Limitations of legal responsibility imposed on officers exercising *Migration Act* powers are at the same time articulations of discretionary authority in migration. As has been observed in relation to policing, police authority is constituted as much by exemptions from liability as by explicit grant.[4] Officers' discretionary power is facilitated by approval implicit from the paucity of judicial censure for wrongdoing and by the wide justifications offered by risk and security for lawful exercise of migration power. The barriers to policing accountability explored in the case studies are not unique to the specific policing powers utilised, but illustrate the disjuncture between the effect of power and the utility of administrative law as an accountability mechanism.

Do migration search warrants constrain or secure discretion?

This part of the chapter examines how migration law treats officers' responsibility for the unlawful or improper use of power. Entry and search operations conducted under warrant provide a useful site to consider this question because the requirement for a warrant itself indicates the significance law attributes to the liberties at stake in these operations. By turning to a point of commonality in the procedural organisation of a migration tribunal hearing and court trial, this part shows how migration law and policing structures the legal marginalisation of officers' wrongdoing in search operations. This is important because it shows how migration law, as part of the broader discipline of administrative law, not only fails to constrain officers' wrongdoing, but also arguably authorises the illegality involved. Before turning to analyse cases of unlawful search, the legal and social context of search warrant operations is set out.

4 David Dixon, *Law in Policing: Legal Regulation and Police Practices* (Oxford: Oxford University Press, 1997), 64.

Migration Act searches – which immigration refers to as 'compliance visits' or 'warrant visits' and others refer to as 'raids' – of private premises such as homes, workplaces and education institutions are an ordinary part of immigration work. Police accompaniment is generally limited to warrant visits for more serious immigration offences,[5] and an Ombudsman's audit in 1999 indicates police accompany immigration in about 7 per cent of all warrant visits conducted under s 251 of the *Migration Act*, primarily to support immigration officers in case of potential violence.[6]

The general power to enter, search and seize items under warrant for the location of non-citizens living unlawfully or in breach of their visa conditions in homes and workplaces has been part of the *Migration Act* since its enactment in 1958 in substantially the same terms.[7] An officer may be issued a warrant under s 251 to enter and search a premise if the officer has reasonable cause to believe that the following will be found: an unlawful non-citizen; any passport, identity document or travel ticket of an unlawful non-citizen (or person who will be removed or deported); or a non-citizen subject to work restrictions.[8] The *Migration Act* provides the power to enter and search under a number of provisions, but s 251 (the 'search warrant power') is the focus of this study.[9]

Evidence given to a Senate Committee inquiry in 2005 by Vincent McMahon, the Executive Coordinator of the Department of Immigration and Multicultural and Indigenous Affairs (DIMIA) Border Control and Compliance Division, described the warrant process as follows:

> Probably half the circumstances would be that we get information relating to a person who is believed to be working illegally or whatever. We then undertake some checks. For example, there is no use getting information which says that there are Korean tilers working on a building site and when we look it up on the web the building site is only at the stage of digging the footings. We would not attend. We normally look for some level of verification. It could be the history. Particularly in respect of brothels, for example, we would look to see whether or not the person had a history of employing illegal workers. We might also look to see whether an employer was checking against our systems to see whether or not the people were legal. Once we form a picture, the person requesting the warrant, under our policy, must form a reasonable cause to believe that there is either a

5 Weber, *Policing Non-Citizens*, 84.

6 Commonwealth Ombudsman, 'Investigation into the Exercise of the Powers of Entry, Search and Seizure under Sub-Sections 251(4)–(6) of the Migration Act 1958: Report under Section 15(2) of the Ombudsman Act 1976', December 1999, 33.

7 *Migration Act 1958* (Cth) ss 37 (1958–December 18, 1989), 90 (December 19, 1989–August 31, 1994), 251 (September 1, 1994 onward).

8 *Migration Act* s 251(6); *Migration Regulations 1994* (Cth) reg 5.32(2), sch 10, form 2.

9 Since 2001, a search warrant may be granted to enter the premises of an education provider to monitor student visas and, from 2012, to obtain evidence relating to employer sanctions offences: see *Migration Act* ss 268CA, 268CD, 487D, 487E.

> person there who is working illegally or an overstayer. A warrant request is made. The person who then approves the warrant then needs to be satisfied that the person has formed a reasonable cause to believe. The warrant is then served and, at the time, the person serving is required under the act to have formed that belief as well.[10]

The conduct of search warrant visits must be understood in the broader context of migration powers that undermine the apparent limits dictated by search warrant policy. Policy states that the scope of the search is restricted to only those individuals and items specified in the warrant, it 'should not be regarded merely as a search for any lawful non-citizen or visa holder with limited work rights who happens to be found on the premises'.[11] However, after entry, the immigration detention power empowers the detention of an individual unrelated to the warrant.[12] McMahon went on to explain in 2005:

> If we went in there and, even if it were not related to the warrant, we saw a person about whom we formed the view at that time that they were an illegal, it would not be the warrant that was providing power; it would be the [A]ct itself.[13]

Non-citizens and advocates interviewed in the period 2007–10 similarly indicated that it is not uncommon for search operations to name one person as the target for attention but detain others not specified in the search warrant.

Migration Act search warrants have very little foothold in administrative jurisprudence. In the 20 years since the September 1994 introduction of the most recent version of the search warrant power in *Migration Act* s 251, merely five reported instances reference migration search warrant powers.[14] In these cases, Federal Court and tribunal consideration of search warrant powers arises only

10 Evidence to Senate Standing Committee for the Scrutiny of Bills, Parliament of Australia, Canberra, March 11, 2005, 11 (Vincent McMahon, Executive Coordinator, Border Control and Compliance Division, DIMIA).

11 DIAC, 'Procedures Advice Manual 3' (Canberra, 2010), National Compliance Operational Instructions [P A136.33], 33.4. The courts have adopted a strict approach to interpretation of statutory authority for search warrants more generally and, in the past, courts have struck down warrants where police have seized items that did not reasonably fit within the warrant authority: *R* v. *Tillett; Ex parte Newton* (1969) 14 FLR 101, 108 (Fox J); *Bartlett* v. *Weir* [1994] FCA 1143; (1994) 72 A Crim R 511.

12 *Migration Act* ss 189, 192.

13 Evidence to Senate Standing Committee for the Scrutiny of Bills, 13 (Vincent McMahon).

14 The following cases were identified utilising the LexisNexis search for legislation judicially considered and the AustLII note up search for this provision: *Hoang* v. *Minister for Immigration* [2013] FCCA 89; *Coleman* v. *Minister for Immigration and Citizenship* [2007] FCA 1500; *Ruddock* v. *Vadarlis (includes corrigendum dated 20 September 2001)* [2001] FCA 1329; (2001) 180 ALR 1; *Majeed, Jahanghir Abdul* [2002] MRTA 6429 (October 31, 2002) ('*Majeed*'); *Alam* [2004] FMCA 583; (2004) 187 FLR 120 (and the associated case of *Alam* [2005] FCAFC 132; (2005) 219 ALR 629), not included for the purpose of the number of cases).

tangentially in the context of merits review for visa cancellation, review of legal error and examination of the legality of detention. In only two of these matters, involving Jahanghir Abdul Majeed and Mahabub Alam, the presiding decision-maker mentioned that officers had potentially breached warrant grounds.

Searches of students Majeed and Alam

In 2001, immigration undertook a migration warrant visit to a house where it located Jahanghir Abdul Majeed, an engineering student in Victoria, and also found a diary that appeared to record his paid work history. A delegate of the Minister for Immigration and Multicultural Affairs (MIMA) cancelled Majeed's student visa on the grounds that he had exceeded the number of hours he was permitted to work each week as a student.[15] In a similar scenario in 2002 noted at the start of this chapter, immigration officers seized pay slips found in New South Wales student Mahabub Alam's drawer, and likewise cancelled his visa.[16] In both cases, the student's visa cancellation decision was later set aside. However, this was due to grounds other than the officers' breach of search rules. In Majeed's case, the Migration Review Tribunal ('MRT') was not satisfied that Majeed had in fact worked more than the permitted hours, and the Federal Magistrates Court set aside Alam's visa cancellation because the delegate had misconstrued the meaning of 'week' and consequently incorrectly applied the law to calculate Alam's purported breach of visa conditions. Neither had breached the restricted work conditions of their student visas. It appears that, in both cases, officers breached search warrant laws.

Like other police powers, the power to execute a search warrant is best understood as an exemption from liability for acts that would otherwise be a criminal or civil wrong.[17] The rationale for requirement for issue of a search warrant to authorise entry is set out in immigration policy, which acknowledges that powers of entry, search and seizure 'necessarily involve an invasion of a person's privacy and property interests that the common law has always valued highly and gone to great lengths to protect'.[18] Immigration policy also acknowledges that

> a person has a fundamental right to their dignity, to their privacy, to the integrity of their person, to their reputation, to the security of their residence and any other premises, and to respect, as a member of a civil society.[19]

15 The facts relied on for this case study are set out in *Majeed* [2002] MRTA 6429 (October 31, 2002).

16 The facts relied on for this case study are those set out in *Alam* [2004] FMCA 583; (2004) 187 FLR 120 and *Alam* [2005] FCAFC 132; (2005) 219 ALR 629.

17 Dixon, *Law in Policing*, 64.

18 DIAC, 'Procedures Advice Manual 3', National Compliance Operational Instructions [P A136.1], 1.2.

19 Ibid.

A search without a warrant amounts to trespass,[20] and the wrong done in a search warrant visit might involve trespass, false imprisonment, and assault. The legality of a search warrant visit thus depends on how the warrant is executed and the interactions in the encounter. For example, a search without warrant will be lawful if the occupier consents to entry and search in particular statutorily defined circumstances.[21]

In Majeed's case, the search was conducted pursuant to a search warrant issued for the premises where Majeed was found, but the MRT decision record states that officers did not expect to find the review applicant there (because immigration held a different address for Majeed), which suggests that Majeed was not named in the search warrant, though this was not commented upon in the decision. More particularly, after reviewing the statutory limitations for the scope of entry and search warrants and the power to search persons without a warrant, the MRT observed that it 'seems likely that the powers of search do not extend to a document purporting to show only a breach of a visa condition'.[22]

In Alam's case, the officers' breach was egregious. Not only was the search undertaken without a warrant, without legal authority and without Alam's consent, it was also conducted in a way that Judge Wilcox described as 'heavy-handed'.[23] The full Federal Court finalising the matter three years after the search expressed strong concern about officers' methods. Alam's affidavit, extracts of which were included in the decision, describes the events set out at the start of this chapter:

> The DIMIA officers entered my house. They were very rude. They searched my belongings and room without showing me a warrant. They found my payslips during the search in one of my drawers. I did not agree to them searching my belongings or my room.
>
> I was kept in my house by the DIMIA officers for about an hour. I was then told to go with them. I had a singlet on. To the best of my recollection, the following words or words to the following effect were said:
>
> ME: Can I put a shirt on.
>
> DIMIA: No. You look fine.
>
> I was taken to the Lee Street office of DIMIA. I was made to wait again, in a room. Mr Shah Alam was also taken to Lee Street.[24] [Note: immigration officers had attended the house looking for Shah Alam, a friend and not relative of, Mahabub Alam.]

20 *Bathurst City Council* v. *Saban* (1985) 2 NSWLR 704, 706; *Victoria Park Racing and Recreation Grounds Co Ltd* v. *Taylor* [1937] HCA 45; (1937) 58 CLR 479, 494; see also state and territory criminal law statutes such as the *Inclosed Lands Protection Act 1901* (NSW) s 4.

21 *Migration Act* s 251(1).

22 *Majeed* [2002] MRTA 6429 (October 31, 2002) [41]; see also *Migration Act* ss 251, 252.

23 *Alam* [2005] FCAFC 132; (2005) 219 ALR 629, 633 [17].

24 Extract of Alam's affidavit: ibid., 634 [25]. Note paragraph numbers omitted in the extract.

Alam was interviewed at the DIMIA offices, and officers cancelled his visa. Alam immediately became an 'unlawful non-citizen'. At this point, officers hold the discretion to issue a 'bridging visa' (which is a non-substantive visa that 'bridges' the time until a visa decision such as an application for review of visa cancellation is finally determined) or to detain a person. Officers may require a security deposit before granting a bridging visa, which then became the subject of discussion between the immigration officer and Alam at around 11 pm that night:

> After I signed the [visa cancellation related] forms, to the best of my recollection, the following words or words to the following effect were also said:
>
> DIMIA: If you pay a bond of $10,000 you can leave.
>
> ME: I can't get $10,000 now. I might be able to get $5000. It is late. Can I call my sister to get money.
>
> DIMIA: No – you can't talk with anyone.
>
> (the DIMIA officer then took my wallet and my two mobile phones)
>
> ...
>
> DIMIA: I can't let you go if you don't pay. You will have to go to Villawood [immigration detention centre]. You will be released tomorrow. It is easy to get your release. Just explain it to the officer at Villawood.
>
> Because I could not pay the bond, I was taken to Villawood and locked up. I am very upset at the way I have been treated.[25]

The Court accepted Alam's account of events as correct, which was not disputed by counsel for the Immigration Minister. The Court was scathing of immigration's conduct of the raid. Judge Allsop stated that, '[u]nexplained, the evidence led before the Federal Magistrate and her findings reveal a trespass and false imprisonment',[26] given officers conducted a search of home and belongings 'without apparent cause or warrant', restrained Alam during the search, arrested him without lawful warrant, conveyed and held him at immigration offices where he was interrogated, and subsequently incarcerated him at Villawood Detention Centre for almost three weeks.[27] Note that, in evidence later provided to a Parliamentary Inquiry, immigration explained that they had held Alam under their questioning detention powers. These powers allow immigration to detain a non-citizen holding a visa that may be cancelled for up to four hours.[28]

Judge Wilcox was particularly critical of officers' refusal of Alam's 'entirely reasonable'[29] request to put on a shirt over his singlet before being taken to

25 Ibid.

26 *Alam* [2005] FCAFC 132; (2005) 219 ALR 629, 644 [70].

27 Ibid., 644 [69].

28 Questions Taken on Notice, Immigration, Multicultural and Indigenous Affairs Portfolio, Senate Legal and Constitutional References Committee Inquiry into the Administration and Operation and the Migration Act, December 5, 2005; see also *Migration Act* s 192.

29 *Alam* [2005] FCAFC 132, (2005) 219 ALR 629, 632 [17].

the DIMIA offices: 'Unless it was to humiliate him, what reason could the DIMIA officers have had to refuse this request?'[30] Judge Wilcox also questioned the possible basis for refusing Alam the opportunity of calling his sister for assistance with the security bond, given the unlikelihood of Alam carrying A$10 000 on his person. The Court was highly critical of the conduct of officers, noting that both tortious liability of the Commonwealth and personal liability of officers arise from the facts,[31] and emphasised Alam's grievance to be legitimate.[32]

A Senate Inquiry into the *Migration Act* the year following the finalisation of the Federal Court case and four years after the actual search found the case 'troubling' in its documentation of the very concerns that advocates had highlighted in relation to immigration's approach to enforcement of student visa conditions.[33] The federal government's response to criticism of the actions of the visa compliance department was to establish a College of Immigration for training purposes, which opened in July 2006,[34] the limitations of which will be discussed further below.

Administrative tribunals and trials: permitting officers' wrongdoing

Complaints, as well as civil and criminal litigation against the government and its officers, are common forms for the oversight and accountability for officers' wrongdoing. Each has its benefits and detriments. Complaint mechanisms facilitate access through their informality, but do not result in legally binding outcomes. The outcome of litigation is legally binding on parties and potentially provides compensation for damage suffered. However, litigation involves considerable costs for legal representation, stress and uncertainty in the lengthy periods until resolution and, at least for criminal trials, requires a criminal standard of proof that can be difficult to achieve.[35] The significance of these hurdles led the Australian Law Reform Commission ('ALRC') to comment, in their review of the rules of evidence prior to the introduction of uniform statutory evidence laws across the nation, on the value of evidentiary rules in addressing infringements. It is not enough, the ALRC argued, to exclude evidence of an officer's illegality or impropriety only if affected the *reliability* of evidence. Adopting a narrow approach to the exclusion of evidence 'would ignore the

30 Ibid., 632–3 [17].
31 Ibid., 644 [70] (Allsop J).
32 Ibid., 638 [39] (Stone J).
33 Senate Legal and Constitutional References Committee, 'Inquiry into the Administration and Operation of the Migration Act 1958' (Canberra: Commonwealth of Australia, 2006), 316.
34 Ibid., 317–18. See also 'College of Immigration', Australian Government Department of Immigration and Border Protection, accessed October 9, 2016, www.border.gov.au/about/reports-publications/reviews-inquiries/inquiry-detention-cornelia-rau-vivian-alvarez/department-of-immigration-and-multicultural-affairs-college-of-immigration.
35 See, for example, Australian Law Reform Commission ('ALRC'), 'Managing Justice: A Review of the Federal Civil Justice System' (Sydney, 2000); Community Law Australia, 'Unaffordable and Out of Reach: The Problem of Access to the Australian Legal System' (2012).

reality that, on occasion, there are *no real alternative methods* to obtain justice available to an individual citizen whose rights have been infringed'.[36] The form of oversight and accountability offered by evidentiary rules allows insight into how, through the inapplicability of evidence law in migration, irresponsibility for illegal or improper action by state officials is structured into the law.

The rules of evidence operate as a key mechanism through which the judiciary effects oversight over officers' exercise of investigatory powers which is integrated into substantive litigation. Australian courts hold discretion to exclude unlawfully or improperly obtained evidence in civil and criminal proceedings. The basis for the argument for exclusion of such evidence rests on the 'public interest in minimising the extent to which law enforcement agencies act outside the scope of their lawful authority'.[37] The ALRC explained the purpose of exclusion of unlawfully obtained evidence may take account of the interest in disciplining officers, deterring illegality, encouraging lawful investigatory methods, protecting individual rights, and supporting the legitimacy of the executive and judiciary.[38] Uniform statutory evidence laws were introduced in 1995, and today provision for the exclusion of unlawfully obtained evidence has been described at least in part, for better or worse, as a 'collateral means of disciplining wrongdoers and vindicating rights'.[39]

Regardless of the extent to which the exclusion of unlawfully obtained evidence deters improper behaviour, a question arises as to whether inclusion of such evidence amounts to tribunal and judicial sanctioning of unlawful or improper action of the state. In other words, should the inclusion of unlawfully obtained evidence be regarded as legal authorisation for unlawful practices by state officers like police and immigration? In deciding whether to include such evidence, the statutory rules of evidence across Australia require the court to balance competing considerations, reflecting the common law emphasis that this discretionary process involves 'broader questions of high public policy' that go beyond fairness to the accused or affected individual.[40] The courts must find the balance 'between the desirable goal of bringing to conviction the wrongdoer and the undesirable effect of curial approval, or even encouragement, being given to the unlawful conduct of those whose task it is to enforce the law'.[41] In this context, the inclusion of unlawfully obtained evidence is generally said to risk undermining the legitimacy of the judiciary as an institution of legal adjudication,[42] but not to go so far as to authorise the wrongful actions of state officials.

36 ALRC, 'Evidence (Interim) ALRC Report 26' (Canberra, 1985), [960] (emphasis added).

37 Ibid., [958]; Jeremy Gans and Andrew Palmer, *Uniform Evidence* (Melbourne: Oxford University Press, 2010), 325–6.

38 ALRC, 'Evidence (Interim) ALRC Report 26' [958]; Gans and Palmer, *Uniform Evidence*, 325–6.

39 Gans and Palmer, *Uniform Evidence*, 325–6.

40 *Evidence Act 1995* (Cth) s 138, *Bunning* v. *Cross* [1978] HCA 22; (1978) 19 ALR 641, 659; see also *Ridgeway* v. *The Queen* [1995] HCA 66; (1995) 184 CLR 19, 31.

41 *Bunning* v. *Cross* [1978] HCA 22; (1978) 19 ALR 641, 659.

42 Gans and Palmer, *Uniform Evidence*, 326.

The procedural regime: organising non-responsibility

How then should we understand the categorical inapplicability of the rules of evidence from tribunals and consequently court trials addressing migration matters? The procedural regime governing avenues for the address of officers' misconduct supports a more robust reading that the law permits wrongdoing by police and immigration officers exercising *Migration Act* powers. This is generated by four features of the procedural regime in relation to non-citizens.

The first salient feature is that no legal avenue exists for non-citizens seeking recognition and redress for officers' wrongdoing that is *integrated* into their main substantive litigation. Because pursuing, for example, litigation against an officer's wrongdoing in search practices or a complaint is unrelated to a person's eligibility or application for a substantive visa, this means it does not provide grounds for legal stay in Australia.[43] Yet allegations of unlawful action by immigration or police arise precisely in contexts where a non-citizen either did not hold a visa or whose visa has been cancelled. For unlawful non-citizens, as well as those with temporary visas, permission to remain in Australia to pursue redress for the wrong suffered is essential, and its absence is a strong disincentive. It is the *integration* of the rules of evidence into criminal and civil litigation, unlike in migration, that goes some way to bringing litigants and practices of accountability into synchronous relation. The absence of an opportunity for oversight integrated into review and litigation processes in which the non-citizen is already engaged is a barrier to bringing wrongdoing to light.

The integration of the rules of evidence into litigation through the means of a *voir dire* (a preliminary examination conducted in tandem with trials, here, to consider the admissibility of evidence to trial) can be understood by reference to Mariana Valverde's notion of 'path dependence'. Valverde used this term to elaborate the 'chain reaction' of the operation of jurisdiction which, through sorting out what law applies where and to whom, renders questions of *how* law ought to be practised as merely technical legal issues that are the result of the earlier sorting process.[44] For non-citizens, the decision to pursue action against officers' wrongdoing is conditioned by a 'path dependence' conditioned by the social and legal constraints discussed above that structures the legal possibilities for judicial oversight of policing practice.

Second, and most importantly, evidence law as a key mechanism for address of state officials' investigatory wrongdoing does not apply as part of visa-related litigation. Visa decisions reviewable by administrative tribunals under the *Migration Act* are 'not bound by technicalities, legal forms or *rules of evidence*; and … shall act according to substantial justice and the merits of the case'.[45]

43 *Migration Regulations 1994* (Cth) sch 2, subclass 050, 050.212.

44 Mariana Valverde, 'Jurisdiction and Scale: Legal "Technicalities" as Resources for Theory', *Social and Legal Studies* 18, no. 2 (2009): 141.

45 *Migration Act* s 353 (emphasis added). See also s 420, which provides for substantively the same terms for the Refugee Review Tribunal.

The exclusion of evidence law does not mean that evidence law has no impact on the conduct of administrative tribunal hearings; rather, the potential for the exclusion of evidence to act as a mechanism for accountability is remote.

The inapplicability of the rules of evidence is a traditional characteristic of administrative tribunals. In 1989, when the first independent immigration-specific merits review tribunal in Australia, the Immigration Review Tribunal ('IRT'), was established, then Minister for Immigration and Ethnic Affairs, Senator Robert Ray explained this provision was intended to promote 'informality and an absence of legalism' as distinctive characteristics of the IRT.[46] In other words, administrative tribunals are not required to apply the *Evidence Act 1995* (Cth) ('*Evidence Act*') discretion to exclude unlawfully or improperly obtained evidence. Moreover, claims that a search (or other investigatory practice) was conducted unlawfully will not necessarily be adduced into evidence in a tribunal hearing – it depends on what the applicant brings to the attention of the tribunal, and also on how tribunal decision-makers understand what it means to not be bound by the rules of evidence and to implement the statutory mandate to 'act according to substantial justice'.[47]

In 1996, soon after the enactment of the *Evidence Act*, Richard Philips, then a Senior Member of the IRT, commented on the scant guidance from the courts as to precisely what it means for administrative tribunals to dispense with the rules of evidence.[48] In a basic sense, tribunals must make decisions based on evidence; thus they may set aside a decision because there is no evidence to support it. Dispensing with the rules of evidence means that tribunals may take account of logically probative evidence, regardless of its legal admissibility.[49] Sixteen years later in 2013, the Justice Duncan Kerr, President of the Administrative Appeals Tribunal ('AAT') put it more strongly when he argued that administrative tribunals are intended to develop a different framework for justice. In his construction of the AAT statute, Justice Kerr argued that the provision for the tribunal not to be bound by the rules of evidence

> is not a grant of power occasionally to depart from the strict application of the rules of evidence; rather it presupposes and establishes a scheme for the reception of evidence in which … compliance with those rules is intended to be foreign.[50]

In practice, tribunals work in a space of tension between the inapplicability of the rules of evidence and the statutory mandate to have regard to fairness and

46 Commonwealth, *Parliamentary Debates,* Senate, April 5, 1989, 926 (Robert Ray) cited by Richard Phillips, 'The Immigration Review Tribunal and Evidence', *Canberra Bulletin of Public Administration* 79 (1996): 141.

47 *Migration Act* s 353, 420.

48 Ibid., 142.

49 Ibid., 142–3.

50 Duncan Kerr, 'Keeping the AAT from Becoming a Court', in *Australian Institute of Administrative Law (NSW) Seminar* (Sydney), 4.

justice. This is encapsulated in the statutory requirement that the AAT (which incorporated the Migration Review Tribunal and Refugee Review Tribunal on July 1, 2015) 'pursue the objective of providing a mechanism of review that is fair, just, economical, informal and quick'.[51] Tribunals might legitimately exclude unlawfully obtained evidence because its inclusion would be unfair in some circumstances, but not because it should be excluded to comply with the rules of evidence.

In the only empirical study on this topic, Terese Henning and John Blackwood found that the rules of evidence do shape how (at least some) tribunals conduct their operations, though it is unclear when, how and the rationale that tribunals use in determining when the rules of evidence will be applied.[52] Henning and Blackwood concluded that requiring tribunals not be bound by the rules of evidence:

> entrenches at a practical level the theoretical uncertainty of the application of the rules of evidence in proceedings of quasi-judicial tribunals. Represented and unrepresented parties as well as lay members of tribunals are, therefore, unable to predict with any degree of confidence just how particular rules of evidence are likely to operate from case to case. It also creates the environment for inconsistencies to occur in the operation of the rules. The findings of this study, particularly with respect to the hearsay rule, reveal evidence of just such inconsistency. Finally, it creates the environment for the rules to be manipulated unfairly.[53]

No empirical study examines how tribunals treat allegedly unlawfully or improperly obtained evidence, nor specifically studies tribunals with a migration or refugee jurisdiction.[54] The *Majeed* decision reflected Henning and Blackwood's findings that, although they are not bound by the rules of evidence, tribunals sometimes keep them in mind, though their effect on how tribunals come to a decision and what decision is made remains unclear.[55] Even if a tribunal documents apparent investigatory illegality in the decision record, however, this does not necessarily result in judicial oversight.

51 *Administrative Appeals Tribunal Act 1975* (Cth) s 2A. Prior to the merger, the same objective was stipulated in the statute establishing these tribunals (*Migration Act* ss 353, 420).

52 Terese Henning and John Blackwood, 'The Rules of Evidence and the Right to Procedural Fairness in Proceedings of Four Tasmanian Quasi-Judicial Tribunals', *Australian Journal of Administrative Law* 10, no. 2 (2003).

53 Ibid., 103.

54 Ibid. The study was restricted to examination of the hearsay rule, the opinion evidence rule and the relevance rule in the following tribunals: the Medical Council of Tasmania, the Guardianship and Administration Board of Tasmania, the Anti-Discrimination Tribunal of Tasmania, and the Resource Management and Planning Appeals Tribunal of Tasmania. On disclosure of evidence, see John Blackwood and Terese Henning, 'Tribunals' Power to Control Their Own Procedures and the Requirements of Procedural Fairness', *Australian Journal of Administrative Law* 11, no. 1 (2003): 5–33.

55 See, for example, *Majeed* [2002] MRTA 6429 (October 31, 2002) [41].

The point of this exploration is not to argue that if tribunals making migration decisions were bound by the rules of evidence this would adequately constrain migration policing powers. Indeed, the exclusion of evidence has been described as a 'haphazard approach' for breaches of privacy and liberty, and one that does not guarantee consistent application by individual decision-makers.[56] But the formal exclusion of the rules of evidence from migration decision-making contributes to a legal structure which treats the problem of unlawful or improper policing practice as insignificant.

The third feature that structures disregard for bringing officers' impropriety into judicial purview is founded on the limited remit of judicial review of migration law itself. The scope of judicial review has formed a site of contestation between the court's understanding of its role under the *Australian Constitution* and the legislature's attempts to make decisions under the *Migration Act* final.[57] Judicial review in migration itself provides little scope for the courts to have regard to the legality of officers' investigatory conduct. The admissibility of evidence does not arise at judicial review stage because the court is concerned with legal and jurisdictional error not with assessing the merits of the application.[58] To return to *Alam* (2005) by way of example, the officers' unlawful search was brought into the record only because the court raised the question whether the conduct of the search justified the court ordering the Immigration Minister pay Alam's costs;[59] it was not directly part of the substantive matter before the Full Federal Court. This represents a marked difference from criminal and civil trials. In these forums, not only is the potential for exclusion of unlawfully obtained evidence embedded in trial process, while it is not completely settled, it appears that appellate courts have broad scope to review lower courts' exercise of the discretion to exclude unlawfully or improperly obtained evidence.

56 ALRC, 'Evidence (Interim) ALRC Report 26', [959], [63].

57 See, for example, the 2001 introduction of a 'privative clause', which sought to make migration decisions final and conclusive and so simultaneously expand the legal validity of administrative decisions and narrow the grounds for challenge in the Federal and High Courts: *Migration Act* s 474 (introduced by *Migration Legislation Amendment (Judicial Review) Act 2001* (Cth) sch 1 [7]). See also *Plaintiff S157* v. *The Commonwealth* [2003] HCA 2; (2003) 211 CLR 476; Robyn Bicket, 'Controlling Immigration Litigation: The Commonwealth Perspective', *Australian Institute of Administrative Law Forum* 63 (2010): 40. See also Mary Crock, 'Judging Refugees: The Clash of Power and Institutions in the Development of Australian Refugee Law', *Sydney Law Review* 26, no. 1 (2004): 176; Mary Crock and Edward Santow, 'Privative Clauses and the Limits of the Law', in *Australian Administrative Law: Fundamentals, Principles and Doctrines*, ed. Matthew Groves and H. P. Lee (Cambridge: Cambridge University Press, 2007); Mary Crock and Hannah Martin, 'Refugee Rights and the Merits of Appeals', *University of Queensland Law Journal* 32, no. 1 (2013).

58 Note on legal and jurisdictional error, see the sources noted above and discussion in Duncan Kerr, 'Privative Clauses and the Courts: Why and How Australian Courts Have Resisted Attempts to Remove the Citizen's Right to Judicial Review of Unlawful Executive Action', *Queensland University of Technology Law and Justice Journal* 5, no. 2 (2005).

59 The court has discretion to order payment of indemnity costs only where there are good reasons, such as the inappropriate or unreasonable conduct of one party during the trial.

Review goes beyond examining whether the decision is in error and includes whether the judgment exercised was sound.[60]

Finally, it is generally in the non-citizen's interest to submit or not seek the exclusion of the unlawfully or improperly obtained evidence. This is for the simple reason that it is often relevant to the matter being determined at both merits and judicial review stage. In reviews of immigration decisions to cancel a non-citizen's visa, common grounds for an applicant's review include that immigration did not provide valid notification that they intended to cancel the non-citizen's visa, and legal interpretations of the substantive basis for visa cancellation. Evidence gained unlawfully may be relevant to the non-citizen's case for both these grounds. Staying with this chapter's spotlight on Alam's experience of DIMIA's search of his residence, the admission of Alam's allegedly unlawfully obtained payslips (which showed that he had worked for 22.25 hours in one period of seven consecutive days) was necessary for the court to determine whether the MRT correctly applied the meaning of 'week' to calculate if Alam had complied with his visa conditions which permitted him to work up to 21 hours per week.[61] It is only in the interests of non-citizens to submit unlawfully obtained evidence because there is no provision for administrative decisions to exclude relevant factual information because of the way it was obtained. It is part of the broader character of migration control as an administrative process whose purpose is to regulate the coming into and presence of non-citizens in Australia.[62]

These four related features of migration law – the procedural separation between visa-related litigation and mechanisms for officers' accountability and, more specifically, the inapplicability of the rules of evidence, the limited remit of judicial review, and the incentive for non-citizens to bring unlawfully obtained evidence before the tribunal and court – structure a disregard of the significance of officers' wrongdoing in exercise of *Migration Act* powers. Does this equate to legal permission for wrongdoing in migration policing? The features embed a social and legal structure of disregard for officers' wrongdoing that sustain a reading that officers' deviance from investigatory requirements is institutionalised in law itself. The findings of Doreen McBarnet in her study of the tension between law's rhetoric of procedural requirements for arrest law and law's practice in the criminal law context resonate here. McBarnet argues that procedural law 'does not so much set a standard of legality from which the police deviate as provide a licence to ignore it'.[63] The admission of unlawfully or improperly obtained evidence into immigration decision-making, in the context of insufficient alternatives for constraint of officers' powers in migration, contributes to

60 Stephen Odgers, *Uniform Evidence Law*, 11th edn (Pyrmont: Lawbook Co, 2014), 895–6.

61 Considered in *Alam* [2004] FMCA 583; (2004) 187 FLR 120; *Alam* [2005] FCAFC 132; (2005) 219 ALR 629. See also *Majeed* [2002] MRTA 6429 (October 31, 2002) [42].

62 *Migration Act* s 4.

63 Doreen J. McBarnet, 'The Police and the State: Arrest, Legality and the Law', in *Power and the State*, ed. Gary Littlejohn *et al.* (London: Croom Helm, 1978), 213.

the constitution of policing power as well as to their legality. The absence of effective constraints on unlawful police conduct divests content from the enactment of legal standards for state conduct, securing rather than constraining unlawful conduct.

The broader problem of migration search powers

Although, as mentioned, judicial mention of search practices and search warrants is extremely rare, searches themselves are common. At around the time the searches of Majeed and Alam were undertaken, in 2001 and 2002 respectively, considerable numbers of warrant visits took place. In 2001–02, 1286 migration search warrants were issued, and 1609 in the following year.[64] In the period 2002–03 to 2004–05 immigration had been involved in 17 134 raids and cancelled 24 567 student visas.[65] No empirical research has quantified the extent to which officers contravene search warrant laws, but anecdotal evidence provided to parliamentary senate inquiries and reports by the Ombudsman paint a picture of long-term and persistent problems in this area of compliance operations.

After a series of complaints, the Commonwealth Ombudsman first commenced an own motion investigation of immigration's use of entry and search powers in 1997, finalising its report two years later.[66] It found a deeply concerning practice of abuse of immigration search warrant powers for unauthorised purposes by agencies otherwise unable to obtain authorisation. In one instance, NSW Police had insufficient information to obtain a search warrant for criminal investigation of a brothel, police then prompted immigration to undertake a search and, in addition to providing support to immigration in the search, the Ombudsman reported that police also sought intelligence and evidence about 'rumoured links between the brothel and Asian organised crime (Triads)' and other criminal activity.[67] Although police accompaniment on search warrant operations is intended to ensure immigration have peaceful access to the premises, the Australian Federal Police said 'it was "not unusual" to use DIMA warrants for "follow-on" searches to locate criminal suspects'.[68] In another instance, the migration search warrant was similarly used by National Crime

64 DIMIA, 'Department of Immigration and Multicultural and Indigenous Affairs Submission to the Senate Standing Committee for the Scrutiny of Bills Inquiry into the Government's Response to the Previous Report by the Senate Standing Committee for the Scrutiny of Bills on Entry and Search Provisions Tabled in 2000' (2004), 3. Given the steady increase in the number of compliance visits (at least since 2009 when figures have been consistently reported), it is reasonable to suppose that the number of search warrants has similarly increased: DIBP, 'Annual Report 2014–15' (Belconnen, 2014), 173.

65 Simon Marginson *et al.*, *International Student Security* (Melbourne: Cambridge University Press, 2010), 6.

66 Commonwealth Ombudsman, 'Investigation into the Exercise of the Powers of Entry, Search and Seizure'.

67 Ibid., 34.

68 Ibid., 37, 39–42.

Authority officers primarily to gain intelligence on activity. The use in these instances was not authorised by the warrant itself nor by the legislative migration search warrant power, which does not empower search for the investigation of criminal offences under migration or other laws. The migration search warrant power is limited to matters related to the identity and status of a person.

Immigration officers' understanding of their authority was no better than that of police. Officers failed to appreciate that their search warrant power did not extend to migration fraud-related offences where persons were not unlawful non-citizens.[69] In this same report, the Ombudsman reported that immigration used the search powers for more than that permitted by the *Migration Act*: 'Case studies identified risks of invading individual's privacy and property without proper authority; the risk of serious challenge to the legitimacy and reasonableness of DIMA compliance activity; and the risk of court challenges to evidence obtained'.[70]

In the years that followed, reports of 'a lot of excesses' continued to be made, such as 'cases where compliance officers effectively just turn up on someone's doorstep and demand entry',[71] and instances of

> late-evening visits ... [where] six people turned up and the style of questioning was reported to us as being extremely intimidating. In both cases, there were small children who were extremely distressed. On both occasions, they stayed there for upwards of 45 minutes.[72]

The Ombudsman, again prompted by complaints about immigration compliance activity dominated by dissatisfaction with entry and search practices (having finalised 26 complaints about immigration compliance activity in 2004–05),[73] established ongoing monitoring and inspection of immigration compliance activity in 2006–07.

From the time abuses of the search warrant power first came to light in 1997 the Ombudsman has framed the problem as two-fold. The first arena of problem relates to how officers understood their powers and thus led to recommendations for policy development, training for immigration and other agencies.[74] These recommendations, and others such as the need for record-keeping,

69 Ibid., 33–43.

70 Submission No. 8, 6–7 (Commonwealth Ombudsman) cited in Senate Standing Committee for the Scrutiny of Bills, 'Entry and Search Provisions in Commonwealth Legislation' (Canberra: Commonwealth of Australia, 2000), 114.

71 Evidence to Senate Legal and Constitutional References Committee Administration and Operation of the Migration Act 1958, Parliament of Australia, Melbourne, September 27, 2005, 77 (Mr Michael Thornton, Committee Member Law Institute Victoria).

72 Ibid., Sydney, September 28, 2005, 33 (Ms Tamara Domicelj, Coordinator, Asylum Seekers Centre).

73 Commonwealth Ombudsman, 'Annual Report 2004–05' (Canberra, 2005), 47.

74 Commonwealth Ombudsman, 'Investigation into the Exercise of the Powers of Entry, Search and Seizure', 8–11.

recurred through later annual reports.[75] Immigration has responded to these recommendations with the establishment of a College of Immigration, policy development and so on. Other recommendations also address operational issues by suggesting the need for clarity in relationships between agencies, databases and monitoring of compliance work.

It is the second type of problem – the law itself – which has seen no traction. In the Ombudsman's early discussions of the search warrant power, legislative amendments to the regulation of immigration searches were seen as vital. In its 1999 report, the Ombudsman clearly regarded immigration as engaged in law enforcement and argued that immigration's powers should be subject to the same minimum standards of protection from arbitrary search as other agencies. In particular, it favoured law reform requiring judicial (rather than immigration staff) authorisation at least for warrants to enter and search for ***unidentified*** unlawful non-citizens.[76] As recently as 2006 the government rejected a similar recommendation, made by the Senate Standing Committee, that the power to issue a warrant should be conferred on judicial officers. The government explained that the delay involved in consulting a judicial officer is unacceptable 'where DIMIA officers require a warrant as a matter of urgency to assist in apprehending an illegal migrant believed to be at a particular residence'.[77]

Similarly, the government has not amended the breadth of the search warrant power, which exceeds that available to most police across Australia, and has sustained long-standing criticism.[78] The statute permits an officer to enter and search a premise if the officer has reasonable cause to believe that a non-citizen subject to work restrictions will be located, which is acknowledged by immigration as an unnecessarily wide category.[79] Individuals holding visitor, long-stay business, working holiday maker, other temporary visas and student visas all face work restrictions that would provide grounds for a search warrant, and in December 2009 the total number of these visa holders was significant, estimated

75 Commonwealth Ombudsman, 'Annual Report 2003–04' (Canberra, 2004), 51; Commonwealth Ombudsman, 'Annual Report 2004–05' (Canberra, 2005) 47; Commonwealth Ombudsman, 'Annual Report 2005–06' (Canberra, 2006), 81; Commonwealth Ombudsman, 'Annual Report 2006–07' (Canberra, 2007), 87; Commonwealth Ombudsman, 'Annual Report 2007–08' (Canberra, 2008), 94, 96; Commonwealth Ombudsman, 'Annual Report 2008–09' (Canberra, 2009), 89; Commonwealth Ombudsman, 'Annual Report 2009–10' (Canberra, 2010), 101.

76 Commonwealth Ombudsman, 'Investigation into the Exercise of the Powers of Entry, Search and Seizure', 5.

77 Senate Standing Committee for the Scrutiny of Bills, 'Entry, Search and Seizure Provisions in Commonwealth Legislation' (Canberra: Commonwealth of Australia, 2006), 343.

78 Commonwealth Ombudsman, 'Investigation into the Exercise of the Powers of Entry, Search and Seizure', 18.

79 *Migration Act* s 251(6); *Migration Regulations 1994* (Cth) reg 5.32(2); sch 10, form 2; Commonwealth Ombudsman, 'Investigation into the Exercise of the Powers of Entry, Search and Seizure', 44; Senate Standing Committee for the Scrutiny of Bills, 'Entry and Search Provisions in Commonwealth Legislation', 103.

at 964 118 migrants.[80] Although policy has long provided that officers should search only if they have formed reasonable cause to believe that the person has breached a work condition,[81] this limitation on the search power has not been incorporated in statute and does not make a warrant issued on the wider ground invalid. It is clear from reports from those working with non-citizens in this category that searches conducted targeted those subject to work restrictions in the absence of specific suspicion of breach. One advocate recounts a couple of search warrant visits in 2005:

> In both cases, the questions related to how that family was surviving in the community. I suppose there was an implicit threat that, if they were in any way breaching their bridging visa, which did not permit them to work, they would be detained. The point I have raised on that front with DIMIA is that all of our clients are in that situation.[82]

Despite recent indications of improvement,[83] the lengthy history of flaws and illegalities at all stages of the search warrant process suggests it is unrealistic to believe there is universal compliance with search laws today. While the legislative, policy and common law proclaims certain protections, the legal framework for oversight suggests a structure of permissiveness that effectively configures illegalities in search practices lawful. This organised permissiveness concentrates discretion at the front end of the process, distancing officers' actions from the potential accountability.

Speed, arrest and rapid removal: making policing practices lawful

'Arrest' in migration occurs when a person is detained without notification. This may occur by apprehension on the street or in immigration compliance fieldwork 'raids' as explored in Chapter 2. In these contexts, migrants experience their apprehension as a violent disruption involving fear, force and humiliation, features characteristic of an arrest for a criminal offence. This part of the chapter argues that another immigration process operates as 'arrest' – when

80 This is based on figures from the DIAC Update, July to December 2009: Stephen Howells, 'Report of the 2010 Review of the *Migration Amendment (Employer Sanctions) Act* 2007' (Belconnen: Commonwealth of Australia, 2011), 22.

81 Commonwealth Ombudsman, 'Investigation into the Exercise of the Powers of Entry, Search and Seizure', 44.

82 Evidence to Senate Legal and Constitutional References Committee Administration and Operation of the Migration Act 1958, Parliament of Australia, Sydney, September 28, 2005, 33 (Ms Tamara Domicelj, Coordinator, Asylum Seekers Centre).

83 Commonwealth Ombudsman, 'Annual Report 2013–14' (Canberra, 2014), 53; Commonwealth Ombudsman, 'Annual Report 2014–15' (Canberra, 2015), 14, 52. Note the Ombudsman's monitoring in these years involved file inspections, observation of parts of staff training and selected fieldwork.

immigration chooses to notify a non-citizen of their visa cancellation at the same time the person is taken into detention; that is, when the timing between a series of processes is compressed. This part analyses migration law to illustrate how it has produced authority for policing practice without explicit statutory articulation. In other words, it is about how immigration 'arrest' and rapid removal is made legal.

This form of immigration 'arrest' is an outcome of officers' control over processes that may be triggered by a commonplace immigration activity – visa cancellation. Visas may be cancelled on a broad range of grounds including breach of the character test, providing incorrect information to immigration, breach of *Migration Act* obligations, and as a consequence of the visa cancellation of another visa held by the non-citizen or visa holder.[84] The effect of cancellation is the same: it causes a visa to cease to be in effect and the former visa holder becomes an unlawful non-citizen.[85] The change in immigration status takes effect from the Immigration Minister's decision, which causes a record of that decision to be made.[86] This is critically important because it means that a person may become unlawful *without knowing* their status has changed, and *before* being notified of that fact.

The Immigration Minister's choice of notification method reflects decisions about whether a non-citizen will be detained immediately upon notification or will be permitted to remain at liberty in the Australian community while lodging and awaiting decision for review of that visa cancellation. The written visa cancellation decision can be handed to the person directly, delivered to a person who appears to live or work at the last residential or work address of the former visa holder, or by posting, faxing or emailing the decision (unless a person is in immigration detention or it involves a student visa cancellation).[87] The Immigration Minister may decide to provide notification of visa cancellation in person if intending to effect detention at the same time.

Conceptually, the differences between these forms of notification reflect the contrast between the immediacy of arrest as a mechanism for initiating criminal proceedings as distinct from summons (sometimes referred to as a 'court attendance notice') to attend court to answer charges. Notification coupled with detention mirrors the sudden deprivation of liberty engaged by arrest, whereas alone it simply alerts a non-citizen to the visa cancellation and review process. As noted in Chapter 2, in some circumstances proceeding by arrest rather than by summons may be inappropriate and even unlawful, in recognition that arrest itself involves punishment. For example, if police know the name and address of the alleged offender and the alleged offence is minor,

84 *Migration Act* ss 501, 109, 116, 119, 101–105, 107, 140.

85 Ibid., s 15.

86 Ibid., ss 15, 138. A different process follows for breach of student visa education conditions – visas are automatically cancelled after the expiry of a period of time from notice of breach: *Migration Act* s 137J.

87 *Migration Regulations 1994* (Cth) regs 2.45, 2.42, 2.55, 5.02.

then charge should proceed by summons in accordance with the principle that arrest is a last resort. In migration law, the form of notification is at the Minister's discretion. It is not guided by analogous legal principles as in arrest. Even if the notification of visa cancellation is not given in the prescribed form, the cancellation remains valid[88] and thus the subsequent detention and removal will be lawful.

If notification, detention and removal occur in rapid succession in a single arrest process, it effectively fast tracks the *Migration Act* temporal requirement to remove unlawful non-citizens 'as soon as reasonably practicable'.[89] Speeding up this process is not unlawful of itself as the *Migration Act* does not establish minimum periods between these processes. But the consequence is that administrative law exercises limited constraint over the policing power exercised when officers speed up migration processes. The previous part of this chapter explored how merits and judicial review of immigration decisions reveal a structure of disregard for improper or illegal use of investigatory powers. Analysis of the case that follows further illustrates the limitations of administrative law in making officers responsible for migration policing powers, but in this case, demonstrates how administrative law produces these powers as lawful.

Arrest and rapid removal of Scott Morrison

Scott Morrison is a citizen of the United Kingdom ('UK'). He arrived in Australia in 1977 at 12 years of age with his family but never became an Australian citizen. He remained in Australia, never leaving until he was removed 30 years later in May 2007.[90] At the time of his apprehension in a Perth suburb in Western Australia ('WA'), he was an unlawful non-citizen. The Immigration Minister had cancelled his visa two months earlier on the basis of convictions (including violent offences) for which he had been sentenced to more than seven years' imprisonment. He had an extensive criminal history. By mid-2006 Morrison had been convicted of about 90 other offences, and at the time of his apprehension was on bail for further charges (which were later discontinued). The operation that detained and removed Morrison was planned over a number of months and was undertaken with assistance from WA Police and correctional services. The normative question as to whether immigration was justified in its quick removal of Morrison is largely beside the point in this exploration. Rather, the case study illustrates the *effect* of control over the timing of immigration processes as an example of the breadth of lawfully permitted front-end discretion, and explores the mismatch between the exercise of temporal controls that effect rapid arrest and removal and accountability measures in administrative law.

88 *Migration Act* s 127.

89 Ibid., s 198.

90 Information about this case study has been drawn from *Morrison* v. *Minister for Immigration and Citizenship* [2008] FCA 54 ('*Morrison*').

Speeding up notification, detention and removal processes intensifies the violence involved in apprehension. On May 8, 2007 at about 10 am Morrison and his fiancée, Maria Roberts, had just finished attending to some banking and were about to purchase a present for their daughter who had turned five years old that day. They were in the bank's car park when several plainclothes WA Police officers, including the Tactical Response Group, tasered Morrison. Morrison collapsed to the ground, resulting in a gash above his eye and severe grazing to his knees, and while on the ground was handcuffed and had four taser barbs and wires removed from his body. Officers did not warn Morrison of their intention to take him into custody or indicate that they were legally authorised officials undertaking the arrest. The Immigration Minister accepted that Morrison was detained in a violent fashion, but argued that it was justified because of the special risks he posed. Forceful arrest before notification of visa cancellation was a planned strategy, and also reversed the usual sequence of events that makes notification of visa cancellation the first step followed by detention.

Controlling when Morrison would be advised of his impending removal was an important part of effecting rapid removal. As an initial step, the Immigration Minister did not advise Morrison of his visa cancellation until more than two months after his decision. Further, immigration explained that providing Morrison with the standard minimum 48 hours' notice of removal risked disrupting his removal. Thus, although Morrison was apprehended at 10 am, he was notified that he was to be removed only at 1 pm, just hours before the plane was due to depart.[91]

From Morrison's standpoint, the rapid process seriously hampered his capacity to seek meaningful legal assistance regarding his removal. Even accepting immigration's evidence (as the Court did) that Morrison was afforded a telephone call after he was advised of his removal, he had less than four hours to lodge an interim injunction to restrain departure. (Morrison gave evidence that he was offered a telephone call just 20 minutes prior to the plane's planned departure.[92]) In any case, although the Federal Court accepted that because Morrison had been tasered he was 'stunned for most of the day, confused, dazed',[93] this did not assist his case. Studies on the effect of taser shots support the argument that Morrison's capacity to pursue review options may have been compromised,[94] yet the Federal Court did not take his confused state into

91 Note that Morrison claimed he was informed even later.

92 As it turned out, the plane was delayed due to a technical repair, which allowed Morrison to lodge an interim injunction prior to it leaving at 6.43 pm, though from the court record it appears that immigration did not know the flight would face delays at the time they notified Morrison of his removal.

93 *Morrison* [2008] FCA 54, [126].

94 Western Australia Police, 'Post Implementation Review of Taser', *Research Report prepared for the Corporate Executive Team* (Perth, 2010), 57–8. The use of the taser on Morrison appears (to the extent ascertainable through the account in the Federal Court decision) to have been contrary to WA Police policy on the use of tasers because it was used in drive-stun mode, and apparently outside of circumstances where use is necessary to prevent injury to any person.

account for this purpose. Instead, evidence of the effect of the tasers on Morrison's memory of the events meant that the Federal Court viewed officers' testimony that Morrison was not denied telephone calls as more reliable.

Control over the timing of processes also achieves a rapid removal. After his apprehension, Morrison was taken to the police station, then the airport, and, by 5 pm, Morrison was on a plane being removed from Australia to the UK. He was removed the same day as he was detained, as intended by immigration.

The doctrinal role of purpose and risk

As part of his review application, Morrison's lawyer argued that the Immigration Minister did not act to remove him as soon as reasonably practicable (in accordance with the *Migration Act* powers) 'but rather acted to remove the Applicant in circumstances where he was denied his right to seek a review by the Federal Court of the Respondent's decision to cancel the Applicant's visa'.[95] The legality of the Immigration Minister's and the Department of Immigration and Citizenship's (DIAC) actions turned on the administrative legal doctrine of 'improper purpose'.[96] What was DIAC's purpose in rapidly removing Morrison and providing him with just four hours' notice prior to boarding the plane? If the Federal Court found that the DIAC and the Immigration Minister sought to deprive Morrison of his appeal rights, this would be a purpose collateral to removal and beyond immigration's jurisdiction. The dilemma thus was for the court to distinguish between immigration's ostensible and real purpose in carrying out the operation in that way.

The problem for Morrison's argument is that an expansive range of policing actions can properly be seen as part of effecting removal, and the onus on the party alleging improper purpose is heavy. The courts are said to take a deferential approach, particularly if the decision is made at the highest level of government or involves political or national security interests.[97] Immigration removal from Australia involves security interests of a routine kind, as in this case, where the immediate purpose of government action at each stage was said to address the risk and danger posed by Morrison. In this case, the Federal Court relied primarily on the stated intention of governmental agents to determine their purpose, rather than the circumstances and effects of their actions on Morrison. For example, the Immigration Minister and DIAC stated that they explicitly controlled the circumstances of Morrison's notification, detention and removal so as to remove him quickly and efficiently. The immediacy of removal was in exception to the usual notice period and before the expiration of the 28-day period for application for judicial review. But they argued this all aided removal because of the risk Morrison

95 *Morrison* [2008] FCA 54, [4].

96 *The Queen* v. *Toohey; Ex parte Northern Land Council* [1981] HCA 74; (1981) 151 CLR 170.

97 H. P. Lee, 'Improper Purpose', in *Australian Administrative Law: Fundamentals, Principles and Doctrines*, ed. Matthew Groves and H. P. Lee (Cambridge: Cambridge University Press, 2007), 203–4, 11.

posed. In particular, DIAC and the other agencies involved considered that Morrison posed a high risk of escape during movement, and a risk of violence to himself and to custodial officers that obligated a maximum security rating, on the basis of his past convictions and allegations that Morrison had made threats towards immigration officers. The risk of violence was seen as a problem, as recorded in the first line of the DIAC's reasons, because of its potential to 'disrupt the removal'.[98] Thus controlling Morrison's knowledge of impending removal was identified as crucial because of its capacity to 'trigger' disruption.[99]

But report of the circumstances of Morrison's removal, combined with attention to how it was experienced, brings into question whether the government was motivated by more than concerns about the risk of violence in rapidly removing him. For instance, if the rationale for controlling the timing of the removal process was to avoid disruption of removal, the possibility that Morrison would lodge a judicial review application upon notification of removal could be classified as similarly disruptive. Certainly, the physical and legal logistics involved in planning for immediate removal suggest that delaying removal would pose significant difficulties for immigration. Ten officers were allocated as escorts for Morrison, and the last six rows of an international flight were booked. It was an expensive operation that would increase in cost if delayed.

In addition, prior to Morrison's removal, immigration had prepared an affidavit to be lodged in court should Morrison seek an interim injunction preventing removal.[100] The Federal Court treated this as evidence that immigration did not intend to deprive Morrison of appeal rights as its preparation showed that immigration contemplated the possibility of an interim application. Yet the prepared affidavit would also sustain the contradictory inference that immigration sought to maintain the goal of immediate removal.[101] The Federal Court gave more weight to their reading of the prepared affidavit than practical matters (such as the fast pace of events and Morrison's compromised physical and mental condition following his violent apprehension) that made it difficult for Morrison to pursue review, and instilled a state of mind in Morrison that discouraged him from lodging an application for an injunction to prevent removal. (Note though that while at the airport Morrison did seek urgent interlocutory relief to restrain the Immigration Minister from causing his removal to occur, which was declined.)

Quick and lawful

Speeding up particular migration processes is produced as a lawful practice by certain conventions in migration law. Migration law does not prescribe one way that notification of visa cancellation, apprehension and removal is to be carried out. This process may lawfully be conducted in a single day (although policy

98 *Morrison* [2008] FCA 54, [41].
99 *Morrison* [2008] FCA 54.
100 Ibid., [127].
101 Ibid., [85].

suggests 48 hours' notice for removal), or might be carried out over a year. Though the rationale for the compression of processes that resulted in Morrison's detention and rapid removal was to address the 'extraordinary' risks Morrison's removal posed,[102] the logic of risk provides an inherent flexibility for justifications, even for more ordinary security risks.

Further, the administrative law doctrine of *improper purpose* provides little recourse to restrain officers from speeding up migration processes. That is not to say that the purpose of government action will never be found improper in migration. A number of cases have found deportation orders to be improper, in one instance because the order sought to effect extradition and in another because the purpose of the order was to detain persons in custody to secure their availability to provide witness evidence in a criminal prosecution.[103] But the doctrine is particularly unsuited to restraining governmental action based on addressing the risks of disruption, violence or self-harm. This is because removals potentially carry some risk of self-harm that might disrupt removal, and thus speeding up these processes remains within the latitude afforded by the proper purpose of removal. In the absence of the government admitting a positive intention to deprive an applicant of judicial review, it is hard to envisage a circumstance where the courts might find the government held an improper purpose. Even if action is prompted by a mixture of purposes, if the 'substantial purpose' is removal, the purpose remains proper, unless detention and removal would not have taken place if the government had not sought to give effect to an improper purpose.[104] The problem is that, in addition to the well-established analysis that the onus of proof sets a high bar for improper purpose, the doctrine is simply unsuitable as a mechanism of restraint over speeding up processes.

The timing of some migration decisions is prescribed by statute. Various time limits are set for considering a step in a visa application.[105] A strict time period is allowed for persons to lodge review applications if immigration has refused a person's visa application.[106] The review tribunal is required to allow a certain time period to respond to an invitation for an applicant to provide information.[107] The Immigration Minister is required to provide a specified time period for former visa holders to show a reason why their visa should not have been cancelled,[108] and so on. But neither statute nor common law stipulates that officers must conduct notification, apprehension and removal at a particular speed or in a particular order.

102 Ibid., [35].

103 *Schlieske* v. *Minister for Immigration and Ethnic Affairs* [1988] FCA 48; (1988) 84 ALR 719; *Park Oh Ho* v. *Minister for Immigration and Ethnic Affairs* [1988] FCA 274; (1988) 91 ALR 288, 315; see also *Ang* v. *Minister for Immigration and Ethnic Affairs* [1994] FCA 952; (1994) 121 ALR 95.

104 See the discussion of the 'substantial purpose' test in *Samrein Pty Ltd* v. *Metropolitan Water Sewerage and Drainage Board* (1982) 56 ALJR 678; (1982) 41 ALR 467, 468–9.

105 *Migration Act* s 61.

106 Ibid., ss 347, 412.

107 Ibid., ss 359B, 424B; *Migration Regulations 1994* (Cth) regs 4.17, 4.35.

108 *Migration Act* s 129.

Why does the legal framework fail to constrain the conduct of apprehension and removal at a particular speed? In other words, why is control over the timing of migration policing actions viewed as rightly left to the discretion of immigration officers, police and other *Migration Act* officers exercising these powers? Theoretical approaches to the relationship between types of legal orders suggest that the preventative risk-based logic engaged by policing generally is 'at odds with other, more visible legal logics'.[109] Police-style regulation is said to involve discretionary power that decentres individual rights amenable to litigation.[110] The clash might be understood as that between the 'national' scale of legal entitlements litigated through migration and citizenship forums, and migration policing practices which are inherently interlegal, often engage a risk-based logic and do not conform neatly to the national scale of migration legal forums.[111]

A contrast in the logic underpinning types of migration processes arguably provides some explanation for the discrepancy in the stringency of laws that regulate the pace of migration processes. The regulation of the speed of migration processes in relation to visa decision-making is strict and, as noted above, is commonly set out in statute and regulations. Such laws communicate specific expectations of procedural fairness in relation to substantive visa decisions about migration legal status. They are concerned with fairness to the individual, or broadly with 'rights'. In contrast, migration processes, such as notification of visa cancellation, detention and removal, may be viewed as more classically procedural as they do not directly determine migration legal status. Decision-making in these processes may sometimes be informed by a logic of risk. As explored above, administrative law conventions such as the doctrine of improper purpose impose comparatively weak constraint and support the expansive lawful power of officers to set the pace in relation to these migration processes.

Temporal control

The control over timing in immigration 'arrest' and rapid removal is not unique within the broader framework of migration policy. Various migration and refugee policies explicitly seek to control the timing of global mobility. Temporal controls or 'temporal borders' are part of the broader proliferation of borders, important to the production of 'governable mobile subjects'.[112] Sandro Mezzadra and Brett Neilson explain that temporal borders do not necessarily match spatial borders, but 'serve to reconfigure, strengthen and attenuate them'.[113] Temporal borders are a

109 Valverde, 'Jurisdiction and Scale', 150.

110 Ibid.

111 See Chapter 1.

112 Efthimia Panagiotidis and Vassilis Tsianos, 'Denaturalizing "Camps": Überwachen Und Entschleunigen in Der Schengener Ägäis-Zone', in *Turbulente Ränder. Neue Perspektiven Auf Migration an Den Grenzen Europas*, ed. Transit Migration Forschungsgruppe (Bielefeld: Transcript Verlag, 2007), 82 cited by Sandro Mezzadra and Brett Neilson, *Border as Method, or, the Multiplication of Labor* (Durham: Duke University Press, 2013), 149.

113 Mezzadra and Neilson, *Border as Method*, 150.

critical method of reorganisation of the global labour market, through a range of policies including temporary work visas, restrictive work limits and circular migration policies that seek to control the flow of migrant labour.[114] Further, a range of refugee status determination policies designed to enable early identification of unmeritorious asylum applications and rapid removal, speed up appeals processes and generally, accelerate processing reflect a 'restrictionist drive', documented by Saulo Cwerner in relation to UK asylum policies.[115] Literature directly addressing temporality in migration focuses on speed as a form of domination controlling the mobility of bodies; however, slowness or delay as form of domination is equally evident. Refugees in Australia on temporary three-year protection visas, part of Australian policy from 1999 to 2008, experienced a 'life in limbo'.[116] Temporary protection visa holders were unable to sponsor family, faced study restrictions and lived without certainty of ongoing protection upon their visa expiry, and stand testament to the oppressive experience of a staged approach to refugee recognition.[117] The temporalities engaged in such policies and processes engage in a 'time politics' that works to exert power over asylum seekers.[118]

In contrast, migration policing practices enable temporal control even in the absence of policies with an explicit time dimension. The discretionary policing engaged in the apprehension and removal of non-citizens thus can be understood both as a precursor and concurrent power to explicit policy approaches to temporal control over removal such as 'fast track' asylum processing passed by Australian Parliament in December 2014.[119] The fast track process utilises restricted forms of review, specifies that an officer is not required to consider whether the person subject to removal engages Australia's non-refoulement obligations before removing that person,[120] and seeks to achieve a 'more timely removal from Australia of

114 Ibid.

115 Saulo B. Cwerner, 'Faster, Faster and Faster: The Time Politics of Asylum in the UK', *Time and Society* 13, no. 1 (2004): 77–9.

116 Michael Leach and Fethi Mansouri, *Lives in Limbo: Voices of Refugees under Temporary Protection* (Sydney: University of New South Wales Press, 2004).

117 Ibid.

118 Cwerner, 'Faster, Faster and Faster'.

119 *Migration and Maritime Powers Legislation Amendment (Resolving the Asylum Legacy Caseload) Act 2014* (Cth).

120 This statutory inclusion arose in response to jurisprudence that interpreted *Migration Act* provisions (including the s 198 removal power) as intending to be compliant with Australia's various non-refoulement obligations under the *Convention Relating to the Status of Refugees*, 189 UNTS 150 (opened for signature July 28, 1951, entered into force April 22, 1954); *Protocol Relating to the Status of Refugees*, 616 UNTS 267 (opened for signature January 31, 1967, entered into force October 4, 1967); and the *Convention against Torture and Other Cruel, Inhuman or Degrading Treatment or Punishment*, 1465 UNTS 85 (opened for signature December 10, 1984, entered into force June 26, 1987). See, for example, *Plaintiff M61/2010E* v. *Commonwealth of Australia; Plaintiff M69 of 2010* v. *Commonwealth of Australia* [2010] HCA 41 [27]; (2010) 243 CLR 319; *Plaintiff M70/2011* v. *Minister for Immigration and Citizenship* [2011] HCA 32; (2011) 244 CLR 144; 280 ALR 18; *Minister for Immigration and Citizenship* v. *SZQRB* [2013] FCAFC 33; (2013) 296 ALR 525.

those who do not engage Australia's protection obligations'.[121] Unlike the limited asylum-based remit of 'fast track' processing, rapid removal practices potentially apply to all non-citizens because they may be activated by visa cancellation or unlawful status more generally. In this way, migration policing practices extend temporal controls beyond those for which they form an explicit policy mandate.

Conclusion

It is not surprising that law's rhetoric of protection of personal liberties against state intrusion fails to gain traction over migration policing practices, given the well-documented hollowness of rule of law protections over criminal justice practices. But in migration this failure adopts a particular form because the administrative arena of review in migration not only provides little censure for officers' wrongdoing, it supports the erasure of migrant experiences of abuse of power. This chapter has shown how the failure to gain traction for accountability fails before it begins because of the fundamental incompatibility between how migration policing is practised and the structure of accountability offered by law.

The incompatibility between migration policing practices and accountability is illuminated first by the institutional features of migration law itself. Key features of migration law structure a disregard for officers' wrongdoing that amounts to permission for such acts. These include the procedural separation between visa-related litigation and mechanisms for officer's accountability, the inapplicability of the rules of evidence, limited remit of judicial review, and the lack of incentive for non-citizens to bring unlawfully obtained evidence before the tribunal and court. These are organising elements of migration law's disavowal of responsibility for violent practices. Within a rule of law model, the failure of avenues for effective account can be read as a missed opportunity for administrative law to deter police misconduct in investigation in the broader context where many, including the ALRC, have recognised that discretion over the exclusion of evidence in the standard trial process provides the most effective and accessible means for redress of investigatory impropriety.[122] But, more importantly, the case study on the regulation of search reveals that, despite legal rhetoric expressed by search warrants' seeming acknowledgement of the importance of personal liberties, the warrant itself serves to secure improper action, rather than constrain it.

Migration policing's discretionary legal authority to exercise temporal control is also indicative of an incompatibility between the logic of policing practices and rights-focused national scale of migration legal forums. The law affirms the legality of policing control over the timing of processes where the timing is not

121 Explanatory Memorandum, Migration and Maritime Powers Legislation Amendment (Resolving the Asylum Legacy Caseload) Bill 2014 (Cth) 2.

122 ALRC, 'Evidence (Interim) ALRC Report 26', [960].

otherwise positively articulated by statute and, in so doing, generates a migration policing power of arrest and rapid removal. The embedded character of temporal control in policing elides its connection with legislative articulations of rapid removal procedures, which are now an important part of the policy landscape in Australia and elsewhere. The arrest and rapid removal power adds an expansive and flexible form of temporal control that is relatively unregulated. Like Cwerner's analysis of the effect of speeding up asylum interviews, the compression of time between notification of visa cancellation, detention and removal also 'proceeds to silence, delegitimize and partially obliterate the temporal complexity'.[123]

The mismatch between policing exercise of power and the juridical structures of responsibility has major impacts. The result amplifies the phenomenon of 'front-end' loading in law-making practices discussed in Chapter 2. The expansiveness of migration policing discretion imbues the processes before any independent review, whether by tribunal or court, with significant weight over the definition of migrant illegality. By charting *how* juridical structures make policing practices lawful, either by explicitly affirming the legality of police exercise of discretionary power or by withholding opportunities for effective redress for police wrongdoing, it is apparent how the law structures the weight of discretion in the hands of immigration officers.

The mismatch also obscures the voices of non-citizens living without a visa or in breach of visa conditions and their experiences of migration policing. The irrelevance of investigatory misconduct to tribunal and court decision-making means there is little incentive for non-citizen applicants to draw attention to their experiences through the judicial record, and little reason for tribunals to explore alleged misconduct in any detail. As practices that are expansively empowered and marginal to judicial oversight, migration policing practices remain outside the broader context of the politically charged 'traditional national dance' between legislative reforms directed at controlling migration litigation and judicial resistance to infringements on the courts' role.[124]

The finding that non-responsibility for migration policing powers in search and arrest operations is embedded in the structure of administrative law and procedure rests on the premise that accountability mechanisms integrated into visa-related litigation must be regarded as the key framework to judge the legal responsibilities of officers. Mechanisms for accountability rest on initiation of complaint about practice and thus this premise is critical to evaluating accountability because it foregrounds the experience and needs of the policed non-citizen. From a practical perspective, the ability of many non-citizens to pursue

123 Cwerner, 'Faster, Faster and Faster', 73.

124 Bicket, 'Controlling Immigration Litigation: The Commonwealth Perspective', 40; see also Crock, 'Judging Refugees', 176; Crock and Santow, 'Privative Clauses and the Limits of the Law'; Crock and Martin, 'Refugee Rights and the Merits of Appeals'; Catherine Dauvergne, *Making People Illegal: What Globalization Means for Migration and Law*, Law in Context (New York: Cambridge University Press, 2008).

a complaint and litigation rests on their presence in Australia so they can self-represent, properly instruct representation and sometimes access pro bono legal services. Legal status, which enables stay in the community, is thus a factor which shapes the likelihood of pursuit of legal action and thus judicial oversight over searches and 'arrests'. The next chapter explores how legal status has been mobilised as a means of selective and arbitrary control over those released from immigration detention.

4 'Mums', 'mafia' and 'ransom money'

Release from immigration detention

In interviews with former detainees, three words stood out in the way they talked about the conditions of their release from immigration detention. Some talked about their community sponsors as 'mums'. This term captured the intense familial sentiment that former detainees developed with sponsors, who provided guarantees in the form of security deposits for their release and contributed to the everyday costs of living in the community.[1] Others described various refugee support groups as 'mafia', a term suggestive of powerful familial networks protective of its members, embedded with coerced obligations and extensive surveillance.[2] Several released detainees referred to bonds as 'ransom money', or else spoke about how the security bond required for release made them feel trapped and held hostage.[3] All identified the right to work as essential or the denial of work rights as the main constraint and source of precarious legal status afforded by a bridging visa on release.

Bridging visas, and other mechanisms of release ameliorate the violence of mandatory and indefinite immigration detention. However, it is clear historically and today that release from detention is not equivalent with liberty. Nor does it mean the end of conditions of the kind that defined incarceration. Former detainees report indefinite periods of temporary legal status, often in poverty without permission to work in circumstances where re-detention is a constant possibility because their release is conditional. The considerable mental distress experienced by many while living on a Bridging E Visa ('BVE') has led some to suicide. These features underscore the continuity between violence in detention and after release. Ahmed Al Kateb described his release from detention into the community on a bridging visa as a move from 'a small detention to big detention'.[4] It is crucial not to overlook how the release regime has enabled the constraint of liberty in community settings, and mobilised legal status as a mechanism of selective and arbitrary control.

1 Interviews with M3, M5 and M11.
2 Interviews with M1 and M2.
3 Interview with M1.
4 Ahmed Al Kateb, 'Submission No 86 to the Senate Legal and Constitutional References Committee Inquiry into the *Administration and Operation of the Migration Act 1958*' (2005), 1.

But while release from detention does not equate to liberty, nor should the constraints imposed be understood as merely reproducing detention outside the institution. This chapter analyses release from immigration detention or, in other words, the conditions that make a person marginally lawful. Release involves the policing of status by making release and continued legal status (and thus stay in the community) conditional. This chapter focuses on the specific and unique effects of conditional release on a bridging visa. It argues that bridging visas produce a restricted form of liberty, subject to arbitrary controls, which make legal status precarious. In order to develop this argument, the chapter explores the key features that have dominated the conditions of release on a bridging visa at various times and reflects on how the subjugation they produce might be conceptualised. The study exposes a deep contradiction between the rhetoric and practice of release from detention. Release decisions are ostensibly contingent on officers' prediction of detainees' compliance with visa conditions upon release, but, in practice, conditional release sets people up for non-compliance due to the arbitrariness of conditions and their enforcement.

This chapter relies on two main sources to understand the effect of conditions in relation to each other over time: snapshots of law and policy placed in their historical context; and insight from those affected by the conditional nature of BVE release. It draws on interviews with 12 non-citizens conducted in the period 2008–10 and publicly available accounts of those released after 2011 to build a picture of the experiences of release from detention and living in the community without the right to work. It also draws on interviews with six non-legal advocates, who had each been involved in community immigration justice advocacy for between five and eight years, to shed light on sponsorship as a particular type of release condition. Analysis of release practices in their historical context enables the character of the release regime to become visible. Despite shifting conditions of release, the subjugation it produces is part of its ordinary operation not isolated exceptional moments in policy development. The analysis advanced in the chapter shows that the transition out of detention does not equate to the cessation of violent conditions for non-citizens.

The argument is advanced by examination of three features of the release regime at selected times from the establishment of the bridging visa release scheme in 1994 until 2016. These features each illuminate fundamental ways in which the marginal legal status provided by a bridging visa (and thus migrant illegality) is regulated. The first part of the chapter examines immigration's requirement for 'sponsorship' of release from detention. It illustrates how the constraints imposed by sponsorship requirements were experienced by sponsors and former detainees as financially and intimately disruptive. The second part explores policy regulation of work rights after release from detention and the experience of prohibition on work. The financial and temporal dimension of constraint shaped by the denial of work rights on release has been an important feature since the inception of bridging visas. These practices suggest that it is not legal status itself that is important for release from detention, but the conditions it imposes which function as a means of retaining executive control over those released. The third feature of bridging visas, explored in the third part of the chapter, turns to a more recent condition introduced in 2013 that makes lawful status for 'illegal maritime arrivals' ('IMAs') contingent on compliance with a Code of Behaviour ('the Code'). The Code manifests the intimate constraints of sponsorship but fosters internalised surveillance and, like the prohibition on work, conveys the precarity of their legal status to former detainees through broad and vague behavioural standards contravention of which risks visa cancellation. The chapter concludes by reflecting on the issues of state responsibility invoked by release from detention. Before turning to these perspectives, a brief introduction to bridging visas for release from detention is necessary.

Bridging visas for release from detention

Bridging visas were part of a radical set of reforms that took effect from 1994. These reforms introduced two elements that fundamentally define the contemporary migration system: the requirement for every non-citizen in Australia to hold a visa, and the requirement that those not holding a visa ('unlawful non-citizens') be detained.[5] Bridging visas for release from detention are the product of these two requirements, also known as the *universal visa system* and *mandatory detention*. A BVE provides temporary legal status so that 'detention or continued detention is no longer mandatory'.[6] It provides legal status that 'bridges' the period between visa lodgment and decision or removal, but does not provide the substantive status provided by grant, for example, of a relationship, refugee or skilled migration visa. Unlawful non-citizens 'who satisfy certain minimum criteria will be eligible for the grant of a "bridging visa"',[7] and released subject to conditions that may include work and study prohibition, lodgment of a security deposit, regular reporting for BVE renewal, and the requirement to live at a specified address.[8] Bridging E visa grants from detention thus illustrate the base conditions to be 'legal'.

Today, BVEs are not the only mechanism permitting detainees to reside in the community. After overwhelming evidence of the negative mental health consequences of prolonged detention, litigation challenging the indefinite detention of stateless non-citizens the government had failed to remove, and reports that explicitly stated detention was no place for children,[9] the federal government

5 See the *Migration Reform Act 1992* (Cth), which came into effect on September 1, 1994.

6 Explanatory Memorandum, Migration Reform Bill 1992 (Cth); Migration (Delayed Visa Applications) Tax Bill 1992 (Cth), 10.

7 Ibid., 9.

8 *Migration Regulations 1994* (Cth) sch 8, 8101, 8207, 8401, 8506; sch 2, 050.224.

9 See, for example, Zachary Steel *et al.*, 'Psychiatric Status of Asylum Seeker Families Held for a Protracted Period in a Remote Detention Centre in Australia', *Australia and New Zealand Journal of Public Health* 28, no. 6 (2004). See also *Al Masri* v. *Minister for Immigration and Multicultural and Indigenous Affairs* [2002] FCA 1009; (2002) 192 ALR 609 ('*Al Masri* (2002)'); *Al Khafaji* v. *Minister for Immigration and Multicultural and Indigenous Affairs* [2002] FCA 1369 ('*Al Khafaji* (2002)'); *Al-Kateb* v. *Godwin* [2004] HCA 37; (2004) 219 CLR 562 ('*Al-Kateb*'); Human Rights and Equal Opportunity Commission, 'A Last Resort? The National Inquiry into Children in Immigration Detention' (Human Rights and Equal Opportunity Commission, 2004); Petro Georgiou, 'Why We Need a New Policy on Refugees', *The Age*, May 26, 2005, www.theage.com.au/news/Opinion/Why-we-need-a-new-policy-on-refugees/2005/05/25/1116950753630.html.

introduced new measures into the release regime. Three initiatives commenced in 2005, each designed to enable release at the personal discretion of the Immigration Minister. The Immigration Minister gained the power to grant any kind of visa to a person in detention if the Minister 'thinks that it is in the public interest to do so'.[10] A new Removal Pending Bridging Visa ('RPBV') provided an option for the Minister's exercise of personal power and enabled the release of detainees who were cooperative with efforts for their removal, but for whom removal was not reasonably practicable at the time.[11] Finally, 'community detention' allowed the Minister to transfer non-citizens into a designated residence legally recognised as detention but in a community setting, and was initially used almost exclusively for families with children.[12] In these reforms, the discretionary character of release decisions is writ large in its authority, whereas the discretionary nature of BVEs is more starkly evident from policy development over a long period. Despite the 2005 reforms, BVEs remain the primary form of release from detention, granted on the basis of satisfaction of eligibility criteria but also via exercise of the Immigration Minister's personal power to grant visas where eligibility is not satisfied. Continuities and changes in release conditions can best be studied through examining the operation of BVEs.

Many of the policy reforms relating to release from detention have been prompted by broader asylum politics. Indeed, the very initiation of mandatory detention which makes discussion of release so critical, sought to address concerns about the unauthorised maritime arrival of Chinese, Cambodian and Vietnamese asylum seekers.[13] Asylum politics also influenced policy approaches towards the eligibility for a bridging visa for release from detention, and the conditions imposed on release. In ushering in the contemporary form of mandatory detention in 1994, former Immigration Minister Gerry Hand explained that those arriving without a visa would generally not be entitled to a bridging visa so as to send 'a clear signal … that migration to Australia may not be achieved by simply arriving in this country and expecting to be allowed into the community'.[14] In discussion in the lead-up to the introduction of bridging visas, the Joint Standing Committee summarised immigration's basis for the new visa – the creation of a new distinction between authorised and unauthorised arrivals. Non-citizens who had overstayed their visas had otherwise 'submitted themselves to a proper application and entry process offshore', whereas those who had bypassed that process – such as unauthorised boat arrivals (primarily those

10 *Migration Act 1958* (Cth) s 195A ('*Migration Act*') inserted by *Migration Amendment (Detention Arrangements) Act 2005* (Cth) s 3 and sch 1 item 10.

11 *Migration Regulations 1994* (Cth) reg 2.20 (12) inserted by SLI 76 of 2005, reg 3 and sch 1 item 5, with effect from May 11, 2005.

12 *Migration Act* ss 197AA–197AG, inserted by *Migration Amendment (Detention Arrangements) Act 2005* (Cth) s 3 and sch 1 item 11.

13 For a history of immigration detention see *Al-Kateb* [2004] HCA 37; (2004) 219 CLR 562 [86]–[90] (Gummow J), [201]–[209] (Hayne J).

14 Commonwealth, *Parliamentary Debates*, House of Representatives, May 5, 1992, 2371 (G Hand, Minister for Immigration, Local Government and Ethnic Affairs).

seeking safety), those jumping ship or stowaways – had 'avoided the relevant offshore processing'.[15] It was thus necessary, immigration argued, to categorically deny release in order to maintain access to unauthorised arrivals during visa application processing and for removal if later required.[16]

The distinction between authorised and unauthorised arrivals prejudices those seeking safety and remains an important factor in eligibility for release. Access to work rights plays an equally important and sometimes overlapping role. In 2008, a new risk-based approach to detention was implemented through adoption of the 'key immigration detention values'.[17] Although attempts to incorporate these values into legislation failed,[18] they are part of detention procedure set out in the non-legally binding immigration procedure manual,[19] and provide that only three groups will be subject to mandatory detention:

- all unauthorised arrivals, for management of health, identity and security risks to the community;
- unlawful non-citizens who present unacceptable risks to the community; and
- unlawful non-citizens who have repeatedly refused to comply with their visa conditions.

The third group specified includes those who have worked without permission.

Given criteria that targets those seeking safety in Australia, who represent almost all those who arrive in Australia without prior authorisation, this chapter draws on a number of examples of policy and practice that intersect with asylum politics. However, because bridging visa policy and conditions are not limited to those seeking safety, these examples provide insight into the experience, effect and purpose of conditional release more generally.

Sponsorship requirements: financial and intimate constraints

'Sponsorship' is an informal term that refers to: (i) undertakings made by an Australian citizen or permanent resident to meet the housing and living needs of a non-citizen after release; and/or (ii) lodgment of a security bond to be

15 Joint Standing Committee on Migration, 'Asylum, Border Control and Detention' (Canberra, February 1994), 109.

16 Ibid., 110.

17 DIAC, 'Annual Report 2008–09' (Belconnen, 2009), 7, 17, 118.

18 *Migration Amendment (Immigration Detention Reform) Bill 2009* (Cth); see also Chris Evans (Minister for Immigration and Citizenship), 'Detention Values to Be Enshrined in Law', Media Release, June 25, 2009.

19 DIAC, 'Procedures Advice Manual 3' (Canberra: Commonwealth of Australia, 2010), Detention – Detention Services Manual – Legislative and Principles Overview [P A 133.2] 2 2 Immigration Detention Values (updated May 21, 2015).

forfeited if the bridging visa holder breaches BVE conditions. In the period 2002–10 studied here, the absence of sponsorship did not exclude eligibility for release on a BVE for most applicants, but the undertaking of sponsorship was a positive factor in release decisions.[20] The requirement of sponsorship for release has not completely ceased. The 2011 change in government policy that permits work rights and some government-funded support to unauthorised maritime arrival refugee claimants upon their release effectively means that release of the bulk of the former detainee population has not been contingent on sponsorship.[21] But for those not within that cohort, it remains relevant.

Sponsors active in that period saw sponsorship as important for various reasons – as a deliberate political strategy, an act of solidarity and humanitarian support to assist the chance that detainees would be released, as part of friendship, family ties, an act of love and responsibility. From immigration's perspective, sponsorship was relevant in its predictive assessment of the likelihood that a non-citizen would abide by 'no-work' conditions upon release and not 'disappear' into the community if their visa application was unsuccessful.[22] In other words, for immigration, sponsorship was envisaged to hold potential to enhance compliance or 'police at a distance'. This part of the chapter will first evaluate the legal techniques utilised to corral sponsors into 'policing at a distance' and the disruption this engendered to people's lives and then explore how sponsorship effected constraint over intimate social bonds.

Community sponsorship: policing at a distance?

The constraints imposed on sponsors by the BVE regime, reflect the notion that community members could play a role in monitoring visa compliance. The notion of 'policing at a distance' or 'governing at a distance' refers to a range of activities that are not undertaken directly by the police organisation or, more broadly, by government.[23] De Lint and Hall explain that, in the strategy of policing at a distance, 'police professionalism is not understood so much in tactical delivery, but in tactical oversight'.[24] The potential for

20 In contrast asylum seekers who had arrived without authorisation were not eligible for release unless they demonstrated adequate post-release community support arrangements; and were aged under 18 years, or 75 years or over, or had health needs (including as a result of torture and trauma) that could not be met in a detention environment: see *Migration Act* s 72; *Migration Regulations 1994* (Cth) reg 2.20, sch 2 subclass 051 Bridging (Protection Visa Applicant).

21 See the second part of this chapter.

22 *Migration Regulations 1994* (Cth) sch 2 subclass 050 Bridging (General), subclass 051 Bridging (Protection Visa Applicant).

23 Nikolas Rose and Peter Miller, 'Political Power Beyond the State: Problematics of Government', *The British Journal of Sociology* 43, no. 2 (1992); Mariana Valverde, *Law's Dream of a Common Knowledge* (Oxford: Princeton University Press, 2003); Willem De Lint and Alan Hall, 'Making the Pickets Responsible: Policing Labour at a Distance in Windsor, Ontario', *Canadian Review of Sociology/Revue canadienne de sociologie* 39, no. 1 (2002).

24 De Lint and Hall, 'Making the Pickets Responsible'.

immigration adopting a tactical oversight of released detainees was debated early on. Prior to the introduction of bridging visas in 1994, immigration considered that its direct post-release monitoring of bridging visa holders could potentially be quite minimal. One of the options immigration floated was that '[r]eporting conditions need not involve the department at all', and that 'reporting could be to the responsible [community-based] organisation, with only breaches reported to the department', provided release was accompanied by a surety.[25] However, numerous community groups rejected the idea of policing any conditions of release,[26] and the enactment of the bridging visa regime did not impose legal requirements on community members to report suspected breaches.

In the period studied, immigration viewed sponsorship as important to ensure the post-release visa compliance of former detainees. This was apparent from the fact that, at this time, it was not easy for those who had been found living without a visa in the community or who entered Australia without a visa or on false documents to obtain release. Many former detainees reported that their applications were repeatedly refused. In contrast, post-release conditions required detainees to report for bridging visa renewal, sometimes each week, month or sometimes three months depending on the visa period granted.[27] There was thus a significant difference between the intense state surveillance effected by the close immigration detention environment and the contact with immigration post-release. Immigration's direct post-release supervision of individuals involved passive, episodic contact when non-citizens attended immigration offices for renewal of their short-term bridging visas. There was also the chance of ad hoc contact if a non-citizen happened to be present during an immigration search warrant visit ('raid').

Sponsorship as financial constraint

To date, community support arrangements do not formally require community 'sponsors' to report breaches to immigration. Yet sponsors must abide by their undertakings, such as to provide residential support and, much like bail bonds for criminal offences, risk forfeit of any security bond should the released detainee breach conditions such as not leaving Australia when required. Third-party lodgment of a surety is important to understand the constraints imposed by sponsorship conditions. The bridging visa regime did not subject community

25 Department of Immigration and Ethnic Affairs, 'The Official View: Extract of Submission to the Joint Standing Committee Inquiry into Detention Practices Prepared by the Department of Immigration and Ethnic Affairs', in *Protection or Punishment: The Detention of Asylum Seekers in Australia*, ed. Mary Crock (Leichhardt: Federation Press, 1993), 133.

26 Joint Standing Committee on Migration, 'Asylum, Border Control and Detention', 130, 53. This heightened the Joint Standing Committee's Inquiry into Detention Practices' concern that there would be few safeguards to deter unauthorised arrivals from absconding upon release.

27 Interviews with A5 and A8.

sponsors to what Lorraine Mazerolle and Janet Ransley refer to as a 'legal lever', that is a legal sanction that encourages the alignment of civil actor activities with police goals.[28] However, the risk of losing security bonds deposited for detainees as a release condition did form a sanction, albeit one voluntarily assumed. The amount of the requisite security bond, set anywhere between $1500 and $50 000,[29] was identified to be a major problem by advocates. As one explained, 'they are so large, most people just can't get them, and so choose to stay in Villawood'.[30] The decision to provide a bond, whether by individuals or by the Bridge for Asylum Seekers Fund ('BASF'), was weighty. Individual sponsors were not wealthy, fund resources were limited, obtaining a bond amount sometimes involved a fair amount of negotiation and even lobbying,[31] and bonds were returned only when immigration had granted a substantive Australian visa or the applicant had returned to their country of origin.[32] As one sponsor explained, '[T]he money is tied up for so long.... No matter how much you trust [the sponsored person] it can sometimes take a couple of years without that money'.[33] And if those released on a bond 'disappeared', the bond was lost. Bonds constrained the potential for release of detainees, and financially constrained sponsors when lodged.

Disruption of social bonds

Sponsorship effected a disruption of the potential for relationships of solidarity, and produced an uneasy and unequal power relationship between sponsors and those released. In the words of Tamara Domicelj, then Director of the Asylum Seekers Centre of NSW, the destitution resulting from denial of work rights can lead to non-citizens being released 'beholden to the people who have contributed to that [security bond] and they are immediately in debt'.[34] This was a dynamic to which sponsors were deeply attuned. One sponsor recalled: 'With Mr Zhou [alias] he tried to make himself scarce, and he'd do things like sweeping up the paths, and do all the washing up for me, and make himself as scarce

28 Lorraine Green Mazerolle and Janet Ransley, *Third Party Policing* (Cambridge: Cambridge University Press, 2005), 171–92.

29 Interviews with A5, A6, A7, A8 and A9; see also Parliament of the Commonwealth of Australia Joint Standing Committee on Migration, 'Immigration Detention in Australia: A New Beginning, Criteria for Release from Immigration Detention, First Report of the Inquiry into Immigration Detention in Australia' (Canberra, 2008), 160.

30 Interview with A6.

31 An advocate, A6, explained: 'One time we had a final negotiation with the intervention of famous powerful people, you know, people whom have the ear of the Minister. That's what got them on a bond we could afford'.

32 Bridge for Asylum Seekers Foundation, accessed September 14, 2015, asylumseekersfoundation.com/index.html; see also interviews with A6, A7 and A9.

33 Interview with A6.

34 Evidence to Joint Standing Committee on Migration, Parliament of Australia, Sydney, May 7, 2008, 40 (Tamara Domicelj).

as he possibly could'.[35] But residential sponsorship was more complex and a challenge for sponsors' time and energy 'It's a lot more involved than just providing accommodation. It's largely related to their needs'.[36]

Frequently, the sponsorship relationship also entailed the intimate proximity of sharing a home. The sponsorship relationship may be close but unequal, and may be simultaneously comforting, nurturing, cloistering and overbearing. A common experience of the women involved in direct support work for people seeking safety during the Howard government era was the development of a maternal role towards those they supported. Many reported that their caring acts, their age, and the asylum seekers' separation from their own families led to asylum seekers referring to them as 'mother'.[37] One community advocate commented of a young man who stayed with her for three weeks after first staying with some younger people:

> When he came to see me he thought my place was quieter and it was easier for him to live in and ... there was a lack of a mum that he desperately needed ... he was [in his twenties] and he had been in detention for four years.[38]

Those released from immigration detention spoke similarly with affection, but also deeply conscious of the discrepancy in power and authority, and the surveillance enabled by intimate proximity to their sponsors.

Janet, a refugee in her early twenties, had grown up in a small remote area in her country, and could not read or write in her own language.[39] Janet was detained for about nine months and would not have been released without sponsorship including an undertaking to provide accommodation by a family involved in refugee support who had been visiting her in detention for some time, and a security bond of A$15 000, very high for the time. Janet's perception that the family was connected to the Australian government because of their sponsorship formed the lens through which she understood the authority of advice made by members of the family. This was strengthened as Janet's sponsor had accompanied her to her legal appointments, and Janet relied on her sponsor for reminders about what her visa conditions meant in practice. As a result, Janet imbued her sponsor's advice with the authority of law. She felt she had no autonomy. Even after she held a substantive refugee visa, she felt that if she didn't do as her former sponsor bid – not to work and not to start a romantic relationship – she might be removed from Australia. Janet's temporary protection visa permitted her to pursue both these things.[40] However, Janet found

35 Interview with A8.

36 Ibid.

37 Fiona Rutkay, 'Welcome to the Mother Country', *newmatilda.com*, February 5, 2010, https://newmatilda.com/2010/02/05/welcome-mother-country.

38 Interview with A9.

39 Account derived from interview with M3.

40 *Migration Regulations 1994* (Cth), reg 2.08F; sch 1, 1401 Protection (Class XA); sch 2 Subclass 785 Temporary Protection Visa.

it difficult to distinguish between the legal requirements of her visa and the advice her sponsors gave her.

Katrina and her husband Ben's situation was not unusual, nor should their experience be considered unique to the study period. They had lived for almost six years on a bridging visa (five of which without work permission) and for that time depended almost completely on Katrina's Australian citizen uncle and his wife.[41] The uncertainty of the eventual outcome of their visa application exacerbated the experience of this period: '[F]ive years is just five years but it looked like fifty years, you know'.[42] The financial support and loans from their relatives effectively developed into a situation of unpaid domestic service where Katrina and Ben undertook driving, cooking and cleaning for their relatives, often walking half an hour to deliver food they had cooked. It compromised their ability to make plans, even day to day, as the structure of their days was defined by what was needed of them by their relatives. In an understated manner, Katrina exclaimed it was: 'No, not okay. You know, they have two kids. For them very difficult. So we have to help a lot', and they felt, 'We must be lovely a face'. That dependence started to change as BASF, which they felt understood the circumstances facing those on BVEs, granted Katrina and Ben income support of A$60 per week. However, that grant was not sufficient to meet the needs of themselves and their child.

Released detainees' dependence on sponsors goes beyond financial dependence and reflects the structural and social inequalities facing those with temporary visa status. Community sponsors reported providing cultural and practical orientation to former detainees, including matters as diverse as safe crossing of the road, dealing with cars, transport, shopping and so on.[43] One explained: '[S]ome have never experienced anything except straight from airport to Villawood [immigration detention], so it's huge'.[44] Often sponsors acted as a 'gateway' to non-citizens gaining entitlements. Sponsors utilised personal networks with individuals in educational institutions, government and corporate bodies to facilitate access to entitlements that might otherwise be refused. Even mundane matters, such as obtaining sufficient identification to open a bank account, was not possible for many non-citizens without individuals in identification-issuing institutions finding creative pathways or making exceptions. Similarly, former detainees with permission to study would ordinarily face obstacles to study because of the requirement to pay hefty overseas student fees. But there were numerous examples of technical and further education ('TAFE') institutions making fee exceptions that enabled former detainees to study, largely English language courses.[45] Sponsors and advocates played a role in

41 Account and quotes derived from interviews with M5 and M6.

42 Interview with M5.

43 Interview with A8; see also Parliament of the Commonwealth of Australia Joint Standing Committee on Migration, 'Immigration Detention in Australia' (2009), 90.

44 Interview with A8.

45 Interview with M5.

contributing to the social entitlements of released bridging visa holders. However, the sponsorship relationship was disruptive to social bonds between sponsors and former detainees, and proceeded within a context of financial constraint on both.

Denial of work rights: the threat of re-detention

The denial of work rights on bridging visas has been central to defining the post-release life of former detainees. The resultant constraint is easy to understand. Work is necessary for survival in the absence of other income support. The necessity of work illuminates just how denial of work rights regulates migrant illegality. This section considers first how denial of work rights makes legal status insecure as it provides little protection from detention, and second notable occasions where people were released from detention without a visa. These practices suggest that it is not legal status itself that is important for release from detention, but the conditions it imposes which function as a means of control. The arbitrariness of policy decisions about who has access to work rights, and who might be detected for breach, is also evident.

Many types of bridging visas automatically permit work. Bridging E visas are the most restrictive because they categorically deny work rights in visa applications that have been rejected by a review tribunal. In other circumstances, work rights on a BVE are discretionary and take account of whether an applicant has a compelling need to work, as well as other factors. Many seeking release from detention may also need to contend with the adverse inferences of prior visa non-compliance. To provide a sense of the affected population during the period my interview participants held BVEs, at June 30, 2008, 5923 general BVEs and 2 protection BVEs were in effect, 280 of those having been granted on release from detention in 2007–08.[46] No official figures are available on the number of BVE holders without permission to work, but estimates suggest anywhere between 40 and 95 per cent were denied work permission in 2005 and 2006.[47] Eligibility for work permission on a bridging visa granted on release from detention reflects a complex and stratified legal regime and practice, one that has been subject to considerable policy change over time. But the history of government-funded income support for those released is much simpler. Two main phases can be discerned: prior to and post-2009.

46 DIAC, Submission 129f to Joint Standing Committee on Migration Responses from the Department of Immigration and Citizenship, *Inquiry into Immigration Detention in Australia*, October 15, 2008, 8; submission 1290 to Joint Standing Committee on Migration, *Inquiry into Immigration Detention in Australia*, March 17, 2009, 1.

47 Andrew Markus and Jessie Taylor, 'No Work, No Income, No Medicare – The Bridging Visa E Regime', *People and Place* 14, no. 1 (2006): 46 citing 'Rural Australians for Refugees', www.ruralaustraliansforrefugees.org/template.php3?area=facts&content=costs; and Anna Burke, 'Bridging Visa to Where?', *Online Opinion: Australia's e-journal of Social and Political Debate*, July 29, 2005, www.onlineopinion.com.au/view.asp?article=3709.

The introduction of a national program of government-funded income support scheme in 2009 – the Status Resolution Support Services ('SRSS') – was the culmination of years of advocacy and parliamentary recommendations for the expansion of work rights and provision of some income support.[48] The SRSS operated as a pilot scheme from 2006.[49] Prior to this, government-funded income support was available only to a limited class of asylum seekers and was administered by the Red Cross through the Asylum Seekers Assistance Scheme ('ASAS'). SRSS extended support for the first time not only for vulnerable asylum seekers (in addition to the existing ASAS), but also to vulnerable individuals in the migration stream.[50] Despite being positive programs, the financial assistance provided by ASAS and SRSS was set at 89 per cent of the national welfare payment. The minimum payment did not meet the basic costs of rent, food and bills.[51] This chapter focuses on the pre-2009 period because it is this period where the basic impact of the denial of work rights on survival is most starkly evident.

'No work' conditions: requiring the impossible?

Until 2009, almost all people released on bridging visas without work rights were expected to make their own arrangements for financial support. This represented a stark difference from detention, where the government provided food, shelter and healthcare. For some detainees the material support made detention preferable to making a BVE application.

> Actually a lot of them are now just waiting in detention. They say it is better to stay in detention where at least they get food, and housing and have people they can talk to and their friends are there.[52]

48 See Senate Select Committee on Ministerial Discretion in Migration Matters, 'Senate Select Committee on Ministerial Discretion in Migration Matters Report', 78–80; Senate Legal and Constitutional References Committee, 'Inquiry into the Administration and Operation of the Migration Act 1958' (Canberra: Commonwealth of Australia, 2006), 254–60. For more on the streams of assistance, see Luke Buckmaster, 'Australian Government Assistance to Refugees: Fact v. Fiction', *Parliamentary Library Background Notes* (Canberra: Parliamentary Library, 2012); and for the most up-to-date details, see 'SRSS Programme', Department of Immigration and Border Protection, accessed October 12, 2016, www.border.gov.au/Trav/Refu/Illegal-maritime-arrivals/status-resolution-support-services-programme-srss.

49 Joint Standing Committee on Migration, 'Immigration Detention in Australia: Community-Based Alternatives to Detention, Second Report of the Inquiry into Immigration Detention in Australia', 58.

50 To be regarded as vulnerable, a person would be required to meet at least one vulnerability criteria such as suffering from torture and trauma, having significant mental health issues or a serious medical condition, or being an unaccompanied minor or a minor at risk: see International Detention Coalition, 'Case Management as an Alternative to Immigration Detention: The Australian Experience' (June 2009), 7.

51 Caroline Fleay and Lisa Hartley, '"I Feel Like a Beggar": Asylum Seekers Living in the Australian Community without the Right to Work', *Journal of International Migration & Integration* 17 (2016): 1031. doi: 10.1007/s12134-015-0453-x(2015); see also United Nations High Commissioner for Refugees Regional Representation, 'Asylum-Seekers on Bridging Visas in Australia: Protection Gaps UNHCR Consultation, 2013' (December 16, 2013).

52 Interview with A6.

One man who had lived without a visa in Sydney for 21 years suffered so much stress, poverty and loneliness during that time that he eventually contacted police and was detained.[53] These reflections go some way to illustrate the untenable choice between basic survival needs for food, shelter and health and breach of visa conditions for those released from detention without work rights.

Extreme poverty was not unusual. Some BVE holder participants interviewed in 2008 and 2009 described not having funds for public transport, and had trouble meeting regular reporting requirements at immigration.[54] Another recounted having a garage sale a week before she was due to give birth to raise the hospital fee for delivery, selling everything which meant that on her return home there were no chairs for seating, nor any furniture.[55] She said:

> After I got the no work visa I lost everything. So I'm feeling depression. I don't want to see anybody. I don't want to bring anybody to my house. I'm very ashamed, nothing to my house. So yeah, when I delivered him, the nurse came to my place. She cannot sit on the floor; very difficult for her. I said I'm sorry, I don't have any chairs ... she was trying to sit on the floor.[56]

This account reflects earlier research that found denial of work rights to be both physically debilitating and psychologically distressing. Studies in the early 2000s have documented the direct link between the no-work requirements binding BVE holders and chronic poverty, homelessness and poor health.[57] The 'no work' visa condition prevented entitlement for public medical services and public housing, in circumstances where evidence showed BVE conditions generated new health problems.[58] The conditions were so brutal that some argued it amounted to a form of constructive refoulement. Without work, Graham Thom of Amnesty International put it bluntly, asylum seekers may be 'starved out' of Australia.[59] More recent studies that collate findings of mental health experts on the constellation of factors affecting former detainees, specifically those who have travelled to Australia for safety, argue that, in the context of

53 Interview with A8.

54 This is also documented elsewhere: see United Nations High Commissioner for Refugees Regional Representation, 'Asylum-Seekers on Bridging Visas in Australia', 7; Asylum Seeker Project Hotham Mission, 'Welfare Issues and Immigration Outcomes for Asylum Seekers on Bridging Visa E' (Melbourne: Asylum Seeker Project – Hotham Mission, November 2003), 20.

55 Interview with M5.

56 Ibid.

57 Asylum Seeker Project Hotham Mission, 'Welfare Issues and Immigration Outcomes for Asylum Seekers on Bridging Visa E', 19; Anne McNevin, 'Seeking Safety, Not Charity: A Report in Support of Work-Rights for Asylum Seekers Living in the Community on Bridging Visa E' (Melbourne: Network of Asylum Seeker Agencies Victoria, March 2005).

58 Asylum Seeker Project Hotham Mission, 'Welfare Issues and Immigration Outcomes for Asylum Seekers on Bridging Visa E', 20–22; McNevin, 'Seeking Safety, Not Charity', 43.

59 Evidence to Joint Standing Committee on Migration, Parliament of Australia, Sydney, May 7, 2008, 20 (Graham Thom, Chair of the Asylum Seekers Interagency forum, and Refugee Coordinator of Amnesty International).

prolonged uncertainty about refugee claims, despite income support, the denial of work rights has negative mental health consequences.[60]

Some bridging visa holders and community advocates interviewed explained that they or many they knew felt that they had no choice but to work without permission to survive. One explained, 'We are very scared, but after I think two years without work permit, it was very difficult to find the money so we can eat'.[61] Another interview participant described the bridging visa regime as 'creating criminals'[62] because working without immigration authorisation was and is a criminal offence punishable by a maximum of A$10 000 fine.[63] In practice, working without permission is not targeted for criminal prosecution. The real danger for a non-citizen who is found in breach is that immigration will cancel any visa, detain and, if possible, remove the individual from Australia.[64]

In legal philosophy, the unreasonable choice between survival and obeying a BVE prohibition on work would call into question the identity of the BVE and its conditions as lawful at all. Laws that require the impossible are classically viewed as contrary to the basic purpose of a legal order, which is to set rules capable of observance. Lon Fuller contends that such laws offend the internal legitimacy of law because they cause injustice for those who contravene and because tolerating non-compliance risks undermining respect for the law itself.[65] Yet it is well documented that, particularly prior to 2009, immigration released some non-citizens without work rights in circumstances that created an 'impossible' choice. The practice of prohibiting work in circumstances where compliance is impossible, or at least difficult, reveals that conditional release produces non-compliance. This opens up the question of how BVE holders experience the security or insecurity afforded by the legal status of a BVE.

Insecure legal status

BVE holders do not have the legal right to permanently remain in Australia, have marginal social citizenship entitlements that may (or may not) include defined short periods of work permission, and face strict conditions that mean lawful status is not secure. These characteristics have been referred to as creating 'precarious legal status'.[66] The concept captures the contingencies that make

60 Fleay and Hartley, '"I Feel Like a Beggar"'.

61 Interview with M5.

62 Interview with M8.

63 *Migration Act* s 235.

64 See Chapters 2 and 3; see also Louise Boon-Kuo, 'The Policing of Immigration: Raids, Citizenship and the Criminal Law', in *Criminalisation and Criminal Responsibility in Australia*, ed. Thomas Crofts and Arlie Loughnan (Melbourne: Oxford University Press, 2015), 276–91.

65 Lon L. Fuller, *The Morality of Law* (New Haven: Yale University Press, 1969), 71, 79.

66 Luin Goldring, Carolina Berinstein and Judith K. Bernhard, 'Institutionalizing Precarious Migratory Status in Canada', *Citizenship Studies* 13, no. 3 (2009): 240–1; Luin Goldring and Patricia Landolt, 'Precarious Legal Status in Canada: Theorizing Non-Citizenship and Conditionality', in *Producing and Negotiating Non-Citizenship: Precarious Legal Status in Canada*, ed. Luin Goldring and Patricia Landolt (Toronto: University of Toronto Press, 2013), 14–15.

continuing lawful status uncertain, and the way in which these conditionalities undermine sharp and comprehensive distinctions between the experience of authorised and unlawful status.

For BVE holders without work rights, the BVE was experienced as an insecure legal status and fostered non-citizens' internalisation of surveillance. Life on a bridging visa was characterised by a constant vigilance, on guard for potential exposure. As one interview participant stated, 'You are just taking precautions for everything'.[67] This meant adhering to legal rules, being careful to pay for transport tickets, being particularly aware of persons in uniform, and noticing even while sleeping at night whether a car stops in front of their residence.[68] It also disrupted BVE holders' social relationship and connections with ethnic and religious communities. It is pertinent that, when recounting their lives on a bridging visa in the community, interview participants often returned to their experiences of living without a visa. There is a slippage that arises between the insecurity of the legal status afforded by a bridging visa without work rights, and the experiential similarities with unlawful migration status. The sense of insecurity of legal status was strengthened by the typically short BVE periods which required attendance at immigration to seek renewal and invariably caused BVE holders great anxiety. Precarity of BVE status instituted a consciousness of rules and promoted isolation from community support that immigration has viewed as prompting the threat that former detainees will 'disappear' into the community.

Ironically, the precarious legal status produced by denial of work rights is so insecure that it invokes the experience of illegality, and reduces incentives for regularisation of legal status. One interview participant, Andy, reported that he chose not to report himself to immigration when he was living without a visa. He explained that living illegally and undetected was preferable to living on the short periods of legality offered by bridging visas, with no permission to work, and the added risk that when he presented for renewal of the bridging visa he might be detained instead.[69] Rather, Andy stated, 'I will just keep falling'.[70]

'Illegal' in the community

It is important to unpack the apparent lack of security afforded by the lawful status provided by a BVE without work rights further, because this finding from my research is in direct opposition to the principles underlying the universal visa system and mandatory detention regime. The importance of these regimes in defining the contemporary migration system since 1994 cannot be overstated. After all, the entire mandate for a BVE is to provide legal status for release from

67 Interview with M10.
68 Interviews with M8, M5 and M11.
69 Interview with M8.
70 Ibid.

detention. Moreover, immigration legal status has been definitive in finding immigration detention to be constitutionally lawful.[71] The High Court in *Lim* held that 'the involuntary detention of a *citizen* in custody by the State is penal or punitive in character' and ordinarily only lawful as a consequence of judicial criminal adjudication of guilt.[72] In contrast, the *Lim* majority held that it was constitutionally lawful for the executive to detain *aliens* provided detention was reasonably necessary to assess a visa application or arrange removal.[73] Thus, in *Lim*, the difference between the status of citizens and aliens is laid bare 'in the vulnerability of the alien to exclusion or deportation'.[74]

However, in the context of release from detention, a strong tension exists between the legal rhetoric of the universal visa system and mandatory detention and legal practice in which '[t]he idea of aliens being in Australia without a visa is not entirely alien to our history'.[75] In practice, contrary to rhetoric, the mandate for a BVE is not to provide lawful status upon release. This is not only evident from BVE holders' *experiences* of precarious status, but is also strongly supported by the instances where government has permitted non-citizens to stay in the Australian community without a visa.

Release without a visa

In 2003, up to about 30 detainees were released without a visa in the 15-month period between the Federal Court decision at first instance of *Al Masri* (2002) and the High Court's 2004 decision of *Al-Kateb*.[76] Some detainees were

71 See, for example, Mary Crock, ed. *Protection or Punishment: The Detention of Asylum Seekers in Australia* (Leichhardt: Federation Press, 1993); Mary Crock, 'Climbing Jacob's Ladder: The High Court and the Administrative Detention of Asylum Seekers in Australia', *Sydney Law Review* 15, no. 3 (1993).

72 *Chu Kheng Lim* v. *Minister for Immigration, Local Government and Ethnic Affairs* [1992] HCA 64; (1992) 176 CLR 1 [23] (Brennan, Deane and Dawson JJ) ('*Lim*') (emphasis added).

73 Ibid., [32]–[34].

74 Ibid., [26]. More recently, commentators have observed that the 2014 High Court decision of *Plaintiff S4/2014* v. *Minister for Immigration and Border Protection* [2014] HCA 34; (2014) 253 CLR 219 shows a renewed focus 'on the key difference between aliens and citizens, namely, their immigration status': Joyce Chia, 'Back to the Constitution: The Implications of Plaintiff S4/2014 for Immigration Detention', *UNSW Law Journal* 38, no. 2 (2015): 651.

75 Transcript of Proceedings, *Behrooz* v. *Secretary DIMIA, SHDB* v. *Godwin, MIMIA* v. *Al Khafaji* [2003] HCATrans 458 (November 13, 2003) (Kirby J).

76 The Federal Court initially released Al Masri in 2002 and soon after Al Khafaji. Then, following Al Masri's Full Federal Court decision in April 2003, about 12 people including Al-Kateb were reportedly released, and an estimated 31 Palestinian and Iraqi persons in immigration detention were potentially affected by the Al Masri outcome and may have been released: see *Al Masri* [2002] FCA 1009; (2002) 192 ALR 609; *Al Khafaji* [2002] FCA 1369; *Al-Kateb* [2004] HCA 37; (2004) 219 CLR 562; David Marr, 'Escape from a Life in Limbo', *The Sydney Morning Herald*, October 27, 2007, www.smh.com.au/articles/2007/10/26/1192941339538.html; Natalie Bugalski, 'A Taste of Freedom from Limbo in Woomera', *Alternative Law Journal* 27, no. 5 (2002): 241. The figures that Bugalski relied on were derived from a letter from Fr Frank Brennan SJ, Director of the Uniya Jesuit Social Justice Centre to the Minister for Immigration dated August 20, 2002.

released on *habeas corpus* grounds (a writ used to contest the legality of imprisonment)[77] as a result of Federal Court orders, and others because immigration decided to release persons in similar circumstances to those the subject of orders. The releases were instigated by an action brought by Akram Ouda Mohammad Al Masri, a stateless Palestinian. Al Masri's application for refugee status had been refused and despite his request the Australian government had not been able to arrange his return to the Gaza Strip.[78] The Federal Court in *Al Masri* (2002) found the power to detain was not authorised when there is no real likelihood or prospect of removal in the reasonably foreseeable future, and ordered his release, which was upheld on appeal.[79] However, in August 2004, the High Court in *Al-Kateb* decided no such limit existed.[80] The majority found that, even if there are no prospects for removal, continued detention is not punitive because its legality is determined by the purpose of detention, not by the duration. In other words, in *Al-Kateb* the High Court held indefinite detention to be lawful.

The cases of *Al Masri* and *Al-Kateb* are remembered mostly for their legal legacies concerning the lack of limits on the executive detention of aliens who cannot be removed. Here I am interested in the light they shed on how government has viewed the relative necessity of legal status for release. The Immigration Minister did not make provision for grant of legal status when the court ordered release. Instead, the Minister seemed satisfied with the conditions imposed by the court, which were broadly similar to BVE conditions: notification of address, no work, reporting requirements, and undertaking to submit to the custody of the Immigration Minister if arrangements were made for removal.[81] It seems the Immigration Minister had input into the conditions imposed in at least some

77 George Williams and Tony Blackshield, *Australian Constitutional Law and Theory: Commentary and Materials*, 2nd edn (Sydney: The Federation Press, 1998). Note there is some debate as to whether the Federal Court has the power to make an order of *habeas corpus* (see *Ruddock* v. *Vadarlis* [2001] FCA 1329; (2001) 110 FCR 491, 509–14 (Black CJ), 517–18 (Beaumont J), 546–8 (French J); see also *Al-Kateb* [2004] HCA 37; (2004) 219 CLR 562 [24]–[29] (Gleeson CJ). As a result, some applicants at that time sought orders 'in the nature of' *habeas corpus*.

78 *Al Masri* [2002] FCA 1009; (2002) 192 ALR 609.

79 Ibid.; *Minister for Immigration and Multicultural and Indigenous Affairs* v. *Al Masri* [2003] FCAFC 70; (2003) 126 FCR 54 [18]. Note that Mr Al Masri was returned to Gaza in September 2002 prior to the Full Federal Court case and was killed in 2008: Paul Bibby *et al.*, 'Deported Refugee Shot Dead', *The Sydney Morning Herald*, August 2, 2008, www.smh.com.au/news/world/deported-refugee-killed/2008/08/01/1217097536265.html?page=fullpage.

80 *Al-Kateb* [2004] HCA 37; (2004) 219 CLR 562.

81 For Mr Al Masri, see *Al Masri* [2002] FCA 1037; Bugalski, 'A Taste of Freedom from Limbo in Woomera'. For Mr Al-Kateb, see Al Kateb, 'Submission No 86 to the Senate Legal and Constitutional References Committee Inquiry into the *Administration and Operation of the Migration Act 1958*', 2; *Al-Kateb* [2004] HCA 37; (2004) 219 CLR 562 [107] (McHugh); Transcript of Proceedings, *Behrooz* v. *Secretary DIMIA, SHDB* v. *Godwin, MIMIA* v. *Al Khafaji* [2003] HCATrans 458 (November 13, 2003) (O'Connor, counsel for Mr Al-Kateb). For Mr Al Khafaji, see Transcripts of Proceedings, *Behrooz* v. *Secretary DIMIA, SHDB* v. *Godwin, MIMIA* v. *Al Khafaji* [2003] HCATrans 458 (November 13, 2003) (Tilmouth, counsel for Mr Al Khafaji); *Minister for Immigration and Multicultural and Indigenous Affairs* v. *Al Khafaji* [2004] HCA 38 [34] (Hayne J).

cases.[82] Like Al Masri and Al-Kateb, these were mostly stateless persons, from the Occupied Palestinian Territories or Iraq, who the Australian government had been unable to remove to their countries of former habitual residence. It was the subjugating conditions that formed the minimum requirements for release, not grant of legal status. In the following year, as mentioned in the first part of this chapter, the Immigration Minister introduced RPBVs to enable the release of those in analogous situations. Nevertheless, my argument is that this example of release should not be regarded simply as the result of an administrative lag prior to the introduction of RPBVs, but indicative of the relative insignificance of legal status for release from detention. This view is strengthened by the next example of a person permitted stay without a visa.

Authorised stay without a visa

In the period November 25, 2011 to November 2013, an estimated 27 000 people seeking safety who had arrived in Australia by boat and without authorisation had been released and were living on BVEs in the community.[83] The vast majority were released in 2012–13.[84] Bridging visas for these cohorts had been granted for limited periods and, upon the Coalition government taking office in September 2013, immigration ceased renewing expired BVEs, resulting in some former detainees living in the community without a visa.[85] Despite non-citizens alerting immigration that their visas had expired,[86] in March 2014 the Sydney-based Refugee Advice and Casework Service ('RACS') was not 'aware of anyone being taken to detention by the Department of Immigration because their bridging visa has expired, although this remains possible'.[87] Refugee legal advocates advised those whose visas had expired to maintain contact with immigration, to continue to comply with prior visa conditions, and not to work even if previously permitted.[88] By April 2015, some former detainees reported that immigration had started renewing bridging visas.[89] But three years after the Immigration Minister had frozen bridging visa renewals, immigration advised advocates that at April 4, 2016 there were about 300 non-citizens of the group

82 See, for example, *Al-Kateb* [2004] HCA 37; (2004) 219 CLR 562 [107].

83 Fleay and Hartley, '"I Feel Like a Beggar"'.

84 DIAC, 'Annual Report 2012–13' (Belconnen, 2013), 219; *M79/2012* v. *Minister for Immigration and Citizenship* [2013] HCA 24; (2013) 252 CLR 336, 343 [10] (French CJ, Crennan, Bell JJ); 298 ALR 1.

85 Fleay and Hartley, '"I Feel Like a Beggar"'; Refugee Advice and Casework Service, 'Recent Changes' (Sydney, March 2014), 6, www.australianchurchesrefugeetaskforce.com.au/wp-content/uploads/2014/03/Recent-changes.pdf.

86 United Nations High Commissioner for Refugees Regional Representation, 'Asylum-Seekers on Bridging Visas in Australia'.

87 Refugee Advice and Casework Service, 'Recent Changes', 6, www.australianchurchesrefugeetaskforce.com.au/wp-content/uploads/2014/03/Recent-changes.pdf

88 Ibid.

89 Fleay and Hartley, '"I Feel Like a Beggar"', 4.

that had arrived post-August 13, 2012 who were unlawful.[90] This represents an extended period of government-enforced illegality within the community.

The most outstanding feature of the release of this cohort was the executive discretion that structured it at every stage. This was not a scenario where the detainees met minimum criteria for BVE eligibility as intended by the scheme, but one where the legal regime established in 2001 made BVE criteria irrelevant. Following the highly publicised stand-off between the Australian Special Armed Services and the *Tampa* in 2001, the Howard government introduced new laws that sought to deter people seeking safety by transferring unauthorised boat arrivals offshore to a third country for detention and refugee processing.[91] The first iteration was known as the 'Pacific Solution' (2001–08), and the second as 'Regional Processing' (2012–present), and both utilised Nauru and Papua New Guinea's Manus Island for offshore processing centres. There are important differences between these two periods of offshore processing, the latter of which is harsher and provides that those found to be refugees would never be resettled in Australia. However, one part of the legal architecture has remained substantially the same: people arriving by boat without authorisation are barred from lodging a valid application for any Australian visa.[92]

Initially the bar on making a valid visa application applied to people arriving at excised places (such as Australia's Christmas Island) and it was later expanded to apply to people arriving at any part of Australia. Not only does this bar mean unauthorised maritime arrivals cannot apply for refugee protection, it also bars application for a BVE for release from detention, unless the Immigration Minister exercises the personal and non-compellable power to 'lift the bar' in the 'public interest'.[93] From 2005, the Immigration Minister was also granted the personal power to grant a visa to a person in detention whether or not the person had lodged an application if the Minister thinks it is in the 'public interest'.[94] It was this latter power that the Minister utilised to release unauthorised maritime arrivals. The Immigration Minister issued a temporary safe haven visa of short duration and a BVE at the same time, because the former visa included a statutory bar that would again prevent grantees from making any

90 Unclassified information provided by the DIBP, statistics current as at April 4, 2016.

91 For a gripping journalistic account of the Tampa affair, see David Marr and Marian Wilkinson, *Dark Victory* (Crows Nest: Allen & Unwin, 2003); for a legal account, see Mary Crock, 'In the Wake of the Tampa: Conflicting Visions of International Refugee Law in the Management of Refugee Flows', *Pacific Rim Law & Policy Journal* 12 (2003); for commentary on offshore processing in Australia, see Susan Kneebone, 'The Pacific Plan: The Provision of "Effective Protection"?', *International Journal of Refugee Law* 18, no. 3–4 (2006); Savitri Taylor, 'The Pacific Solution or a Pacific Nightmare: The Difference between Burden Shifting and Responsibility Sharing', *Asian-Pacific Law and Policy Journal* 6, no. 1 (2005); Janet Phillips, 'A Comparison of Coalition and Labor Government Asylum Policies in Australia since 2001', *Parliamentary Library Research Paper 2013–14* (Canberra: Parliamentary Library, 2014).

92 *Migration Act* s 46A, inserted by the *Migration Amendment (Excision from the Migration Zone) Act 2001* (Cth).

93 *Migration Act* s 46A.

94 *Migration Act* s 195A.

valid visa application (which would otherwise have been available upon BVE grant).[95] This meant that, even after release from detention, any BVE renewals (or refusals to renew) were at the personal mercy and absolute control of the Minister.[96]

For the Immigration Minister, the 'public interest' concerns were informed by highly pragmatic concerns about the pressure to accommodate large numbers of people in Australian detention. In the intermission between offshore processing regimes, those arriving by boat on Australian shores were held in detention. In the 2010 calendar year numbers exceeded 6000, placing pressure on the detention system.[97] In November 2011, the government announced a policy change and the Immigration Minister utilised his personal power to issue bridging visas with the right to work and access to health services.[98] Then, in August 2012, the Gillard government reintroduced offshore processing, meaning that those arriving would be sent to Nauru and Manus Island Papua New Guinea. However, it was clear that the dramatically increased numbers of asylum seekers arriving, which had reached 17 204 in the 2012 calendar year, could not all be accommodated in the offshore centres, the ultimate capacity of which was planned to reach 2100 people.[99] The government announced that those who could not be transferred would be released from immigration detention on BVEs in the community. Those arriving after August 13, 2012 would be subject to the 'no advantage' test designed to ensure those arriving by boat receive no benefit over those awaiting resettlements in camps around the world, and thus were not eligible for work rights on release. Both the reason that detainees were released and the reason why they remained unlawful were the result of executive discretion.

It is also worth noting that a significant characteristic of executive control is expressed through arbitrary character of denial of work rights. In this example, access to work rights upon release was determined by the date of arrival, not any individual concerns of a BVE holder's need to work or predicted compliance with visa conditions. It sought to institute the deterrence policy of 'no

95 *M79/2012* v. *Minister for Immigration and Citizenship* [2013] HCA 24; (2013) 252 CLR 336, 298 ALR 1.

96 *Migration Act* s 91L.

97 For a summary of the number of boats and people arriving by calendar and financial year from 1976–2014, see Janet Phillips, 'Boat Arrivals in Australia: A Quick Guide to the Statistics', *Parliamentary Library Research Paper 2013–14* (Canberra: Parliamentary Library, 2014), 2. For an overview of policy since 2009, see Chia, 'Back to the Constitution: The Implications of Plaintiff S4/2014 for Immigration Detention', 634–7.

98 Chris Bowen (Minister for Immigration and Citizenship), 'Bridging Visas to Be Issued for Boat Arrivals', Media Release, November 25, 2011.

99 Simon Cullen, 'First Asylum Seekers Arrive on Manus Island', *ABC News Online*, November 21, 2012, www.abc.net.au/news/2012-11-21/first-asylum-seekers-arrive-on-manus-island/4383876; Phillip Coorey and Bianca Hall, 'The Limbo Solution: Free, but Not to Work', *The Sydney Morning Herald*, November 22, 2012, www.smh.com.au/federal-politics/political-news/the-limbo-solution-free-but-not-to-work-20121121-29qep.html#ixzz3z5Xlx9Oi.

advantage'.[100] It can also be seen earlier in the categorical denial of work rights to people who lodged a protection visa more than 45 days after arrival, the '45-day rule', effective in the period 1997–2009. Former Immigration Minister Phillip Ruddock said restrictions sought to counter the refugee application process being used as a gateway to, in the Minister's words, 'a $30 work visa'[101] with accompanying access to healthcare, though no evidence of alleged exploitation was offered.

In these examples of the legal practice of release from detention, the significance of immigration legal status as the mandate for release recedes. The precarity of legal status experienced by BVE holders undermines the protection it ostensibly offers. And despite legal rhetoric that every non-citizen is required to hold a visa to remain in the community, the conditions of release and the retention of executive control are more important factors in a person's release than formal legal status itself.

The code of behaviour for asylum seekers

The Immigration Minister Scott Morrison introduced a Code of Behaviour ('the Code') in December 2013, and as the most recent significant addition to bridging visas conditions, it came into effect in February 2014.[102] From that date, all people who arrived by boat without authorisation and sought to apply for or renew a bridging visa were required to sign the Code for grant of a bridging visa. The Code epitomises dimensions of the regulation of conditional release that have been discussed in this chapter. Like sponsorship, it has a social dimension that involves an intimate regulation, but unlike sponsorship it is not mediated by a civil actor. Like the denial of work rights, the Code institutes a sense of the precarity of legal status to former detainees that does not rely on apprehension by the authorities for its effect. But unlike the exacting requirement of no work, the Code requirements are ill-defined mythical values. Recalling that BVE conditions are not experienced in isolation, the particularities of the Code intensify the constraints discussed in the chapter thus far.

The Code stipulates first that BVE holders 'must not disobey any Australian laws' and then goes on to require adherence to specific existing laws, including not making 'sexual contact with another person without that person's consent'. Morrison first flagged his commitment to the implementation of 'behaviour protocols'

100 Immigration Minister Chris Bowen said: 'Consistent with "no advantage", people from this cohort going onto bridging visas will have no work rights and will receive only basic accommodation assistance, and limited financial support': see Chris Bowen, 'No Advantage Onshore for Boat Arrivals'.

101 Commonwealth, *Parliamentary Debates*, House of Representatives, June 19, 1997, 5857–8 (Phillip Ruddock, Minister for Immigration and Multicultural Affairs).

102 *Migration Amendment (Bridging Visas – Code of Behaviour) Regulation 2013* (Cth) came into effect in February 2014. It is now incorporated into *Migration Regulations 1994* (Cth) sch 4 public interest criterion 4022, sch 8 visa condition 8566.

while he was in opposition after a refugee claimant was charged with indecent assault.[103] Two years after the enactment of the Code he was acquitted of the offence.[104] Of most concern to BVE holders and commentators are the Code's open-ended prohibitions that a holder must not 'bully' any person or 'engage in any anti-social or disruptive activities that are inconsiderate, disrespectful or threaten the peaceful enjoyment of other members of the community'. Immigration explains this includes 'making threats, spreading rumours', 'spitting or swearing in public', to 'persistently irritate' another person, or 'disturb someone or something'.[105] The Code also requires cooperation with all 'reasonable requests' from immigration, such as requests to attend interviews or to provide or obtain identity and/or travel documents.

The Code sought to address what the Immigration Minister saw as limited capacity to cancel BVEs for behaviour unacceptable to the Australian community.[106] However, advocates emphasised that the Code was unnecessary.[107] A range of laws were already available to address the behaviour of BVE holders, including the general law, long-standing powers to cancel visas for bad character (see Chapter 5), as well as amendments adopted earlier in 2013 that enhanced broad cancellation powers on public safety grounds.[108] The consequences of breach go further than criminal or civil prosecution and visa cancellation. The Code empowers immigration to cease or reduce any income support, cancel visas and re-detain and prevent future BVE eligibility for those considered to have breached the Code.

About 29 000 BVE holders have signed the Code, but at June 30, 2016 only two had faced cancellation and re-detention for breach of the Code: Ali Sadaat, and Sarwar. In the first program year of the Code's operation, it was reported in the media that immigration made one cancellation, although immigration did not report on the numbers that year.[109] Ali Sadaat, 19, was stopped by police for carrying an open bottle of beer while travelling on the train. In addition to a

103 Lenore Taylor and Judith Ireland, '"Behaviour" Rules Vilify Asylum Seekers – Lib', *The Age*, February 28, 2013, www.theage.com.au/federal-politics/political-news/behaviour-rules-vilify-asylum-seekers--lib-20130227-2f6d4.html.

104 AAP, 'Asylum-Seeker Cleared of Indecent Assault', *SBS News Online*, March 11, 2016, www.sbs.com.au/news/article/2016/03/11/asylum-seeker-cleared-indecent-assault.

105 See DIBP, 'Code of Behaviour for Subclass 050 Bridging (General) Visa Holders Form 1443'.

106 See, for example, Commonwealth, *Parliamentary Debates*, Senate, July 14, 2014, 4863–6 (Michaela Cash, Assistant Minister for Immigration and Border Protection and Minister Assisting the Prime Minister for Women).

107 Karen Barlow, 'Asylum Seekers Required to Follow Government's New Code of Conduct', *ABC News Online*, February 4, 2014, www.abc.net.au/news/2013-12-16/an-asylum-seekers-required-to-follow-code-of-conduct/5160118.

108 *Migration Amendment (Disclosure of Information) Regulation 2013* (Cth).

109 DIBP, 'Annual Report 2013–14' (Belconnen, 2014); Ben Doherty and Abdul Karim Hekmat, '"We Are the Forgotten People": The Anguish of Australia's "Invisible"' Asylum Seekers', *Guardian*, April 13, 2016), www.theguardian.com/australia-news/2016/apr/13/we-are-the-forgotten-people-the-anguish-of-australias-invisible-asylum-seekers; Refugee Action Coalition, 'Concerns Increase for Re-Detained Christmas Island Iranian Hunger Striker', Refugee Action Coalition, December 24, 2015, www.refugeeaction.org.au/?p=4568.

fine and a nine-month good behaviour bond imposed by the criminal justice system, in late 2013 immigration cancelled his BVE and re-detained him. Sadaat was detained first at Villawood in Sydney, where he had been residing while awaiting the Minister's decision on his refugee claims, and was then moved to Darwin and then Christmas Island where he has been detained now for over two years. In 2014–15, immigration cancelled a second BVE on breach of Code grounds.[110] Sarwar showed the *Guardian* a document from his immigration file that stated he was re-detained for 'public threat to suicide; security issue and suicidal threats; working illegally as a farmer'.[111] In the program year 2015–16, Immigration identified 281 persons in potential breach of the Code, but did not proceed to make any cancellations.[112] Overall, the number of BVE holders found in breach of the Code is negligible.

Regardless, the Code has had a profound impact on BVE holders. Its operation does not rely on detection and enforcement, but on the sense of precarious legal status it conveys. Its fundamental function is in its power over the mind of the BVE holder. The Code builds a metaphysical prison within the community through the internalisation of surveillance.[113] In the first year of its operation, asylum seekers reported that they were staying indoors to avoid breaching the Code.[114] An Afghan Hazara using the alias Karim describes living in constant fear of doing even mundane things outside the house. He feared using the wrong ticket to catch a train or otherwise inadvertently breaching the Code. 'I've been here two years and I'm physically safe, but I'm not mentally safe ... It [the Code] is very complicated, it is not very specific and you don't know what is in it and what is not'.[115]

The uncertainty of what is captured within the Code's remit, coupled with its dire consequences, produces a surveillance that penetrates and transforms the intimate space of the home of people seeking safety. In a 2016 theatre production in Sydney titled *Tribunal*, one of the writers and performers, Mahdi Mohammadi, who travelled from Afghanistan seeking safety in Australia, dances with Jawad Yaqoubi, speaking of the solace music and dance brought during the interminable wait for a refugee visa and worry for family back home. Mohammadi then speaks of a friend, who after having had a neighbour threaten to call the police because of noise from their home threw their stereo out the

110 DIBP, 'Annual Report 2014–15' (Belconnen, 2015), 187.

111 Doherty and Hekmat, '"We Are the Forgotten People"'.

112 DIBP, 'Annual Report 2015–16' (Belconnen, 2016), 51. In that year, however, 5 BVE holders had a formal counselling session with an immigration officer to emphasise expected conduct standards, and 19 had discussions with their non-government service provider (for example, Australian Red Cross).

113 Michel Foucault, *Discipline and Punish – The Birth of the Prison*, trans. Alan Sheridan (Middlesex: Penguin Books, 1977), 101, 187, 201–2.

114 Cited in Mohamed Taha and Allan Clarke, 'Asylum Seekers "Staying Indoors" after Signing Federal Government's Code of Behaviour', *ABC News Online*, November 29, 2014, www.abc.net.au/news/2014-11-29/refugee-code-of-conduct-stressful-asylum-seekers-say/5923700.

115 Cited in ibid.

window fearful of disturbing neighbours. Mohammadi explains the Code means that there's 'no more party'.[116]

It is clear that the government intended for the Code to work on the mind of those released. In Federal Parliament, responding to an Australian Greens motion to disallow the law instituting the Code, the Assistant Minister for Immigration Michaelia Cash argued for the Code's necessity as 'an educative tool'.[117]

> When you release into the community thousands of people who have arrived here illegally by boat from very different backgrounds, then, as a government, we should at the very least, explain to these people what is expected of them in terms of their behaviour. Examples include people from Iran, Iraq or Afghanistan, who either do not speak English or have very limited knowledge of the English language. These people might come from cultures that are fundamentally different to our own – for example, cultures where women are not equal to men and who have had little to no exposure to Australian society.
>
> The regulations that are sought to be disallowed are necessary as they provide the framework for the government to address community concerns about the behaviour of illegal maritime arrivals, who are in Australia temporarily as the holders of bridging visas.... The code of behaviour makes it clear that antisocial as well as criminal behaviour will not be tolerated.[118]

In this parliamentary speech, the concerns of the Australian community are invoked as both the impetus for the Code and justification for scrutiny of 'antisocial' BVE holders. The intention for the Code to operate automatically through self-surveillance by asylum seekers is evident from Cash's emphasis that the 'grant of a bridging visa to an IMA is a privilege; it is not a right' and that the consequences of violation are assured as '[t]his government has a zero tolerance approach to those who violate the privilege'.[119] Despite Cash's exhortation that the behavioural expectations conveyed by the Code are clear, for asylum seekers its meaning remains vague, and the conduct that would amount to contravention elusive. This can be seen from some BVE holders' anxious

116 Karen Therese (dir.) 2016, *Tribunal*, by Paul Dwyer, Katie Green, Rhonda Grovenor Dixon, Mahdi Mohammadi, Karen Therese, Jawad Yaqoubi, theatre performance, August 12–20, 2016, Powerhouse Youth Theatre, Griffin Theatre Company, viewed August 20, 2016; Keith Gallasch, 'A Just Hearing in the Court of Theatre', *RealTime* 134 (August–September 2016), www.realtimearts.net/article/issue134/12367.

117 Commonwealth, *Parliamentary Debates*, Senate, July 14, 2014, 4863 (Michaela Cash, Assistant Minister for Immigration and Border Protection and Minister Assisting the Prime Minister for Women).

118 Ibid., 4863–5 (Michaela Cash, Assistant Minister for Immigration and Border Protection and Minister Assisting the Prime Minister for Women).

119 Commonwealth, *Parliamentary Debates*, Senate, July 14, 2014, 4865 (Michaela Cash, Assistant Minister for Immigration and Border Protection and Minister Assisting the Prime Minister for Women).

attachment to the Code text: 'More than one of the asylum seekers the Guardian spoke to carries a copy of the code with them, unfolding it, worn with age and repeated rereadings, from a pocket or wallet'.[120]

The circumstances facing the cohort of BVE holders subject to the Code have been particularly difficult. They are all people who have fled their homelands seeking safety in Australia, who have arrived by boat and without authorisation. They have been at the mercy of Ministerial decision-making, and have experienced long periods of uncertainty. Some have waited for more than five years for the Immigration Minister to consider their cases. But with legal changes in 2014 they are now eligible only for a three-year temporary protection visa ('TPV') or a five-year safe haven enterprise visa ('SHEV') and have no pathway to permanent protection. Temporary protection visas and SHEVs do not allow visa holders to sponsor family to Australia, and there is no guarantee of being permitted back in the country if they leave, unless the Minister gives written approval on the basis of compassionate or compelling circumstances justifying the travel.[121]

It is not surprising that there have been many suicides by BVE holders in the community.[122] Leo Seemanpillai (October 2014), Raza (June 2015), Khodayar Amini (October 2015), Reza Alizadeh (October 2015), Mohammad Nazari (April 2016) and Mohammad Hadi (June 2016) are some of the men reported to have committed suicide while living in the community on a bridging, and in the case of Saeed Hassanloo (September 2016) on a SHEV, visa.[123] A recent study of asylum seekers on BVEs explains that the adverse mental health consequences of prior detention and traumatic experiences prior to arrival in Australia are compounded by long periods of uncertainty in refugee determination, fears of being returned to country of origin, fears for family outside of Australia, loneliness and inactivity.[124]

120 Doherty and Hekmat, '"We Are the Forgotten People"'.

121 *Migration and Maritime Powers Legislation Amendment (Resolving the Asylum Legacy Caseload) Act 2014* (Cth) was passed on December 5, 2014, and many of the new laws commenced December 16, 2014.

122 For insight into the impact of immigration detention on mental health, see Steel *et al.*, 'Psychiatric Status of Asylum Seeker Families Held for a Protracted Period in a Remote Detention Centre in Australia'; G. J. Coffey *et al.*, 'The Meaning and Mental Health Consequences of Long-Term Immigration Detention for People Seeking Asylum', *Social Science and Medicine* 70, no. 12 (2010).

123 Rachel Wells and Nicole Hasham, 'Hazara Community Shocked, Angered at Death of Afghan Asylum Seeker', *The Age*, October 20, 2015, www.theage.com.au/victoria/hazara-community-shocked-angered-at-death-of-afghan-asylum-seeker-20151020-gkdxdo.html.; Doherty and Hekmat, '"We Are the Forgotten People"'; Abdul Karim Hekmat, 'Asylum Seekers Are Taking Desperate Actions as Bridging Visas Leave Them in Limbo', *The Sydney Morning Herald*, September 25, 2016, www.smh.com.au/national/asylum-seekers-are-taking-desperate-actions-as-bridging-visas-leave-them-in-limbo-20160919-grjgac.html.

124 Fleay and Hartley, '"I Feel Like a Beggar"', 10–11. See also Shakeh Momartin *et al.*, 'A Comparison of the Mental Health of Refugees with Temporary Versus Permanent Protection Visas', *Medical Journal Australia* 185, no. 7 (2006); Zachary Steel *et al.*, 'Impact of Immigration Detention and Temporary Protection on the Mental Health of Refugees', *British Journal of Psychiatry* 188 (2006).

Many of the men who have died are from the Hazara community, one of the largest groups of people seeking safety in Australia. Shukufa Tahiri, who arrived in Australia as a refugee in 2006, described this as 'a kind of epidemic unfolding before the nation's eyes in Australia – in my Hazara community alone there have been six suicides in the past 12 months'.[125] Tahiri told ABC's *Q&A* program in October 2016 that suicide and self-harm are the direct result of asylum policies: 'It is the endemic result of prolonged delays, prolonged uncertainty, prolonged uncertainty'.[126] The despair conveyed by these suicides, previously more strongly associated with the distress of detention, challenges the notion that the conditions of release provide any succour.[127] It also prompts serious questions about who is responsible for the conditions experienced by those released from detention.

Responsibility for the conditions of release from detention

The failure of release from detention to enable financial and social independence of former detainees prompts the broader question of how the movement out of detention affects responsibility for the welfare of former detainees. This question has arisen in policy forums over the years. In 2006, a Senate Inquiry commenting on the denial of work rights and access to basic services on BVEs concluded that a 'policy which renders a person destitute is morally indefensible and an abrogation of responsibility by the Commonwealth'.[128] It regarded the government as having primary responsibility 'for ensuring … minimum standards essential to the survival and wellbeing of all people in Australia' and went on to state that necessity of reliance on charities and other agencies for survival 'represents a significant cost-shifting by the Commonwealth'.[129]

Discussion of the legal position of state responsibility after release has not been prominent probably because litigation has focused on clarifying state responsibility for conditions in detention centres run by private contractors. The courts have found that, in immigration detention, the government is under a non-delegable duty to 'ensure that reasonable care is taken of the detainees who, by reason of their detention cannot care for themselves'.[130]

125 ABC TV, 'Australia's Sovereign Borders', *Q&A*, October 10, 2016.

126 Ibid.

127 For insight into the impact of immigration detention on mental health, see Steel *et al.*, 'Psychiatric Status of Asylum Seeker Families Held for a Protracted Period in a Remote Detention Centre in Australia'; Coffey *et al.*, 'The Meaning and Mental Health Consequences of Long-Term Immigration Detention for People Seeking Asylum'.

128 Senate Legal and Constitutional References Committee, 'Inquiry into the Administration and Operation of the Migration Act 1958', 258.

129 Ibid., 259.

130 *S* v. *Secretary, Department of Immigration and Multicultural and Indigenous Affairs* (2005) FCA 549 [212]; (2005) 143 FCR 217; 216 ALR 252 ('*S*').

The duty cannot be avoided by outsourcing detention management to private companies as is the case for immigration detention in Australia.[131]

No case regarding state responsibility for a former detainee released from detention living in the community within Australia has gone to trial, but a recent case flags the possibility for this development. In 2016, the Federal Court found the Australian government held a duty of care towards a refugee living in the community on Nauru after release from detention in the Regional Processing Centre.[132] Drawing on extensive authority, the court in *Plaintiff S99/2016* held a multi-factorial approach is the correct way to determine the existence of a duty of care.[133] It held that in a case such as this one where the Minister holds statutory power or discretion, it is especially important to consider particular factors, such as the coherence of a duty with the statutory scheme and policy considerations, as well the extent of control exercised by the defendant (the Australian government), the reliance of the plaintiff on the government, the degree of vulnerability of the plaintiff and any assumption of responsibility by the government.

In future cases, a court might conceivably find that the government owes a duty of reasonable care for the physical and mental health of those released on the bases of its imposition of contingent conditions which create a risk or danger for those released; the former detainees' reliance on government for food, shelter and healthcare; and their vulnerability, not least derived from their period of detention.[134] The more difficult question is likely to be whether a breach of duty can be established. What would amount to failure to provide for reasonable care for the physical and mental health of former detainees?

Conclusion

The destitution, dependency and distress produced by conditional release from detention is not new, but the constellation of conditions in effect since 2011 produces intensified forms of violence in community settings. The constraints that former detainees face are not simply the result of enforced poverty, as is evident from the post-November 2011 releases of unauthorised maritime arrivals who received basic, though insufficient, income support if they were not permitted to work or were unable to find work. The conditions impose financial,

131 *S* (2005) FCA 549; (2005) 143 FCR 217; 216 ALR 252; Australian National Audit Office, 'Management of the Detention Centre Contracts – Part A Department of Immigration and Multicultural and Indigenous Affairs' (Canberra, 2004), 69–71; Lynda Crowley-Cyr, 'Contractualism, Exclusion and "Madness" in Australia's "Outsourced Wastelands"', *Macquarie Law Journal* 5 (2005).

132 *Plaintiff S99/2016* v. *Minister for Immigration and Border Protection* [2016] FCA 483 ('*Plaintiff S99/2016*').

133 *Plaintiff S99/2016* [2016] FCA 483 [229].

134 See *Plaintiff S99/2016* [2016] FCA 483 [216] citing *Amaca Pty Ltd* v. *the State of New South Wales* [2004] NSWCA 124; (2004) 132 LGERA 309 [21], [230], and [225] discussing *Crimmins* v. *Stevedoring Industry Finance Committee* [1999] HCA 59; (1999) 200 CLR 1 [93].

social and temporal constraints that mean that release from detention does not provide relief from many of the strictures that former detainees experienced in immigration detention. Although the requirements for release have fluctuated with policy change, it is evident that conditional release from detention cannot be equated with liberty, and that this has been evident in some features of the bridging visa regime since its inception. This is demonstrated by the specific and unique effects of sponsorship, work rights and behavioural codes as contingent conditions of release on a bridging visa.

The character of sponsorship as an act of familial or community solidarity enabled sponsored former detainees into the social life of a community in which their marginally lawful status would otherwise form a barrier. But it did so in circumstances where sponsors were subject to financial constraints, former detainees were financially dependent on sponsors, in conditions which at times undermined the autonomy and independence of former detainees. The impossibility of compliance with no work requirements in the absence of income support, which predominated in the 1994–2009 period, produced BVE legal status as intensely precarious. Bridging E visa status was precarious because immigration was empowered to cancel a visa upon breach and re-detain the person. Further, the precarity created by the denial of work rights in combination with other factors – such as the short periods granted and requirement for renewal and the uncertainty of substantive visa claims – defined former detainees' perceptions of their lawful status. For those unauthorised maritime arrivals released from detention post-2011, the introduction of a Code of Behaviour for BVE holders illustrated the government's renewed commitment to reminding BVE holders of the precarity of their status and the potential for visa cancellation on vaguely elaborated behavioural expectations. These mechanisms mobilised legal status as a mechanism of selective and arbitrary control.

What does the study of release from detention reveal about the central themes of this book: the policing of status and issues of responsibility over how people are made 'illegal'? Bridging visas are issued to those who meet the minimum conditions for release. However, the practice of release challenges the rhetoric that bridging visas are intended to provide *lawful* status on release from detention. The precarious legal status BVEs afford reveals that lawful status itself is decentred, which is starkly illustrated by examples of state-enforced illegality. An important implication here is that the social experience of migrant illegality is much more fluid than suggested by the binary 'unlawful non-citizen' and 'lawful non-citizen' status articulated in the *Migration Act*. Some former detainees holding lawful BVE status lived in a state of incipient illegality as they were unable to comply with visa conditions. Others were known to immigration but were permitted to remain in the community without a visa. Release practices police a person's status by making release and continued lawful status (and thus stay in the community) conditional and subject to arbitrary controls.

For immigration, the High Court has long established that immigration detention is constitutional provided detention is reasonably necessary for a visa application to be considered or for removal to be effected.[135] Thus, even if visa conditions cumulatively amounted to a deprivation of liberty, the law would remain constitutionally valid if directed to those ends. The question of responsibility that conditional release from immigration detention raises is whether the state's creation of harmful conditions, coupled with the reliance and vulnerability of former detainees on the state, means that the state itself holds a legal duty of care to persons in the community that must be discharged. The institution of immigration detention does not exclusively define the experience of migrant illegality nor represent the sole forum of state violence, and thus should not set the limits for state responsibility. While this chapter has examined the conditions that make a person marginally lawful, the next chapter turns to a condition which determines substantive legal status – the requirement that all non-citizens be of good character.

135 *Chu Kheng Lim* v. *Minister for Immigration, Local Government and Ethnic Affairs* [1992] HCA 64; (1992) 176 CLR 1 [32]–[34] (Brennan, Deane and Dawson JJ).

5 Profiling bad character

> In a general sense I have formed the view that I have too much power. The act [Migration Act] is unlike any act I have seen in terms of the power given to the minister to make decisions about individual cases. I am uncomfortable with that not just because of a concern about playing God but also because of the lack of transparency and accountability for those ministerial decisions, the lack in some cases of any appeal rights against those decisions and the fact that what I thought was to be a power that was to be used in rare cases has become very much the norm. There is an industry in appealing to the Minister for Immigration and Citizenship, I have noticed ... there is a real sense of the appeal to the minister becoming very much part of the process. Rather than being a check on the system it has become institutionalised.[1]
>
> (Immigration Minister Chris Evans, 2008)

In the extract above, Immigration Minister Chris Evans addressed a parliamentary committee soon after he took office as part of the new Labor government after 12 years of a conservative Coalition government. The Minister expressed discomfort that the broad powers he held (including exclusion for bad character), which were intended only to address exceptional matters not adequately covered by visa rules, had become an ordinary part of migration process. The character test is a key mechanism that makes people illegal, intended to protect 'Australian values'.[2] Failure of the character test empowers the Immigration Minister or immigration to cancel a non-citizen's visa or to refuse to grant a visa, regardless of their length of residence in Australia.

The Immigration Minister has long held the power to refuse or grant a visa because of concern about a non-citizen's character.[3] But when Parliament passed

1 Evidence to Senate Standing Committee on Legal and Constitutional Affairs Additional Budget Estimates, Parliament of Australia, Canberra, February 19, 2008, 31 (Senator Chris Evans, Minister for Immigration and Citizenship).

2 Commonwealth, *Parliamentary Debates*, House of Representatives, December 17, 1992, 4121 (Gerald Hand).

3 See, for example, *Migration (Offences and Undesirable Persons) Amendment Act 1992* (Cth) s 180A, which was preceded by *Migration Regulations 1989* (Cth) regs 2(1), 4 ('*Migration Regulations*'). For a brief review of the legal history of the character provisions see *MIMIA* v. *Nystrom* [2006] HCA 50; (2006) 230 ALR 370, 405 (Heydon and Crennan JJ) ('*Nystrom* (2006)').

laws intending to strengthen the character provisions that commenced in mid-1999, it intensified the character provision as a particularly flexible and opaque method of exclusion. From that point onward, it took its contemporary label as a 'character test' and placed the onus of proof on non-citizens to satisfy the Minister that the person passes the character test.[4] The 1999 reforms also gave personal powers to the Immigration Minister, which became the subject of Chris Evans' concern ten years later. The reforms provided the Immigration Minister with personal powers to set aside tribunal decisions on character as well as intervene to make character decisions which were not subject to review. Upon its enactment, then Immigration Minister Philip Ruddock explained that his personal power was for 'exceptional or emergency circumstances'[5] (in line with the role of Ministerial discretions in migration generally). Yet during Ruddock's Ministership, use of the personal power became routine. In the period 2002–03, about 80 per cent of the character cancellation decisions were made personally by the Minister.[6] Subsequent Immigration Ministers made far fewer personal decisions on character; these accounted for 15 per cent in 2003–04, and 19 per cent in 2006–07.[7] Following the change of federal government from the Coalition to Labor in November 2007, despite the retention of such personal power, personal decisions by the Minister on character became almost non-existent.

It is a mistake to view the now negligible use of the personal powers of the Immigration Minister as indicative of the elimination or even reduction of discretion in character test practices. The textual openness of the character test allows it to be mobilised to target the production of illegality. Some of the targeting is directly evident on the face of the legislation; for example, the focus on categorically excluding non-citizens who have been sentenced to imprisonment for 12 months or more. Other targeting is evident from the practice of excluding individuals immigration has determined pose a defined kind of risk, including risk to security or of inciting discord, discussed below. The most open ground under the character test allows for exclusion if the Immigration Minister or delegate regards the person is not of good character because of their past and present criminal and/or general conduct ('general conduct provision').[8] The wording for this part of the character test has remained the same since the commencement of the contemporary character test in mid-1999, despite notable changes to types of crimes and the meaning of a 'substantial criminal history' in another part of the character test.

4 *Migration Legislation Amendment (Strengthening of Provisions Relating to Character and Conduct) Act 1998* (Cth), which came into effect June 1, 1999; Commonwealth, *Parliamentary Debates*, House of Representatives, December 2, 1998, 1229–30 (Phillip Ruddock).
5 Commonwealth, *Parliamentary Debates*, House of Representatives, December 2, 1998, 1230 (Phillip Ruddock).
6 Commonwealth and Immigration Ombudsman, 'Department of Immigration and Multicultural Affairs Administration of S501 of the *Migration Act 1958* as it Applies to Long-Term Residents' (Canberra: Commonwealth of Australia, 2006), 9.
7 Ibid., 10; DIAC, 'Annual Report 2006–07' (Belconnen, 2007), 113.
8 *Migration Act 1958* (Cth) s 501(6)(c) ('*Migration Act*').

This chapter develops the argument that 'nationality' has been utilised to particularise and stabilise the broad subjective discretion empowered by the general conduct provision in the character test. In the legal setting of tribunal decisions 'nationality' provides an ostensibly neutral basis for interpreting and organising disparate factors, making sense of subjective issues of credibility, and coming to a decision on character. In technologies utilised to profile the intent of visa applicants and entrants, nationality is an element that forms part of the basic building blocks profiling the risk that travellers will stay past the period authorised or will otherwise breach their visa conditions. Both the statistical and discursive links made between nationality and illegality highlight how nationality remains an important element in the gendered racialisation of immigration status. Here I am concerned with how law and technical expertise bolster the legitimacy of viewing illegality as having a national register, though my focus is primarily on how nationality and illegality is rendered in law. The legitimacy of nationality as a factor relevant to defining a non-citizen's 'character' is established by much more than what is examined in this chapter, given the significance of the nation-state as an organising principle in modern governance. But through a close examination of how nationality is construed to make sense of the honesty and character of visa applicants, the chapter explores how it is sustained and naturalised as a meaningful classification.

The argument unfolds in three steps. The first part of the chapter contextualises the general conduct provision within the function of the character test and as part of the broader legal regime regulating migration offences that government discourse refers to as 'visa integrity'. Here, through a legal frame, visa integrity is shown to be a moral issue of character, which is elaborated most fully through the character test. The second part reports on two ways general conduct decisions by the Administrative Appeals Tribunal ('AAT') harnessed nationality: first, as a way to assess dishonesty as a character trait; and, second, to inform tribunal decisions as to whether the deterrence was an appropriate matter to take into account in determining visa refusal or cancellation. The cases examined were selected from a review of 365 AAT general conduct decisions from July 1, 1995 to June 31, 2007, and demonstrate how and what stereotypes about nationality are established and perpetuated. While the first two parts of this chapter focus on the legal regulation of visa integrity, the third part situates the AAT findings in the broader visa integrity assemblage in which risk-profiling technologies play a vital part. By comparing the extent to which nationality plays a visible role in legal decisions and statistical risk-profiling practices, this part suggests that legal renderings of bad character bolster the authority and legitimacy of less visible statistical and algorithmic expertise of risk-profiling technologies. The chapter concludes with comments on character testing within the book's thematic explorations of discretion and authority for the violent effects of the law and policing of migrant illegality.

A legal test of character

Character exclusion in Australia performs two main functions: it polices the benefits of citizenship by making the test a visa requirement, and it protects 'Australian values'. In its power to force removal, the applicability of the character test to all non-citizens has been become 'a mechanism for reconfiguring established members of the community as aliens'.[9] The character test's role in this respect, as traced by Mike Grewcock, is evident from its historical trajectory as part of the criminal deportation regime. Law reform in the 1980s set limits on who could be deported because of their criminal history. Criminal offenders who had been lawfully resident in Australian for at least ten years could not be removed under the criminal deportation provision. This policy approach recognised that, after a certain period of residence, the state simply needed to accept that Australia had moulded and shaped the character of long-term residents, an issue that the government of the time viewed as particularly acute in the case of immigrants who had arrived as children. However, the introduction of character grounds for visa cancellation in 1992, and subsequent amendments in 1998 that specified a person would fail the character test if they had been sentenced to prison for 12 months or more, permitted cancellation of any non-citizen's visa regardless of length of residence. By 2002, visa cancellation on character grounds, which were unburdened by the ten-year residence restriction of the criminal deportation provision, had displaced criminal deportation as a measure to address non-citizen offenders.

A key problem addressed by character exclusion on the basis of a substantial criminal history is thus acutely directed towards policing the citizenship of long-term residents.[10] The applicability of the provision to long-term permanent residents, particularly those arriving as minors, has been the main critique of the provision in judicial and policy discussions.[11] In Australia and in other jurisdictions,

9 Michael Grewcock, 'Reinventing "the Stain" – Bad Character and Criminal Deportation in Contemporary Australia', in *Routledge Handbook on Crime and International Migration*, ed. Sharon Pickering and Julie Ham (Abingdon: Routledge, 2014), 124.

10 Ibid., 125; Michael Grewcock, 'Punishment, Deportation and Parole: The Detention and Removal of Former Prisoners under Section 501 *Migration Act 1958*', *The Australian and New Zealand Journal of Criminology* 1 (2011); Michael Grewcock, 'Multiple Punishments: The Detention and Removal of Convicted Non-Citizens', *University of New South Wales Legal Research Series* 41 (2009); Michelle Foster, '"An 'Alien' by the Barest of Threads" – The Legality of the Deportation of Long-Term Residents from Australia', *Melbourne University Law Review* 33 (2009): 504–7.

11 For judicial discussion, see *Nystrom* v. *MIMIA* [2005] FCAFC 121[27]; (2005) 143 FCR 420; *Nystrom* [2006] HCA 50 [2], [46], [66]–[69], [70], [74], [135], [161]–[169]; (2006) 230 ALR 370. For policy discussion, see: Commonwealth and Immigration Ombudsman, 'Department of Immigration and Multicultural Affairs Administration of S501 of the *Migration Act 1958* as it Applies to Long-Term Residents', 33, 44; Senate Legal and Constitutional References Committee, 'Inquiry into the Administration and Operation of the *Migration Act 1958*' (Canberra: Commonwealth of Australia, 2006), 295, see also 80–95; Australian Human Rights Commission, 'Background Paper: Immigration Detention and Visa Cancellation under Section 501 of the Migration Act' (Sydney, 2010); Human Rights and Equal Opportunity Commission, 'Submission to the Joint Standing Committee on Migration Inquiry into Immigration Detention in Australia' (Sydney, 2008), [60]–[68].

scholars have also argued that visa cancellation for criminal offending insults the criminal law principle against double jeopardy.[12] The argument is developed on two bases: that visa cancellation (and subsequent removal) institutes additional consequences to that imposed by the criminal justice system for the same offence, and that (at least for long-term residents) removal is a consequence so severe that it amounts to punishment.[13] The severity can be illustrated by a couple of significant cases. Most well-known is Stefan Nystrom, who had lived in Australia for more than 30 years having arrived aged 27 days, and was removed in 2006, after which it appeared that his mental health deteriorated and he became homeless. In a similar case, Robert Jovicic migrated to Australia with his parents at two years of age and was deported to Serbia at the age of 36 in 2004, a country to which he had never been and whose language he did not speak.[14] In November 2005, a year after his deportation from Australia, he was penniless, faced serious physical and mental health issues and, homeless and in desperation, slept outside the Australian Embassy in Belgrade. Jovicic later stated: 'I've explained to the embassy, if I am considered Australian trash, then I will rot on Australian soil'.[15] Jovicic's experience garnered a public profile in the media at a time when the issue of deportation of long-term residents was becoming controversial because of its harsh impacts. He was permitted to return to Australia in 2006, but lived in limbo on a temporary visa for about two years, which arguably performed a punitive function similar to deportation. As Grewcock rightly argues, criminal deportation via character-based visa cancellation 'increasingly is a vehicle for constructing citizenship as a privilege to be earned'.[16]

The character test has also provided a flexible provision to exclude people whose entry or stay is produced as controversial in some way. One of the most well-known examples is the 1993 exclusion of Holocaust denier David Irving, who was refused permission to visit Australia to promote his books on the basis that there was a significant risk his visit would be disruptive to a segment of the community.[17] In another example, in 2007, the Immigration Minister cancelled

12 See, for example, Grewcock, 'Multiple Punishments'; Michael Grewcock, 'Conviction, Detention and Removal: The Multiple Punishment of Offenders under Section 501 Migration Act', *University of New South Wales Legal Research Series* 49 (2009).

13 See Daniel Kanstroom, 'Deportation, Social Control, and Punishment: Some Thoughts about Why Hard Laws Make Bad Cases', *Harvard Law Review* 113 (2000).

14 The details of Jovicic's removal and return to Australia are derived from: ABC, 'Family Pleads for Deportee's Return', *Lateline*, November 23, 2005 (Margot O'Neill); ABC, 'Jovicic's Deportation "Disproportionate Punishment"', *Lateline*, November 23, 2005 (Tony Jones); ABC, 'Deportee Allowed to Return to Australia', *Lateline*, March 2, 2006 (Brett Evans); ABC, 'Jovicic Awaits Residency Decision', *Lateline*, March 9, 2006; ABC, 'Jovicic Asked to Apply for Serbian Citizenship', *Lateline*, March 10, 2006 (Tom Iggulden); Lindy Kerin, 'Jovicic's Permanent Residency a "Wonderful Surprise"', *ABC News*, February 23, 2008, www.abc.net.au/news/2008-02-23/jovicics-permanent-residency-a-wonderful-surprise/1051468.

15 ABC, 'Family Pleads for Deportee's Return'.

16 Grewcock, 'Reinventing "the Stain"', 133.

17 *Re David John Cawdell Irving and MILGEA* [1993] FCA 228; (1993) 115 ALR 125 ('*Irving* (1993)').

the visa of Gold Coast doctor Mohamed Haneef because of his association with his second cousins who had been apprehended in connection with the attempted car bombing of Glasgow airport passenger terminal. (Note that the Federal Court later reinstated Haneef's visa on the basis that the cancellation relied on an 'innocent' familial association that did not make Haneef of bad character.[18]) More recently, in 2015, anti-abortion campaigner Troy Newman was denied a visa because he presented a threat to good order.[19]

For controversial visa applicants or visa holders, the character test enables exclusion to symbolically communicate Australian values. At the time character-based exclusion was first introduced into legislation,[20] the then Immigration Minister explained: 'The power is intended to be exercised in a manner consistent with well-accepted Australian values, such that it is aimed at those persons who may regard entry to this country as a means to attack those values'.[21] The symbolic role of the character test was evident in papers placed before the Minister to assist consideration of one of David Irving's visa applications. An immigration officer's minute noted that community opposition to Irving's visit should not persuade the Minister to exclude because (as later summarised by the Federal Court) 'the Australian government had amply demonstrated its credentials on the Holocaust through long and expensive war crimes, investigations and trials … [and] racial vilification legislation recently drafted by the government'.[22] This statement illuminates a key function of character exclusion – its capacity to send a message to the public.

General conduct bad character: honesty and morality

In the cases examined where non-citizens were excluded because of their general conduct, some had been present in Australia for lengthy periods prior to their conduct coming into question, and thus the character test functioned to police their progression towards eventual citizenship.[23] Many general conduct cases justified exclusion on the basis that binding policy states that the behavioural expectations of the Australian community is a primary consideration, or in other words functioned to protect 'Australian values'.[24] However, the general conduct

18 *Haneef* v. *MIAC* [2007] FCA 1273; (2007) 161 FCR 40; 242 ALR 290 ('*Haneef*').

19 ABC News Online, 'Anti-Abortion Activist Troy Newman to Be Deported after Losing Court Bid to Stay in Australia', October 2, 2015, www.abc.net.au/news/2015-10-02/anti-abortionist-troy-newman-lose-court-bid-to-stay-in-australia/6823952; Transcript of Proceedings, *Newman-Mariotti* v. *MIBP* [2015] HCATrans 250 (October 1, 2015); *Newman-Mariotti* v. *MIBP* [2015] HCATrans 251 (October 2, 2015).

20 *Migration (Offences and Undesirable Persons) Amendment Act 1992* (Cth).

21 Commonwealth, *Parliamentary Debates*, House of Representatives, December 17, 1992, 4121 (Gerald Hand).

22 *Irving* [1993] FCA 228; (1993) 115 ALR 125, 131.

23 See, for example, *Jreige and MIMA* [1999] AATA 237 (April 7, 1999) ('*Jreige*').

24 MIMA, 'Ministerial Direction [No. 21] – Visa Refusal and Cancellation under Section 501' (August 23, 2001), [2.12].

provision has a more particular, consistent and definitive function in the protection of 'Australian values'. It almost exclusively deals with issues of 'visa integrity'. This includes the alleged provision of false information, statements and documents, or fraud, in migration processes.

By excluding people for administrative findings of fraud, the character test constitutes visa integrity as a matter of personal moral character. Given the increasing prominence of visa integrity regulation as a matter of technical determination through predictive technologies of 'intent management' and subsequent exclusion, the character test might be seen as an anomaly. But it is more accurate to regard the regulation of visa integrity as involving a hybrid form of regulation. It mobilises a mode of authority that Nikolas Rose and Mariana Valverde suggest has, since the mid-nineteenth century, 'frequently been established and defended through alliances between the different legitimacies conferred by law and expertise'.[25] In the broader array of legal provisions regulating visa integrity, the legitimacy conferred by the character test is derived from its selected targets, its role in a spectrum of calibrated consequences, and its nature as moral judgment.

The general conduct part of the character test provides broad grounds for exclusion. It enables exclusion on the basis of conduct that does not constitute an offence and does not require the person to have a criminal conviction. It states:

> a person does not pass the *character test* if…
>
> c having regard to either or both of the following:
>
> i the person's past and present criminal conduct;
> ii the person's past and present general conduct;
>
> the person is not of good character.[26]

The general conduct provision primarily seeks to address visa integrity. In his second reading speech for the 1998 introduction of the character provision in test form, then Immigration Minister Philip Ruddock positioned the character test as part of a broader program of border control, intended to send 'a very clear and unequivocal message that the immigration program is one of integrity'.[27] From 2001, legally binding policy guidance has directed decision-makers to focus on whether the applicant had been involved in activities indicating contempt or disregard for the law, such as breaches of immigration law, or had provided a bogus document or made a false or misleading statement.[28] From 2009, the rules were relaxed somewhat, with policy guidance that directed

25 Nikolas Rose and Mariana Valverde, 'Governed by Law?' *Social Legal Studies* 7, no. 4 (1998): 550.
26 *Migration Act* s 501(6).
27 Commonwealth, *Parliamentary Debates*, House of Representatives, December 2, 1998, 1243 (Phillip Ruddock).
28 Minister for Immigration and Multicultural Affairs (Cth), 'Ministerial Direction [No. 21]', [1.9].

decision-makers to consider whether the applicant had a history of *serious* breaches of migration law.[29] Today, character remains an essential part of the institutional networks that address fraud allegations for both prospective visa applicants and visa cancellations.[30]

The general conduct character provision is just one legal option among many if the Immigration Minister, delegate or tribunal member is satisfied that a person has breached immigration law. The wide range of options situates the consequences of character exclusion as more serious than other forms of administrative exclusion and as qualitatively different than criminal prosecution. In terms of administrative options, where the bona fides of a person's intent in Australia is not accepted, a visa may simply be refused on the grounds that the eligibility criteria have not been met. The Minister also has wide-ranging powers to cancel a visa for the provision of incorrect information or other grounds.[31] The same conduct may sustain exclusion for bad character; the difference is that the consequences are more serious. Character-based visa refusal or cancellation results in a three-year ban, with limited exceptions that permit, for example, grant of refugee protection and, for some cancellation grounds, reduction of the ban for compelling or compassionate circumstances.[32] Those whose visa has been cancelled because of criminal conduct face a permanent ban on return to Australia.[33] These other options underscore the seriousness of addressing a visa integrity issue using character exclusion.

A wide array of criminal provisions supplement administrative address of visa integrity issues. It is a criminal offence, for example, to provide a forged or false document, make a false or misleading statement, use a visa granted to another, or make arrangements to help a person obtain a relationship-based visa.[34] These offences are punishable by a maximum period of ten years' imprisonment and/or a hefty fine, equivalent to the penalty for the basic people smuggling offence,[35] again indicating seriousness of offence. However, immigration's policy is to refer only serious breaches of immigration law for prosecution,[36] which thus focus on offences such as people smuggling and passport offences such as damaging or dishonestly obtaining an Australian passport. The numbers prosecuted are small (in 2015–16 the Commonwealth prosecutorial service dealt with 42 summary and 176 indictable charges under the *Migration Act*)[37] and reflect

29 Minister for Immigration and Citizenship, 'Ministerial Direction [No. 41] – Visa Refusal and Cancellation under Section 501' (June 3, 2009), [7.3.2].

30 ANAO, 'Managing Compliance with Visa Conditions: Department of Immigration and Border Protection, Performance Audit' (Barton, 2015), 29–30, 37–8.

31 *Migration Act* ss 109, 116.

32 See *Migration Act* s 501E; *Migration Regulations* sch 4, Public Interest Criteria 4013, 4020.

33 Note that ban is lifted if the decision is revoked or the Minister personally grants a permanent visa: *Migration Regulations* sch 5, Special Return Criteria 5001.

34 *Migration Act* ss 234, 236, 240, 241.

35 *Migration Act* s 233A.

36 DIAC, 'Annual Report 2012–13' (Belconnen, 2013), 163.

37 CDPP, 'Annual Report 2015–16' (Canberra, 2016), 32.

that prosecution for minor matters is not a priority. Beyond prosecution, the labelling of particular breaches of immigration law as criminal offences plays a role in character test determination. Criminalisation of particular activities is used as a proxy to locate the seriousness of certain conduct and as evidence of community expectations.[38] Character exclusion enables an administrative mechanism to address visa integrity without the requirement to meet a criminal standard of proof, with profound consequences for those excluded.

The general conduct provision develops visa integrity as a matter of morality. The moral dimension is a feature of the character test more generally, even though the general conduct provision is the sole character test ground that explicitly requires the Immigration Minister to weigh up whether the conduct in question means a person is not of 'good character'. The otherwise absent stipulation of good character in other character test grounds moved counsel for the Immigration Minister Kevin Andrews to argue in 2007 that the title of the character provision, 'the character test', was 'just a convenient definition' and that a person can fail the character test because of their 'association' even if that association does not adversely reflect on the non-citizen's character.[39] However, the Federal Court rejected this argument. It is now settled that all parts of the character test entail character assessment, even when not explicit in the legislative text.[40]

'Character' has been interpreted in its ordinary sense to mean 'the enduring moral qualities of a person'.[41] Thus, while conduct 'may lay character bare very tellingly', even criminal conduct does not necessarily mean a person is of bad character.[42] One need not have an 'exemplary or saintly character' to be of good character;[43] rather, it is dependent on the 'aggregate' qualities of a person objectively assessed in accordance with ordinary community standards of good behaviour.[44] Nor is an assessment of character static. Rehabilitation and later conduct may demonstrate good character.[45] The AAT has emphasised the significance of truth in general conduct character matters, explaining:

> The observance of truth in dealing with officials in migration matters (particularly where the truth is known only to the person making the statement) is of fundamental importance to the control mechanism which

38 See, for example *Re Lachmaiya and DIEA* [1994] AATA 27, [34]; (1994) 19 AAR 148 ('*Lachmaiya*').

39 *Haneef* [2007] FCA 1273; (2007) 161 FCR 40; 242 ALR 290, 325 [204], [205], [230].

40 Ibid.; *Akpata* v. *MIMIA* [2004] FCAFC 65 (March 25, 2004) [103], [105].

41 *Irving* v. *MILGEA* [1996] FCA 663; (1996) 139 ALR 84, 85 ('*Irving* (1996)').

42 *MIEA* v. *Baker* (1997) 153 ALR 463.

43 *Re Strangio and MIEA* (1994) 35 ALD 676, 683–4 ('*Strangio*').

44 *Strangio* (1994) 35 ALD 676 [33]; see also *Lachmaiya* [1994] AATA 27 [33]; (1994) 19 AAR 148.

45 *Irving* [1996] FCA 663; (1996) 139 ALR 84, 85; citing *Re Davis* [1947] HCA 53; (1947) 75 CLR 409, 416; *Clearihan* v. *Registrar of Motor Vehicle Dealers in the Australian Capital Territory* (1994) 117 FLR 455, 461.

> this country exercises in visa applications when dealing with the many reasons for coming to Australia. To lie consistently, as Mr Lachmaiya has over a period of years, is to subvert the administration and, in the context of the Act to demonstrate that Mr Lachmaiya is not a person of good repute or good character. Australia can have no confidence that he would not again trangress in matters where truth and good faith could be deceptively withheld.[46]

The approach to the meaning of character set out above allows a person's wrongdoing to be understood in context, and in particular it appears important to notions of good character that a person disclose prior misrepresentations. For example, despite Antonio Strangio's failure to disclose his conviction for armed robbery in his initial three visitor visa applications, the AAT took account of the fact that he fully disclosed that conviction in his later spouse visa application. In the eight years since the offence took place, Strangio had only one other minor conviction mitigated by the circumstances, which informed the AAT's evaluation that he demonstrated low risk of recidivism and, coupled with persuasive evidence of his good repute, the AAT found Strangio was not of bad character.

Through this legal frame, visa integrity is rendered a deeply moral issue of character. The character test articulates breach of immigration laws as more than disobedience with a rule. It exemplifies what Michel Foucault traced as the secularisation of confession into governance in the eighteenth and nineteenth centuries wherein the government requires 'not just that the subject tell the truth but that he tell the truth about himself, his faults, his desires, the state of his soul'.[47] In reflecting upon the embedding of the 'ritual[s]of obedience, confession, and examination' in various border practices, Mark Salter highlights how the border trains mobile subjects to discipline themselves, to offer up 'the whole, entire, self-policing truth', a process he argues binds the mobile subject to the sovereign, albeit without bestowal of rights.[48]

However, the disciplining of mobile subjects is never complete; the examiner assesses and ascertains the 'truth'. In so doing, the examination involves facts that are the product of 'complex legal and organizational processes in which reality is socially constructed and reconstructed'[49] and are capable of multiple interpretations. The character test charges the decision-maker with determining whether the alleged conduct occurred, whether it amounts to bad character and, if so, whether the person should be excluded.

46 *Lachmaiya* [1994] AATA 27 [35]; (1994) 19 AAR 148.

47 Michel Foucault, *Ethics: Subjectivity and Truth: Essential Works of Foucault 1954–1984, Volume I*, ed. Paul Rabinow, trans. Robert Hurley (New York: New Press, 1997), 81; Mark B. Salter, 'The Global Visa Regime and the Political Technologies of the International Self: Borders, Bodies, Biopolitics', *Alternatives Global, Local, Political* 31, no. 2 (2006): 180.

48 Salter, 'The Global Visa Regime', 183.

49 Robert Baldwin and Keith Hawkins, 'Discretionary Justice: Davis Reconsidered', *Public Law* (1984): 581.

Immigration 'fraud' at the Administrative Appeals Tribunal

How do decision-makers make sense of subjective issues of credibility and come to a decision about a person's character? The analysis developed here draws on my research into matters finalised by the AAT involving review of character exclusion on general conduct grounds between July 1, 1995 and June 31, 2007. The AAT, discussed in Chapter 3, is an administrative tribunal that reviews immigration's primary decision on the character of non-citizens. The AAT's review of character decisions is conducted in a more formal manner than reviews of many other immigration and refugee matters. In particular, both parties appear at the hearing. This part of the chapter examines how nationality is deployed by tribunal members in making sense of people's alleged conduct and character, and appraises the kind of knowledge that tribunal members relied upon in investing nationality as an important tool for decision-making. Nationality stands out as a factor that is treated as relevant in both law and in statistical analysis for risk profiling, and is important to expose to closer scrutiny. Far from being a neutral marker, nationality is densely invested with racialised, gendered and class stereotypes. This analysis seeks to better understand how nationality has been utilised to navigate the vast discretion available in general conduct character matters. It does not argue that nationality or particular nationalities are always or usually viewed in the ways outlined below.

In the period studied, the AAT finalised 365 reviews of character exclusion on general conduct grounds. Analysis of these cases first charted some basic details for the entire case load: citizenship of the person whose conduct was in issue, the visa type sought, whether general conduct or criminal conduct (in the general conduct provision) was at issue, the type of conduct at issue, whether the decision involved visa refusal or cancellation, the decision-maker and the outcome. After reviewing a sample of about 30 cases, themes emerged that tied incentives for dishonesty to nationality, and indicated information networks were important in influencing 'deterrence'. Because deterrence emerged as a theme in almost 75 per cent of the cases, I identified words referenced in the sample to narrow down the selection. I added to the selection by searching for references to the cases in the sample that illuminated how the tribunal deployed nationality, and further cases concerning persons of the same nationality, and selected 72 to analyse in depth. Further cases are not directly referenced in the analysis, but informed the theorising.

This research found that almost all matters involving review of character exclusion on general conduct grounds concerned persons who were alleged to be dishonest (355, or 96 per cent), and that dishonesty was almost exclusively in relation to their dealings with immigration. Most of the alleged conduct at issue in these cases involved false and misleading statements,[50] and many cases

50 See, for example, *Morales and MIMA* [1996] AATA 741 (August 2, 1996); *Hamida Jalal and MIMA* [1997] AATA 292 (August 15, 1997); *Phan Van Xuan and MIMA* [1997] AATA 295 (August 18, 1997); *Read and MIMA* [1997] AATA 931 (August 25, 1997) ('*Read*'); *Edwards and DIMA* [1998] AATA 86 (February 13, 1998).

included submission of false documents,[51] staying past the permitted period,[52] illegal entry into Australia,[53] illegal work in Australia,[54] fraudulent application for refugee status[55] and contrived marriage.[56] Numerous cases involved more than one instance of dishonesty. Unless these instances of dishonesty resulted in criminal conviction, the tribunal treated them as matters of general conduct.[57] The conduct at issue in the matters unrelated to dishonesty regarded allegations of child abuse and domestic violence,[58] criminal charges[59] and past criminal conduct including drug-related offences.[60] Another defining feature of this caseload was that they overwhelmingly related to relationship visas. It comprised almost 75 per cent spouse or interdependency, almost 10 per cent parent/child/remaining relative, and about 5 per cent prospective marriage visas.

The period studied encompassed two consecutive articulations of the legislative requirements for character. Before June 1999, immigration was empowered to exclude if a person's 'general conduct' meant they were not of good character and, after June 1999, statute provided a person does not pass the character test if, having regard to their past and present criminal or general conduct, the person is not of good character.[61] However, the bulk of the matters continued to involve general not criminal conduct under this provision.

51 See, for example, *Joseph Annecchini and MIMA* [1997] AATA 153 (May 7, 1997).

52 See, for example, *Phuoc Tuong Tran and DIMA* [1997] AATA 436 (October 30, 1997) ('*Phuoc Tuong Tran*').

53 See, for example, *Kwong Leung Lam and MIMA* [1997] AATA 196 (June 11, 1997); *Vinh Tran and MIMA* [1997] AATA 463 (November 7, 1997) ('*Vinh Tran*'); *Novi Medyanto and MIMA* [1997] AATA 522 (November 28, 1997) ('*Novi Medyanto*'); *Cesar Torres and MIMA* [1997] AATA 565 (December 15, 1997); *Shirley Edwards and MIMA* [1997] AATA 591 (December 22, 1997) ('*Shirley Edwards*').

54 *Novi Medyanto* [1997] AATA 522 (November 28, 1997); *Shirley Edwards* [1997] AATA 591 (December 22, 1997); *Romeo and MIMA* [1998] AATA 87 (February 12, 1998) ('*Romeo*').

55 See, for example, *Romeo* [1998] AATA 87 (February 12, 1998); *Emmanuel Mariano Frijas and MIMA* [1998] AATA 773 (October 2, 1998); *Shukri and MIMIA* [2003] AATA 997 (October 3, 2003); *Natalie Kaufman and MIMA* [1998] AATA 897 (November 23, 1998); *Hongvilai and MIMIA* [2003] AATA 998 (October 3, 2003); *Brennan and MIMIA* [2003] AATA 1029 (October 13, 2003); *May and MIMA* [2000] AATA 480 (June 15, 2000) ('*May*'); *Gawronski and MIMA* [2000] AATA 790 (June 26, 2000) ('*Gawronski*').

56 See, for example, *Galang and MIMA* [1998] AATA 240 (April 3, 1998); *Perth City Mission and DIMA* [1998] AATA 457 (June 29, 1998); *Mohammed Hameed Khan and MIMA* [1998] AATA 475 (June 30, 1998); *Ostin and MIMIA* [2005] AATA 313 (April 8, 2005) ('*Ostin*'); *Higgins and MIMA* [1998] AATA 13 (January 19, 1998).

57 *Strangio* (1994) 35 ALD 676, [24].

58 *'Wag' and MIMA* [1996] AATA 264 (July 31, 1996); *Evans and MIMIA* [2004] AATA 171 (February 20, 2004).

59 *Fatma Ilbay and MIMA* [1996] AATA 459 (December 20, 1996).

60 *Ho Song Lu and MIMA* [1998] AATA 966 (December 16, 1998); *Jreige* [1999] AATA 237 (April 7, 1999); *Yusuf and MIMA* [2000] AATA 792 (August 11, 2000); *Konteh and MIMA* [2002] AATA 262 (April 18, 2002); *Stewart and MIMIA* [2004] AATA 1234 (November 22, 2004); *Basic and MIMIA* [2005] AATA 590 (June 10, 2005) ('*Basic*'); *Kertz and MIMA* [2006] AATA 247 (March 15, 2006).

61 *Migration Legislation Amendment (Strengthening of Provisions Relating to Character and Conduct) Act 1998* (Cth), enacted into *Migration Act* s 501(6)(c).

In some cases, applicants admit to an instance of dishonesty, such as entry on false documents, working without permission or overstay, but explain that their later marriage is genuine.[62] In other instances, review applicants maintain they have not been dishonest. In both scenarios, decisions about an applicant's candour involve significant judgment as to whether the applicant is dishonest in the first place, whether their conduct amounts to bad character, and whether failure of the character test should result in exclusion. Two strong themes emerged in the way that nationality was deployed in these cases: it was used as a basis to contextualise immigration history and credibility and to determine whether considerations of deterrence should influence the visa decision.

Profiling dishonesty as a nationality trait

The cases revealed that nationality-based stereotypes were used as a method of navigating the highly subjective terrain of credibility in scenarios of incomplete and often conflicting narratives. Nationality was sometimes used as a framework to conceptualise incentives for migration and migration fraud, the credibility of a person's knowledge of proper migration law and procedure, and whether their provision of false information or documents implied bad character. These three themes are detailed below.

First, in a number of AAT cases, the AAT interpreted the plausibility of non-citizens submitting fraudulent information within a framework of largely unstated assumed knowledge of the comparative economic conditions of foreign countries and Australia. One tribunal member, for example, used the term 'emigrant societies' to refer to countries including Thailand, the Philippines and South Korea.[63] The term is not used neutrally in the sense of the dictionary meaning of those countries from which a person 'leaves their own country in order to settle permanently in another',[64] which would include a wide range of states. Rather, it is used as shorthand to signal countries that provide many migrants to Australia, are comparatively poorer than Australia, and thus are countries where decision-makers perceive there is an incentive for persons to migrate to Australia for employment. The implication is that visa fraud is organised in 'emigrant societies':

> The Philippines has provided many migrants to Australia. As the evidence in this case shows, there is in that country an industry … that assists other Philippine residents to follow in their footsteps, if necessary by means of bogus passports and other documents.[65]

62 See, for example, *Vinh Tran* [1997] AATA 463 (November 7, 1997).

63 *Sorensen and MIMIA* [2006] AATA 96 (February 7, 2006) [29] ('*Sorensen*'); *Howard and MIMA* [2006] AATA 474 (May 31, 2006) [104] ('*Howard*'); *Lim and MIMIA* [2005] AATA 893 (September 15, 2005) [30] ('*Lim*').

64 Oxford Dictionary of English, *Oxford Dictionary of English (3rd edn)* (New York: Oxford University Press, 2010), current electronic version 2015, s.v. 'emigrant'.

65 *Howard* [2006] AATA 474 (May 31, 2006) [105].

The loaded terminology reflects the country classification utilised in some scholarly and policy migration discourse, which distinguishes between 'migration source countries' (broadly referring to poor countries and those in the Global South), 'countries of destination' (referring to rich western/northern counties', and 'transit countries' (through which migrants pass in their journeys). This language embeds assumptions about migrant desires to leave their home countries and conversely the desirability of 'destination' countries, though which countries are regarded as 'emigrant societies' depends on how the social, economic and political circumstances of those counties are perceived at any one time. In other cases, although the AAT has not used the phrase 'emigrant societies', the construction of the country of origin of the visa applicant carries the same connotations:

> The spate of spouse visa cases coming from the Philippines does not appear to be slowing. The reasons are not hard to discern. The Philippines is a poor country and Australia by contrast is a rich country which provides numerous benefits including social security, medical care and education.[66]

These decisions illustrate the deployment of stereotypes of the situation in particular countries and nationals from that country of origin. It is clear that tribunal members were comfortable to record their reasons in their written decisions, which suggests they viewed nationality as having a race-neutral register. However, the classificatory work undertaken in grouping some nations as desirous of emigration mostly on economic grounds, and crafting Australia as a desirable economically attractive destination, is racially coded. It fashions an image of 'emigrant societies' as structurally prone to illegal migration, sorting these nationals as the illegal other, while simultaneously inscribing the Australian state as victim. The examples discussed here illustrate Etienne Balibar's comment that 'the discourses of race and nation are never very far apart'.[67]

Second, in some cases, the AAT's construction of countries as 'emigrant societies' with its concomitant associations was instrumental in providing credence to the finding that an applicant *knew* that their actions were wrong. In *Sorensen*, for example, the tribunal asserted that: 'In emigrant societies such as Thailand, there are said to be strong communication networks conveying information about green cards, work permits, visas and other requirements for settling in the usual host countries'.[68] This statement informed the tribunal's funding that Poonsap Wanwongka's actions in applying for a visa in a street market, rather than at the Australian Embassy, showed she was aware that she was not engaging in lawful travel arrangements, and was instrumental to finding that she came to Australia as a 'knowing participant in some form of people

66 *Reyes and MIMIA* [2003] AATA 497 (May 30, 2003) [45] ('*Reyes*').

67 Etienne Balibar and Immanuel Wallerstein, *Race, Nation, Class: Ambiguous Identities*, trans. Chris Turner (London: Verso, 1991), 37.

68 *Sorensen* [2006] AATA 96 (February 7, 2006) [29].

smuggling operation'.[69] The resultant finding of multiple migration law violations eclipsed her explanations of the circumstances that led to her staying and working in Australia, which were not viewed as mitigating factors.[70]

In another case, the AAT found it implausible that Tae Doo Ban, an applicant for a contributory parent visa, did not know he was not permitted to work when he had arrived in Australia 17 years earlier.[71] The grounds for this finding were partly inferred from his personal characteristics at the time of his arrival as a 'mature man aged 34 … a successful businessman', and also from knowledge of Australian migration law that the AAT imputed to Ban as a person from an 'emigrant society'.[72] No evidence that South Koreans were actually aware of Australian law was put forward to base this finding.

> Especially in emigrant societies such as South Korea, from which many people migrate to western countries in search of work or business opportunities, there is today a considerable degree of public awareness about the importance and availability of green cards, work permits and similar documents. Mr Ban is an intelligent and enterprising man and it is not credible that he would have landed in Australia in 1988 with no idea about whether he was permitted to work or not or, if he was in any doubt on the point, that he had no idea how to go about obtaining information on the subject.[73]

The AAT also utilised identity, loaded with stereotypes, as an anchor to evaluate the veracity of visa sponsors' evidence in character proceedings. For example, in one case, an Australian citizen Jiang Shu Qin sought to sponsor her husband Wang Guo Zhang in a spouse visa application. The genuineness of the marriage was not in question. But immigration alleged that Wang had previously made false statements in relation to the visa on which he had entered Australia and in its subsequent extension, in a refugee application, and had also been unlawful in Australia for more than three years over three separate periods. At the hearing, Jiang gave evidence that she did not know the details of her husband's visa situation, but the tribunal regarded her responses as evasive and said:

> Given that Ms Jiang is *herself an immigrant*, and given also that visa matters are a *central topic of interest in migrant communities*, I think it most probable that she was aware of, or strongly suspected, Mr Wang's migration status from early in their relationship. She was undoubtedly aware of it by the time they were married in June 2003.[74]

69 Ibid., [29], [88].
70 Ibid., [69]–[70], [96].
71 *Lim* [2005] AATA 893 (September 15, 2005).
72 Ibid., [30].
73 Ibid.
74 *Jiang and MIMA* [2005] AATA 666 (July 12, 2005) [69] (emphasis added).

Jiang's 'immigrant' status as a naturalised Australian citizen is produced and made meaningful by the tribunal. By classifying Jiang as an 'immigrant', the tribunal drew in national origin again as a way to authorise 'common sense' notions about what an immigrant would know.

A large part of the tribunal's work in these settings involves deciding what people 'know', and when they are telling the 'truth'. The tribunal's evaluations of witnesses as forthright or 'evasive' is a significant kind of 'judgecraft'.[75] As a craft more than a science,[76] the skill set that judges bring to resolving legal disputes involves not solely legal knowledge. Judgecraft may involve managing civil litigation as a bargaining process,[77] and/or skilled time management of busy court lists (including switching between passive and interventionist modes to alternately expedite and pause in court matters to maintain the legitimacy of judicial decisions),[78] and also draws on accumulated personal and shared experience on the bench. Determinations of credibility or evasiveness fall very much in the latter realm of experience and the assumed knowledge called 'common sense'. One of the dangers of deriving impressions of witness honesty from a common-sense approach to physical and linguistic indicators is that indicators (such as lowered eyes or statements that the witness is not sure) are culturally specific, not universal.[79] Although psychological expertise exists (for instance, building knowledge of the non-linear recall and recounting of events associated with post-traumatic stress disorder),[80] this form of expertise was not primary to character decision-making, where social stereotypes and common sense prevailed in assessing credibility.

The third situation where nationality-based stereotypes were used to navigate credibility was where the AAT distinguished between applicants whose activities stemmed from a genuine fear of harm 'clutching at the offer of safe haven'[81] and those where all applicants 'wanted was to have a better life'.[82] This arose in cases where the AAT sought to determine whether a prior unsuccessful refugee visa application of the visa applicant was duplicitous and, if so, what weight to place

75 Herbert Kritzer, 'Toward a Theorization of Craft', *Social and Legal Studies* 16, no. 3 (2007); Nigel G. Fielding, 'Judges and Their Work', *Social and Legal Studies* 20, no. 1 (2011); Kathy Mack and Sharyn Roach Anleu, '"Getting through the List": Judgecraft and Legitimacy in the Lower Courts', *Social and Legal Studies* 16, no. 3 (2007).

76 Kritzer, 'Toward a Theorization of Craft'.

77 Fielding, 'Judges and Their Work', 100.

78 Mack and Anleu, '"Getting through the List"'.

79 Heather Douglas, 'The Cultural Specificity of Evidence: The Current Scope and Relevance of the Anunga Guidelines', *University of New South Wales Law Journal* 21 (1998); Ken Liberman, 'Ambiguity and Gratuitous Concurrence in Inter-Cultural Communication', *Human Studies* 3 (1980).

80 Jane Herlihy, Peter Scragg and Stuart Turner, 'Discrepancies in Autobiographical Memories – Implications for the Assessment of Asylum Seekers: Repeated Interviews Study', *British Medical Journal* (2002), 324.

81 *Priori and MIMIA* [2005] AATA 1288 (December 22, 2005) [50] ('*Priori*').

82 *Sorensen* [2006] AATA 96 (February 7, 2006) [97].

on that prior falsehood in assessing good character. Outside a specialised refugee status determination process this is a difficult distinction to determine and risks inadequate attention to the subjective circumstances faced by the applicant. It is well established in refugee law that economic deprivation can amount to refugee persecution, and that mixed motives such as a fear of harm and a desire for a better life, do not preclude refugee status.[83] Applicants may thus have mixed reasons for departing their home country, but nevertheless have lodged genuine – albeit unsuccessful – claims for protection.

The AAT's approach to the honesty of Filipina women who had unsuccessfully lodged refugee applications in the past suggests that evaluation of individual visa applicants was undermined by the tribunal's concern about the prevalence of fraudulent visa applications by Filipina women. The profile of Filipina women is discussed further in the next section, but here a case illustrates how nationality and gender provided a framework to distinguish the genuineness of refugee applications. In *Golding*, for example, the applicant admitted that one ground of her refugee application was false, but maintained the truthfulness of the other ground. In this case the AAT viewed the earlier refusal of refugee protection as support for the finding that the applicant's protection application was disingenuous:

> The evidence before me points to a desire, from the outset, on the part of Mrs. Golding to become resident in Australia. This arose purely for economic reasons and not for reasons of persecution. The Philippines may be a Catholic country and it may be that there is something of a stigma against single mothers, *but it is difficult to believe that there is actual persecution of what must, in this day and age, be a considerable number of citizens of the country similarly placed*. In any event, the single-mother ground did not amount to one which constituted sufficient ground for the grant of a protection visa.[84]

At the time of *Golding* it does not appear that a refugee claim on the grounds of being a single mother in the Philippines had been successful, but, since then, unmarried mothers of foreign national children have been found in some circumstances to be refugees.[85] But the apparent prevalence of false protection visa claims by Filipina women overshadowed Juliet Golding's explanation that at least one ground of her failed refugee application was genuine.[86] Coupled with

83 Michelle Foster, *International Refugee Law and Socio-Economic Rights: Refuge from Deprivation* (Cambridge: Cambridge University Press, 2007), 1; UNHCR, 'Handbook on Procedures and Criteria for Determining Refugee Status under the 1951 Convention and the 1967 Protocol Relating to the Status of Refugees' (1992 edn), [63]–[64]; *Chan Yee Kin* v. *MIEA* [1989] HCA 62; (1989) 169 CLR 379, 430 (McHugh J).

84 *Golding and MIMA* [2000] AATA 956 (November 2, 2000) [13] ('*Golding*') (emphasis added).

85 *1001289* [2010] RRTA 310 (April 21, 2010).

86 See, for example, *Golding* [2000] AATA 956 (November 2, 2000).

evidence of repeated migration offences, the tribunal found Golding was not of good character and affirmed refusal of her visa.

In contrast, in *Priori*, the otherwise 'reprehensible'[87] action of entering Australia using a false passport diminished in seriousness because the action was that of Franko Cenaj when he was a traumatised boy, 15 years of age, fleeing the war zone in Kosovo, who believed his parents had recently been killed and his home destroyed. In those circumstances, the AAT accepted that a person 'may lie out of fear without necessarily laying bare any enduring deficiency of integrity or character'.[88] It was important to the AAT that Cenaj had lodged a refugee application in his real name soon after arrival in Australia and did not conceal his method of entry and, although his protection claim was in fact refused, he did not fail the character test in relation to the prospective marriage visa he then sought. In this case, the AAT assessed Cenaj's actions in light of the circumstances as he subjectively perceived them. Despite coming to different conclusions on the character of the visa applicants, the AAT in both *Golding* and *Priori* relied on a common-sense appreciation of the applicant's intent. This kind of anecdotal knowledge, underpinned by stereotypes, provides an unstable footing in circumstances where the need for caution in dismissal of a genuine basis of refugee applications is particularly acute.

Profiling subjects for deterrence

The tribunal contemplated the deterrent effect of exclusion for failure of the character test on general conduct grounds in almost 75 per cent of the cases in the study cohort. Decision-makers were legally bound to take the general deterrent effect of visa refusal and cancellation into account in the period from mid-1999 until 2009, marking the bulk of the period studied here.[89] Yet it was a factor considered in some cases even before it was legally required.[90] Deterrence arose as an issue for consideration if the tribunal found that the applicant had failed the character test and was not of good character. At that point, the tribunal held discretion to decide if such failure should lead to the applicant's visa being refused or cancelled. To reiterate, deterrence did not have any role in determining whether a person was of good or bad character; rather, it was one of the factors considered in exercising the discretion to exclude.

Policy set out primary and other relevant considerations the tribunal was bound to take into account in deciding whether to exclude someone deemed to be of bad character. In assessing one of the primary considerations – the protection of the Australian community – the tribunal was required to consider 'the

87 *Priori* [2005] AATA 1288 (December 22, 2005) [43].

88 Ibid., [49].

89 MIMA, 'Ministerial Direction [No. 21]'; 'Ministerial Direction [No. 17] – Visa Refusal and Cancellation under Section 501' (June 16, 1999).

90 See, for example, *Phuoc Tuong Tran* [1997] AATA 436 (October 30, 1997); *Vinh Tran* [1997] AATA 463 (November 7, 1997); *Novi Medyanto* [1997] AATA 522 (November 28, 1997).

likelihood that visa refusal or visa cancellation would prevent (or inhibit the commission of) like offences by other persons'.[91] That is, the potential of exclusion for general deterrence. Policy stated that, while deterrence was 'not a conclusive factor in itself, general deterrence is an important factor'.[92] The tribunal was also required to consider the seriousness and nature of the conduct, likelihood that the conduct may be repeated, the expectations of the Australian community and best interests of any Australian citizen child of the non-citizen (or other child for whom there was a parental or other close relationship).[93] The requirement to consider deterrence established a site of authority that provided extensive latitude for immigration and the AAT to define who should be seen as potential migration offenders and thus prime subjects for deterrence and exclusion.

Deterrence is a key principle of punishment in criminal justice. General deterrence is engaged as a principle in sentencing when an offence is so serious that the severity of the sentence should take account of its practical and symbolic impact on discouraging similar behaviour by others. Its rationale is thus utilitarian and forward looking. The principle of general deterrence in criminal justice is controversial because it shapes punishment of an individual not on the basis of the actions of the individual concerned, but on their future impact on others. The argument developed here is that in the AAT's envisaging of the others intended to be deterred, the deployment of nationality to identify those 'others' invests in stereotypes that produce a gendered racialisation of immigration status. Several factors support the purchase and perpetuation of such nationality-based stereotypes: a symbolic rather than empirical approach to the utility of deterrence; an approach to deterrence that views the prevalence of migration offences by nationals of that country as significant; and the reliance on 'local knowledge' of immigration, which is anecdotal rather than technical. The deployment of stereotypes works to constitute whole countries as potential migration frauds, and some Australian citizens as 'immigrants'.

A symbolic role for deterrence

In many cases, the AAT gave weight to deterrence without considering the practical likelihood of the effect of exclusion on character grounds on deterring others from immigration wrongdoing. Instead, the AAT often viewed evidence that exclusion would achieve deterrence as evidenced by the symbolic function of the AAT decision itself in 'sending a message'. The rationale for taking deterrence into account in character exclusion for many tribunal members can be summed up as follows:

91 MIMA, 'Ministerial Direction [No. 21]', [2.11]; 'Ministerial Direction [No. 17]'.
92 MIMA, 'Ministerial Direction [No. 21]', [2.11].
93 Ibid.

> The deterrent effect of a particular decision is impossible to prove in advance and the concept is perhaps better expressed in positive form by saying that if bad behaviour is rewarded, there will be more of it. That is a principle well known to parents, teachers, managers and most other members of the community. It suffices to say that granting a visa in the present case would send entirely the wrong message to those contemplating acts violating Australian migration law.[94]

Far from being discomfited by the impossibility of predicting the deterrent effect, Walker DP, who repeated the above text in many of his decisions, favoured a broad-brush approach to deterrence. He stated in a later case that the incorporation of deterrence into binding policy direction 'may be simply a reflection of the need for decision-makers to consider the long-term effects of their decisions, not merely the short-term results'.[95] Thinking of deterrence in terms of its long-term effects allowed the AAT to view deterrence as relevant as a matter of general principle:

> It has sometimes been suggested that individual cases of visa application rejection do not become generally known in the community, and are thus of limited deterrent value, but I subscribe to the view that a consistency in approach by decision-makers soon *filters through to those persons who require permission to enter or stay in this country.* Knowledge that criminal or anti-social behaviour may jeopardise that prospect must surely act as a deterrent to such individuals in the same way that imprisonment and other penalties provide deterrence.[96]

For some members, character exclusion was important to maintain 'a visible probability of sanctions', and was influenced by the notion that higher penalties and the probability of punishment deterred the commission of crime.[97] But for others, the symbolic approach gave weight to deterrence even when the tribunal held the view it would not in fact deter:

> Deterrence is a major problem area in a case such as this. *I do not think that this decision will deter anyone in Korea currently embarking on much the*

94 *Sorensen* [2006] AATA 96 (February 7, 2006) [97]. See also *Golding* [2000] AATA 956 (November 2, 2000) [11]:

> It must be said that having regard to the very considerable number of matters involving women from the Philippines ... one has to wonder whether refusals do indeed have a negative effect. It may be that it is more apt to put the matter in the negative; that it is to say that the grant of a visa in these circumstances might send entirely the wrong signal.

95 *Rodgers and MIMA* [2006] AATA 723 (August 21, 2006) [93].

96 *Basic* [2005] AATA 590 (June 10, 2005) [25] (emphasis added).

97 *Re Sam and MIMIA* [2004] AATA 1003 (September 24, 2004) [31]; *Howard* [2006] AATA 474 (May 31, 2006) [103].

> *same path.* Recent experience involving Korea (and for that matter other countries) indicates that to live in Australia is so desirable that it is thought to justify dishonest conduct of any kind. Australia of course has the right to determine who can and who cannot take up residence in Australia. These are mere words, and having no real meaning to persons such as the Visa Applicant and her family. To grant a visa would on any basis send a message which would be grossly improper.[98]

Positioning deterrence in terms of its symbolic rather than empirical effect means that it may always be relevant and thus concentrates authority in the tribunal. Within this frame, the main question for the tribunal is whether the message that a person has been excluded for migration fraud would be heard among potential offenders and, relatedly, how to conceive of 'potential offenders'. These issues overlap. The sections that follow explore how the tribunal conceived the audience for a deterrent message in nationality and ethnicity-based terms, first, through construing networks of communication amongst nationals outside Australia and 'immigrants' within, and second, by particularising the 'nation' as the group identity of potential offenders by reference to the apparent prevalence of migration fraud in that nation. By conceiving of the proper subjects for deterrence in nationality-based terms the tribunal positions these nationals as potential 'illegals' and invokes a racial register for 'illegal' migration and migrant illegality in Australia.

Deterrence and 'immigrant networks'

There were many instances where the tribunal attributed importance to the consideration of deterrence based on the idea that networks of communication exist in 'emigrant societies' that would promulgate that immigration misconduct is met with exclusion.[99] The tribunal used the notion of 'emigrant societies' to make sense of the plausibility of a visa applicant's story, as discussed above. Here I show that the tribunal relied on various sources to establish the utility of deterrence based on the existence of such networks. These sources include cases that have come before the tribunal, information from immigration, and external publications. For example, in a case not yet mentioned, the AAT placed weight on the – at best, anecdotal – evidence of immigration staff at overseas posts that 'the Philippines community is generally very close knit and the fact of a visa refusal tends to become widely known'.[100] Another case noted that immigration staff at the Islamabad office advised 'there is an effective information network in

98 *Moon and MIMA* [2005] AATA 652 (July 7, 2005) [71] (emphasis added).

99 See, for example, *Ribarich and MIMIA* [2005] AATA 1014 (October 31, 2005) ('Ribarich'); *Sorensen* [2006] AATA 96 (February 7, 2006) [30]; *Howard* [2006] AATA 474 (May 31, 2006) [105].

100 *Tuipulotu and MIMA* [2001] AATA 451 (May 28, 2001) [11]; *Serifovski and MIMIA* [2005] AATA 241 (March 22, 2005).

Pakistan which quickly disseminates the latest intelligence concerning the operation of migration laws in Australia and other countries that accept immigrants'.[101] In another, immigration staff in Phnom Penh noted briefly that visa refusal would act as a 'general deterrent to the community who seeks to obtain benefits that they would otherwise not be entitled to through illegal means', and the tribunal was satisfied that refusal would circulate based on their knowledge that the visa applicant and sponsoring spouse both have family members in Cambodia and 'presumably relatives and friends of Ms Pin and Mr Hem have been made aware of the refusal of the spouse visa application'.[102] It appears little is needed to establish the notion of a network for circulation of a deterrent message. The tribunal made generalisations about the economic standing of the non-citizen's country of origin to authorise the significance of deterrence:

> Assisted by her sister, and with the aid of unscrupulous persons in Vietnam and Australia, Ms Lam has been involved in a sophisticated scheme to obviate the legitimate and planned migration program established in this country. Those engaged in the lucrative and growing business of migration fraud would take encouragement from a decision to allow Ms Lam to come to Australia, despite her proven wrongdoing. The cynical business of trafficking *in the plight of persons living in crushing poverty and deprivation in countries like Vietnam* may not be ended through a case like this, but it may well be deterred.[103]

In at least a couple of general conduct cases (but also cases on other character grounds), the AAT has supported its statements regarding the existence of immigration networks by reference to scholarly studies.[104] In *Sorensen*,[105] a case regarding a Thai visa applicant, the AAT relied on a study of family and community networks in Mexico–US migration as evidence of networks of communication about migration, without attention to the different social relationships in Thailand. It also referenced a text that theorised about migrant entrepreneurial networks with regard to the transmission of economic information for this purpose, yet did not acknowledge such networks might be distinct from networks that involve breaches of foreign law.[106] In fact, the latter study referenced

101 *Muhammed and MIMIA* [2004] AATA 878 (August 20, 2004) [59].

102 *Hem and MIMIA* [2004] AATA 645 (June 22, 2004) [34]–[35] ('*Hem*').

103 *Vinh Tran* [1997] AATA 463 (November 7, 1997) (emphasis added).

104 *Sorensen* [2006] AATA 96 (February 7, 2006) [29]; *Howard* [2006] AATA 474 (May 31, 2006); *Azar and MIMIA* [2005] AATA 1061 (October 24, 2005) [37].

105 *Sorensen* [2006] AATA 96 (February 7, 2006) [29] citing P. Winters, A de Janvry and E. Sadoulet, *Family and Community Networks in Mexico–US Migration*, vol. 99–12, Working Paper Series in Agricultural and Resource Economics (Armidale, NSW University of New England, 1999), 14–16.

106 *Sorensen* [2006] AATA 96 (February 7, 2006) [29] citing Ivan Light, Parminder Bhachu and S. Karageorgis, 'Immigrant Networks and Entrepreneurship', in *Immigration and Entrepreneurship*, ed. Ivan Light and Parminder Bhachu (New Brunswick: Transaction Books, 2004).

by the AAT undermines the AAT's finding about the applicant's knowledge of Australian migration requirements because it highlights that not all migrants exist within 'immigrant networks', and cautions against equating studies of one network with another, reminding that immigrant networks are the unique products of ideologies, cultures and beliefs.[107] The problem with reliance on studies that document the existence of immigrant networks in relation to migration fraud is that it cannot be inferred from an applicant's nationality that they might be involved in any such network.

The constitution of diasporic migrant and ethnic communities as vectors for information about illegal migration and migration controls, thus making them the proper audience for a deterrent message, was evident in many cases. The deployment of deterrence in these cases revealed a racialised construction of 'migrants' that produced migrants in relation to their ethnic affiliation (or, in Edward Said's term, their 'Otherness'),[108] rather than Australian nationality. It is a construction that contrasts with legal notions of naturalised citizenship and policy visions of belonging in a multicultural society. The effectiveness of deterrence here rested on the premise that knowledge of visa refusal would become known within ethnic communities in Australia of which the applicant is a member, and that ethnic communities have transnational communication networks about migration and migration fraud.[109]

In some of the cases, positioning the diasporic community as one that should properly be deterred from committing a migration offence was presented without even a tenuous connection to fraud, as indicated by this statement: 'In relation to deterrence, this decision might not be known in Pakistan but it will be known amongst the Pakistani community in Australia'.[110] In another case, community networks were evidenced simply by attendance at the hearing: 'As regards deterrence I note that to grant a visa would send entirely the wrong message to the Korean community (some of whose members were present on the third hearing day)'.[111]

In other cases, the importance of deterrence was established by ethnic affiliation or membership, coupled with general concern about the prevalence of fraud from a particular country:

> Such a message could be diffused through the migrant community's information networks … Mr Chen's evidence suggested that he had some contact with such a network, via the [Sydney organisation] Fujian Clansmen's

107 Light, Bhachu and Karageorgis, 'Immigrant Networks and Entrepreneurship', 26, 39.

108 Edward W. Said, *Orientalism* (London: Routledge & Kegan Paul, 1978).

109 See, for example, AAT cases in relation to the Bolivian, Pakistani and Korean communities in Australia: *Machin and MIMIA* [2005] AATA 187 (March 7, 2005) [102]; *Azad and MIMIA* [2005] AATA 185 (March 7, 2005) [76] ('*Azad*'); *Kim and MIMIA* [2005] AATA 239 (March 18, 2005) [123] ('*Kim*').

110 *Azad* [2005] AATA 185 (March 7, 2005) [76].

111 *Kim* [2005] AATA 239 (March 18, 2005) [123].

> Association. Given the incidence of fraudulent migration documentation emanating from China, it is desirable that wrong messages should not be sent in cases such as the present one [AAT case references omitted].[112]
>
> In the present matter, if the visa applicant's visa is refused, that would presumably become known to friends or acquaintances of Mr Bibashani, particularly those in the Albanian community in South Australia and in Albania itself. If a 'black market' for Australian visas has developed (or is developing) in Albania, the need to maintain a visible probability of sanctions is imperative.[113]

The 'common sense' that it is nationals from poorer countries that are likely to seek illegal entry invoked constructed dichotomies of countries as developed/undeveloped, destination/source which were also discussed earlier in their deployment to frame migrant incentive, and recur here in the tribunal's evaluation of the audience for a deterrent message:

> Sham marriages are a continuing problem in the administration of Australian migration law, and indeed the *experience is similar in all developed countries* that allow spouse migration. Refusal of a visa in this case is likely to be noticed in the Australian Russian community and possibly more widely.[114]

This approach adds a class component by identifying the problem of illegal migration as one that may be addressed by viewing diasporic communities in Australia connected to 'undeveloped' countries as the proper subjects for deterrence.

The AAT's constitution of diasporic ethnic communities in Australia as the audience for deterrent messages provides a strong example of the slippage between nationality-based classifications and racial or ethnic classifications. The racial underpinnings of nationality-based classifications were also apparent by the way that the AAT viewed the group identity of potential offenders as their nationality, rather than viewing the targeting of deterrent messages through the lens of potential fraudulent activity. This was assisted by instances where the tribunal figured the utility of deterrence by reference to the nationality-based prevalence of migration fraud.

Nationality and the prevalence of fraud

Deterrence was justified, either explicitly or implicitly, by reference to the apparent prevalence of fraudulent conduct by nationals of particular countries. Evidence of a high rate of overstay by citizens of Samoa,[115] a finding that while 'lying may be endemic in the culture of the Philippines, lying is not acceptable to the

112 *Guo and MIAC* [2007] AATA 1099 (March 6, 2007) [65].
113 *Bibashani and MIMIA* [2005] AATA 1207 (December 6, 2005) [54].
114 *Ostin* [2005] AATA 313 (April 8, 2005) [150] (emphasis added).
115 *Tautuliu and MIMA* [2000] AATA 968 (November 6, 2000) [19].

Australian community',[116] that 'applications containing false material are commonplace in Cambodia and that corrupt officials and unqualified migration "agents" compound the problem'[117] are some of the value-laden ways through which the tribunal has made it clear that the nationality-based prevalence of migration offending is relevant to character exclusion. What is often less clear in the decisions is the authority for these statements. Is prevalence a matter of the rate of breach/offence as a proportion of all visa applicants from that country? Does prevalence have a threshold rate that indicates its seriousness? These issues did not often arise in the tribunal decisions reviewed. What counts as 'prevalence' is overwhelmingly developed by reference to a mixture of common or assumed knowledge and a sense of expertise developed from on-the-job experience at the tribunal or immigration. For example, in one case, the tribunal simply explained that '[p]ast cases before the tribunal disclose a regular incidence of fraudulent applications and attempted fraud originating in China', which thus made deterrence important.[118]

The knowledge developed by immigration offices overseas was treated as providing a kind of specialised 'local knowledge' about the extent of migration fraud, suspicious identity profiles as well as the general character of the applicants. *Gawronski* and the preceding case of *May*, both decisions of Deputy President Chappell in 2000, exemplify this approach.[119] These cases relied on evidence submitted by Sally Reay-Young, the principal immigration compliance officer at the Australian Embassy in Manila at the time, and highly influenced the tribunal's weighting of the relevance of migration fraud prevalence to deterrence, particularly for Filipino visa applicants.[120]

In *Gawronski*, for example, the apparent prevalence of migration fraud provided a basis for viewing deterrence as an important consideration in deciding exclusion.[121] The AAT did not explicitly consider whether networks of migration fraud would promote the message of deterrence. The tribunal nevertheless found that the applicant's conduct

> must be viewed in the context of the convincing and authoritative evidence provided in Ms Reay-Young's statement about the pervasive nature of the

116 *Damakas and MIMIA* [2002] AATA 355 (May 16, 2002) [36] ('*Damakas*').

117 *Chau and MIMA* [2001] AATA 485 (June 5, 2001) cited by *Chim and MIMIA* [2002] AATA 1340 (December 19, 2002); *Lim and MIMIA* [2002] AATA 1341 (December 23, 2002); *Wei and MIMA* [2006] AATA 398 (May 8, 2006); *Yan and MIAC* [2007] AATA 1369 (May 25, 2007); *Hem* [2004] AATA 645 (June 22, 2004).

118 *Kaveh and MIMIA* [2004] AATA 1331 (December 14, 2004) [64].

119 *Gawronski* [2000] AATA 790 (June 26, 2000); *May* [2000] AATA 480 (June 15, 2000).

120 One or both of these cases were cited with approval in: *Golding* [2000] AATA 956 (November 2, 2000) [10]; *Peljha and MIMA* [2000] AATA 967 (November 6, 2000) [7]; *Wyatt and MIMA* [2001] AATA 29 (January 22, 2001) [16(c)]; *Batula and MIMA* [2001] AATA 496 (June 6, 2001) [8(f)]–[8(g)]; *Mungcal-Fabian and MIMIA* [2003] AATA 362 (April 22, 2003) [64]–[65]; *Reyes* [2003] AATA 497 (May 30, 2003) [43], [45].

121 *Gawronski* [2000] AATA 790 (June 26, 2000) [39].

> false claims made by Filipino citizens for protection visas in order to allow them to remain in Australia for economic and allied reasons.[122]

In *Gawronski*, the tribunal treated the evidence of Reay-Young that Manila was viewed as a high-risk source of fraudulent visa applications as authoritative because she had dealt with over 1000 visa applications. Reay-Young presented a particular suspect profile from the Philippines:

> Ms Reay-Young said there was a strong culture of working overseas to remit money back to the Philippines and one of the major issues she confronted in her duties in regard to visitor applications to Australia was that people claimed that they were going to Australia to visit family. They were often sponsored by their family members and then attempted to find employment in Australia. In her statement, Ms Reay-Young said:
>
>> One of the most common ways for Filipinos to obtain permission to work is to apply for a protection visa. Most typically the applicant lodges a review with the RRT if the application is refused and then seeks Ministerial intervention under section 417 of the Migration Act. The whole process takes approximately two years. It is interesting to note that only three protection visa applications lodged by Philippine nationals were granted in 1996–97 and none in subsequent years.
>>
>> Upon return to the Philippines many previous PV applicants will apply for migration to Australia on spouse grounds. 97 per cent of these have admitted that they willingly submitted false claims through the whole protection visa process to obtain permission to work. Whilst some advised that their agent persisted with the preparation of the application most admit that they know that they are applying for refugee status and that they will do anything to be able to work in Australia.[123]

Even earlier, in the mid-1990s, at least some migration officers in the Manila office and the Australian High Commission in Singapore were 'very suspicious and cautious about female Filipinos wishing to enter Australia in general'.[124] Although AAT decision-making is not bound by precedent of factual interpretation, whether by departmental officers or fellow tribunal members, the AAT placed weight on its prior acceptance that single Filipina women with a particular immigration history are subjects in need of deterrence. In *Reyes*, for example, the AAT formed the view that '[t]o grant a visa in the face of conduct such as this would send entirely the wrong message' and went on to say:

> Many of the cases coming before me have a *common theme*; a young and single woman obtains a visitor's visa. She enters Australia and starts working

122 Ibid., [44].
123 Ibid., [37]–[38].
124 *Read* [1997] AATA 931 (August 25, 1997) [23].

> within a short period; within one month she applies for a protection visa on grounds which are spurious. The refusal of a protection visa leads to an appeal to the RRT and when that fails, there is a further application to the Respondent [the Immigration Minister] under section 417 of the Act. Marriage occurs a short time before she returns to the Philippines.[125]

False protection (that is, refugee) applications attract particular ire; as the tribunal noted in the oft-cited passage in *Gawronski*, false claims to obtain the right to work and residency are 'an affront to these displaced persons, as well as to the Australian community at large'.[126] But the rationale for the significance of deterrence was the prevalence of fraud, set out as a particular fraud profile. Even in cases where deterrence was held to be less important, the tribunal still conceived this in terms of nationality-based prevalence of fraud, stating, for instance, in *Hegarty*: 'There was no evidence to suggest there is a wide-spread practice of Peruvians coming to Australia on false passports, making this factor less of a concern'.[127]

Against deterrence

A contrary stream of cases were sceptical of the potential deterrent effect of exclusion, viewing it as 'only … a matter of speculation',[128] and as 'quite incapable of demonstration'.[129] The likelihood of deterrence suffers from the defect that it relies on whether the visa applicant will reveal the reason for their return,[130] the cultural attitudes to a person's return (which pertaining to the return of an expectant mother to Cambodia was accepted would 'be seen by the community in Cambodia as a result of her failing to be a good spouse'),[131] and the ability of unscrupulous agents to rationalise a person's return without reference to falling foul of Australia's migration laws.[132] In some cases, even if the AAT was prepared to accept that networks of communication about migration might exist in a particular country, it found considerations of deterrence ought to be given little weight if there was nothing to link the visa applicant with persons who shared information about migration or migration fraud, or who intended to enter Australia by violating the *Migration Act*.[133]

125 *Reyes* [2003] AATA 497 (May 30, 2003) [45] (emphasis added).
126 *Gawronski* [2000] AATA 790 (June 26, 2000) [45].
127 *Hegarty and MIMA* [2001] AATA 421 (May 18, 2001) [14].
128 *Konteh and MIMA* [2000] AATA 291 (April 14, 2000) [25].
129 *Esguerra and MIMA* [2000] AATA 554 (July 6, 2000) [24] ('*Esguerra*').
130 *Mahoni and MIMIA* [2004] AATA 465 (May 12, 2004) [109].
131 *Ly and MIMA* [2000] AATA 339 (April 28, 2000) [78] ('*Ly*').
132 Ibid., [79].
133 *Ribarich* [2005] AATA 1014 (October 31, 2005); *Sorensen* [2006] AATA 96 (February 7, 2006) [70]; *Yap and MIMA* [2006] AATA 510 (June 13, 2006) [54]. Conversely, see cases where the AAT found deterrence was an important factor because there was some evidence of the applicant's link to fraudulent activity, for example, *Peng and MIMIA* [2003] AATA 991 (October 2, 2003); *Vinh Tran* [1997] AATA 463 (November 7, 1997); *Novi Medyanto* [1997] AATA 522 (November 28, 1997).

A number of cases specifically rejected the notion that the prevalence of fraud in the applicant's country of nationality should affect assessment of the likelihood of a deterrent effect. In *Esguerra*, a case decided shortly after *Gawronski* and *May*, a differently constituted tribunal dismissed the value of a substantively similar submission by Reay-Young on migration fraud in the Philippines.[134] In cross-examination Reay-Young explained much of the statement was based on anecdotal statements made by others, and the tribunal regarded the evidence as of uncertain statistical reliability and as prejudicial because it could not be tested.[135] *Esguerra* not only rejected the apparent prevalence of fraud in the Philippines reported in *May*, *Gawronski* and other cases, it also rejected the premise that the prevalence of fraud has any relevance in determining deterrence at all. The tribunal said:

> The document has a value, no doubt, as an intelligence report to compliance authorities in the Department. As a piece of evidence in dealing with an application by an individual seeking to review a Departmental decision, it has no value.[136]

The tribunal's reflections in *Esguerra* underscore the dangers of reifying stereotypes as a source of knowledge informing the value of deterrence. Similarly, in *Ribarich*, the tribunal rejected the relevance of the immigration statement that the

> Islamabad caseload is characterised by a high rate of attempted fraud and false claims and identities. The culture in Pakistan encourages sharing of all personal information and it is generally the case that applicants share information on visa applications and decisions with a wide range of people

to the issue of deterrence.[137] The tribunal cautioned that

> there is nothing which links Mr Ahmad to persons who do share or exchange such information (if such persons do exist). Mr Ahmad must be treated on his merits, based on his circumstances, and his character. It is not fair or correct to assess his character by regard to him as a member of a nationality or class of persons.[138]

In 2009, a new binding policy was issued by the Immigration Minister which removed consideration of deterrence for character exclusion, and a further

134 *Esguerra* [2000] AATA 554 (July 6, 2000) [21]–[25].
135 Ibid.
136 Ibid., [25].
137 *Ribarich* [2005] AATA 1014 (October 31, 2005) [12].
138 Ibid., [70].

iteration in 2014 did not reincorporate deterrence.[139] However, the stereotypes deployed in the discussion above might equally be mobilised in the requirements decision-makers are bound to consider today. In assessing the primary consideration of the 'protection of the Australian community', decision-makers must consider the seriousness and nature of the non-citizen's conduct and the risk to the Australia community that the conduct or other serious conduct may be repeated.[140] These and other considerations potentially sustain similar stereotypical assumptions as is seen, for example, in the tribunal's focus on the prevalence of migration fraud in particular national settings.

In drawing attention to the cases discussed here, my argument is not that the AAT's particular factual findings of migration fraud are unreliable, an argument that would be limited because this analysis relies on the AAT decision records, not the whole range of evidence before the AAT. I have sought rather to unpack how the category of nationality has been deployed to authorise and defend the AAT's analysis of a person's character and the utility of deterrence in the matters discussed here, and to show how nationality is not a neutral marker of identity.

The persistence of common and experiential knowledge in character-based decisions in tribunal settings illustrates Mariana Valverde's contention that the 'expert domination' of what she calls 'high-status' knowledges, such as psychiatry, medicine and statistics, remains limited in socio-legal settings.[141] AAT character determination is not unique in this respect. Research on the Australian Refugee Review Tribunal suggests utilisation of stereotypes is a normal mode of tribunal operation. For example, the grasp of sexuality-based narratives was found to be constrained by the tribunal's linear approach to understanding the development of sexual identity,[142] culturally specific Westernised notions of homosexuality,[143] evidentiary practices that sustained homophobic stereotyping,[144] and the importance that assessment of the credibility of claimed sexuality, sometimes poorly grounded, played in refugee determination.[145] Given the remit of tribunals as merits-based review,

139 MIAC, 'Ministerial Direction [No. 41]', MIBP (Cth), 'Ministerial Direction [No. 65] – Visa Refusal and Cancellation under Section 501 and Revocation of a Mandatory Cancellation of a Visa under Section 501CA' (December 22, 2014).

140 MIAC, 'Ministerial Direction [No. 41]', [10.1]; MIBP, 'Ministerial Direction [No. 65]', [9.1].

141 Mariana Valverde, *Law's Dream of a Common Knowledge* (Oxford: Princeton University Press, 2003), 2–3.

142 Laurie Berg and Jenni Millbank, 'Constructing the Personal Narratives of Lesbian, Gay and Bisexual Asylum Claimants', *Journal of Refugee Studies* 22, no. 2 (2009).

143 Jenni Millbank, 'From Discretion to Disbelief: Recent Trends in Refugee Determinations on the Basis of Sexual Orientation in Australia and the United Kingdom', *The International Journal of Human Rights* 13, no. 2 (2009).

144 Catherine Dauvergne and Jenni Millbank, 'Burdened by Proof: How the Australian Refugee Review Tribunal Has Failed Lesbian and Gay Asylum Seekers', *Federal Law Review* 31 (2003).

145 Jenni Millbank, '"The Ring of Truth": A Case Study of Credibility Assessment in Particular Social Group Refugee Determinations', *International Journal of Refugee Law* 21, no. 1 (2009).

their disposition as forums where common knowledge shapes decision-making is unlikely to change.

Nationality, authority and risk profiling

This last part of the chapter positions the legal determination of character in its relation to the technological risk-profiling practices that contribute to the identification of potential character concern. Discussion of statistical and algorithmic profiling has not featured in the book thus far because the primary focus has been on policing and legal responsibility for arrest, raids and release from detention. But technical expertise plays a huge part in the policing of migrant illegality. As explicitly advertised and promoted by government, the legal framework of the universal visa system is part of a 'layered' border management system that manages mobile subjects by 'pushing the border offshore'.[146] It is not possible to do justice to the role of predictive risk management in migration, but it is necessary to at least position character determination within the domain of technical expertise because, in this area of migration law, the role of technical expertise in 'front-end' filtering is particularly acute. What I am interested in is how the contrasting registers of visibility in law and expertise produce authority. So far, the book has traced different sites where the low visibility of legal and policing practices have been important to how these practices have sustained their authority, even in the face of legal rhetoric which would mask their violent effects. Here I suggest that the highly visible legal renderings of character contribute to the authority of the less visible statistical and algorithmic expertise of risk-profiling technologies. Before turning to this argument, I set out the procedural relationship between risk-profiling technologies and character determination.

Pre-law character concern

Few people are excluded on character grounds each year despite immigration and tribunal decisions making findings that statements made by applicants lack credibility, suggesting a great deal of selection is involved in identifying who might be of concern to migration law's character test. Immigration grants about 4.3 million visas each year[147] and, at any one time, about 1.4 million non-citizens are present in Australia, all of whom are required to meet the character test.[148] But in the period 1996–2014 immigration rarely excluded more than

146 DIMIA, 'Managing the Border: Immigration Compliance' (Belconnen, 2004).

147 DIAC, 'Annual Report 2009–10' (Belconnen, 2010), 2. Note this number has since increased with 7.2 million temporary visas granted in 2014–15: Department of Immigration and Border Protection, 'Annual Report 2014–15' (Belconnen, 2015), 5.

148 ANAO, 'Administering the Character Requirements of the *Migration Act 1958* Department of Immigration and Citizenship' (Barton, 2011), 13.

250 people on character grounds each year.[149] In 2014–15, the number of character exclusions dramatically rose to 723 due to a range of law reforms that broadened the grounds for failure of the character test (including for conviction for offences committed during or after an escape from immigration detention and reasonable suspicion of involvement in particular crimes regardless of the absence of a conviction), and mandated visa cancellation for certain types of criminal sentences, leaving little room for discretion to revoke the decision.[150]

Since about 2007, relatively clear avenues have existed to identify potential failure of the character test due to a criminal sentence of one year or more (the 'substantial criminal history' ground) – primarily relying on referrals from police, prisons and non-citizens' submissions of criminal history certificates as part of visa applications.[151] In contrast, the process for identifying people of character concern on other grounds has been neglected by immigration.[152] It remains remarkably unsystematic and uncoordinated. The cases that came to the AAT provide insight into how they were initially identified as raising potential character concern. People had admitted prior immigration misconduct, had an immigration history that documented periods in Australia without a visa or other breaches, or immigration had found their prior visa application lacked plausibility and involved false statements. Given that visa applicants at the AAT were seeking a further visa application, generally either a permanent visa or a provisional visa en route to a permanent visa, it is reasonable to expect that the officers handling these applica-

149 DIMA, 'Annual Report 1996–97' (Canberra, 1997) Sub-program 8.1 Investigation and Compliance, Character provisions; DIMA, 'Annual Report 1997–98' (Canberra, 1998), Sub-program 2.4 Border Control, Character requirements; DIMA, 'Annual Report 1998–99' (Canberra, 1999), Program 1 Border Control and Compliance, Character requirements; DIMA, 'Annual Report 1999–00' (Canberra, 2000), Output 1.3 Enforcement and Immigration Law, Character; DIMIA, 'Annual Report 2001–02' (Canberra, 2002) [1.3.4]; DIMIA, 'Managing the Border: Immigration Compliance 2004–05 Edition' (Belconnen, 2005), 45, 79, 83; DIMIA, 'Annual Report 2005–06' (Canberra, 2006), 146; DIAC, 'Annual Report 2006–07' (Canberra, 2007), 113; DIAC, 'Annual Report 2007–08' (Canberra, 2008), 113; DIAC, 'Annual Report 2008–09' (Canberra, 2009), 124; DIAC, 'Annual Report 2009–10' (Canberra, 2010), 157; DIAC, 'Annual Report 2010–11' (Canberra, 2011), 160; DIAC, 'Annual Report 2011–12' (Canberra, 2012), 174; DIAC, 'Annual Report 2012–13' (Canberra, 2013), 163; DIBP, 'Annual Report 2013–14' (Canberra, 2014), 169; DIBP, 'Annual Report 2014–15' (Canberra, 2015), 159.

150 The *Migration Amendment (Character and General Visa Cancellation) Act 2014* (Cth) commenced on December 11, 2014 and inserted provisions including ss 501(3A), 501(3B), 501CA, 501BA into the *Migration Act*.

151 See ANAO, 'Administering the Character Requirements', 60–1; Commonwealth and Immigration Ombudsman, 'Department of Immigration and Multicultural Affairs Administration of S501 of the *Migration Act 1958* as it Applies to Long-Term Residents', 20, 40; DIAC, 'Annual Report 2011–12' (Belconnen, 2011), 150; DIBP, 'Annual Report 2013–14' (Belconnen, 2014), 248.

152 ANAO, 'Administering the Character Requirements', 14, 18. For example, ANAO reviewed preliminary assessments of 639 visa holders by the immigration's National Character Consideration Centre in 2009–10 and identified 65 cases, some involving really serious harm or the supply and manufacture of drugs, which, although they did not meet the threshold of a sentence of at least one year, potentially warranted further assessment for character test failure based on the visa holder's past and present criminal conduct.

tions flagged them as raising potential character concern. Identification of visa applicants' immigration histories would have been assisted by checks of risk management technologies such as the automated risk-profiling system the Safeguards System ('Safeguards') or the Border Risk Identification System ('BRIS'), which analyses huge amounts of data from multiple systems to predict the intent of travellers. These technological practices play an important role in what David Lyon neatly termed 'social sorting',[153] distinguishing between those deemed 'legitimate'/'trusted'/'low risk', while at the same time managing resources to concentrate on those deemed 'illegitimate'/'distrusted'/'high risk'.[154]

The classificatory exercise performed by algorithmic expertise is commonly presented as involving a rational discrimination not subject to the human foibles of prejudice. In reality, scholarly studies have amply demonstrated that the expertise produced through risk-management technologies is never completely automated or isolated from the human inflected interpretation. The values of designers are encoded into the very risk categories and objectives and even the technical capacity of a whole range of technologies involved in risk tiering – from algorithmic calculative, biometric inscription to geolocation.[155] Moreover, officials' use of technology inevitably brings a human element into the risk-tiering process, not least as noted in the use of Safeguards in Australia because officers may be aware that information in the database is outdated or the action to be taken following a profile match may be unclear.[156] In other words, the 'reality is a far messier mix of technical and human curating'.[157] Despite this, risk-profiling technologies retain a strong authority because they present risk as a technical rather than political issue and position classification and discrimination as 'rational'.

153 See, for example, David Lyon, *Surveillance Society: Monitoring Everyday Life* (Buckingham: Open University Press, 2001).

154 See, for example, Louise Amoore, 'Biometric Borders: Governing Mobilities in the War on Terror', *Political Geography* 25 (2006): 340; Tamara Vukov, 'Target Practice: The Algorithmics and Biopolitics of Race in Meerging Smart Border Practices and Technologies', *Transfers* 6, no. 1 (2016); Peter Adey, 'Facing Airport Security: Affect, Biopolitics, and the Preemptive Securitisation of the Mobile Body', *Environment and Planning D: Society and Space* 27 (2009).

155 See, for example, Browne's discussion of facial scan technology in airports which she argues enacts 'epidermal thinking' by being optimised towards 'lighter skin' and thus has higher fail rates for others leading to greater intervention: Simone Browne, 'Digital Epidermalization: Race, Identity and Biometrics', *Critical Sociology* 36, no. 1 (2010); see also Vukov, 'Target Practice'.

156 Commonwealth and Immigration Ombudsman, 'Department of Immigration and Citizenship: The Safeguards System' (Canberra, 2008), 7. For the US, see Janet Gilboy, for example, writing about her observational work of immigration inspectors at an airport. Gilboy noted that inspectors work from the understanding that intelligence records are incomplete, dated and unreliable and, given language difficulties are a disincentive to pursue questioning of travellers, 'inspectors tend to rely on what they know about similar types of travellers to guide their decisions', in particular relying on nationality: Janet A. Gilboy, 'Deciding Who Gets In: Decisionmaking by Immigration Inspectors', *Law and Society Review* 25, no. 3 (1991): 580.

157 Cynthia Dwork and Deidre K. Mulligan, 'It's Not Privacy, and It's Not Fair', *Stanford Law Review* (2013), www.stanfordlawreview.org/online/privacy-and-big-data/its-not-privacy-and-its-not-fair.

Public access to risk profiles – a history

As risk profiles have become a more important mechanism for predicting travellers' actions, public access to the basis for risk profiles, in particular the nationality basis, has diminished. This suggests the Australian government has a particular and increasing unease in relation to the release of nationality-based risk profile information. It is perhaps not surprising that the shift in transparency charted below – from Risk Factor List to Safeguards and the BRIS – also tracks a transition from a legal to a technological mechanism of risk, and I will return to this point below.

The Risk Factor List ('RFL'), operational in the period 1991–2009, was considered a new and 'bold control experiment'.[158] It was the first time risk profiles were used as a tool to predict and 'prevent temporary entrants who may be potential overstayers or residence applicants from entering Australia'.[159] Initially it was directed to identify the risk that people would stay past their visa expiry and become unlawful non-citizens; later it also accounted for those who did not return after their entry visa (because for example they obtained a further visa); and even later removed all European listings.[160]

During its operation, the form of the RFL ensured the basis of risk was visible in a way that it is not today. The RFL formulated crude profiles based on just three factors – nationality, gender and age characteristics – all specified in the form of a table. The RFL was issued by the Minister, and its four iterations were published in the form of a list by government *Gazette*.[161] The RFL operated as part of a legislative instrument that placed the onus on applicants who fitted the profile to satisfy decision-makers there was very little likelihood they would remain after their visa expired.[162] In other words, those listed faced a higher bar for visa grant. The legislative basis for the RFL meant failure to satisfy immigration provided grounds for visa refusal.

The statistical basis of the RFL sought to address perceived concerns that offshore posts were discriminatory in identifying persons likely to stay past their

158 Kathryn Cronin, 'A Culture of Control: An Overview of Immigration Policy-Making', in *The Politics of Australian Immigration*, ed. James Jupp and Marie Kabala (Canberra: AGPS, 1993), 96.

159 Ibid.

160 MIMA, *'Public Interest Criteria – Risk Factor', Migration Regulations* reg 1.17, sch 4, para 4011(2)(b), December 12, 2000; MIAC, *'Class of Persons – Public Interest Criteria – Risk Factor (Paragraph 4011(2)(b)' Migration Regulations* reg 1.17, sch 4, para 4011(2)(b), IMMI 08/033, May 12, 2008; MIAC, *'Class of Persons – Public Interest Criteria – Revocation of Risk Factor List (Paragraph 4011(2)(b)'* in Commonwealth Government *Gazette*, Legislative Instrument Number F2009L01316, IMMI 08/119, May 15, 2009. See also Commonwealth and Immigration Ombudsman, 'The Safeguards System', 9, 14; Philip Ruddock (Minister for Immigration and Multicultural and Indigenous Affairs), 'Community Leaders Encouraged to Help with Visa Compliance Media Release, MPS 55/2003', Media release, August 27, 2003.

161 *Migration Regulations* sch 4, Public Interest Criteria 4011; Commonwealth and Immigration Ombudsman, 'The Safeguards System', 9–10.

162 Since the demise of the RFL, this higher bar applies to applicants deemed a risk because they have applied for a visa to permanently reside in Australia in the past five years: *Migration Regulations* sch 4, Public Interest Criteria 4011.

visa period,[163] and represented an early method whereby nationality, gender and age were established as authoritative factors for distinguishing who should be permitted in Australia. Yet the infrequent updates of the RFL led to decisions based on outdated data, allegations of unfairness should an applicant be 'unable to ascertain that he has this evidential burden',[164] and it was disbanded in 2009 because of criticism that it was 'an inflexible tool'.[165]

In July 2004, immigration introduced Safeguards – an automated system used to identify visa applicants who match predetermined characteristics of concern developed into risk-based profiles relating to visa integrity, security or potential fraud.[166] Safeguards remains in use today. In contrast to the RFL, which openly justified which nationalities, age groups and genders faced a barrier to entry, Safeguards profiles are much less visible on a number of levels. The profiling undertaken by Safeguards is held 'in confidence',[167] and thus is not published. A little insight is available from an Ombudsman's report from which it can be gleaned that, of 300 active profiles in 2008, at least one profiled Sri Lankan visitor visa applicants and another related to the general skilled migration visa caseload.[168] But otherwise the specific basis for risk is not public beyond broad generalities. Risk profiles in Safeguards are derived from statistics, trends and intelligence, and are composed of characteristics that may include nationality, country of birth, age, gender, visa class sought, travel document type, occupation type, migration agent, and sponsor or employer, or nominated education provider.[169] Some profiles include personal information, for example, the name of a migration agent or the name of a particular sponsor/employer.[170]

Safeguards is explained as a 'processing tool only', which has several implications for visa applicants' access to information used in their matters.[171] A match with a Safeguards profile alerts decision-makers that the applicant may present a higher risk and prompts further checking of the application.[172] But because 'Safeguards has no legislative basis', it is not lawful to refuse a visa on the grounds of a Safeguards match.[173] Nor are decision-makers required to provide a person opportunity to respond to information that there has been a Safeguards match or to adverse information of which they may not be aware. Thus

163 Commonwealth and Immigration Ombudsman, 'The Safeguards System', 9.
164 Cronin, 'A Culture of Control', 96.
165 MIAC, '*Class of Persons – Public Interest Criteria – Revocation of Risk Factor List (Paragraph 4011(2)(b))*'.
166 DIAC, 'Procedures Advice Manual 3, Generic Guidelines A, Visa Systems, Alerts and Data Bases Instructions' (2010), [45000.2].
167 Commonwealth and Immigration Ombudsman, 'The Safeguards System', 5.
168 Ibid., 4, 7.
169 DIAC, 'Procedures Advice Manual 3', [45000.6] 6.3.
170 Ibid., [45000.4]–[45000.5].
171 Ibid., [45000.5] 5.3.
172 Ibid., [45000.2]; DIMIA, 'Annual Report 2004–05' (Canberra, 2005), 33.
173 DIAC, 'Procedures Advice Manual 3', [45000.5].

immigration policy states that '[s]taff are not to mention a Safeguards match in a decision record or mention it to the applicant or their agent' and are not to include Safeguards profiles or alert message screen shots in paper or electronic files.[174] The exclusion of Safeguards identification from the legal record, and thus from scrutiny, makes it, to borrow Karen Glover's phrase, 'pretextual'.[175] The shift from the legal mode of the RFL to the technological processing of Safeguards has thus resulted in diminishing transparency. A recent glimpse suggests a particular contemporary sensitivity to publicising nationality based risk information.

In 2009, the increasing importance accorded to a technical risk-management approach was signalled by immigration's establishment of the Risk, Fraud and Integrity Division,[176] and later use of networked or 'Big Data' in the BRIS.[177] An expanding amount of data from diverse sources is utilised to generate predictive risk models for what immigration refers to as 'intent management'. Nationality, country of birth, other demographic details and immigration and movement histories are key factors in the compilation of risk profiles. These profiles work in a similar way to Safeguards in that they identify persons matching risk profiles for further scrutiny, and risk profiling is similarly regarded as a processing tool only. Two public presentations by immigration staff provided some rare insight into the actual composition of a profile. In 2010, Gavin McCairns shared an example of a risk profile, which included the specific data that calculated that there was a 64.3 per cent chance that a passenger matching this profile would be a person of interest. Under the attributes it listed the specific visa classes, birth countries, airlines, citizenship at the time of movement and immigration posts granting the visa for the movement and port of arrival that together articulated the risk prediction.[178] Two years later, Klaus Felsche used a modified version of this profile with the birth country and citizenship at the time of movement details removed. It is impossible to know the rationale behind the later removal of this information, but the selective removal of country of birth citizenship details does suggest this information is more sensitive.[179]

174 Ibid., [45000.5], [45000.25]. But see also Commonwealth and Immigration Ombudsman, 'The Safeguards System', 5.

175 Karen S. Glover, *Racial Profiling: Research, Racism and Resistance* (Maryland: Rowman and Littlefield, 2009), 4; see also David A. Harris, '"Driving While Black" and All Other Traffic Offences: The Supreme Court and Pretextual Traffic Stops', *Journal of Criminal Law and Criminology* 87 (1997): 544–82.

176 DIAC, 'Annual Report 2012–13', 278.

177 Australian Government Information Management Office, 'The Australian Public Service Big Data Strategy: Improved Understanding through Enhanced Data-Analytics Capability' (Department of Finance and Deregulation, 2013), 14.

178 Gavin McCairns, 'Serious and Organised Crime: Promoting Visa Integrity – DIAC's Response to the Commission of Serious Migration Offences', in *International Serious and Organised Crime Conference 2010* (Melbourne, Australian Institute of Criminology, October 18, 2010).

179 Felsche, 'Real-Time Analytics Challenges for Immigration'.

Authority from law and expertise

The increasing role of 'front-end' predictive risk-profiling technologies that are regarded as processing tools not legal decisions arguably represents a strategy for management of potential criticism of discriminatory visa decision-making. This transition also suggests that the role of law is diminishing or at least changing in the regulation of human mobility. It is in this setting that I suggest that the symbolic role of law in renewing the central importance of nationality as a legitimate discriminator does some work in bolstering authority for the nationality basis of risk-profiling technologies.

The contrast between legal renderings of character and risk-profiling technologies can fruitfully be understood through Jean-Paul Brodeur's frame of 'high policing'.[180] Brodeur developed the model of 'high policing' at a time when it was assumed that policing in liberal democracies was directed towards crime repression, patrolling and through the deterrent effect of prosecution and punishment (which Brodeur characterised as 'low policing').[181] In contrast, Brodeur sought to highlight 'high policing' practices that elevated intelligence gathering (in which crime control may offer one avenue for intelligence), intelligence analysis and surveillance as a method for preventative control 'of any group or individual perceived as threatening the established order'.[182] Today, high policing targets what David Bayley and David Weisburd refer to as 'macro-crimes', that is, those crimes regarded as threats to society in general, such as terrorism, drug trafficking and illegal immigration.[183]

A major contrast between high and low policing is their visibility to the public. Risk-profiling technologies reflect high policing's methodological emphasis on strategies of pre-emption and disruption that are operationally based on secret intelligence. Character exclusion embodies low policing's legally oriented practices that enable insight into the charge, the evidence against the defendant and how that evidence was collected. The operation of both high and low policing in a policing strategy has varied effects. Accountability challenges may arise with the incorporation of high policing practices into general-duties 'low' policing.[184] Shifts in institutional functions have been observed as border policing is militarised while, conversely, military institution is civilianised.[185] In the broader regulation of visa integrity, character-based exclusion plays a minor role in comparison to the

180 Jean-Paul Brodeur, 'High Policing and Low Policing: Remarks About the Policing of Political Activities', *Social Problems* 30, no. 5 (1983).

181 Peter K. Manning, 'Jean-Paul Brodeur on High and Low Policing', *Champ pénal/Penal field [En ligne]* 9 (2012): 5.

182 Brodeur, 'High Policing and Low Policing', 514.

183 David H. Bayley and David Weisburd, 'Cops and Spooks: The Role of Police in Counterterrorism', in *To Protect and to Serve: Policing in an Age of Terrorism*, ed. David Weisburd *et al.* (New York: Springer, 2011), 82.

184 See, for example, Maggy Lee, *Trafficking and Global Crime Control* (London: Sage Publications, 2011), chapter 6; Bayley and Weisburd, 'Cops and Spooks', 94–5.

185 Lee, *Trafficking and Global Crime Control*, 107–6.

vast processing work of risk profiling. This emphasises the symbolic role of legal determinations of character. Reflecting on the secrecy over the basis and purpose of particular nationality discriminators in risk profiling, the tribunal's discursive production of a nationality-based hue for bad character can be understood as bolstering authority in risk technologies in the visa integrity assemblage.

Conclusion

Character exclusion forms part of substantive visa decision-making. Every non-citizen must satisfy the character test for the grant and continued validity of a visa. In that sense, the vantage point for examination of the policing and legal regulation of migrant illegality is different to that previously pursued in this book. Prior chapters have engaged with the exercise of migration's police-like powers to focus on the discretion exercised in locating people who are already of unlawful status or in breach of visa conditions, and with discretionary power to grant marginal legal status for release from immigration detention. In these prior chapters, an orthodox view regards the migration powers at issue as procedural powers that assist the administration of the visa regime, but are not part of the substantive visa criteria that dictates who will hold a visa. But the case studies in the chapters on 'arrest', raids and release from detention and in this chapter on character testing illustrate various ways in which the conventional distinction between procedural and substantive law becomes irrelevant. Legal practices that are ostensibly procedural materially shape access to substantive lawful status. And the law of character demonstrates that profiling, regarded as a procedural mechanism, animates discretion in courtrooms over substantive visa determination, just as much as in the streets and raids.

Empirically, this chapter has charted how nationality was deployed in tribunal determinations of character in the period 1997–2006, a time span that represents the bulk of the Howard Coalition government's time in office. It has focused largely on the most open ground of the character test, which empowers exclusion if a person's past or present criminal and/or general conduct means they are not of good character. Nationality is an irrelevant consideration in determining character given judicial interpretations that position character in terms of enduring morality. But its deployment in tribunal decisions as a lens through which the honesty and character of visa applicants is determined traces a practice which makes nationality a meaningful attribute of character testing. At least some tribunal members' comfort in making broad generalisations that, for example, 'lying may be endemic in the culture of the Philippines, lying is not acceptable to the Australian community'[186] signifies how profoundly nationality-based distinctions are treated as neutral in a way that racial distinctions are not.

In the character decisions examined, nationality was instrumental for the promulgation of stereotypes as a mechanism to frame and make sense of often

186 *Damakas* [2002] AATA 355 (May 16, 2002) [36].

conflicting narratives of immigration and the visa applicant. The tribunal's insertion of 'common-sense' assumptions – which in another context might be relatively innocuous – into legal decision-making provided a vital step to authorise exclusion on character grounds. The tribunal relied on key assumptions with regards to the relative economic and welfare circumstances of nations, the existence of communication networks among those wishing to travel to Australia and among ethnic communities within Australia, and the nature of migration fraud as an organised, rather than individualistic, affair. These notions enabled the tribunal to ascribe motivations and knowledge of immigration procedures to visa applicants on the basis of their nationality, and the utility of deterrence, and make these findings appear a matter of common sense. Yet, by utilising nationality in this way, the tribunal adopted a deeply problematic categorical treatment of character that in simple terms treated people from particular countries as migration frauds, and racialised citizens within Australia as similarly involved and supportive 'immigrants'. This research reveals that, for people of certain nationalities, during this period the discursive suspicion of Filipina women was particularly evident; the character test arguably provided a forum which allowed renewal of a 'color line'.[187] In light of the character test's rationale as protection of 'Australian values' the use of nationality-based stereotypes is of deep concern.

Theoretically this chapter has been concerned with the authorisation of discretion in legal practices. It has been included to underline that extraordinary discretion is interwoven throughout migration legal practices that go beyond the conventional recognition of discretion's prominence in sites of police practice and residual ministerial discretion. Discretion in factual assessments within legal decisions is particularly powerful because it recreates reality through unacknowledged and biased frames, but this new reality becomes verified as objective truth through its legal process. Nationality has been instrumental in producing the truth about people's character. In this way, the chapter has further developed the book's enquiry into the marginalisation of the voice of migrant illegality.

It is important to note that the tribunal's verification of facts has an extended life as character exclusions are incorporated as part of the intelligence stored, assembled and analysed through Big Data technologies. This has long-lasting material repercussions on the future mobility of the particular non-citizens judged who are not only banned from entering Australia for varying periods, but may also face barriers upon entry into the many counties that require disclosure of prior exclusions as a condition of entry. Character exclusions are aggregated as part of intelligence that informs the prediction of intent of other travellers with a range of specified attributes, including nationality. Thus nationality-based stereotypes recursively affect the regulation of visa integrity.

187 W. E. B. Du Bois, *The Souls of Black Folk* (Boulder: Project Gutenberg, eBook Collection (EBSCOhost).

Further, the tribunal's visible affirmation of the legitimacy of nationality as a factor for character classification lends authority to its use as a basic building block in the technical expertise of risk profiling. Character profiling, through both law and technology, through common sense knowledge and technical expertise, are thus central and connected mechanisms of policing status. Animating decisions about substantive legal status and procedural practices, the centrality of discretionary authority in migration's legal order is evident from its effects on the lived experience and legal determination of membership, which are taken up in the concluding chapter.

Conclusion

'The umbrella of legality'

On February 26, 2011, the Australian Customs and Border Protection Service intercepted and boarded 'suspect illegal entry vessel 231'. They detained a number of people for people smuggling, including SU and BS, pseudonyms allocated by the court to Indonesian nationals of 16 and 14 years of age respectively.[1] At that time, a fierce public antagonism portrayed people smuggling as, in Prime Minister Julia Gillard's words, 'an evil trade to be punished'.[2] Initially SU and BS were taken into immigration detention, first at Christmas Island, a remote Australian island 1500 nautical miles west of Darwin, and later in immigration detention facilities for unaccompanied minors in Darwin on the mainland's Northern Territory.

SU and BS did not contest the legality of their immigration detention under the *Migration Act 1958* (Cth) ('*Migration Act*'). They instead claimed their detention became illegal from about 12.15 am on June 30, 2011, when they were woken up and Serco transferred them to Sydney Police Centre in Surry Hills for the purpose of arrest.[3] At 10.15 am that same day the Australian Federal Police ('AFP') arrested them and charged them with aggravated people smuggling offences under s 233C(1) of the *Migration Act*. The AFP denied bail and SU and BS were taken before the magistrate at Central Local Court who subsequently refused bail that afternoon. SU and BS were then held in an adult remand centre in Silverwater, NSW until December 2011, when the charges against each of them were discontinued for reasons unrelated to age, and they were returned to an immigration detention centre and then removed to Indonesia.

The court found that the police had unlawfully arrested SU and BS because police had not supplied a reason why a summons for their attendance at court

1 This account has been developed from *SU* v. *Commonwealth of Australia* [2014] NSWSC 241; *SU* v. *Commonwealth of Australia; BS* v. *Commonwealth of Australia* [2016] NSWSC 8; (2016) 307 FLR 357 ('*SU*'); 'Case Study: Residual Liberty, False Imprisonment and Asylum Seekers', *O'Brien Solicitors Blog*, March 30, 2016, http://obriensolicitors.com.au/case-study-su-v-commonwealth-of-australia-bs-v-commonwealth-of-australia/.

2 'Julia Gillard's Speech to the Lowy Institute on Labor's New Asylum-seeker Policy for Australia', *The Australian*, July 6, 2010, www.theaustralian.com.au/archive/politics/julia-gillards-speech-to-the-lowy-institute-on-labors-new-asylum-seeker-policy-for-australia/news-story/5ffb94b349ee46e1778da4ca67c3fed2.

3 Serco was the immigration detainee transport service provider at the time.

> would not ensure their appearance.[4] Consequently, the court was required to decide whether the period they were detained in the police cells after arrest and before the magistrate's decision to refuse bail was unlawful. From the Commonwealth's point of view, the unlawfulness of the arrest did not make subsequent detention unlawful because SU and BS were unlawful non-citizens at all times while present in Australia.[5] The court disagreed, finding that SU and BS were not detained in the Sydney Police Centre cells because they were in immigration detention, but because they were there to be arrested and dealt with as remand prisoners. Hamill J explained: 'In this respect, the legal nature of their detention was different. One of the residual liberties that the plaintiffs enjoyed was the right to be dealt with according to the law … Nothing in the *Migration Act* alters the requirements for a lawful arrest'.[6]

This 2016 New South Wales Supreme Court case grapples with many of the themes in this book: the state's disregard for the liberty of non-citizens; coercive policing practices in the context of immigration law's interrelation with criminal law; and legal conventions that institutionalise non-responsibility for state violence. It also offers a fundamental insight that is emblematic of how officials imagine the authority that immigration law extends. The immigration detention provisions provided, in counsel for the Commonwealth, Peter Semmler QC's words, an 'umbrella of legality'.[7] Hamil J commented: 'No doubt, because the plaintiffs were at all times in immigration detention, those who brought the charges against them did not see any relevant distinction between arresting them and bringing the charges by way of summons'.[8] A more foundational indistinction is routinely made by the Commonwealth through its migration jurisdiction. While the criminal law in principle guards liberty as the freedom from arbitrary interference and detention by the state for both citizens and non-citizens alike, the *Migration Act* demands arbitrary detention on the basis of unlawful status. This underlying policy animates the migration policing of status.

The arrest practice in this case should not be regarded as an isolated incident. As the accounts that have surfaced in this book show, this case should be regarded as a rare example in which the daily tensions of migration policing made it into the legal record. The case sheds light on the apparent confidence of senior Australian Border Force (ABF) officials in the planned Operation Fortitude, which opened the book, in announcing that immigration officers would be positioned in Melbourne city speaking to, and thus presumably stopping, any individual 'we cross paths with'.[9] It appeared that the ABF, as has been observed

4 *Crimes Act 1914* (Cth) s 3W.
5 *SU* [2016] NSWSC 8; (2016) 307 FLR 357, 359 [8], 364 [29].
6 Ibid., 369 [47].
7 Ibid., 360 [8], 364 [29].
8 Ibid., 364 [24].
9 Australian Border Force, 'ABF Joining Inter-Agency Outfit to Target Crime in Melbourne CBD', Media release, August 28, 2015.

in many policing encounters, was thinking of the law not in terms of the authority it provided to stop individuals but rather as a resource for the later justification of immigration detention and criminal charges. In other words, it appears the ABF was thinking of law as creating an overarching environment of permissive intervention.

Through its recognition that unlawful non-citizens retain the right to 'residual liberty',[10] *SU* might be read optimistically as signalling the possibility of legal recognition of the violence justified by migration powers; that is, the violence inflicted by the state upon non-citizens through law and its administration to be detained indefinitely and without recourse. The danger is that the case of *SU* be treated as simply one about the proper exercise of arrest powers. This would elide the broader lesson of the dangers and complexities of legal authority for practices at the intersection of immigration law and criminal law. Like many of the examples in this book, it was at the intersection of these laws that migration powers were treated as providing an overarching power that made procedural criminal law irrelevant or broadened the discretionary authority available to police. Immigration law has provided a placeholder-style authority for detention in circumstances where legal authority to arrest for a criminal offence was unclear, and made police reasons for initial intervention legally unaccountable. It is not surprising that the legal limitations of the *Migration Act* detention powers emerged from a contest over the conduct of arrest for a criminal offence. It is when immigration practices collide with those areas of regulation that have long-established and protected safeguards, such as the criminal law of arrest (no matter their problems in practice), that state inattention to the legal rhetoric of liberty becomes more acutely obvious.

Policing Undocumented Migrants has charted how migration legal practices are organised through discretionary authority. Discretionary authority must be viewed as central to the legal order of migration. It must be taken seriously as a source of jurisprudence. The implications are opposite to Adam Smith's eighteenth-century demarcation of high jurisprudence from that of the lowly mean matters addressed through police regulation which could not be so termed.[11] This demarcation separated the high jurisprudence of rights and justice from that within the remit of police concerns with matters such as waste disposal and the enforcement of justice. Yet discretionary authority is central to both substantive legal decisions about migration status and to procedural powers which shape the lived social experience of migration status. In other words, discretionary authority is central to the constitution of legal and social senses of membership that invoke high jurisprudential issues of rights. Discretionary authority generates legal policy – establishing authority and modes of

10 Residual liberties are those civil liberties that statute has not excluded expressly or by necessary implication, see *SU* [2016] NSWSC 8; (2016) 307 FLR 357, [32].

11 Mariana Valverde, 'Jurisdiction and Scale: Legal "Technicalities" as Resources for Theory', *Social and Legal Studies* 18, no. 2 (2009): 148–9.

responsibility for such practices. The organisation of discretionary authority shows how policy is developed through practices in the interrelation between legal disciplines of migration and criminal law, between delegated powers within these disciplines, and between procedures. It is the logic of discretion over the policing of status that makes migration 'law'.

A further matter in *SU* connects with a key theme in the book: the mismatch between discretionary practices and legal practices of review. *SU* conforms with Mariana Valverde's observation that policing tends to become visible only in its conflicts with 'higher' law, such as constitutional rights.[12] It is instructive that the challenge (and clarification) to migration legal power was enunciated in the review of the exercise of criminal procedural law. In this it manifests the disjuncture between the national 'scale', developed by Boaventura de Sousa Santos, of citizenship/migration law, and what Valverde refers to as the 'urban jurisdiction' of policing. 'Urban' regulation and the risk logic embedded in policing produce an interlegality that does not conform neatly with national or local scales of legal frameworks of review.

The 'interlegality' of migration legal practices is evident throughout the book. While migration law defines the entitlements of people based on status, which reflects the national scale of citizenship, its practices do not easily map onto the national scale. Migration's discretionary authority is produced partly through the interrelation of migration and criminal law. The identification of unlawful non-citizens, for example, was instigated by diverse factors including suspicion of drug possession and public order concerns that have little to do with the formal concerns of legal citizenship. Migration's discretionary authority is further enacted through the interrelation between citizenship and policing. It enabled grant of legal status for the purpose of administrative convenience as detention centres became overcrowded. And, in protecting 'Australian values' via character determination, it relied on nationality to make sense of non-citizens' honesty. The interlegality of policing status is performed in 'zones of non-responsibility'.[13]

Organised non-responsibility

Key features of the legal accountability framework of migration law organise 'zones of non-responsibility' for legal and policing practices discussed in this book. These features include conventions of administrative law, such as the inapplicability of the rules of evidence, as well as judicial interpretations of statute and legal doctrine which enable flexible interpretations of decisions made to manage risk and security, the restriction of judicial review to matters of jurisdictional error, broad discretion structured into every layer of decision-making,

12 Ibid., 149.

13 Scott Veitch, *Law and Irresponsibility: On the Legitimation of Human Suffering* (New York: Routledge-Cavendish, 2007).

and the many practical barriers facing non-citizens seeking to pursue complaint or litigation against their treatment or status. These features make it difficult for accounts of migration law's violence to surface in legal forums and records.

Time and management over time formed a common theme in how non-responsibility was organised throughout the case studies. By limiting the period of responsibility for coercive practices, and extending the period in which non-citizens remain vulnerable to migration powers, migration policing practices are implicated in the performance of temporal borders. 'Temporal borders', as Sandro Mezzadra and Brett Neilson explain, operate to block, delay and accelerate migrant mobility and, in doing so, mediate differential social inclusion.[14] Temporal borders are a critical method for reorganisation of the global labour market through policies that regulate the speed of mobility, including temporary visas and circular migration policies, which arrange for repeated temporary stays between host and home states and detention centres.[15] The potential for adverse effects of temporary migration on the working conditions and social entitlements of low-wage workers is well documented.[16] Temporal borders do not uniformly articulate with spatial borders, but may reinforce and remake them, creating hierarchies in mobility.[17]

In the practices examined in this book, some forms of temporal control are explicit on the face of the law. The use of time periods to mark changes in policy is a persistent characteristic in migration law that makes migration legal advice such a specialist area. Strict time periods highlight the arbitrary practice and thus the concentration of executive power. The reason for policy change is not informed by any change in the actions of the policed population. For example, Chapter 4 recorded how the date of a person's arrival without visa by boat determined whether the person would be subject to an indefinite period of mandatory detention, or released from detention, and their eligibility for work rights on release. The population of about 27 000 people, referred to in official discourse as the 'asylum legacy caseload' to signify those who arrived by boat after the Labor government abolished the 'Pacific Solution', is affected by this policy. Many in this population have waited since 2011 for the Immigration Minister's personal permission to allow lodgment of their refugee visa application and in late 2014 were told they are eligible only for Temporary Protection Visas or Temporary Safe Haven Enterprise Visas. The recent suicides and prevalence of psychological distress from this cohort living in the community illustrates how the slowness of migration legal process effects a form of punishment.

14 Sandro Mezzadra and Brett Neilson, *Border as Method, or, the Multiplication of Labor* (Durham: Duke University Press, 2013), 131–66.

15 Ibid.

16 See, for example, Laurie Berg, *Migrant Rights at Work: Law's Precariousness at the Intersection of Immigration and Labour* (Abingdon: Routledge, 2016); Leah F. Vosko, Valerie Preston and Robert Latham, eds. *Liberating Temporariness? Migration, Work and Citizenship in an Age of Insecurity* (Montreal: McGill-Queen's University Press, 2014).

17 Mezzadra and Neilson, *Border as Method*, 150.

These approaches reflect how explicit policy and legislative criteria use time to organise differential social entitlements with violent effects outside the detention context.

In contrast to the use of delay, migration policing practices may also use speed and expediency as an explicit form of violence, even in the absence of policies with a specified time dimension. In this way, migration policing practices extend temporal controls beyond those for which they form an overt policy mandate. It is a particular and long-standing characteristic of policing that police exist to respond to the situation where 'Something-ought-not-to-be-happening-about-which-something-ought-to-be-done-NOW!'[18] The capacity to institute and act in an emergency is not exceptional.[19] As discussed in Chapter 3, the speeding up of migration processes charges the character of migration practice with violence. It facilitates the creation of immigration 'arrest' and rapid removal, sometimes in the same day. Hastened processes may be empowered by the absence of specific time periods with practice itself constituting the legal authority for speed. Justified by a classically flexible aspect of policing – discretion to deal with 'emergencies' and security risks – it is the future-oriented logic of prevention and risk management that escapes legal frameworks of constraint.

By understanding discretion as a process unfolding through time, the interpretative frame of 'front-end' discretion enables the concentration of administrative power to emerge more fully. Pre-trial processes are the mainstay and indeed mandate of administrative practice, and, as shown through practices of immigration 'arrest' in the street and in raids, involve violence. Yet, as is discussed in Chapter 2, the migration law framework of accountability limits responsibility by quarantining the time period of officers' actions relevant for review, adopting a 'snapshot' model of responsibility that manifests in two ways. First, unlike provision in a criminal trial, migration process does not predicate the legality of 'arrest' (taking a person into detention) on the propriety of an officer's conduct preceding exercise of the detention power. This is despite the fact that this initial intervention by the state in public spaces has been understood by courts as one of the most important to protect, and by scholars as a site that often involves racial profiling, in articulation with stereotypes about class, age and gender. Police thus have more discretion and less responsibility imposed for how they conduct immigration detention than when using arrest powers. Second, responsibility for 'arrest' is also limited by the exclusion of compensation for detention effected on what later often becomes known as a misunderstanding of an individual's legal status. These limited forms of responsibility show how speed can facilitate the lawfulness of violence. At the micro level of the border, coercive powers exercised by police and immigration have implications for the speed of removal of unlawful non-citizens, and thus for the production of temporal borders.

18 Egon Bittner, 'Florence Nightingale in Pursuit of Willie Sutton: A Theory of Police', in *The Potential for Reform of Criminal Justice*, ed. H. Jacob (Beverly Hills: Sage, 1974).

19 Mark Neocleous, 'The Problem with Normality: Taking Exception to "Permanent Emergency"', *Alternatives* 31(2006): 208.

Policing status

Migration law and legal practices police status in multiple ways. They make people illegal via visa refusal or cancellation for bad character, security concerns, and the provision of incorrect information in visa applications. In character determination, as developed in Chapter 5, the Administrative Appeals Tribunal demonstrated law's policing function through profiling practices that deployed nationality as a mechanism to make sense of the honesty and character of non-citizens. The policing of status involves multiple institutions in finding and apprehending unlawful non-citizens, and in reporting and monitoring non-citizens. It imposes conditions that make lawful status contingent on their satisfaction and continued adherence. Each of these examples produce particularised forms of status – or, in other words, targeted regimes of social entitlements – which mediate non-citizens' experiences of 'deportability'.[20]

Policing status involves extensive discretion at the front end of migration process. The profusion of rules in migration, which set out the requirements for visa eligibility in minute detail, does not always or necessarily constrain discretion. The openness of discretion is facilitated by the doctrinal approach to migration legal status as a binary classification, that is, one that does not rely on assessment of conduct. Status-based distinction institutes broad discretion in the identification and elimination of threats, from street clearing to the social and spatial regulation of non-citizens through detention and release, and determination of character through assessments of honesty. Further, in practice, the policies viewed as the two fundamental pillars of the Australian immigration control regime – the universal visa requirement and the mandatory detention of unlawful non-citizens – are exposed as organised through discretionary authority in important ways. The Immigration Minister's effective permission for a specific cohort of lapsed Bridging E Visa holders to remain in the community without a visa is the most dramatic example. Although a relatively recent scenario, occurring since 2013, it is not isolated. Historically, the denial of work rights upon release from detention in circumstances where no government support is available is analogous, because many were unable to comply with the work prohibition, which arguably provides an example of tacit acknowledgement of breach coupled with the capacity to recall individuals to detention. In other words, it is the executive government's management of the conditions of stay in the community that is central, not legal status itself. Legal status is a way to produce those conditions. In this way, legal status is used as a means for power, able to be manipulated for changing government strategies. But because policing status is authorised as the central mandate in migration law, the concentration of discretion is presented in law as natural, and the significance of discretion obscured.

20 Nicholas P. De Genova, 'Migrant "Illegality" and Deportability in Everyday Life', *Annual Review of Anthropology* 31(2002): 439.

Constructing differential regimes

The significance of the organisation of discretionary authority and non-responsibility in migration is illuminated through the differential regimes of entitlements it creates. Differential regimes of entitlements constitute, as a number of scholars have argued, a form of apartheid. Systems of apartheid are sometimes considered to be predicated on explicit ideologies of racial inferiority, but, in keeping with contemporary forms of raciality, are also articulated through differential construction of citizenship.[21] The economic inclusion but political exclusion of non-EU nationals within the EU has been described, by Etienne Balibar, as 'an apartheid being formed at the same time as European citizenship itself'.[22] Canadian policies that deny permanent legal status to migrant workers who may spend their entire lives in Canada and relegate some migrants to temporary or illegal status have similarly been described by Nandita Sharma as bolstering a system of 'global apartheid'.[23] The concern expressed by these scholars is not restricted to these jurisdictions. Across the globe nations have systems in place in which migrant workers may live and work but without the rights and entitlements of citizens.

Analysis of the differential oversight over policing powers exercised under migration and criminal law shows that the constitution of legal regimes of differential entitlements cannot be mapped precisely and wholly onto citizenship status itself. Study of the policing of status shows the instability of apparent legal binaries between citizenship and non-citizenship, and between lawful and unlawful non-citizenship. The differentiated model of responsibility for police violence offered by criminal law and migration law thus does not simply reflect a law for citizens and a law for non-citizens. The saturation of discretion through every stage of migration law and legal process makes room for the policing of migration legal status as imbricated with other embedded social hierarchies. In particular, the practices traced in this book suggest that the differences between protections from state violence are generated in articulation with 'race', class, gender and sexuality, in various relations to migration legal status. In street-based policing, 'race' and gender was understood by those policed to be a factor that promoted police intervention. In character determination, notions of 'race', gender, sexuality and class shaped assessments of honesty and produced illegal subjects through visa refusal or cancellation. In some decisions, the AAT cast citizens as 'immigrants', and proceeded on the assumption that they were associated with networks of migration fraud because of their country of origin and naturalised citizenship status.

21 Nandita Sharma, 'Global Apartheid and Nation-Statehood: Instituting Border Regimes', in *Nationalism and Global Solidarities: Alternative Projections to Neoliberal Globalisation*, ed. James Goodman and Paul James (London: Routledge, 2007), 71–89.

22 Etienne Balibar, *We, the People of Europe? Reflections on Transnational Citizenship*, trans. James Swenson (Princeton: Princeton University Press, 2004), 9, 31–50.

23 Sharma, 'Global Apartheid and Nation-Statehood', 72; Nandita Sharma, 'Anti-Trafficking Rhetoric and the Making of a Global Apartheid', *NWSA Journal* 17, no. 3 (Fall 2005): 88–111, 89.

The institutionalisation of status-based classification promoted by migration law means that status is at issue in the most critical social sites: homes, schools, hospitals, workplaces, social security, airports, overseas embassies to name but a few. This is why the compensation that the state has paid does not provide measure of the extent of harm arising from practices of direct coercive violence in unlawful detention and other harms in community settings. The Australian government paid over A$27 million in compensation between 1999 and 2013 to persons who claimed they were unlawfully detained or that the government had breached its duty of care to them while in immigration detention.[24] Many of these cases were settled prior to court hearing and, as such, have not been a productive source for learning about who is subject to migration policing and how that policing is enacted. Aside from a few Ombudsman investigations, little is known about the circumstances of the immigration detention of persons who either held visas or were Australian citizens. It is unclear how many citizens are questioned about their migration legal status in circumstances where they are not free to leave or are otherwise affected by assumptions about their status. The harm done to those affected by migration law through either the use of 'police-like' powers to identify and apprehend suspected unlawful non-citizens and those in breach or the use of legal status and visa conditions as a means of control is largely absent on legal records.

Conclusion

It is clear that extraordinary discretionary authority is engaged in policing status. Discretionary authority *produces* people as illegal and marginally legal in arbitrary and racialised ways. Discretionary authority thus forms the substance of migration laws that make people illegal. And it does so through legal practices that challenge central conventional binaries in migration analysis between the citizen and non-citizen, and between lawful and unlawful status. The fluidity of these binaries has implications for approaches to policing and migration research. It demands studies of policing that are not solely focused on criminal law in order to better understand how policing produces differential inclusion through social, spatial and temporal ordering. It requires migration scholarship take discretionary authority seriously as productive of citizenship and particularly of stratified citizenship. It opens up the need to explore the intersection between migration legal practices and racialised hierarchies that reach beyond non-citizens. It calls for further attention to the interrelation between criminal law and migration law as a means to unpack the extent to which non-citizens are governed fundamentally by migration law. These are research questions that are sidelined when the practice and significance of discretionary authority in migration is overlooked.

24 Australian Lawyers Alliance, 'Freedom of Information Request – FOI 13/69', accessed October 12, 2016, www.lawyersalliance.com.au/documents/item/13.

The analysis in this book challenged the notion that discretion is secondary to law in migration by examining the organisation of legal authorisation of discretionary practices at the level of the individual encounter, bureaucratic routines and decision-making. Attending to the organised operation of discretionary legal authority provides a new perspective through which responsibility for migration legal practices can be better understood and evaluated, and reveals the ways in which it marginalises responsibility for migration law's violence. Migration's powerful discretion is reinforced by the legal framework of accountability: major conventions of administrative law marginalise these decisions from tribunal and judicial oversight; and the incompatible logics within each arena make such exclusions appear natural.

Temporary migration to Australia, as in many Global North states, in circumstances where legal citizenship is not necessarily the desired outcome, is growing.[25] The increase in the speed of migration centres the policing of status in all its forms – substantive practices of determination and conditioning of legal status, and practices of identification, apprehension, detention and removal of those suspected to be unlawful or in breach – for the management of migration. We are living in a world in which migratory movement and its management through the policing of status have become, and will continue to be, vital forums through which questions of state power and responsibility are being negotiated. If the differential regimes of entitlements produced by migration laws bolster a system of 'global apartheid', then it is even more important that the law's work in marginalising the voices of those it makes illegal be understood and resisted.

25 Stephen Castles, 'Rethinking Australian Migration', *Australian Geographer* 47, no. 4 (2016): 394.

Bibliography

Books and articles

Adey, Peter. 'Facing Airport Security: Affect, Biopolitics, and the Preemptive Securitisation of the Mobile Body'. *Environment and Planning D: Society and Space* 27 (2009): 274–95.

Alexy, Robert. 'A Defence of Radbruch's Formula'. In *Recrafting the Rule of Law: The Limits of Legal Order*, edited by David Dyzenhaus. Oxford: Hart, 1999.

Aliverti, Ana. 'Making People Criminal: The Role of the Criminal Law in Immigration Enforcement'. *Theoretical Criminology* 16, no. 4 (2012): 417–34.

Alldridge, Peter. *Relocating Criminal Law*. Aldershot: Ashgate, 2000.

Amoore, Louise. 'Biometric Borders: Governing Mobilities in the War on Terror'. *Political Geography* 25 (2006): 336–51.

Baldwin, Robert, and Keith Hawkins. 'Discretionary Justice: Davis Reconsidered'. *Public Law* (1984): 570–99.

Balibar, Etienne, and Immanuel Wallerstein. *Race, Nation, Class: Ambiguous Identities*. Translated by Chris Turner. London: Verso, 1991.

Banton, Michael. *Policeman in the Community*. New York: Tavistock, 1964.

Bauder, Harald. 'Why We Should Use the Term "Illegalized" Refugee or Immigrant: A Commentary'. *International Journal of Refugee Law* 26, no. 3 (2014): 327–32.

Bayley, David H., and David Weisburd. 'Cops and Spooks: The Role of Police in Counterterrorism'. Chap. 4 in *To Protect and to Serve: Policing in an Age of Terrorism*, edited by David Weisburd, Thomas Feucht, Idit Hakimi, Lois Mock and Simon Perry, 81–99. New York: Springer, 2011.

Beaton-Wells, Caron. 'Judicial Review of Migration Decisions: Life after S157'. *Federal Law Review* 33, no. 1 (2005): 142–75.

Benjamin, Walter. 'Critique of Violence (1920–1)'. Translated by Edmund Jephcott and Kingsley Shorter. In *One Way Street and Other Writings*, 132–54. London: New Left Books, 1979.

Berg, Laurie. *Migrant Rights at Work: Law's Precariousness at the Intersection of Immigration and Labour*. Abingdon: Routledge, 2016.

Berg, Laurie, and Jenni Millbank. 'Constructing the Personal Narratives of Lesbian, Gay and Bisexual Asylum Claimants'. *Journal of Refugee Studies* 22, no. 2 (2009): 195–223.

Bicket, Robyn. 'Controlling Immigration Litigation: The Commonwealth Perspective'. *Australian Institute of Administrative Law Forum* 63 (2010): 40–53.

Bittner, Egon. 'The Capacity to Use Force as the Core of the Police Function'. In *The Police and Society: Touchstone Readings*, edited by V. E. Kappeler, 127–37. Illinois: Waveland Press Inc., 1995.

Bittner, Egon. *The Functions of Police in Modern Society.* Chevy Chase, MD: National Institute of Mental Health, 1970.

Bittner, Egon. 'Florence Nightingale in Pursuit of Willie Sutton: A Theory of Police'. In *The Potential for Reform of Criminal Justice*, edited by H. Jacob. Beverly Hills: Sage, 1974.

Blackwood, John, and Terese Henning. 'Tribunals' Power to Control Their Own Procedures and the Requirements of Procedural Fairness'. *Australian Journal of Administrative Law* 11, no. 1 (2003): 5–33.

Blommaert, Jan. 'Investigating Narrative Inequality: African Asylum Seekers' Stories in Belgium'. *Discourse Society* 12, no. 4 (2001): 413–49.

Boon-Kuo, Louise. 'The Policing of Immigration: Raids, Citizenship and the Criminal Law'. In *Criminalisation and Criminal Responsibility in Australia*, edited by Thomas Crofts and Arlie Loughnan, 276–91. Melbourne: Oxford University Press, 2015.

Bostock, Chantal. 'The Effect of Ministerial Directions on Tribunal Independence'. *Australian Institute of Administrative Law Forum* 66 (2011): 33–42.

Brodeur, Jean-Paul. 'High Policing and Low Policing: Remarks About the Policing of Political Activities'. *Social Problems* 30, no. 5 (1983): 507–20.

Brown, David. 'Giving Voice: The Prisoner and Discursive Citizenship'. Chap. 19 in *The Critical Criminology Companion*, edited by Thalia Anthony and Chris Cunneen, 228–39. Sydney: Hawkins Press, 2008.

Browne, Simone. 'Digital Epidermalization: Race, Identity and Biometrics'. *Critical Sociology* 36, no. 1 (2010): 131–50.

Bruer, Jeremy, and John Power. 'The Changing Role of the Department of Immigration'. Chap. 6 in *The Politics of Australian Immigration*, edited by James Jupp and Marie Kabala, 105–23. Canberra: AGPS, 1993.

Buckmaster, Luke. 'Australian Government Assistance to Refugees: Fact v. Fiction'. *Parliamentary Library Background Notes.* Canberra: Parliamentary Library, 2012.

Bugalski, Natalie. 'A Taste of Freedom from Limbo in Woomera'. *Alternative Law Journal* 27, no. 5 (2002): 239–41.

Calavita, Kitty. 'A "Reserve Army of Delinquents": The Criminalization and Economic Punishment of Immigrants in Spain'. *Punishment & Society* 5, no. 4 (2003): 399–413.

Calavita, Kitty. 'Immigration, Law, and Marginalization in a Global Economy: Notes from Spain'. *Law & Society Review* 32, no. 3 (1998): 529–66.

Castles, Stephen. 'International Migration at a Crossroads'. *Citizenship Studies* 18, no. 2 (2014): 190–207.

Castles, Stephen. 'Rethinking Australian Migration'. *Australian Geographer* 47, no. 4 (2016): 391–8.

Chia, Joyce. 'Back to the Constitution: The Implications of Plaintiff S4/2014 for Immigration Detention'. *UNSW Law Journal* 38, no. 2 (2015): 628–68.

Churches, Steven. 'Civil and Political Rights: Flow-on from Findings of Lack of Legislative Reach or Invalidity: False Imprisonment and Compulsory Examinations Founded in Invalid Summonses'. *Australian Journal of Administrative Law* 16 (2008): 12–15.

Clothier, Michael. 'Changing Custody Regimes for Illegal Entrants'. In *The Criminal Justice System in a Multicultural Society*, 1–7. Melbourne: Australian Institute of Criminology, 1993.

Coffey, G. J., I. Kaplan, R. C. Sampson and M. Tucci. 'The Meaning and Mental Health Consequences of Long-Term Immigration Detention for People Seeking Asylum'. *Social Science and Medicine* 70, no. 12 (2010): 2070–9.

Collet, Bruce A. 'Confronting the Insider-Outsider Polemic in Conducting Research with Diasporic Communities: Towards a Community-Based Approach'. *Refuge* 25, no. 1 (2008): 77–83.

Coombs, Moira. 'Excising Australia: Are We Really Shrinking?' *Research Note.* Information and Research Service. Canberra: Parliamentary Library, 2005.

Coombs, Moira. 'Excisions from the Migration Zone-Policy and Practice'. *Research Note.* Information and Research Service. Canberra: Parliamentary Library, 2004.

Coutin, Susan Bibler. *Legalizing Moves: Salvadoran Immigrants' Struggle for U.S. Residency.* Ann Arbor: University of Michigan Press, 2000.

Coutin, Susan Bibler. 'Reconceptualising Research: Ethnographic Fieldwork and Immigration Politics in Southern California'. Chap. 6 in *Practicing Ethnography in Law: New Dialogues, Enduring Methods,* edited by June Starr and Mark Goodale, 108–27. New York: Palgrave Macmillan, 2002.

Cover, Robert. 'Violence and the Word'. *Yale Law Journal* 95 (1986): 1601–29.

Crock, Mary. 'Climbing Jacob's Ladder: The High Court and the Administrative Detention of Asylum Seekers in Australia'. *Sydney Law Review* 15, no. 3 (1993): 338–56.

Crock, Mary. 'In the Wake of the Tampa: Conflicting Visions of International Refugee Law in the Management of Refugee Flows'. *Pacific Rim Law & Policy Journal* 12 (2003): 49–96.

Crock, Mary. 'Judging Refugees: The Clash of Power and Institutions in the Development of Australian Refugee Law'. *Sydney Law Review* 26, no. 1 (March 2004): 51–73.

Crock, Mary. ed. *Protection or Punishment: The Detention of Asylum Seekers in Australia.* Leichhardt: Federation Press, 1993.

Crock, Mary, and Laurie Berg. *Immigration, Refugees and Forced Migration: Law, Policy and Practice in Australia.* Annandale: The Federation Press, 2011.

Crock, Mary, and Hannah Martin. 'Refugee Rights and the Merits of Appeals'. *University of Queensland Law Journal* 32, no. 1 (2013): 137–55.

Crock, Mary, and Edward Santow. 'Privative Clauses and the Limits of the Law'. In *Australian Administrative Law: Fundamentals, Principles and Doctrines,* edited by Matthew Groves and H. P. Lee, 345–67. Cambridge: Cambridge University Press, 2007.

Cronin, Kathryn. 'A Culture of Control: An Overview of Immigration Policy-Making'. Chap. 5 in *The Politics of Australian Immigration,* edited by James Jupp and Marie Kabala, 83–104. Canberra: AGPS, 1993.

Crowley-Cyr, Lynda. 'Contractualism, Exclusion and "Madness" in Australia's "Outsourced Wastelands"'. *Macquarie Law Journal* 5 (2005): 81–102.

Cunneen, Chris. 'Law, Policing and Public Order: The Aftermath of Cronulla'. In *Lines in the Sand: The Cronulla Riots, Multiculturalism and National Belonging,* edited by Greg Noble, 220–31. Sydney: Sydney Institute of Criminology, 2009.

Cwerner, Saulo B. 'Faster, Faster and Faster: The Time Politics of Asylum in the UK'. *Time and Society* 13, no. 1 (2004): 71–88.

Darian-Smith, Eve. *Laws and Societies in Global Contexts: Contemporary Approaches.* New York: Cambridge University Press, 2013.

Dauvergne, Catherine. *Making People Illegal: What Globalization Means for Migration and Law.* Law in Context. New York: Cambridge University Press, 2008.

Dauvergne, Catherine, and Jenni Millbank. 'Burdened by Proof: How the Australian Refugee Review Tribunal Has Failed Lesbian and Gay Asylum Seekers'. *Federal Law Review* 31 (2003): 299–342.

David, Fiona. 'Trafficking of Women for Sexual Purposes'. In *Research and Public Policy Series.* Canberra: Australian Institute of Criminology, 2008.

Davis, Kenneth Culp. *Discretionary Justice: A Preliminary Inquiry.* Baton Rouge: Louisiana State University Press, 1969.

De Genova, Nicholas P. 'Migrant "Illegality" and Deportability in Everyday Life'. *Annual Review of Anthropology* 31 (2002): 419–47.

De Genova, Nicholas P. 'The Queer Politics of Migration: Reflections on "Illegality" and Incorrigibility'. *Studies in Social Justice* 4, no. 2 (2010): 101–26.

De Lint, Willem, and Alan Hall. 'Making the Pickets Responsible: Policing Labour at a Distance in Windsor, Ontario'. *Canadian Review of Sociology/Revue canadienne de sociologie* 39, no. 1 (2002): 1–27.

Department of Immigration and Ethnic Affairs. 'The Official View: Extract of Submission to the Joint Standing Committee Inquiry into Detention Practices Prepared by the Department of Immigration and Ethnic Affairs'. Chap. 15 in *Protection or Punishment: The Detention of Asylum Seekers in Australia*, edited by Mary Crock, 129–37. Leichhardt: Federation Press, 1993.

Dillon, Michael, and Luis Lobo-Guerrero. 'Biopolitics of Security in the 21st Century: An Introduction'. *Review of International Studies* 34 (2008): 265–92.

Dixon, David. *Law in Policing: Legal Regulation and Police Practices.* New York: Clarendon Press, 1997.

Dixon, David, A. K. Bottomley, C. A. Coleman, M. Gill and D. Wall. 'Reality and Rules in the Construction and Regulation of Police Suspicion'. *International Journal of the Sociology of Law* 17, no. 2 (1989): 185–206.

Dixon, David, Clive Coleman, and Keith Bottomley. 'Consent and the Legal Regulation of Policing'. *Journal of Law and Society* 17, no. 3 (1990): 345–62.

Doná, Giorgia. 'The Microphysics of Participation in Refugee Research'. *Journal of Refugee Studies* 20, no. 2 (2007): 210–29.

Douglas, Heather. 'The Cultural Specificity of Evidence: The Current Scope and Relevance of the Anunga Guidelines'. *University of New South Wales Law Journal* 21 (1998): 27–54.

Du Bois, W. E. B. *The Souls of Black Folk.* Boulder; Champaign: Project Gutenberg, eBook Collection (EBSCOhost).

Dubber, Markus D. 'The New Police Science and the Police Power Model of the Criminal Process'. In *The New Police Science: The Police Power in Domestic and International Governance*, edited by Markus D. Dubber and Mariana Valverde, 107–44. Stanford: Stanford University Press, 2006.

Dubber, Markus D. *The Police Power: Patriarchy and the Foundations of American Government.* New York: Columbia University Press, 2005.

Dubber, Markus D. 'The Possession Paradigm: The Special Part and the Police Power Model of the Criminal Process'. In *Defining Crimes: Essays on the Special Part of the Criminal Law*, edited by R. A. Duff and Stuart Green. Oxford: Oxford University Press, 2005.

Dubber, Markus D., and Mariana Valverde. 'Perspectives on the Power and Science of Police'. In *The New Police Science: The Police Power in Domestic and International Governance*, edited by Markus D. Dubber and Mariana Valverde, 1–16. Stanford: Stanford University Press, 2006.

Duvell, Franck, Anna Triandafyllidou and Bastian Vollmer. 'Ethical Issues in Irregular Migration Research, Clandestino, European Union Citizens and Governance in a Knowledge-Based Society'. In *CLANDESTINO Undocumented Migration: Counting the Uncountable, Data and Trends Across Europe*: Research DG, 2008.

Dwork, Cynthia, and Deidre K. Mulligan. 'It's Not Privacy, and It's Not Fair'. *Stanford Law Review* (2013). www.stanfordlawreview.org/online/privacy-and-big-data/its-not-privacy-and-its-not-fair.

Dworkin, Ronald. *Taking Rights Seriously*. London: Duckworth, 1978.

Ericson, Richard. *Reproducing Order: A Study of Police Patrolwork*. Toronto: University of Toronto Press, 1982.

Feeley, Malcolm M. *The Process Is the Punishment: Handling Cases in a Lower Criminal Court*. New York: Russell Sage Foundation, 1992.

Felsche, Klaus. 'Real-Time Analytics Challenges for Immigration'. *CeBIT BigData Conference 2012*. Sydney, October 31–November 1, 2012.

Fielding, Nigel G. 'Judges and Their Work'. *Social and Legal Studies* 20, no. 1 (20): 97–115.

Findlay, Mark. 'The Ambiguity of Accountability: Deaths in Custody, and the Regulation of Police Power'. *Current Issues in Criminal Justice* 6, no. 2 (1994): 234–51.

Findlay, Mark. *The Globalisation of Crime: Understanding Transitional Relationships in Context*. Cambridge: Cambridge University Press, 1999.

Findlay, Mark, and Ralph Henham. 'Integrating Theory and Method in the Comparative Contextual Analysis of Trial Process'. Chap. 5 in *Research Methods for Law*, edited by Mike McConville and Wing Hong Chui. Research Methods for the Arts and Humanities, 104–32. Edinburgh: Edinburgh University Press, 2007.

Fleay, Caroline, and Lisa Hartley. '"I Feel Like a Beggar": Asylum Seekers Living in the Australian Community without the Right to Work'. *Journal of International Migration & Integration*. doi: 10.1007/s12134-015-0453-x (2015): 1–18.

Fontana, Andrea, and James H. Frey. 'The Interview: From Neutral Stance to Political Involvement'. In *The Sage Handbook of Qualitative Research*, edited by Norman K. Denzin and Yvonna S. Lincoln, 695–727. Thousand Oaks: Sage Publications, 2005.

Foster, Michelle. '"An 'Alien' by the Barest of Threads": The Legality of the Deportation of Long-Term Residents from Australia'. *Melbourne University Law Review* 33 (2009): 483–541.

Foster, Michelle. *International Refugee Law and Socio-Economic Rights: Refuge from Deprivation*. Cambridge: Cambridge University Press, 2007.

Foucault, Michel. *Ethics: Subjectivity and Truth: Essential Works of Foucault 1954–1984, Volume I*. Translated by Robert Hurley, edited by Paul Rabinow. New York: New Press, 1997.

Foucault, Michel. *Discipline and Punish: The Birth of the Prison*. Translated by Alan Sheridan. Middlesex: Penguin Books, 1977.

Foucault, Michel. *Security, Territory, Population: Lectures at the Collège De France, 1977–78*, edited by Michel Senellart, gen. ed. François Ewald and Alessandro Fontana, English series ed. Arnold I. Davidson, translated by Graham Burchell. Houndmills: Palgrave Macmillan, 2007.

Foucault, Michel. *Society Must Be Defended: Lectures at the Collège De France, 1975–1976*. Translated by David Macey, edited by Mauro Bertani, Alessandro Fontana, Francois Ewald and Arnold I. Davidson. London: Penguin Books, 2004.

Freckelton, Ian. *Administrative Decision-Making in Australian Migration Law*. ANU eText, 2015.

Fuller, Lon L. *The Morality of Law*. New Haven: Yale University Press, 1969.

Galbraith, Janet. 'Processes of Whiteness and Stories of Rape'. *Australian Feminist Law Journal* 14 (2000): 71–89.

Galligan, Denis J. *Discretionary Powers: A Legal Study of Official Discretion*. Oxford: Clarendon Press, 1986.

Gans, Jeremy, and Andrew Palmer. *Uniform Evidence*. Melbourne: Oxford University Press, 2010.

Garland, David. *The Culture of Control: Crime and Social Order in Contemporary Society.* Oxford: Oxford University Press, 2001.

Gilboy, Janet A. 'Deciding Who Gets In: Decisionmaking by Immigration Inspectors'. *Law and Society Review* 25, no. 3 (1991): 571–600.

Glover, Karen S. *Racial Profiling: Research, Racism and Resistance.* Lanham: Rowman & Littlefield, 2009.

Goggin, Gerard. 'SMS Riot: Transmitting Race on a Sydney Beach, December 2005'. *M/C Journal* 9, no. 1 (2006).

Goldring, Luin, and Patricia Landolt. 'Precarious Legal Status in Canada: Theorizing Non-Citizenship and Conditionality'. In *Producing and Negotiating Non-Citizenship: Precarious Legal Status in Canada*, edited by Luin Goldring and Patricia Landolt. Toronto: University of Toronto Press, 2013.

Goldring, Luin, Carolina Berinstein and Judith K. Bernhard. 'Institutionalizing Precarious Migratory Status in Canada'. *Citizenship Studies* 13, no. 3 (2009).

Goldstein, Joseph. 'Police Discretion Not to Invoke the Criminal Process: Low-Visibility Decisions in the Administration of Justice'. *Yale Law Journal* 69, no. 4 (1960): 543–94.

Gonzalez, Juan. *Harvest of Empire: A History of Latinos in America.* New York: Penguin Books, 2011.

Grewcock, Michael. 'Conviction, Detention and Removal: The Multiple Punishment of Offenders under Section 501 Migration Act'. *University of New South Wales Legal Research Series* 49 (2009).

Grewcock, Michael. 'Multiple Punishments: The Detention and Removal of Convicted Non-Citizens'. *University of New South Wales Legal Research Series* 41 (2009).

Grewcock, Michael. 'Punishment, Deportation and Parole: The Detention and Removal of Former Prisoners under Section 501 Migration Act 1958'. *The Australian and New Zealand Journal of Criminology* 1 (2011): 56–73.

Grewcock, Michael. 'Reinventing "the Stain" – Bad Character and Criminal Deportation in Contemporary Australia'. In *Routledge Handbook on Crime and International Migration*, edited by Sharon Pickering and Julie Ham. Abingdon: Routledge, 2014.

Griffin, Michael G., Patricia A. Resick, Angela E. Waldrop and Mindy B. Mechanic. 'Participation in Trauma Research: Is There Evidence of Harm?' *Journal of Traumatic Stress* 16, no. 3 (2003): 221–7.

Harris, David A. '"Driving While Black" and All Other Traffic Offences: The Supreme Court and Pretextual Traffic Stops'. *Journal of Criminal Law and Criminology* 87 (1997): 544–82.

Henning, Terese, and John Blackwood. 'The Rules of Evidence and the Right to Procedural Fairness in Proceedings of Four Tasmanian Quasi-Judicial Tribunals'. *Australian Journal of Administrative Law* 10, no. 2 (2003): 84–106.

Hepworth, Kate. *At the Edges of Citizenship: Security and the Constitution of Non-Citizen Subjects.* Farnham, Surrey: Ashgate, 2015.

Herlihy, Jane, Peter Scragg and Stuart Turner. 'Discrepancies in Autobiographical Memories – Implications for the Assessment of Asylum Seekers: Repeated Interviews Study'. *British Medical Journal* 324, no. 7333 (2002): 324–7.

Hugman, Richard, Eileen Pittaway and Linda Bartolomei. 'When "Do No Harm" Is Not Enough: The Ethics of Research with Refugees and Other Vulnerable Groups'. *British Journal of Social Work* 41 (2011): 1271–87.

Hunt, Alan. *Governance of the Consuming Passions: A History of Sumptuary Law.* New York: St. Martin's Press, 1996.

International Detention Coalition. 'Case Management as an Alternative to Immigration Detention: The Australian Experience'. June 2009.

Jordan, Roy. 'Identity Cards and the Access Card'. *E-brief.* Canberra: Parliamentary Library, 2006.

Jowell, Jeffrey. 'The Legal Control of Administrative Discretion'. *Public Law* (1973): 178–220.

Kagehiro, Dorothy K. 'Perceived Voluntariness of Consent to Warrantless Police Searches'. *Journal of Applied Social Psychology* 18, no. 1 (2006): 38–49.

Kanstroom, Daniel. 'Deportation, Social Control, and Punishment: Some Thoughts About Why Hard Laws Make Bad Cases'. *Harvard Law Review* 11 (2000): 1889–1935.

Kelly, Mark. 'Racism, Nationalism and Biopolitics: Foucault's Society Must Be Defended, 2003'. *Contretemps* 4 (September 2004): 58–70.

Kerr, Duncan. 'Keeping the AAT from Becoming a Court'. In *Australian Institute of Administrative Law (NSW) Seminar.* Sydney.

Kerr, Duncan. 'Privative Clauses and the Courts: Why and How Australian Courts Have Resisted Attempts to Remove the Citizen's Right to Judicial Review of Unlawful Executive Action'. *Queensland University of Technology Law and Justice Journal* 5, no. 2 (2005): 195.

Kesby, Alison. 'The Shifting and Multiple Border and International Law'. *Oxford Journal of Legal Studies* 27, no. 1 (2007): 101–19.

Kimber, Julie 'Poor Laws: A Historiography of Vagrancy in Australia'. *History Compass* 11, no. 8 (2013): 537–50.

Klockars, Carl B. *The Idea of the Police.* California: Sage Publications, 1985.

Kneebone, Susan. 'Before the High Court: Ruddock and Others v. Taylor'. *Sydney Law Review* 27, no. 1 (March 2005): 143–66.

Kneebone, Susan. 'The Pacific Plan: The Provision of "Effective Protection"?' *International Journal of Refugee Law* 18, no. 3–4 (2006): 696–721.

Kritzer, Herbert. 'Toward a Theorization of Craft'. *Social and Legal Studies* 16, no. 3 (2007): 321–40.

Lê, Marion. 'Advancing the Asylum-Seeker Cause: A Case for Pragmatism: Address to the Sydney Institute by Marion Lê 5 October 2004'. *The Sydney Papers* 16, no. 4 (2004): 83–93.

Leach, Michael, and Fethi Mansouri. *Lives in Limbo: Voices of Refugees under Temporary Protection.* Sydney: University of New South Wales Press, 2004.

Lee, H. P. 'Improper Purpose'. Chap. 13 in *Australian Administrative Law: Fundamentals, Principles and Doctrines*, edited by Matthew Groves and H. P. Lee, 198–211. Cambridge: Cambridge University Press, 2007.

Lee, Maggy. *Trafficking and Global Crime Control.* London: Sage Publications, 2011.

Levi, Ron, and Mariana Valverde. 'Knowledge on Tap: Police Science and Common Knowledge in the Legal Regulation of Drunkenness'. *Law & Social Inquiry* 26, no. 4 (2001): 819–46.

Liberman, Ken. 'Ambiguity and Gratuitous Concurrence in Inter-Cultural Communication'. *Human Studies* 3 (1980): 65–85.

Light, Ivan, Parminder Bhachu and S. Karageorgis. 'Immigrant Networks and Entrepreneurship'. In *Immigration and Entrepreneurship*, edited by Ivan Light and Parminder Bhachu. New Brunswick: Transaction Books, 2004.

Lyon, David. *Surveillance Society: Monitoring Everyday Life.* Buckingham: Open University Press, 2001.

Mack, Kathy, and Sharyn Roach Anleu. '"Getting through the List": Judgecraft and Legitimacy in the Lower Courts'. *Social and Legal Studies* 16, no. 3 (2007): 341–61.

Manning, Peter K. 'Jean-Paul Brodeur on High and Low Policing'. *Champ pénal/Penal field [En ligne]* 9 (2012).

Mansouri, Fethi, and Melek Bagdas. *Politics of Social Exclusion: Refugees on Temporary Protection Visa in Victoria*. Geelong, Victoria: Deakin University Centre for Citizenship & Human Rights, and Victorian Arabic Social Services, 2002.

Marginson, Simon, Chris Nyland, Erlenawati Sawir and Helen Forbes-Mewett. *International Student Security*. Melbourne: Cambridge University Press, 2010.

Markus, Andrew, and Jessie Taylor. 'No Work, No Income, No Medicare – the Bridging Visa E Regime'. *People and Place* 14, no. 1 (2006): 43–52.

Marr, David, and Marian Wilkinson. *Dark Victory*. Crows Nest: Allen & Unwin, 2003.

Martinez, George A. 'Philosophical Considerations and the Use of Narrative in Law'. *Rutgers Law Journal* 30 (1999): 683–706.

Mazerolle, Lorraine Green, and Janet Ransley. *Third Party Policing*. Cambridge: Cambridge University Press, 2005.

McBarnet, Doreen J. *Conviction: Law, the State and the Construction of Justice*. London: Macmillan, 1981.

McBarnet, Doreen J. 'Legal Form and Legal Mystification: An Analytical Postscript on the Scottish Criminal Justice Act, the Royal Commission on Criminal Procedure, and the Politics of Law and Order'. *International Journal of the Sociology of Law* 10 (1982): 409–17.

McBarnet, Doreen J. 'The Police and the State: Arrest, Legality and the Law'. In *Power and the State*, edited by Gary Littlejohn, Barry Smart, John Wakeford and Nira Yuval-Davis. London: Croom Helm, 1978.

McCairns, Gavin. 'Serious and Organised Crime: Promoting Visa Integrity – DIAC's Response to the Commission of Serious Migration Offences'. In *International Serious and Organised Crime Conference 2010*. Melbourne: Australian Institute of Criminology, October 18, 2010.

McConville, Mike, Andrew Sanders and Roger Leng. *The Case for the Prosecution: Police Suspects and the Construction of Criminality*. London; New York: Routledge, 1993.

Metcalfe, Andrew. 'Administrative Law Evolution: An Administrator's Point of View'. *Admin Review* 59 (2010): 59–69.

Mezzadra, Sandro, and Brett Neilson. *Border as Method, or, the Multiplication of Labor*. Durham: Duke University Press, 2013.

Millbank, Jenni. 'From Discretion to Disbelief: Recent Trends in Refugee Determinations on the Basis of Sexual Orientation in Australia and the United Kingdom'. *The International Journal of Human Rights* 13, no. 2 (2009): 391–414.

Millbank, Jenni. '"The Ring of Truth": A Case Study of Credibility Assessment in Particular Social Group Refugee Determinations'. *International Journal of Refugee Law* 21, no. 1 (2009): 1–33.

Momartin, Shakeh, Zachary Steel, Marianio Coello, Jorge Aroche, Derrick M. Silove and Robert Brooks. 'A Comparison of the Mental Health of Refugees with Temporary Versus Permanent Protection Visas'. *Medical Journal Australia* 185, no. 7 (October 2, 2006): 357–61.

Moon, Jeremy, and Anthony Sayers. 'The Dynamics of Governmental Activity: A Long-Run Analysis of the Changing Scope and Profile of Australian Ministerial Portfolios'. *Australian Journal of Political Science* 34, no. 2 (1999): 149–67.

Moreton-Robinson, Aileen. *The White Possessive: Property, Power, and Indigenous Sovereignty*. Minnesota: University of Minnesota Press, 2015.

Muir, William Ker. *Police: Streetcorner Politicians.* Chicago: University of Chicago Press, 1977.

Neocleous, Mark. *The Fabrication of Social Order: A Critical Theory of Police Power.* London: Pluto Press, 2000.

Neocleous, Mark. 'The Problem with Normality: Taking Exception to "Permanent Emergency"'. *Alternatives* 31 (2006): 191–213.

Newburn, Tim. 'The Commodification of Policing: Security Networks in the Late Modern City'. *Urban Studies* 38, no. 5–6 (2001): 829–48.

Newman, Elana, and Danny G. Kaloupek. 'The Risks and Benefits of Participating in Trauma-Focused Research Studies'. *Journal of Traumatic Stress* 17 (2004): 383–94.

Newman, Elana, and Elizabeth Risch. 'Ethical Issues in Trauma-Related Research: A Review'. *Journal of Empirical Research on Human Research Ethics* 1, no. 3 (2006): 29–46.

Noble, Gregory, ed. *Lines in the Sand: The Cronulla Riots, Multiculturalism and National Belonging.* Sydney: Sydney Institute of Criminology, 2009.

Noble, Gregory. 'Where the Bloody Hell Are We? Multicultural Manners in a World of Hyperdiversity'. In *Lines in the Sand: The Cronulla Riots, Multiculturalism and National Belonging*, edited by Greg Noble. Sydney: Sydney Institute of Criminology, 2009.

Nyers, Peter. 'No One Is Illegal between City and Nation'. *Studies in Social Justice* 4, no. 2 (2010): 127–43.

Odgers, Stephen. *Uniform Evidence Law.* 11th edn. Pyrmont: Lawbook Co, 2014.

O'Malley, Pat. 'Risk, Power and Crime Prevention'. *Economy and Society* 21, no. 3 (1992): 252–75.

O'Malley, Pat. 'Risk and Responsibility'. In *Foucault and Political Reason: Liberalism, Neo-Liberalism, and Rationalities of Government*, edited by Andrew Barry, Thomas Osborne and Nikolas Rose, 189–207. London: UCL Press, 1996.

O'Malley, Pat, and Darren Palmer. 'Post-Keynesian Policing'. *Economy and Society* 25, no. 2 (1996): 137–55.

Parsley, Connal. 'Performing the Border: Australia's Judgment of "Unauthorised Arrivals" at the Airport'. *The Australian Feminist Law Journal* 18 (2003): 55–75.

Phillips, Janet. 'Boat Arrivals in Australia: A Quick Guide to the Statistics'. *Parliamentary Library Research Paper 2013–14.* Canberra: Parliamentary Library, 2014.

Phillips, Janet. 'A Comparison of Coalition and Labor Government Asylum Policies in Australia since 2001'. *Parliamentary Library Research Paper 2013–14.* Canberra: Parliamentary Library, 2014.

Phillips, Richard. 'The Immigration Review Tribunal and Evidence'. *Canberra Bulletin of Public Administration* 79 (February 1996): 137–45.

Powell, Rebecca, Leanne Weber and Sharon Pickering. 'Counting and Accounting for Deaths in Australian Immigration Custody'. *Homicide Studies* 17, no. 4: 391–417.

Poynting, Scott. 'What Caused the Cronulla Riot?' *Race & Class* 48, no. 1 (July 2006): 85–92.

Ransley, Janet, Jessica Anderson and Tim Prenzler. 'Civil Litigation against Police in Australia: Exploring Its Extent, Nature and Implications for Accountability'. *The Australian and New Zealand Journal of Criminology* 40, no. 2 (2007): 143–60.

Reiner, Robert. *The Politics of the Police.* 2nd edn. Hertfordshire: Harvester Wheatsheaf, 1992.

Ridgely, Jennifer. 'Cities of Refuge: Immigration Enforcement, Police, and the Insurgent Genealogies of Citizenship in U.S. Sanctuary Cities'. *Urban Geography* 29, no. 1 (2008): 53–77.

Rose, Nikolas, and Peter Miller. 'Political Power Beyond the State: Problematics of Government'. *The British Journal of Sociology* 43, no. 2 (1992): 173–205.

Rose, Nikolas, and Mariana Valverde. 'Governed by Law?' *Social Legal Studies* 7, no. 4 (1998): 541–51.

Said, Edward W. *Orientalism*. London: Routledge & Kegan Paul, 1978.

Salter, Mark B. 'The Global Visa Regime and the Political Technologies of the International Self: Borders, Bodies, Biopolitics'. *Alternatives Global, Local, Political* 31, no. 2 (2006): 167–89.

Salter, Mark B. 'To Make Move and Let Stop: Mobility and the Assemblage of Circulation'. *Mobilities* 8, no. 1 (2013): 7–19.

Samers, Michael. 'Invisible Capitalism: Political Economy and the Regulation of Undocumented Immigration in France'. *Economy and Society* 32, no. 4 (2003): 555–83.

Santos, Boaventura de Sousa. 'Law: A Map of Misreading. Toward a Postmodern Conception of Law'. *Journal of Law and Society* 14, no. 3 (1987): 279–302.

Sarat, Austin. 'Situating Law between the Realities of Violence and the Claims of Justice: An Introduction'. In *Law, Violence, and the Possibility of Justice*, edited by Austin Sarat. Princeton: Princeton University Press, 2001.

Sassen, Saskia. 'The Repositioning of Citizenship: Emergent Subjects and Spaces for Politics'. In *Empire's New Clothes: Reading Hardt and Negri*, edited by Paul A. Passavant and Jodi Dean, 175–98. New York: Routledge, 2004.

Scarman, Leslie George. *The Scarman Report: The Brixton Disorders 10–12 April 1981, Report of an Inquiry*. Harmondsworth: Penguin, 1982.

Sentas, Victoria. *Traces of Terror: Counter-Terrorism Law, Policing, and Race*. Oxford: Oxford University Press, 2014.

Sharma, Nandita. 'Anti-Trafficking Rhetoric and the Making of a Global Apartheid'. *NWSA Journal* 17, no. 3 (Fall 2005): 88–111.

Sharma, Nandita. 'Global Apartheid and Nation-Statehood: Instituting Border Regimes'. In *Nationalism and Global Solidarities: Alternative Projections to Neoliberal Globalisation*, edited by James Goodman and Paul James, 71–89. London: Routledge, 2007.

Skinner, Stephen. 'Stories of Pain and the Pursuit of Justice: Law, Violence, Experience and Jurisprudence'. *Law, Culture and the Humanities* 5 (2009): 131–55.

Skolnick, J. H. *Justice without Trial*. New York: John Wiley & Sons, 1966.

Smith, David John, Jeremy Gray and Policy Studies Institute. *Police and People in London: The PSI Report*. Aldershot: Gower, 1985.

Smith, Valerie J. 'Ethical and Effective Ethnographic Research Methods: A Case Study with Afghan Refugees in California'. *Journal of Empirical Research on Human Research Ethics* 4 (2009): 59–72.

Steel, Alex. 'Consorting in New South Wales: Substantive Offence or Police Power?' *University of New South Wales Law Journal* 26, no. 3 (2003): 567–602.

Steel, Z., S. Momartin, C. Bateman, A. Hafshagani, D. Silove, N. Everson, K. Roy *et al.* 'Psychiatric Status of Asylum Seeker Families Held for a Protracted Period in a Remote Detention Centre in Australia'. *Australia and New Zealand Journal of Public Health* 28, no. 6 (2004): 527–36.

Steel, Z., D. Silove, R. Brooks, S. Momartin, B. Alzuhairi and I. Susljik. 'Impact of Immigration Detention and Temporary Protection on the Mental Health of Refugees'. *British Journal of Psychiatry* 188 (2006): 58–64.

Stumpf, Juliet P. 'The Process Is the Punishment in Crimmigration Law'. In *The Borders of Punishment: Migration, Citizenship and Social Exclusion*, edited by Katja Franko Aas and Mary Bosworth, 58–75. Oxford: Oxford University Press, 2013.

Taylor, S. Caroline. *Court Licensed Abuse: Patriarchal Lore and the Legal Response to Intrafamilial Sexual Abuse of Children*. New York: Peter Lang, 2004.

Taylor, Savitri. 'The Pacific Solution or a Pacific Nightmare: The Difference between Burden Shifting and Responsibility Sharing'. *Asian-Pacific Law and Policy Journal* 6, no. 1 (2005): 1–43.

Temple, Bogusia, and Rosalind Edwards. 'Limited Exchanges: Approaches to Involving People Who Do Not Speak English in Research and Service Development'. In *Doing Research with Refugees: Issues and Guidelines*, edited by Bogusia Temple and Rhetta Moran, 37–54. Bristol: The Policy Press, 2006.

Thwaites, Rayner. *The Liberty of Non-Citizens: Indefinite Detention in Commonwealth Countries*. Oregon: Hart Publishing, 2014.

Travis, Gail. 'Police Discretion in Law Enforcement: A Study of Section 5 of the NSW Offences in Public Places Act 1979'. In *Issues in Criminal Justice Administration*, edited by Mark Findlay, Sandra J. Egger and Jeff Sutton, 200–33. Sydney: George Allen and Unwin, 1983.

Turton, David. 'Migrants and Refugees'. Chap. 8 in *In Search of Cool Ground: War, Flight, and Homecoming in Northeast Africa*, edited by Tim Allen, 96–110. Trenton: Africa World Press, 1996.

UNHCR. 'Handbook on Procedures and Criteria for Determining Refugee Status under the 1951 Convention and the 1967 Protocol Relating to the Status of Refugees'. 1992 edn.

Valverde, Mariana. 'Jurisdiction and Scale: Legal "Technicalities" as Resources for Theory'. *Social and Legal Studies* 18, no. 2 (2009): 139–57.

Valverde, Mariana. *Law's Dream of a Common Knowledge*. Princeton: Princeton University Press, 2003.

Valverde, Mariana. 'Police, Sovereignty, and Law: Foucaultian Reflections'. In *Police and the Liberal State*, edited by Markus D. Dubber and Mariana Valverde, 15–32. Stanford: Stanford University Press, 2008.

Valverde, Mariana. 'Seeing Like a City: The Dialectic of Modern and Premodern Ways of Seeing in Urban Governance'. *Law & Society Review* 45, no. 2 (2011): 277–312.

Varsanyi, Monica W. 'Documenting Undocumented Migrants: The Matrículas Consulares as Neoliberal Local Membership'. *Geopolitics* 12, no. 2 (2007): 299–319.

Varsanyi, Monica W. 'Interrogating "Urban Citizenship" vis-à-vis Undocumented Migration'. *Citizenship Studies* 10, no. 2 (2006): 229–49.

Varsanyi, Monica W. 'Rescaling the "Alien", Rescaling Personhood: Neoliberalism, Immigration, and the State'. *Annals of the Association of American Geographers* 98, no. 4 (2008): 877–96.

Varsanyi, Monica W. 'Rising Tensions Between National and Local Immigration and Citizenship Policy: Matrículas Consulares, Local Membership and Documenting the Undocumented'. Working Paper 140. San Diego: The Center for Comparative Immigration Studies, University of California, 2006.

Veitch, Scott. *Law and Irresponsibility: On the Legitimation of Human Suffering*. New York: Routledge-Cavendish, 2007.

Vosko, Leah F., Valerie Preston and Robert Latham, eds. *Liberating Temporariness? Migration, Work and Citizenship in an Age of Insecurity*. Montreal: McGill-Queen's University Press, 2014.

Vukov, Tamara. 'Target Practice: The Algorithmics and Biopolitics of Race in Merging Smart Border Practices and Technologies'. *Transfers* 6, no. 1 (2016): 80–97.

Waddington, P. A. J. *Policing Citizens*. London: UCL Press, 1999.

Weber, Leanne. *Policing Non-Citizens*. Oxford: Routledge, 2013.

Weber, Leanne, and Benjamin Bowling. 'Policing Migration: A Framework for Investigating the Regulation of Global Mobility'. *Policing and Society* 14, no. 3 (2004): 195–212.

Williams, George, and Tony Blackshield. *Australian Constitutional Law and Theory: Commentary and Materials.* 2nd edn. Sydney: The Federation Press, 1998.

Wilson, James Q. *Varieties of Police Behavior: The Management of Law and Order in Eight Communities.* Cambridge: Harvard University Press, 1968.

Winters, P., A. de Janvry and E. Sadoulet. *Family and Community Networks in Mexico – US Migration.* Working Paper Series in Agricultural and Resource Economics. Vol. 99–12, Armidale, NSW University of New England, 1999.

Zong, Jie, and Jeanne Batalova. 'Frequently Requested Statistics on Immigrants and Immigration in the United States'. *Migration Information Source.* February 26, 2015. www.migrationpolicy.org/article/frequently-requested-statistics-immigrants-and-immigration-united-states#Unauthorized Immigration.

Official publications and submissions

Al Kateb, Ahmed. 'Submission No 86 to the Senate Legal and Constitutional References Committee Inquiry into the *Administration and Operation of the Migration Act 1958*'. 2005.

Australian Government Information Management Office. 'The Australian Public Service Big Data Strategy: Improved Understanding through Enhanced Data-Analytics Capability'. Department of Finance and Deregulation, 2013.

Australian Human Rights Commission. '2009 El Masri v. Commonwealth (Department of Immigration and Citizenship): Report into Unlawful and Arbitrary Detention and the Right of People in Detention to Humane Treatment (2009) AUSHRC 41'. Sydney, 2009.

Australian Human Rights Commission. 'Background Paper: Immigration Detention and Visa Cancellation under Section 501 of the Migration Act'. Sydney, 2010.

Australian Human Rights Commission. 'The Forgotten Children: National Inquiry into Children in Immigration Detention'. Sydney, 2014.

Australian Law Reform Commission. 'Evidence (Interim) ALRC Report 26'. Canberra, 1985.

Australian Law Reform Commission. 'Managing Justice: A Review of the Federal Civil Justice System'. Sydney, 2000.

Australian National Audit Office. 'Administering the Character Requirements of the Migration Act 1958: Department of Immigration and Citizenship'. Barton, 2011.

Australian National Audit Office. 'Management of the Detention Centre Contracts –Part A Department of Immigration and Multicultural and Indigenous Affairs'. Canberra, 2004.

Australian National Audit Office. 'Managing Compliance with Visa Conditions: Department of Immigration and Border Protection, Performance Audit'. Barton, 2015.

Australian National Audit Office. 'Onshore Compliance: Visa Overstayers and Non-Citizens Working Illegally Department of Immigration and Multicultural and Indigenous Affairs'. Canberra, 2004.

Committee of Review of Prerogative Writ Procedure. 'Report of the Committee of Review of Prerogative Writ Procedure'. Canberra: Commonwealth of Australia, 1973.

Committee on Administrative Discretions. 'Final Report of the Committee on Administrative Discretions'. Canberra: Commonwealth of Australia, 1973.

Committee to Advise on Australia's Immigration Policies. 'Immigration: A Commitment to Australia'. Canberra: Commonwealth of Australia, 1988.

Commonwealth Administrative Review Committee. 'Commonwealth Administrative Review Committee Report'. Canberra: Commonwealth of Australia, 1971.

Commonwealth and Immigration Ombudsman. 'Department of Immigration and Citizenship Report into Referred Immigration Cases: Detention Process Issues'. Canberra, 2007.

Commonwealth and Immigration Ombudsman. 'Department of Immigration and Citizenship: The Safeguards System'. Canberra, 2008.

Commonwealth and Immigration Ombudsman. 'Department of Immigration and Multicultural Affairs Administration of S501 of the Migration Act 1958 as it Applies to Long-Term Residents'. Canberra, 2006.

Commonwealth and Immigration Ombudsman. 'Inquiry into the Circumstances of the Vivian Alvarez Matter: Report under the *Ombudsman Act 1976* by the Commonwealth Ombudsman, Prof. John McMillan, of an Inquiry Undertaken by Mr Neil Comrie AO APM'. Canberra, 2005.

Commonwealth and Immigration Ombudsman. 'Report for Tabling in Parliament by the Commonwealth and Immigration Ombudsman: Under S486o of the Migration Act 1958, Personal Identifier 226/07, Tabled in Parliament 13 February 2008'. Canberra, 2007.

Commonwealth Director of Public Prosecutions. 'Annual Report 2015–16'. Canberra, 2016.

Commonwealth Ombudsman. 'Annual Report 2003–04'. Canberra, 2004.

Commonwealth Ombudsman. 'Annual Report 2004–05'. Canberra, 2005.

Commonwealth Ombudsman. 'Annual Report 2005–06'. Canberra, 2006.

Commonwealth Ombudsman. 'Annual Report 2006–07'. Canberra, 2007.

Commonwealth Ombudsman. 'Annual Report 2007–08'. Canberra, 2008.

Commonwealth Ombudsman. 'Annual Report 2008–09'. Canberra, 2009.

Commonwealth Ombudsman. 'Annual Report 2009–10'. Canberra, 2010.

Commonwealth Ombudsman. 'Annual Report 2013–14'. Canberra, 2014.

Commonwealth Ombudsman. 'Annual Report 2014–15'. Canberra, 2015.

Commonwealth Ombudsman. 'Investigation into the Exercise of the Powers of Entry, Search and Seizure under Sub-Sections 251 (4)–(6) of the Migration Act 1958: Report under Section 15(2) of the Ombudsman Act 1976'. December 1999.

Community Law Australia. 'Unaffordable and Out of Reach: The Problem of Access to the Australian Legal System'. 2012.

Community Relations Commission. 'Submission to the NSW Ombudsman Law Enforcement Legislation Amendment (Public Safety) Act 2005 Review'. February 21, 2007.

Department of Immigration and Border Protection. 'Annual Report 2013–14'. Belconnen, 2014.

Department of Immigration and Border Protection. 'Annual Report 2014–15'. Belconnen, 2015.

Department of Immigration and Border Protection. 'Annual Report 2015–16'. Belconnen, 2016.

Department of Immigration and Border Protection. 'Australia's Migration Trends 2012–13'. Belconnen, 2014.

Department of Immigration and Border Protection. 'Australia's Migration Trends 2013–14'. Belconnen, 2014.

Department of Immigration and Border Protection. 'Corporate Plan 2015–19'. Belconnen, 2015.

Department of Immigration and Citizenship. 'Annual Report 2006–07'. Belconnen, 2007.

Department of Immigration and Citizenship. 'Annual Report 2007–08'. Belconnen, 2008.

Department of Immigration and Citizenship. 'Annual Report 2008–09'. Belconnen, 2009.

Department of Immigration and Citizenship. 'Annual Report 2009–10'. Belconnen, 2010.

Department of Immigration and Citizenship. 'Annual Report 2011–12'. Belconnen, 2011.

Department of Immigration and Citizenship. 'Annual Report 2012–13'. Belconnen, 2013.

Department of Immigration and Citizenship. 'Australia's Migration Trends 2011–12'. Belconnen, 2013.

Department of Immigration and Citizenship. 'Procedures Advice Manual 3, Generic Guidelines A, Visa Systems, Alerts and Data Bases Instructions'. Canberra: Commonwealth of Australia, 2010.

Department of Immigration and Citizenship. Submission 129f to Joint Standing Committee on Migration Responses from the Department of Immigration and Citizenship, *Inquiry into Immigration Detention in Australia*, October 15, 2008.

Department of Immigration and Citizenship. Submission 129o to Joint Standing Committee on Migration, *Inquiry into Immigration Detention in Australia*, March 17, 2009.

Department of Immigration and Multicultural Affairs. 'Annual Report 1996–97'. Canberra, 1997.

Department of Immigration and Multicultural Affairs. 'Annual Report 1997–98'. Canberra, 1998.

Department of Immigration and Multicultural Affairs. 'Annual Report 2000–01'. Canberra, 2001.

Department of Immigration and Multicultural Affairs. 'Annual Report 2005–06'. Canberra, 2006.

Department of Immigration and Multicultural Affairs. 'Protecting the Border: Immigration Compliance'. Belconnen, 1999.

Department of Immigration and Multicultural Affairs. 'Review of Illegal Workers in Australia: Improving Immigration Compliance in the Workplace'. Canberra, 1999.

Department of Immigration and Multicultural and Indigenous Affairs. 'Annual Report 2001–02'. Canberra, 2002.

Department of Immigration and Multicultural and Indigenous Affairs. 'Annual Report 2002–03'. Canberra, 2003.

Department of Immigration and Multicultural and Indigenous Affairs. 'Annual Report 2003–04'. Canberra, 2004.

Department of Immigration and Multicultural and Indigenous Affairs. 'Annual Report 2004–05'. Canberra, 2005.

Department of Immigration and Multicultural and Indigenous Affairs. 'Department of Immigration and Multicultural and Indigenous Affairs Submission to the Senate Standing Committee for the Scrutiny of Bills Inquiry into the Government's Response to the Previous Report by the Senate Standing Committee for the Scrutiny of Bills on Entry and Search Provisions Tabled in 2000'. 2004.

Department of Immigration and Multicultural and Indigenous Affairs. 'Managing the Border: Immigration Compliance 2003–04 Edition'. Belconnen, 2005.

Department of Immigration and Multicultural and Indigenous Affairs. 'Managing the Border: Immigration Compliance 2004–05 Edition'. Belconnen, 2005.

Department of Immigration and Multicultural and Indigenous Affairs. 'Managing the Border: Immigration Compliance'. Belconnen, 2004.

Explanatory Memorandum, Migration and Maritime Powers Legislation Amendment (Resolving the Asylum Legacy Caseload) Bill 2014 (Cth) 2.

Explanatory Memorandum, Migration Reform Bill 1992 (Cth); Migration (Delayed Visa Applications) Tax Bill 1992 (Cth).

Hazzard, Norm. 'Strikeforce Neil Cronulla Riots: Review of the Police Response, Vol. 1'. Sydney: NSW Police, 2006.

Howells, Stephen. 'Report of the 2010 Review of the *Migration Amendment (Employer Sanctions) Act* 2007'. Belconnen: Commonwealth of Australia, 2011.

Human Rights and Equal Opportunity Commission. 'A Last Resort? The National Inquiry into Children in Immigration Detention'. Sydney, 2004.

Human Rights and Equal Opportunity Commission. 'Those Who've Come Across the Seas: Detention of Unauthorised Arrivals'. Sydney, 1998.

Human Rights and Equal Opportunity Commission. 'Submission to the Joint Standing Committee on Migration Inquiry into Immigration Detention in Australia'. Sydney, 2008.

Joint Management Review. 'Immigration Functions Related to Control and Entry'. Canberra: Commonwealth of Australia, July 1978.

Joint Standing Committee on Migration. 'Asylum, Border Control and Detention'. Canberra, February 1994.

Joint Standing Committee on Migration. 'Immigration Detention in Australia: A New Beginning, Criteria for Release from Immigration Detention, First Report of the Inquiry into Immigration Detention in Australia'. Canberra, 2008.

Joint Standing Committee on Migration. 'Immigration Detention in Australia: Community-Based Alternatives to Detention, Second Report of the Inquiry into Immigration Detention in Australia'. Canberra, 2009.

Joint Standing Committee on Migration Regulations. 'First Report: Illegal Entrants in Australia – Balancing Control and Compassion'. Canberra: Commonwealth of Australia, September 1990.

NSW Ombudsman. 'Review of Emergency Powers to Prevent or Control Disorder'. Sydney, September 2007.

Palmer, Mick. 'Inquiry into the Circumstances of the Immigration Detention of Cornelia Rau'. Canberra: Commonwealth of Australia, 2005.

Platform for International Cooperation on Undocumented Migrants. 'PICUM Submission to the UN Committee on the Protection of the Rights of All Migrant Workers and Members of Their Families: Day of General Discussion on the Role of Migration Statistics for Treaty Reporting and Migration Policies'. Geneva, April 22, 2013.

Senate Legal and Constitutional References Committee. 'Inquiry into the Administration and Operation of the Migration Act 1958'. Canberra: Commonwealth of Australia, 2006.

Senate Legal and Constitutional References Committee. 'Migration Amendment (Employer Sanctions) Bill 2006'. Canberra: Commonwealth of Australia, 2006.

Senate Select Committee on Ministerial Discretion in Migration Matters. 'Senate Select Committee on Ministerial Discretion in Migration Matters Report'. Canberra: Commonwealth of Australia, 2004.

Senate Standing Committee for the Scrutiny of Bills. 'Entry and Search Provisions in Commonwealth Legislation'. Canberra: Commonwealth of Australia, 2000.

Senate Standing Committee for the Scrutiny of Bills. 'Entry, Search and Seizure Provisions in Commonwealth Legislation'. Canberra: Commonwealth of Australia, 2006.

South Australia State Coroner. 'Finding of Inquest: An Inquest Taken on Behalf of Our Sovereign Lady the Queen at Adelaide in the State of South Australia, on the 3rd Day of July 2008 and the 16th Day of October 2008, by the Coroner's Court of the Said State, Constituted of Mark Frederick Johns, State Coroner, into the Death of Wah Aun Chan'. 2008.

Western Australia Police. 'Post Implementation Review of Taser'. *Research report prepared for the Corporate Executive Team*. Perth, 2010.

Cases and transcripts

Akpata v. *Minister for Immigration and Citizenship* [2012] FCA 806; (2012) 206 FCR 120.

Akpata v. *Minister for Immigration and Multicultural and Indigenous Affairs* [2004] FCAFC 65.

Al Khafaji v. *Minister for Immigration and Multicultural and Indigenous Affairs* [2002] FCA 1369.

Al Masri v. *Minister for Immigration and Multicultural and Indigenous Affairs* [2002] FCA 1009; (2002) 192 ALR 609.

Alam v. *Minister for Immigration and Multicultural and Indigenous Affairs* [2004] FMCA 583; (2004) 187 FLR 120.

Alderson v. *Booth* [1969] 2 QB 216; (1969) 53 Cr App R 301.

Al-Kateb v. *Godwin* [2004] HCA 37; (2004) 219 CLR 562.

Amaca Pty Ltd v. *the State of New South Wales* [2004] NSWCA 124; (2004) 132 LGERA 309.

Anderson v. *Judges of the District Court of New South Wales* (1992) 27 NSWLR 701.

Ang v. *Minister for Immigration and Ethnic Affairs* [1994] FCA 952; (1994) 121 ALR 95.

Bartlett v. *Weir* [1994] FCA 1143; (1994) 72 A Crim R 511.

Bathurst City Council v. *Saban* (1985) 2 NSWLR 704.

Behrooz v. *Secretary DIMIA, SHDB* v. *Godwin, MIMIA* v. *Al Khafaji* [2003] HCATrans 458.

Bunning v. *Cross* [1978] HCA 22; (1978) 19 ALR 641.

Chan Yee Kin v. *Minister for Immigration and Ethnic Affairs* [1989] HCA 62; (1989) 169 CLR 379.

Chu Kheng Lim v. *Minister for Immigration, Local Government and Ethnic Affairs* [1992] HCA 64; (1992) 176 CLR 1.

Chu Shao Hung v. *R* [1953] HCA 33; (1953) 87 CLR 575.

Clearihan v. *Registrar of Motor Vehicle Dealers in the Australian Capital Territory* (1994) 117 FLR 455.

Coleman v. *Minister for Immigration & Citizenship* [2007] FCA 1500.

CPCF v. *Minister for Immigration and Border Protection* [2015] HCA 1; (2015) 316 ALR 1.

Crimmins v. *Stevedoring Industry Finance Committee* [1999] HCA 59; (1999) 200 CLR 1.

Director of Public Prosecutions v. *Carr* [2002] NSWSC 194; (2002) 127 A Crim R 151.

Fernando v. *Commonwealth* [2014] FCAFC 181; (2014) 231 FCR 251.

Fernando v. *Commonwealth of Australia* [2010] FCA 753; (2010) 271 ALR 521.

George v. *Rockett* [1990] HCA 26; (1990) 93 ALR 483.

Goldie v. *Commonwealth* [2002] FCA 433; (2002) 117 FCR 566.

Grech v. *Heffey* [1991] FCA 50; (1991) 34 FCR 93.

Haneef v. *Minister for Immigration and Citizenship* [2007] FCA 1273; (2007) 161 FCR 40; 242 ALR 290.

Hoang v. *Minister for Immigration* [2013] FCCA 89.

Hyder v. *Commonwealth of Australia* [2012] NSWCA 336; (2012) 217 A Crim R 517.

Irving v. *Minister for Immigration, Local Government and Ethnic Affairs* [1996] FCA 663; (1996) 139 ALR 84.

Kioa v. *West* [1985] HCA 81; 159 CLR 550; 62 ALR 321.

M79/2012 v. *Minister for Immigration and Citizenship* [2013] HCA 24; (2013) 252 CLR 336, 298 ALR 1.

Macpherson v. *Brown* (1975) 12 SASR 184.

Marshall v. *Watson* [1972] HCA 27; (1972) 124 CLR 640.

Minister for Immigration and Citizenship v. *SZQRB* [2013] FCAFC 33; (2013) 296 ALR 525.

Minister for Immigration and Ethnic Affairs v. *Baker* (1997) 153 ALR 463.

Minister for Immigration and Multicultural and Indigenous Affairs v. *Alam* [2005] FCAFC 132; (2005) 219 ALR 629.

Minister for Immigration and Multicultural and Indigenous Affairs v. *Al Khafaji* [2004] HCA 38.

Minister for Immigration and Multicultural and Indigenous Affairs v. *Al Masri* [2003] FCAFC 70; (2003) 126 FCR 54.

Minister for Immigration and Multicultural and Indigenous Affairs v. *Nystrom* [2006] HCA 50; (2006) 228 CLR 566.

Mohammed v. *The Secretary of State for the Home Department* [2014] EWHC 4317 (Admin); [2015] WLR 3349.

Morrison v. *Minister for Immigration and Citizenship* [2008] FCA 54.

Newman-Mariotti v. *Minister for Immigration and Border Protection* [2015] HCATrans 250 (October 1, 2015).

Newman-Mariotti v. *Minister for Immigration and Border Protection* [2015] HCATrans 251 (October 2, 2015).

Nystrom v. *Minister for Immigration and Multicultural and Indigenous Affairs* [2005] FCAFC 121; (2005) 143 FCR 420.

Park Oh Ho v. *Minister for Immigration and Ethnic Affairs* [1988] FCA 274; (1988) 91 ALR 288.

Park Oh Ho v. *Minister for Immigration and Ethnic Affairs* [1989] HCA 54; (1989) 167 CLR 637.

Percy v. *Hall* [1997] QB 924.

Plaintiff M47/2012 v. *Director-General of Security* [2012] HCA 46; (2012) 251 CLR 1; 292 ALR 243.

Plaintiff M61/2010E v. *Commonwealth of Australia; Plaintiff M69 of 2010* v. *Commonwealth of Australia* [2010] HCA 41; (2010) 243 CLR 319.

Plaintiff S4/2014 v. *Minister for Immigration and Border Protection* [2014] HCA 34; (2014) 253 CLR 219.

Plaintiff S10/2011 v. *Minister for Immigration and Citizenship* [2012] HCA 31; (2012) 246 CLR 636; 290 ALR 616.

Plaintiff S99/2016 v. *Minister for Immigration and Border Protection* [2016] FCA 483.

Plaintiff S157/2002 v. *Commonwealth of Australia* [2003] HCA 2; (2003) 211 CLR 476; 195 ALR 24.

Plaintiff M70/2011 v. *Minister for Immigration and Citizenship* [2011] HCA 32; (2011) 244 CLR 144; 280 ALR 18.

Queensland Bacon Pty Ltd v. *Rees* [1966] HCA 21; (1966) 115 CLR 266.

R v. *Governor of Brockhill Prison; Ex parte Evans (No 2)* [2000] UKHL 48; [2000] 4 All ER 15.

R v. *Inwood* [1973] 2 ALL ER 645; (1973) 57 Cr App R 529.

R v. *Rondo* [2001] NSWCCA 540; (2001) 126 A Crim R 562.

R v. *Tillett; Ex parte Newton* (1969) 14 FLR 101.

Re Bolton; Ex parte Beane [1987] HCA 12; (1987) 162 CLR 514.

Re David John Cawdell Irving and Minister of State for Immigration Local Government and Ethnic Affairs [1993] FCA 228; (1993) 115 ALR 125.
Re Davis [1947] HCA 53; (1947) 75 CLR 409.
Re Patterson; Ex parte Taylor [2001] HCA 51; (2001) 207 CLR 391.
Ridgeway v. *The Queen* [1995] HCA 66; (1995) 184 CLR 19.
Ruddock v. *Taylor* [2003] NSWCA 262; (2003) 58 NSWLR 269.
Ruddock v. *Taylor* [2005] HCA 48; (2005) 221 ALR 32.
Ruddock v. *Vadarlis* [2001] FCA 1329; (2001) 110 FCR 491.
S v. *Secretary, Department of Immigration and Multicultural and Indigenous Affairs* (2005) FCA 549 [212]; (2005) 143 FCR 217; 216 ALR 252.
Salemi v. *Mackellar (No 2)* [1977] HCA 26; (1977) 137 CLR 396.
Sales v. *Minister for Immigration & Citizenship* [2008] FCAFC 132; (2008) 171 FCR 56.
Samrein Pty Ltd v. *Metropolitan Water Sewerage and Drainage Board* (1982) 56 ALJR 678; (1982) 41 ALR 467.
Schlieske v. *Minister for Immigration and Ethnic Affairs* [1988] FCA 48; (1988) 84 ALR 719.
Soh v. *Commonwealth* [2008] FCA 520; (2008) 101 ALD 310.
SU v. *Commonwealth of Australia* [2014] NSWSC 241.
SU v. *Commonwealth of Australia; BS* v. *Commonwealth of Australia* [2016] NSWSC 8; (2016) 307 FLR 357.
The Queen v. *Toohey; Ex parte Northern Land Council* [1981] HCA 74; (1981) 151 CLR 170.
Thompson; Hsu v. *Commissioner of Police of the Metropolis* [1997] EWCA Civ 3083; [1998] QB 498.
Uddin v. *Minister for Immigration and Multicultural and Indigenous Affairs* [2005] FMCA 841.
Victoria Park Racing and Recreation Grounds Co Ltd v. *Taylor* [1937] HCA 45; (1937) 58 CLR 479.
Wu Yu Fang v. *Minister for Immigration and Ethnic Affairs* [1996] FCA 106; (1996) 64 FCR 245.

Australian tribunal cases

'*Wag' and Minister of Immigration and Multicultural Affairs* [1996] AATA 264 (July 31, 1996).
1001289 [2010] RRTA 310 (April 21, 2010).
Azad and Minister for Immigration and Multicultural and Indigenous Affairs [2005] AATA 185 (March 7, 2005).
Azar and Minister for Immigration and Multicultural and Indigenous Affairs [2005] AATA 1061 (October 24, 2005).
Basic and Minister for Immigration and Multicultural and Indigenous Affairs [2005] AATA 590 (June 10, 2005).
Batula and Minister for Immigration and Multicultural Affairs [2001] AATA 496 (June 6, 2001).
Bibashani and Minister for Immigration and Multicultural and Indigenous Affairs [2005] AATA 1207 (December 6, 2005).
Brennan and Minister for Immigration and Multicultural and Indigenous Affairs [2003] AATA 1029 (October 13, 2003).

Cesar Torres and Minister of Immigration and Multicultural Affairs [1997] AATA 565 (December 15, 1997).
Chau and Minister Immigration and Multicultural Affairs [2001] AATA 485 (June 5, 2001).
Chim and Minister for Immigration and Multicultural and Indigenous Affairs [2002] AATA 1340 (December 19, 2002).
Damakas and Minister for Immigration, Multicultural and Indigenous Affairs [2002] AATA 355 (May 16, 2002).
Edwards and Department of Immigration and Multicultural Affairs [1998] AATA 86 (February 13, 1998).
Emmanuel Mariano Frijas and Minister for Immigration and Multicultural Affairs [1998] AATA 773 (October 2, 1998).
Esguerra and Minister for Immigration and Multicultural Affairs [2000] AATA 554 (July 6, 2000).
Evans and Minister for Immigration and Multicultural and Indigenous Affairs [2004] AATA 171 (February 20, 2004).
Fatma Ilbay and Minister of Immigration and Multicultural Affairs [1996] AATA 459 (December 20, 1996).
Galang and Minister for Immigration and Multicultural Affairs [1998] AATA 240 (April 3, 1998).
Gawronski and Minister for Immigration and Multicultural Affairs [2000] AATA 790 (June 26, 2000).
Golding and Minister for Immigration and Multicultural Affairs [2000] AATA 956 (November 2, 2000).
Guo and Minister for Immigration and Citizenship [2007] AATA 1099 (March 6, 2007).
Hamida Jalal and Minister of Immigration and Multicultural Affairs [1997] AATA 292 (August 15, 1997).
Hegarty and Minister for Immigration and Multicultural Affairs [2001] AATA 421 (May 18, 2001).
Hem and Minister for Immigration and Multicultural and Indigenous Affairs [2004] AATA 645 (June 22, 2004).
Higgins and Minister for Immigration and Multicultural Affairs [1998] AATA 13 (January 19, 1998).
Ho Song Lu and Minister for Immigration and Multicultural Affairs [1998] AATA 966 (December 16, 1998).
Hongvilai and Minister for Immigration and Multicultural and Indigenous Affairs [2003] AATA 998 (October 3, 2003).
Howard and Minister for Immigration and Multicultural Affairs [2006] AATA 474 (May 31, 2006).
Jiang and Minister for Immigration and Multicultural and Indigenous Affairs [2005] AATA 666 (July 12, 2005).
Joseph Annecchini and Minister of Immigration and Multicultural Affairs [1997] AATA 153 (May 7, 1997).
Jreige and Minister of Immigration and Multicultural Affairs [1999] AATA 237 (April 7, 1999).
Kaveh and Minister for Immigration and Multicultural and Indigenous Affairs [2004] AATA 1331 (December 14, 2004).
Kertz and Minister for Immigration and Multicultural Affairs [2006] AATA 247 (March 15, 2006).

Kim and Minister for Immigration and Multicultural and Indigenous Affairs [2005] AATA 239 (March 18, 2005).
Konteh and Minister for Immigration and Multicultural Affairs [2000] AATA 291 (April 14, 2000).
Konteh and Minister for Immigration and Multicultural Affairs [2002] AATA 262 (April 18, 2002).
Kwong Leung Lam and Minister of Immigration and Multicultural Affairs [1997] AATA 196 (June 11, 1997).
Lim and Minister for Immigration and Multicultural and Indigenous Affairs [2002] AATA 1341 (December 23, 2002).
Lim and Minister for Immigration and Multicultural and Indigenous Affairs [2005] AATA 893 (September 15, 2005).
Ly and Minister for Immigration and Multicultural Affairs [2000] AATA 339 (April 28, 2000).
Machin and Minister for Immigration and Multicultural and Indigenous Affairs [2005] AATA 187 (March 7, 2005).
Mahoni and Minister for Immigration and Multicultural and Indigenous Affairs [2004] AATA 465 (May 12, 2004).
Majeed, Jahanghir Abdul [2002] MRTA 6429 (October 31, 2002).
May and Minister for Immigration and Multicultural Affairs [2000] AATA 480 (June 15, 2000).
Mohammed Hameed Khan and Minister for Immigration and Multicultural Affairs [1998] AATA 475 (June 30, 1998).
Moon and Minister for Immigration and Multicultural Affairs [2005] AATA 652 (July 7, 2005).
Morales and Minister for Immigration and Multicultural Affairs [1996] AATA 741 (August 2, 1996).
Muhammed and Minister for Immigration and Multicultural and Indigenous Affairs [2004] AATA 878 (August 20, 2004).
Mungcal-Fabian and Minister for Immigration and Multicultural and Indigenous Affairs [2003] AATA 362 (April 22, 2003).
Natalie Kaufman and Minister for Immigration and Multicultural Affairs [1998] AATA 897 (November 23, 1998).
Novi Medyanto and Minister of Immigration and Multicultural Affairs [1997] AATA (November 28, 1997).
Ostin and Minister for Immigration and Multicultural and Indigenous Affairs [2005] AATA 313 (April 8, 2005).
Peljha and Minister for Immigration and Multicultural Affairs [2000] AATA 967 (November 6, 2000).
Peng and Minister for Immigration and Multicultural and Indigenous Affairs [2003] AATA 991 (October 2, 2003).
Perth City Mission and Department of Immigration and Multicultural Affairs [1998] AATA 457 (June 29, 1998).
Phan Van Xuan and Minister of Immigration and Multicultural Affairs [1997] AATA 295 (August 18, 1997).
Phuoc Tuong Tran and Department of Immigration and Multicultural Affairs [1997] AATA 436 (October 30, 1997).
Priori and Minister for Immigration and Multicultural and Indigenous Affairs [2005] AATA 1288 (December 22, 2005).

Re Lachmaiya and Department of Immigration and Ethnic Affairs [1994] AATA 27; (1994) 19 AAR 148.

Re Sam and Minister for Immigration and Multicultural and Indigenous Affairs [2004] AATA 1003 (September 24, 2004).

Re Strangio and Minister for Immigration and Ethnic Affairs (1994) 35 ALD 676.

Read and Minister for Immigration and Multicultural Affairs [1997] AATA 931 (August 25, 1997).

Reyes and Minister for Immigration and Multicultural and Indigenous Affairs [2003] AATA 497 (May 30, 2003).

Ribarich and Minister for Immigration and Multicultural and Indigenous Affairs [2005] AATA 1014 (October 31, 2005).

Rodgers and Minister for Immigration and Multicultural Affairs [2006] AATA 723 [93] (August 21, 2006).

Romeo and Minister for Immigration and Multicultural Affairs [1998] AATA 87 (February 12, 1998).

Serifovski and Minister for Immigration and Multicultural and Indigenous Affairs [2005] AATA 241 (March 22, 2005).

Shirley Edwards and Minister of Immigration and Multicultural Affairs [1997] AATA 591 (December 22, 1997).

Shukri and Minister for Immigration and Multicultural and Indigenous Affairs [2003] AATA 997 (October 3, 2003).

Sorensen and Minister for Immigration and Multicultural and Indigenous Affairs [2006] AATA 96 (February 7, 2006).

Stewart and Minister for Immigration and Multicultural and Indigenous Affairs [2004] AATA 1234 (November 22, 2004).

Tautuliu and Minister for Immigration and Multicultural Affairs [2000] AATA 968 (November 6, 2000).

Tuipulotu and Minister for Immigration and Multicultural Affairs [2001] AATA 451 (May 28, 2001).

Vinh Tran and Minister of Immigration and Multicultural Affairs [1997] AATA 463 (November 7, 1997).

Wei and Minister for Immigration and Multicultural Affairs [2006] AATA 398 (May 8, 2006).

Wyatt and Minister for Immigration and Multicultural Affairs [2001] AATA 29 (January 22, 2001).

Yan and Minister for Immigration and Citizenship [2007] AATA 1369 (May 25, 2007).

Yap and Minister for Immigration and Multicultural Affairs [2006] AATA 510 (June 13, 2006).

Yusuf and Minister for Immigration and Multicultural Affairs [2000] AATA 792 (August 11, 2000).

Legislation and regulations

Administrative Appeals Tribunal Act 1975 (Cth).

Administrative Decisions (Judicial Review) Act 1977 (Cth).

Australian Border Force Act 2015 (Cth).

Customs Act 1901 (Cth).

Crimes Act 1914 (Cth).

Education Services for Overseas Students Act 2000 (Cth).
Evidence Act 1995 (Cth).
Immigration Restriction Act 1901 (Cth).
Inclosed Lands Protection Act 1901 (NSW).
Law Enforcement (Powers and Responsibilities) Act 2002 (NSW).
Migration (Offences and Undesirable Persons) Amendment Act 1992 (Cth).
Migration Act 1958 (Cth).
Migration Amendment (Bridging Visas – Code of Behaviour) Regulation 2013 (Cth).
Migration Amendment (Character and General Visa Cancellation) Act 2014 (Cth).
Migration Amendment (Detention Arrangements) Act 2005 (Cth).
Migration Amendment (Employer Sanctions) Act 2007 (Cth).
Migration Amendment (Excision from the Migration Zone) Act 2001 (Cth).
Migration Legislation Amendment (Judicial Review) Act 2001 (Cth).
Migration Legislation Amendment (Strengthening of Provisions relating to Character and Conduct) Act 1998 (Cth).
Migration Legislation Amendment Act (No 1) 2008 (Cth).
Migration and Maritime Powers Legislation Amendment (Resolving the Asylum Legacy Caseload) Act 2014 (Cth).
Migration Regulations 1989 (Cth).
Migration Regulations 1994 (Cth).
Migration Reform Act 1992 (Cth).

Treaties

Convention against Torture and Other Cruel, Inhuman or Degrading Treatment or Punishment, 1465 UNTS 85 (opened for signature December 10, 1984, entered into force June 26, 1987).
Convention Relating to the Status of Refugees, 189 UNTS 150 (opened for signature July 28, 1951, entered into force April 22, 1954).
Protocol Relating to the Status of Refugees, 616 UNTS 267 (opened for signature January 31, 1967, entered into force October 4, 1967).

Index

accountability 10, 4t, 73–4, 93; for officers' wrongdoing 91, 97; legal framework 45–6, 105–8, 110, 184, 186, 190; limitations to migration policing 84–5, 101, 110–11, 177, 184; offered by evidentiary rules 92, 93–8; *see also* responsibility
Administrative Appeals Tribunal (AAT) 26–7, 27n29, 95, 144
Administrative Appeals Tribunal Act 1975 (Cth) 95n51
Administrative Decisions (Judicial Review) Act 1977 (Cth) 27n30
administrative tribunals 26–7, 31, 170; limitations for oversight of investigatory misconduct 91–8; not bound by the rules of evidence 93–4; record of investigatory misconduct rare 84, 87–8, 111; *see also* Administrative Appeals Tribunal; Migration Review Tribunal; Refugee Review Tribunal
Al Khafaji v. Minister for Immigration and Multicultural and Indigenous Affairs 115n9, 128n75, 128n76, 129n81; *see also Minister for Immigration and Multicultural and Indigenous Affairs v. Al Khafaji*
Al-Kateb v. Godwin 113, 113n4, 128–30, 129n81
Al Masri v. Minister for Immigration and Multicultural and Indigenous Affairs 115n9, 128–30, 128n76, 129n78, 129n79, 129n81
Alam v. Minister for Immigration and Multicultural and Indigenous Affairs 83, 87n14, 88–91, 97–8; *see also Minister for Immigration and Multicultural and Indigenous Affairs v. Alam*
Alldridge, P. 67, 67n84
arrest 29, 52, 63, 90, 102–3, 181; use of force 57, 104; violence of 52–3
arrest for criminal offence 48, 52–3, 59, 73, 80, 101, 181–3; powers 53, 82, 183, 186; safeguards 48, 53, 59, 55,183; unlawful 181–2; *see also* immigration 'arrest'
Australian Border Force (ABF) 2, 30, 49, 49n12, 182n9, 183; Operation Fortitude 1, 182
Australian Border Force Act 2015 (Cth) 49n12
Australian Federal Police (AFP) 10n38, 98, 181

Baldwin, R. 28n39, 31n54, 151n49
Balibar, E. 155, 155n67, 188, 188n22
Berg, L. 7n27, 8n29, 9n34, 26n26, 31n55, 170n142, 185n16
Big Data 176, 176n177, 179; *see also* risk profiling and management
border controls *see* immigration controls
Border Risk Identification System (BRIS) *see* risk profiling and management
Bridging E Visa (BVE) 115–16, 140, 187; access and denial of work rights 113, 123–4, 125–7, 132–3; cancellation of 134–5; Code of Behaviour (the Code) for unauthorised maritime arrival BVE holders 115, 133–8; government-funded income support of 124; holders' experience of physical, financial, psychological, stress 113, 122, 124–5, 127, 137–8, 139–40; insecurity of status 22, 123, 126–7, 134–5, 140; introduction of 115, 116; numbers of 123, 130; release from immigration detention upon grant 114, 115–17, 130, 136; *see also* release from immigration detention

bridging visa 53, 83, 90, 59; *see also* Bridging E Visa (BVE); Removal Pending Bridging Visa (RPBV)
Brodeur, J.-P. 177, 177n180, 177n181

Canada 17, 126n66, 188
cancellation of visas in Australia 3, 9, 25, 33, 43, 102; automatic cancellation of student visas 38, 76–7, 102n86; breach of Code of Behaviour 134–5; ministerial discretion in 149; notification of 55, 102–3, 104, 106–7; potential consequences of 76, 102, 110–11, 140, 149; review of 88, 97, 105; threat of 124–7, 133–7; for unlawful work 88, 126; validity of cancellation 75–8, 83, 103; *see also* 'character test' for visas; Bridging E Visa (BVE); insecure legal status
'character test' for visas 20, 75, 142–5, 178–9; Administrative Appeals Tribunal decisions 152–71; consequences of refusal or cancellation 49; deterrence as a factor in exclusion 159–70; exclusion for failure of 142, 146–7, 154, 159; general conduct part of 147–50, 153, 154; historical development of 142–3, 145–7; meaning of character 150–1; numbers excluded for failure of 171–2
children: best interests of Australian citizen in 'character test' exclusion 160; charged with people smuggling offences 181; distressed by immigration compliance activity 99; separated from parent 24; *see also* mandatory detention
Chu Kheng Lim v. Minister for Immigration 52n20, 52n21, 128, 128n72, 141n135
Chu Shao Hung 34–5; *Chu Shao Hung v. R* 35n67
citizenship 3, 36, 42, 60, 147, 188; benefits of 38, 145; conferred legal status 60; evidence of 69; naturalised 164, 188; plural legality of 42–4, 184; privilege to be earned 146; risk profile factor 176; stratified 189
Code of Behaviour (the Code) 115, 133–8; *see also* refugee and asylum policies and processing
compensation 54, 78–9, 91, 189; not available 82; recommendation of 46
consent: cultural specificity of 63n68; quality of in street policing and raids 59–64
Convention against Torture and Other Cruel, Inhuman or Degrading Treatment or Punishment 109n120
Convention Relating to the Status of Refugees 109n120
Coutin, S.B. 3n11, 3n13, 8n28, 16
Cover, R. 24–5
credibility assessment 31; courts and tribunals 144, 154–70; cultural specificity 157n79; immigration officers' 69, 166–7, 169; racialised 155–7, 164–5; of visa sponsors 156–7
criminal law 34–5, 67; character-based visa cancellation for criminal offending 145–6, 172; procedural 29, 63, 68, 97; *see also* immigration-criminal law and policing interrelation
Crock, M. 8n29, 31n56, 96n57, 131n91
Cronin, K. 26, 174n158
Cronulla riot related policing 70–2
customs officers 2, 30, 48; *Customs Act 1901* (Cth) 49n12
Cwerner, S.B. 109, 111

Dauvergne, C. 3, 31n55, 111n124
Davis, K.C. 26, 26n24
De Genova, N.P. 3n11, 17n60
death, of non-citizens in migration policing contexts 57–8; of asylum seekers 137–8; after removal from Australia 129n79
Department of Immigration and Border Protection (DIBP) *see* Immigration Department
Department of Immigration and Citizenship (DIAC) *see* Immigration Department
Department of Immigration and Ethnic Affairs (DIEA) *see* Immigration Department
Department of Immigration, Local Government and Ethnic Affairs (DILGEA) *see* Immigration Department
Department of Immigration and Multicultural Affairs (DIMA) *see* Immigration Department
Department of Immigration and Multicultural and Indigenous Affairs (DIMIA) *see* Immigration Department
deportation 39, 86, 107, 128, 145–6; *see also* removal

detainees released 19, 46, 48, 77–8, 113, 116, 118–20, 132; contingent on security bond 90–1, 113, 119–20; contingent on sponsorship 118–23; post-release no-work condition 123–7, 130, 132–3; without a visa 123, 128–9; *see also* Code of Behaviour
detention, harm arising from 54–8, 82, 113; adverse mental health consequences 115, 137; distress associated with suicide 138; failure to protect privacy 21
detention, legality of 3n12, 40, 50n14, 128–9; based on misunderstanding of legal status in Australia 74–8 and in the UK 76, 78–9; precondition of the formation of 'reasonable suspicion' of unlawful status 65–70, 74; statutory power 48–9, 52, 73; unlawful or wrongful 64–6, 75–6, 77n153, 78, 80–1, 90, 182, 189; *see also* mandatory detention
deterrence: binding policy direction in the 'character test' 147–9, 159–61, 169–70, 179; factor in 'character test' exclusions 152, 159–71; in maritime border policing 9, 132–3
discretion 25, 27–8, 34, 38, 51, 80; arbitrary 9, 100, 112–14, 132, 140, 182, 185, 189; 'front-end' 29–33, 40, 51, 103; historical development in immigration law 26–7, 115–7; legally authoritative 4, 23, 26, 27–8, 29, 32, 84, 179; organising features in migration policing 25–41; *see also* Immigration Minister's personal discretion; immigration-criminal law and policing interrelation
Dixon, D. 63n66, 66n80, 74n130
'dob-in' 6, 37, 37n81
Dubber, M.D. 29, 29n45, 44n115
duty of care 138–9, 189
Dworkin, R. 27, 27n35, 30

Education Services for Overseas Students Act 2000 (Cth) 38n85
employer 86, 175; awareness sessions 33n63, 37; obligations 38, 51n16; sanctions offences 86n9; *see also Migration Amendment (Employer Sanctions) Act*
equality before the law 18, 24, 38, 40, 46
Ericson, R. 29n47, 30n50, 73n122
evidence: of citizenship 69; of immigration status 38, 60–1, 68–70; to obtain search warrant 86–7, 86n9; to support detention 65
Evidence Act 1995 (Cth) 73n125, 92n40, 94, 96n58
evidentiary rules 91–2; exclusion of unlawfully/improperly obtained evidence 73, 91–3; inapplicability of the rules of evidence in immigration law 93–7, 110, 184; seemingly neutral 23n9; value in addressing infringements 91; *see also* responsibility

false imprisonment *see* mandatory detention
Findlay, M. 11n40, 29n47, 41, 41n101
Fleay, C. 124n51, 130n85, 137n124
Foster, M. 78n158, 145n10, 158n83
Foucault, M. 37n78, 44, 44n115, 44n116, 44n118, 44n121, 135n113, 151, 151n47
'front-end' discretion *see* discretion

Galligan, D.J. 25n22, 27–8
Garland, D. 37, 37n78
gender 42, 144, 152, 158, 174–5, 186
Glover, K.S. 33n59, 176, 176n175
Goldie v. Commonwealth 68, 68n94, 69, 73n123
Goldstein, J. 30n50, 73n122
Grewcock, M. 145, 145n9, 145n10, 146, 146n12

Haneef v. Minister for Immigration and Citizenship 147, 147n18, 150n39
healthcare, access to 63, 124–5, 132–3, 139; needs of asylum seekers 118n20; *see also* mental health
Howells, S. 6n20, 7n22, 7n23, 101n80

identification power 59–62
'illegal' migrants: discourse 3–4, 6; 'illegal maritime arrivals' (IMAs) 115, 124n48, 136; *see also* undocumented migrants in Australia; 'unlawful non-citizen'
immigration 'arrest' 18, 51, 52–9; 84–5, 101–2, 108, 186; devalues liberty 59–67, 70–80; Immigration Department incorrect interpretation of 65–6; limited responsibility for 54, 67, 73–4, 74–80, 91–8, 103, 105–8; low visibility of 49, 50, 72–3, 66, 81; precondition of the formation of 'reasonable suspicion' of unlawful status

immigration *continued*
65–70, 74; safeguards lacking for immigration 'arrest' 19, 49, 55–7, 59; speed of 101–5, 106–8; statutory power 48, 52, 57; violence of 51–2, 52–9, 104–5; *see also* detention, legality of

immigration compliance activities 2, 2n6, 2n7, 6n20, 30, 83; categorical approach 60–1; intelligence analysis 169; 175, 177, 179; intelligence from government and civil sources 33; monitoring 36–8, 119; numbers of 51, 98; offshore166–8; risk identification technologies 171, 173–6; selectivity 61; strategies 32–4, 86–7; targeting industries 33, 33n630; *see also* identification power; immigration 'arrest'; mandatory detention; 'officers' under the *Migration Act*; search warrant; risk profiling and management

immigration controls 30; civil actors' involvement in 33n63, 37–8, 51, 77, 86, 102n86, 118–23; historical development in Australia 26–7, 48–50, 53–4, 115–17, 131–2, 142–3, 145–9, 174–6; unauthorised maritime arrivals 8–9, 109n119, 110n121, 115, 116–17, 118, 124n48 130–3, 136, 137n121, 139, 140, 185; visa conditions 34; whole-of-government approach 2, 36, 37; *see also* cancellation of visas; immigration compliance activities; universal visa system

immigration-criminal law and policing interrelation: challenge for classification of legal scale 24, 41–5; devalues liberty 1–2, 59–67, 70–80, 181–4; historical 'prohibited immigrant' criminal offence 34–5; immigration criminal offence 34–5, 149–50, 181; 'interlegality' 42, 45; 'interlegality' of migration law and policing 24, 46, 81, 108, 184, 188–9; misuse of search warrants 98–9; production of discretionary authority 5, 41 (and de facto identification requirements 59–62; including 'placeholder' detention 62–4); 'reasonable suspicion' for detention police vs immigration officers 68–70; removal vs criminal prosecution 63n65; right to 'residual liberty' 182–3; *see also* immigration compliance activities; responsibility

Immigration Department 11–2; multi-agency operations 1–2, 49, 86, 98–9; multi-institutional practice of migration policing 62, 70; name change 11; *see also* immigration compliance activities; 'officers' under the *Migration Act*

Immigration Minister 11–12,

Immigration Minister's personal discretion 27, 27n33,124n48; to cancel or refuse visas 134, 142–3; to enable community detention 116; to grant visas 8, 22, 27, 116, 131, 137, 168; to grant visas for release from detention 130–2; to issue binding policy 10, 147–9, 159–61, 169–70; in the public interest 116, 132; to set aside tribunal decisions 143; transparency, lack of 142; unauthorised maritime arrivals 130–3, 187

immigration officers *see* 'officers' under the *Migration Act*

Immigration Restriction Act 1901 (Cth) 26, 34n65

Immigration Review Tribunal (IRT) 94, 94n46

immigration status 3, 35–6, 128n74; *see also* 'lawful non-citizen'; undocumented migrants in Australia; 'unlawful non-citizen'

immigration status checks 38, 50, 58, 60–2, 63, 72, 68–9; civil actors involvement in 36–8; 'dob-in' line 37; Immigration Status Service (ISS) 37–8, 70

insecure legal status 126–7; in Canada 17, 126n66

international students: automatic visa cancellation 38, 76–7, 102n86; former visa holders as a proportion of the unlawful non-citizen population 7; lawful status reinstated 77; searches of 86n9, 88, 91; visa conditions 38, 88; work rights restricted 88, 100

Irving v. Minister for Immigration, Local Government and Ethnic Affairs 146, 146n17, 147, 147n22, 150n41, 150n45

'lawful non-citizens' 12, 35, 49, 60, 87, 140, 188–9; marginally lawful 19, 114, 140–1; precarious status 126–7; status 9, 32, 46, 53, 63, 75, 115, 128, 140, 178, 187; status lost 48; status reinstated 77

low visibility decisions 3, 8, 30, 142; link to models of responsibility 46, 67–80, 92–8; risk profiling 171, 174–8; street policing encounters 50, 67, 72–3, 80; *see also* responsibility

M79/2012 v. Minister for Immigration and Citizenship 130n84, 132n95
mandatory detention 3n12, 31, 47–50, 182, 185; Alvarez/Solon report 64–6; centres, management outsourced 139; children in 50n14, 53, 56, 115, 115n9, 181; children detained from school 55–6, 56n38, 56n39; community-based 56, 116; in compliance operations 49, 54–5, 60–2, 83, 87, 89–90; discretion in 25, 53–4, 115–17, 187; discretionary questioning detention 90; government duty of care for detainees 138–9; historical development of 48–50, 53–4, 115–17, 131–2; institutional culture 66; interrelation with criminal procedural powers 59–64, 73–4, 80–2, 181–4; low-visibility of 72–4; offshore 8, 131–2, 139; place of 49; Rau report 64–6; re-detention 113, 123, 134, 187; risk-based approach ('key detention values') 53–4, 117; *see also* immigration 'arrest'
Mazerolle, L.G. 119, 120n28
McBarnet, D.J. 23n7, 39, 39n91, 66n80, 97
mental health: former detainees 125–6, 137–8, 139; impact of immigration detention on 115, 137n122, 138n127; people removed from Australia 146; refugees and asylum seekers 124n50, 125–6, 137, 137n124
Mezzadra, S. 30n49, 108, 108n112, 185, 185n14
Migration Act 1958 (Cth): definition of 'officers' 2; detain 52; 'lawful non-citizen' 49, 35–6; mandatory detention 48; 'unlawful non-citizen' 49, 35–6; s 4 39n94, 42n108, 97n62; s 4AA 53n25; s 5 2n9, 47n3, 49n12, 49n13, 52n18, 55n34, 57n45; s 13 49n9; s 14 49n9; s 15 102n85, 102n86; s 18 14n48; s 21 14n48; s 46A 8n32, 131n92, 131n93; s 61 107n105; s 72 118n20; s 91L 132n96; s101 102n84; s 102 102n84; s 103 102n84; s 104 102n84; s 105 102n84; s 107 102n84, s 109 102n84, 149n31; s 116 102n84, 149n31; s 119 102n84; s 127 103n88; s 129 107n108; s 137J 38n86, 102n86; s 138 102n86; s 140 102n84; s 188 60n54; s 189 3n12, 31 n52, 48 n4, 52n18, 57n45, 87n12; s 192 57n45, 87n12, 90n28; s 195A 116n10, 131n94; s196 52n18; s 197AA–197AG 116n12; s 198 103n89, 109n120; s 223 57n46; s 233A 149n35; s 233C 181, s 234 149n34; s 235 126n63; s 236 149n34; s 240 149n34; s 241 149n34; s 245AB 38n87; s 245AC 38n87; s 251 57n46, 86n6, 86n7, 86n8, 86–9, 89n21, 89n22, 98–101, 98n66, 99n74, 100n76, 100n78, 100n79, 101n81; s 252 57n46, 89n22; s 253 57n45; s 261AE 57n46; s 268CA 86n9; s 268CD 86n9; s 347 107n106; s 351 8n30; s 353 93n45, 94 n47, 95n51; s 359B 107n107; s 412 107n106; s 417 8n30, 167–8; s 420 93n45, 94 n47, 95n51; s 424B 107n107; s 474 31n56, 96n57; s486O 21n1; s 487D 86n9; s 487E 86n9; s 499 10n39; s 501 36n6, 36n76, 142–71, 143n6, 143n8, 145n10,145n11, 147n24, 148n26, 149n29, 153n61, 159n89, 170n139, 171n48, 172n150, 172n151, 172n152, 102n84, 178–9; s 501BA 172n150; s 501CA 170n139, 172n150; s 501E 149n32
Migration Amendment (Bridging Visas Code of Behaviour) Regulation 2013 (Cth) 133n102
Migration Amendment (Character and General Visa Cancellation) Act 2014 (Cth) 172n150
Migration Amendment (Detention Arrangements) Act 2005 (Cth) 53n25, 116n10, 116n12
Migration Amendment (Disclosure of Information) Regulation 2013 (Cth) 134n108
Migration Amendment (Employer Sanctions) Act 2007 (Cth) 6n20, 7n22, 7n23, 38n87, 101n80
Migration Amendment (Excision from the Migration Zone) Act (Cth) 2001 131n92
Migration Amendment (Immigration Detention Reform) Bill 2009 (Cth) 117n18
Migration (Delayed Visa Applications) Tax Bill 1992 (Cth) 115n6
Migration Reform Act 1992 115n5
Migration Regulations 1989: regs 2(1), 4 142n3
Migration Regulations 1994: reg 1.17, sch 4 174n160; reg 2.08F 121n40; reg 2.20 116n11, 118n20; regs 2.45, 2.42, 2.55, 5.02 102n87; regs 4.17, 4.35 107n107; sch 1, 1401 121n40; sch 2 93n43,

Migration Regulations 1994 continued 118n22; sch 4 133n102, 149n32, 174n161, 174n162; sch 5 149n33; sch 8 115n8, 133n102; sch 10 86n8, 100n79
Migration Review Tribunal (MRT) 88–9, 95, 97
Minister for Immigration and Multicultural and Indigenous Affairs v. Al Khafaji 128n75, 129n81
Minister for Immigration and Multicultural and Indigenous Affairs v. Al Masri 129n79; *see also Al Masri v. Minister for Immigration and Multicultural and Indigenous Affairs*
Minister for Immigration and Multicultural and Indigenous Affairs v. Alam 83n1, 88–91, 96–8; *see also Alam v. Minister for Immigration and Multicultural and Indigenous Affairs*
Minister for Immigration and Multicultural and Indigenous Affairs v. Nystrom 78n154, 142n3
Mohammed v. The Secretary of State for the Home Department 78, 78n161, 79, 79n163
Morrison v. Minister for Immigration and Citizenship 103–7

nationality: in the 'character test' 144; factor in deterrence for 'character test' exclusion 159–71; factor in risk profile 171–6; trait in assessing dishonesty in the 'character test' 154–9; perception that race-neutral 155
Neilson, B. 108, 108n112, 108n113, 185, 185n14, 185n17
Newman, Troy 147, 147n19
Noble, G. 70n106, 71n107
Nystrom v. Minister for Immigration and Multicultural and Indigenous Affairs 77, 77n152, 78, 145n11, 146; *see also Minister for Immigration and Multicultural and Indigenous Affairs v. Nystrom*

'officers' under the *Migration Act*: conduct of awareness and counselling sessions 33n63, 51n16, 135n112; detain 48, 68–70; discretion 25, 30; firearms 49; identification power 59–60; 'immigration arrest' power 52; perception of own authority 99, 65–6; search power 86–7; statutory definition 2; training of 57–8, 70, 91, 99–100, 101n83; use of force 49, 57; *see also* discretion; immigration-criminal law and policing interrelation; mandatory detention; search warrant
offshore refugee detention and processing 8, 130–2; interception and transfer to a third country 8, 131; Manus Island 8, 131–2, 132n99; Nauru 8, 131–2, 139; 'Pacific Solution' 8, 131, 131n91, 185; 'Regional Processing' 131
overstay 7, 33n61, 87, 116, 154; risk profiling 174; *see also* undocumented migrants in Australia

'Pacific Solution' *see* offshore refugee detention and processing
Plaintiff S157/2002 v. Commonwealth of Australia 31n56
Plaintiff S99/2016 v. Minister for Immigration and Border Protection 139, 139n132, 139n133, 139n134
policing: home 24, 54–5, 57, 83, 86–91, 99; school 55–6, 86–7; street 31, 47–52, 57–9, 60–4, 69–74, 80, 103–4, 188; workplace 21, 47, 56–7, 60–1, 86–7, 98
policing 'at a distance' (or 'responsibilisation') 36–7, 118
policing status 3, 32–8, 187–90; challenge to binary between the citizen and non-citizen 10, 64–7, 70, 188–9; challenge to binary between lawful and unlawful non-citizen 5, 46, 123–33, 133–8, 140, 188; discretionary legal authority 25–41; plural legalities 41–6, 108; policing progression to citizenship 145–7; state police involvement in 49–50, 55, 57–9, 60, 61–5, 70–2, 98–9, 103–6; status-based criminal offence 35; *see also* immigration compliance activities; racialised stereotypes; responsibility
Poynting, S. 70n106, 72n115
'prohibited immigrant' 34; criminal offence of 34–5

racialised stereotypes: avoiding racial discrimination in work entitlement checks 38; citizenship 42, 188; construction of 'immigrant' 156–7, 164–5; credibility assessments linked to 157, 154–9; Cronulla riot related policing 70–2; dictation test 35;

formation of suspicion associated with language 69–70; formation of suspicion in street policing 62, 70, 71–2, 186; government discourse 136; 'local knowledge' linked to 166–8; nationality-based stereotypes linked to 152, 155–7, 179; risk and surveillant technology linked to 173, 173n155, 173n156; selective enforcement in compliance operations 60–1
Ransley, J. 79n167, 119, 120n28
Rau, Cornelia (Rau report) 64–6, 91n34
Re David John Cawdell Irving and Minister of State for Immigration Local Government and Ethnic Affairs 146n17
refugee and asylum policies and processing (Australia) 8–9; 'asylum legacy caseload' 130–2, 137, 185; 'character test' 157–8; Code of Behaviour 115, 133–7, 135n114; detention 56, 128–30; government assistance 124; interviews 63n68; processing speed 109–10, 137–8; sexuality-based claims 170; unauthorised maritime arrivals 118, 130–1; visas 109, 121, 123, 185; *see also* mental health; offshore refugee detention and processing
Refugee Review Tribunal (RRT) 31n55, 93n45, 95, 170, 170n144
Regional Processing *see* offshore refugee detention and processing
release from immigration detention: community support for asylum seekers 117–18, 120–3; conditions and constraints 114, 117, 119–20, 123, 139–40; government assistance 124; no work rights 123–7, 130–3; security bonds 113, 119–20; sponsorship 117–23, 133, 140
removal (deportation) from Australia 25; consequence of 110, 145–7; 'deportability' 3; deportation orders found improper 107; detention pending 52, 68, 117, 128–9; international law obligations 109n120; of long-term residents 78n158, 143n6, 145–6; rapid removal 84, 101–11, 186; return to Australia after 146; standard notice of 104; statutory power 103n89; unlawful 64–5
Removal Pending Bridging Visa (RPBV) 116, 130; *see also* bridging visa
residual liberty 181n1, 182–3, 183n10
responsibility 4, 41–5; differential regimes of 188; limitations of principles, standards and preconditions 53–4, 64, 69, 100–1; limited judicial oversight over the impetus for intervention in street-based migration policing 67–74; limited responsibility for detention based on a misunderstanding of legal status 74–80; limited responsibility for migration policing misconduct embedded in administrative law and procedure 84, 110–1; rules of evidence, model of 73, 91–8; 'snapshot', model of 67–80; tort law, model of 54, 75, 79, 91, 138–9, 189; 'video', model of 67, 73, 78–9; 'zone of non-responsibility' 23, 41, 184–6
risk profiling and management 33–4, 171–8; Border Risk Identification System (BRIS) 173–4, 176; classificatory technologies for 'intent management' 173, 174–6; low-visibility of risk assessments 107–8, 177–8; nationality as a risk factor 152, 174–6;'pre-textual' relationship to law 148, 176; Risk Factor List (RFL) 174–5, 176; risk justifications for detention 53–4, 117; risks posed to compliance operations 104–6; Safeguards System 173, 175–6; technological expertise and authority 148, 171, 173, 177–8; *see also* racialised stereotypes
Rose, N. 37n78, 118n23, 148, 148n25
Ruddock v. Taylor [2003] 54n27
Ruddock v. Taylor [2005] 40n99, 59n53, 68, 68n85, 68n87, 69, 69n102, 74n132, 75, 75n133, 75n136, 76, 76n139, 76n140, 76n141, 76n144, 78, 78n155, 79, 79n164, 208
Ruddock v. Vadarlis 87n14, 129n77

S v. Secretary, Department of Immigration and Multicultural and Indigenous Affairs 138n130
Safe Haven Enterprise Visa (SHEV) 137, 185
Safeguards System *see* risk profiling and management
Sales v. Minister for Immigration & Citizenship [2008] 78, 78n156
Salter, M.B. 44n118, 151, 151n47
Santos, B. de Sousa 41, 41n104, 42, 45, 184

search warrant 60–2, 86–7; abuse of powers 21, 83, 89–91, 98–9; comparison with criminal procedural standards 57, 100; complaints 99; limitations on oversight and responsibility for 91–8, 100–1; multi-agency operations 86, 98–9; numbers of 98; privacy breach 21, 45–6; reform recommendations 99–101; result in death 57; statutory power 86; use of force 57–8; *see also* immigration 'arrest'; mandatory detention
security bonds *see* release from immigration detention
sexuality: 'character test' 188; -based refugee claims 31n55, 170
Soh v. Commonwealth 40n100
speed *see* temporal controls
sponsorship *see* release from immigration detention
SU v. Commonwealth of Australia [2014] 181n1
SU v. Commonwealth of Australia; BS v. Commonwealth of Australia [2016] 181, 181n1, 182, 182n5, 183, 183n10, 184

temporal controls 108–11, 185–6; indefinite detention 128; intensifies violent or harmful effects 53–4, 56–8, 104, 109, 137–8, 186; link to the lawfulness of violence 73–4, 76–8, 80, 104, 106–8, 196; quarantining time period of officer's actions for review ('snapshot' model of responsibility) 67, 74–5; regulating mobility 185; slowness and delay in migration processes 109, 137–8, 185–6; speeding up migration processes of removal and asylum processing 102–3, 106–10, 186; strict time periods for policy application 130–3; temporary legal status 25, 109, 113, 131–2
temporary migration 5, 185, 190
Temporary Protection Visa (TPV) 9n34, 109, 121, 121n40, 137, 185

Uddin v. Minister for Immigration and Multicultural and Indigenous Affairs 77, 77n146, 77n148
undocumented migrants in Australia 3–4, 5–8, 12; decriminalisation of 35, 49; demographics 7; lack of documentation 7–8; marginalisation of voice 4, 16, 22–3, 111, 179; numbers 6–7; numbers of unauthorised ('illegal') maritime arrivals 132; political discourse 9, 17; production and regulation of migrant 'illegality' 3, 4–5, 23, 27, 42, 114, 178; in the US 7–8, 17, 42–3; vulnerability 15, 128, 139; *see also* 'illegal' migrants discourse; 'unlawful non-citizen'
United Kingdom (UK) 63n65, 68, 105; approach to decision founded on a mistaken understanding of law 76, 78–9; asylum policies 109; removal of unaccompanied minor 79
United States (US) 63n65; airport immigration inspectors 173n156; criminal law and trial process 29; legalisation of undocumented status 7; Mexico–US migration 163; sanctuary cities 42–3; undocumented migrant population 17
universal visa system (requirement to hold a visa) 20, 35–6, 115, 127, 128, 171, 187
'unlawful non-citizen' 4–5; administrative classification 35–6, 48–9; barriers for litigation against government 93; mandatory detention of 3, 115, 187; permitted to stay without a visa 128–33, 187; relation to 'lawful non-citizen' status 140, 188; search warrant powers over 86; status produced by overstay 7; status produced by visa cancellation 3; statutory definition 49, 49n9; *see also* immigration compliance activities
use of force 49, 57–8; coercion and consent 62; endorse authority through 25, 62; handcuffs 47, 57–8, 104; removal of persons 145; statutory powers 49, 57; taser 104–5; *see also* violence

Valverde, M. 29n45, 37n78, 41n103, 43–4, 44n115, 44n117, 45, 93, 93n44, 118n23, 148, 148n25, 170, 170n141, 183n11, 184
Varsanyi, M.W. 3n13, 43, 43n111, 43n113, 43n114
Veitch, S. 23, 23n8, 51n17, 84n3, 184n13
violence 2–3, 4, 24–5, 190
visa: bridging vs substantive 18, 83; *see also* Bridging E Visa (BVE); cancellation of visas; Safe Haven Enterprise Visa; Temporary Protection Visa; universal visa system

Weber, L. 5n16, 11n41, 30n49, 36, 36n77, 49, 49n11, 57n49, 63n65, 70n103

For Product Safety Concerns and Information please contact our EU representative GPSR@taylorandfrancis.com
Taylor & Francis Verlag GmbH, Kaufingerstraße 24, 80331 München, Germany

www.ingramcontent.com/pod-product-compliance
Ingram Content Group UK Ltd.
Pitfield, Milton Keynes, MK11 3LW, UK
UKHW021302190926
475701UK00009B/609
* 9 7 8 0 3 6 7 2 7 9 3 6 3 *